ASP.NET MVC in Action

D0932118

ASP.NET MVC
in Action

WITH MVCCONTRIB, NHIBERNATE, AND MORE

JEFFREY PALERMO
BEN SCHEIRMAN
JIMMY BOGARD

MANNING

Greenwich
(74° w. long.)

For online information and ordering of this and other Manning books, please visit
www.manning.com. The publisher offers discounts on this book when ordered in quantity.
For more information, please contact

    Special Sales Department
    Manning Publications Co.
    Sound View Court 3B   fax: (609) 877-8256
    Greenwich, CT 06830   email: orders@manning.com

©2010 by Manning Publications Co. All rights reserved.

No part of this publication may be reproduced, stored in a retrieval system, or transmitted, in
any form or by means electronic, mechanical, photocopying, or otherwise, without prior written
permission of the publisher.

Many of the designations used by manufacturers and sellers to distinguish their products are
claimed as trademarks. Where those designations appear in the book, and Manning
Publications was aware of a trademark claim, the designations have been printed in initial caps
or all caps.

♾ Recognizing the importance of preserving what has been written, it is Manning's policy to have
the books we publish printed on acid-free paper, and we exert our best efforts to that end.
Recognizing also our responsibility to conserve the resources of our planet, Manning books are
printed on paper that is at least 15% recycled and processed without the use of elemental chlorine.

	Development Editor: Tom Cirtin
	Copyeditor: Betsey Henkels
	Proofreader: Elizabeth Martin
Manning Publications Co.	Typesetter: Gordan Salinovic
Sound View Court 3B	Cover designer: Leslie Haimes
Greenwich, CT 06830	

ISBN 978-1-933988-62-7
Printed in the United States of America
1 2 3 4 5 6 7 8 9 10 – MAL – 14 13 12 11 10 09

brief contents

contents

foreword

The final version of ASP.NET MVC 1.0 was released March 2009 during the Mix 09 conference and nobody was caught by surprise with what was inside—and this is a good thing. Before the debut of the final version, the product team had released multiple public previews with full source code in an effort to raise the bar on openness and community involvement for a Microsoft product.

Why would we do this?

Transparency and community involvement are noble goals, but they aren't necessarily the end goal of a project. What we're really after is great product. I like to think of ASP.NET MVC as almost an experiment to demonstrate that transparency and community involvement were great means to achieving that goal.

After Preview 2 of ASP.NET MVC was released, we received a lot of feedback from developers that writing unit tests with ASP.NET MVC was difficult. Jeffrey Palermo, the lead author of *ASP.NET MVC in Action,* was among the most vocal in providing feedback during this time. We took this feedback and implemented a major API change by introducing the concept of action results, which was a much better design than we had before. Community involvement helped us build a better product.

ASP.NET MVC focuses on solid principles such as separation of concerns to provide a framework that is extremely extensible and testable. While it's possible to change the source as you see fit, the framework is intended to be open for extension without needing to change the source. Any part of the framework can be swapped with something else of your choosing. Don't like the view engine? Try Spark view engine. Don't like the way we instantiate controllers? Hook in your own dependency injection container.

ASP.NET MVC also includes great tooling such as the Add View dialog, which uses code generation to quickly create a view based on a model object. The best part is that all the code generation features in ASP.NET MVC rely on T4 templates and are thus completely customizable.

With this book, Jeffrey will share all these features and more, as well as show how to put them together to build a great application. I hope you enjoy the book and share in his passion for building web applications. Keep in mind that this book is not only an invitation to learn about ASP.NET MVC, but also an invitation to join in the community and influence the future of ASP.NET MVC. Happy coding!

PHIL HAACK
SENIOR PROGRAM MANAGER
ASP.NET MVC TEAM
MICROSOFT

preface

My career started in the mid-nineties as one of the early web developers. Web as in HTTP, that is. Netscape Navigator was helping to grow the number of households with internet modems because it was more advanced than anything else at the time. Netscape Navigator 3.0 (1996) and 3.04 (1997) helped households and businesses all over the world open up the internet for common uses. There is no more common a task than shopping! With the advent of ecommerce, the internet exploded with a capitalist gold run.

I started web development in the public sector where we leveraged the first threads of social networking by allowing school district graduates to collaborate with former classmates. I started my career on the Microsoft platform using IDC (*Internet Database Connector*) with HTX (*HTML Extension Template*). Internet Information Services (IIS) 2.0 gave us fantastic flexibility using ODBC data sources. This was my first use of the "code nugget," or <% %> delimiters. IDC/HTX gave way to Active Server Pages (ASP), and I can still recall following the changes as they broke–ASP 2.0 to ASP 3.0 as well as the awesome COM+ integration. I dabbled in CGI, Perl, Java, and C++, but stayed with the Microsoft platform. Observing the Visual Basic explosion from the sidelines, I learned the ropes with small utility apps.

Active Server Pages 3.0 saw the browser wars with Internet Explorer 4, released with Windows 95, competing with Netscape for market share. Writing web applications that worked well with both browsers was difficult. IE 5.0 opened the horizons for intranet applications with proprietary web extensions like the XML data island and better scripting capabilities. Windows XP shipped with IE 6, which effortlessly captured the majority of the web browser market. ASP 3.0 put the programmer intimately in touch with HTTP, HTML, and the GET and POST verbs. I remember pulling out crude frameworks to handle multiple request paths from the same ASP script.

At the same time ASP 3.0 was enjoying widespread adoption, Struts was taking the Java web application world by storm. Struts is probably the best known Java MVC framework, although today there are many popular frameworks for the JVM. With ASP 3.0, I was unaware of the lessons my Java counterparts had already learned, although I felt the pain of myriad responsibilities lumped into a single ASP script.

I adopted ASP.NET 1.0 right out of the gate and converted some of my ASP 3.0 sites to Web Forms. Remember when GridLayout was the default with CSS absolute positioning everywhere? It was clear that Web Forms 1.0 was geared for VB6 developers coming over to .NET and getting onto the web. The post-backs and button click handlers were largely foreign to me, but my colleagues who were seasoned VB6ers felt right at home. ASP.NET 1.1 dropped the GridLayout and forced the developer to understand HTML and how flow layout works. Down-level rendering was great when Internet Explorer was the "preferred" browser, and everything else was *downlevel*. That paradigm started to break down as Firefox climbed in market share and demanded standards-compliant markup.

I became an ASP.NET expert and was a frequent blogger during the .NET 2.0 beta cycle. I knew every feature and every breaking change from ASP.NET 1.1 to 2.0, and helped my team adopt 2.0. During the ASP.NET 2.0 era, I started following Martin Fowler and his Model-View-Presenter writings. I implemented that pattern to pull away logic from the code-behind file, which had become bloated. Java developers, in 2005, were enjoying a choice of several MVC frameworks for the web. I, on the other hand, was wrestling Web Forms into Model-View-Presenter and test-driven development submission. It was exhausting, but what was the alternative?

In 2006, with a job change, I jumped over to software management and smart client development with WinForms. With the familiar clunkiness of the code-behind model, and a development team to manage, I implemented the Model-View-Controller pattern with the WinForm class as the view. It was a breath of fresh air. UI development was seamless, and the controllers were a natural boundary from the domain model to the UI. In 2007, I jumped back into web development and begrudgingly implemented Model-View-Presenter with Web Forms again. In retrospect, I wish I had adopted Mono-Rail, another Model-View-Controller framework for .NET.

In February 2007, Scott Guthrie (ScottGu) created a prototype of what would become the ASP.NET MVC framework. He had heard from many customers about the difficulties with Web Forms and how they needed a simpler, more flexible way to write web applications. At the 2007 MVP Summit, Scott sought input from a small group of Microsoft MVPs. Darrell Norton, Scott Bellware, Jeremy Miller, and I validated the vision of his prototype and gave initial input that would end up coded into the framework.

When Scott Guthrie presented, to an audience in Austin, Texas, a working prototype and vision for ASP.NET MVC at the AltNetConf open spaces conference in October 2007, I knew instantly that this is what I'd wished for all along. As a long-time web developer, I understood HTTP and HTML, and this, I believe, is what ASP.NET 1.0 should have been. It would have been such a smooth transition from ASP 3.0 to

ASP.NET MVC. I can claim the first ASP.NET MVC application in production because I convinced Scott to give me a copy of his prototype and revised my www.partywithpalermo.com registration site, launching it in November 2007 on one of Rod Paddock's servers at DashPoint.

What Microsoft did with the ASP.NET MVC release cycle was an unprecedented project in the Developer Division. The project was released at least quarterly on the CodePlex site, source code and all. It was also developed using test-driven development as the software construction technique. Full unit test coverage is included in the source code download, and ASP.NET MVC 1.0 was released under the MS-PL, and OSI-approved open source license.

ASP.NET MVC works the way the web works; it's a natural fit. Although Microsoft is last to the table with a Model-View-Controller framework for its development platform, this framework is a strong player. Its design focuses on the core abstractions first. It is conducive to extension by the community. In fact, the same week the first Community Technology Preview (CTP) was released, Eric Hexter and I launched the MvcContrib open-source project with an initial offering of extensions that integrated with the ASP.NET MVC Framework.

At the time of publishing this book, the ASP.NET MVC framework is a frequently used tool at Headspring Systems, where I facilitate the consulting practice. For the .NET industry as a whole, I predict that ASP.NET MVC will be considered the norm for ASP.NET development by 2011.

New developers are coming to the .NET platform every day, and for web developers, ASP.NET MVC is easy to adopt and learn. Because of the decreased complexity, the barrier to adoption is lowered, and because of the simplicity, it can grow to meet the demands of some of the most complex enterprise systems.

When Manning Publications approached me to write a book on ASP.NET MVC, I was already a frequent blogger on the topic and had published an article on the framework in CoDe magazine. Even so, I knew writing a book would be a tremendous challenge. This book has been in progress for over a year, and I am excited to see it published. I learned quite a bit from Ben and Jimmy throughout this project, and I learned so much more about the framework by writing about it. This knowledge has direct and immediate benefit to our client projects.

Our hope is that our book will stay with you even after you have written your first application. Writing a book published just after a 1.0 release is challenging because many things are discovered after a technology has been out in the wild. Leveraging it on client projects immediately has definitely helped increase the quality of information contained in the book because it is derived from hands-on experience.

Although other platforms have benefited from Model-View-Controller frameworks for many years, the MVC pattern is still foreign to many .NET developers. This book explains how and when to use the framework; also the theory and principles behind the pattern as well as complimentary patterns. We hope that this book will enlighten your understanding of an indispensable technology that's simple to learn.

JEFFREY PALERMO

acknowledgments

We'd like to thank Scott Guthrie for seeing the need in the .NET space for this framework. Without his prototype, vision, and leadership, this offering would still not exist in the .NET framework. We would also like to recognize the core ASP.NET MVC team at Microsoft, headed by Phil Haack, the Program Manager for ASP.NET MVC. Other key members of the ASP.NET MVC team are Eilon Lipton (Lead Dev), Levi Broderick (Dev), Jacques Eloff (Dev), Carl Dacosta (QA), and Federico Silva Armas (Lead QA). We would also like to extend our thanks to the large number of additional staff who worked on packaging, documenting and delivering the ASP.NET MVC framework as a supported offering from Microsoft. Even though this framework is small compared to others, this move from Microsoft is shifting the mental inertia of the .NET portion of the software industry.

This book employed three working authors, all consultants with multiple projects, along with startup help and a chapter draft by Dave Verwer. The book effort took over a year and a half, starting with the first Community Technology Preview of the ASP.NET MVC Framework. This dynamic required tremendous support from the staff at Manning Publications. We would like to thank them for their patience and support throughout the project. In particular, we would like to thank acquisitions editor Michael Stephens and editor Tom Cirtin for their leadership. Michael saw the need for this book and contacted me about writing it. Tom was very supportive and patient and helped the three of us through our first book publication.

Our independent technical reviewers were outstanding. They offered advice and opinionated viewpoints on each chapter during development, and without that input, the book would not be as good as we hope it is. Our sincere thanks goes to Phil Haack for reviewing the manuscript and writing a brilliant foreword. Many thanks should also go to Freedom Dumlao, who painstakingly reviewed each chapter to ensure the message would apply in the best manner to the target audience. Jeremy Skinner was also a boon to the project. Jeremy tested and retested every code listing and code sample in the book as well as in the many Visual Studio projects that come with the book. His attention to detail, backed up by his vast experience with ASP.NET MVC and Mvc-Contrib, has contributed greatly to this book.

Manning invited the following reviewers to read the manuscript at different stages of development and to send their comments: Mark Monster, Andrew Siemer, Benjamin Day, Frank Wang, Derek Jackson, Tim Binkley-Jones, Marc Gravell, Alessandro Gallo, Josh Heyer, Peter Johnson, Jeremy Anderson, and Alex Thissen.

This book has also benefited from outside technical reviewers who volunteered to read parts of the manuscript and provided feedback: Rod Paddock, Craig Shoemaker, Hamilton Verissimo, Matt Hinze, Kevin Hurwitz, Blake Caraway, Nick Becker, Mahendra Mavani, Eric Anderson, Rafael Torres, Eric Hexter, Tom Jaeschke, Matt Hawley, and Sebastien Lambla.

Before this book went to print, a large number of people purchased the PDF edition of the book by participating in the MEAP, Manning's Early Access Program. We would like to thank those readers for their comments and participation early, and throughout the manuscript portion of the project, especially Eric Kinateder, Ben Mills, Peter Kellner, Jeff P., Orlando Agostinho, Liam McLennan, Ronald Wildenberg, Max Fraser, Gudmundur.Hreidarsson, Kyle Szklenski, Philippe Vialatte, Lars Zeb, Marc Gravell, Cody Skidmore, Mark Fowler, Joey Beninghove, Shadi Mari, Simone Chiaretta, Jay Smith, Jeff Kwak, and Mohammad Azam.

JEFFREY PALERMO

I would like to thank my beautiful wife, Liana, for her support and patience throughout this project. Liana gave birth to our daughter, Gwyneth Rose, shortly before the book was started, and the motivation to spend more time with my growing family pushed me to complete the book. Thanks also to my parents, Peter and Rosemary Palermo, for instilling in me a love of books and learning from an early age.

BEN SCHEIRMAN

My thanks and utmost appreciation go out to my amazing wife, Silvia. Her continued support and encouragement of my extracurricular work led to writing this book in the first place. I would also like to recognize one of my university mentors, Venkat Subramaniam. With his guidance, I found my passion in software development and strived to learn more and push the envelope. He was an inspiration in my career. Finally I'd like to thank my wonderful children, Andréa, Noah, and Ethan (and most recently Isaac and Isabella), who showed immense patience and encouragement while their dad was banging away at the keyboard in the late hours of the night.

JIMMY BOGARD

Thanks to my wife, Sara, without whose love, support, and patience, my contribution to this project would not have been possible. Also, thanks to my family for putting up with a strange little bookworm all those years. Finally, thanks to my high school computer science teacher, Scotty Johnson, who showed me the rewards that a true passion for the craft can bring.

about this book

The ASP.NET MVC Framework was a vision of Scott Guthrie in early 2007. With a prototype demonstration in late 2007 as well as a key hire of Phil Haack as the Senior Program Manager of the feature team, Scott made the vision a reality. At a time when the .NET community was becoming frustrated that other platforms had great MVC frameworks like Tapestry, Rails, and so on, Web Forms was losing favor as developers struggled to make it do things previously unimagined when it became public in 2001. Castle MonoRail was a very capable framework and continues to have strong leadership behind it, but the broader .NET industry needed a change from Web Forms. Phil Haack, with his experience outside of Microsoft as well as in the open source community, immediately came in and led the ASP.NET MVC Framework team to a successful 1.0 release that the .NET community is excited about.

ASP.NET MVC has the benefit of lessons learned from other popular MVC frameworks such as Struts, WebWork, Tapestry, Rails, and MonoRail. It also came about as C# starts to push away its fully statically typed roots. The language enhancements introduced with .NET 3.5 have been fully leveraged in the ASP.NET MVC Framework, giving it a huge advantage over frameworks that came before as well as all the Java frameworks that are tied to the currently supported Java syntax.

For people who have a diversified software background, ASP.NET MVC is a great addition to the Visual Studio development experience. For those who began their software career with .NET 1.0 or later, it is a fundamental shift in thinking since they grew up with Web Forms being "normal" web development.

This book attempts to start at a point that is past the documentation and online tutorials available on the ASP.NET MVC website at http://www.asp.net/mvc/. If you are just getting started with ASP.NET, you will want to read some of the older books covering the ASP.NET pipeline and server runtime. Because ASP.NET MVC layers on to ASP.NET, it is important to understand the fundamentals. If you are a current ASP.NET developer, you will find that this book does not insult your intelligence. It is a fast-paced book aimed at giving you the *why* and not just the *how*.

Since ASP.NET MVC is a new technology offering you can expect several books to cover the topic. This is a framework that is not sitting still. Since its release in March 2009, several books have been released, but the community is finding new and better ways to use the framework. The newest ideas make their way to the Mvc-Contrib project, and to public release frequently as new additions are contributed. Because of this dynamic, this book covers ASP.NET MVC with MvcContrib sprinkled throughout. The authors are all actively developing with the framework, and MvcContrib plays a vital part in every application. This books aims to have a long-lasting place on your bookshelf. The API will evolve, but the principles behind using an MVC framework as well as the ways to structure URLs, tests, and application layers are more durable. With this, we hope that this book serves not only as a rigorous foray into ASP.NET MVC development but also as a guide toward developing long-lived web applications on the .NET platform.

We hope that the arrival of this book is considered good timing because the text was written with the perspective of the roadmap of ASP.NET MVC 2.0 in mind. With the roadmap plans released and the first CTP of v2 already available, the techniques in this book are useful now and are also relevant for ASP.NET MVC v2, which is quickly approaching. We hope this book will help you start on your way to creating many maintainable, long-lived applications on the new version of ASP.NET.

Who should read this book?

This book is written for senior developers working with ASP.NET. The authors are senior and strong leaders in their companies, local community, and the industry. All three authors are recognized by Microsoft with the Microsoft Most Valuable Professional (MVP) award. With that in mind, we felt it appropriate to write a book aimed at senior members of the software team. With the market flooded with beginner books and books that reformat online documentation and tutorials, we attempted to write a book that might leave some beginners behind but at the same time challenge senior developers and architects. Whether or not you are familiar with other MVC frameworks, this book will push your knowledge further than you are accustomed to when reading a technology book.

The book comes with a full reference implementation in production at http://CodeCampServer.com. CodeCampServer was developed by the authors and is open source with many other contributors at this time. CodeCampServer is an ASP.NET MVC application aimed at hosting user group websites and websites for .NET user group conferences, frequently called *Code Camps*. The codebase was developed using Onion Architecture, domain-driven design, test-driven development, and inversion of control. The techniques espoused in the book are implemented in the project. Many of the code examples in the book are detailed explorations of parts of CodeCampServer. Although the project will continue to evolve after this book is published, the principles with which it and the text were written are timeless and portable beyond a single version of the technology.

Because in any real project, like CodeCampServer, you use many libraries for specific things, we did not shy away from using these as well. We feel that avoiding other libraries for the sake of simplicity also makes it difficult for the reader to apply the knowledge gained while reading. With that in mind, we use popular libraries such as MvcContrib, NAnt, NUnit, StructureMap, Windsor, Castle, RhinoMocks, Log4Net, NHibernate, Tarantino, AutoMapper, Iesi.Collections and many others. Because real projects have a collage of libraries, we felt that learning ASP.NET MVC in this realistic setting was most appropriate. We have taken care to separate concerns when necessary. We always separate data access from the domain model and the presentation layer, and we separate presentation model from views; you will not see simplistic examples such as performing a query directly from a UI controller. This is bad practice in anything but the most trivial applications such as that serving http://PartyWithPalermo.com (a three-page site). Real applications have many screens, the embedding data access and other logic in the UI is a recipe for a codebase that is very costly to maintain.

We've done our best to call out where we expect existing ASP.NET knowledge to tie the example together, but if you find yourself wondering what an HTTP module is, you will probably want to read one of the earlier ASP.NET books.

Roadmap

Chapter 1 throws the reader directly into code by picking apart the default project template. After a primer on routes, the text moves through a simple controller and view and moves to initial maintainability. The chapter follows up by covering the basics of testing controllers.

Chapter 2 moves into the model. It covers not only the domain model of the application but also the need for different types of models depending on usage, such as a presentation model. Because the authors consider using a presentation model, commonly called *view model*, essential for the maintainability for nontrivial systems, it is used right away.

Chapter 3 covers controller details. The controller can be very simple or quite complex, and the text covers both. The chapter explores working with form values and querystring values, and it covers model binding, which is one of the most-needed abstractions for ASP.NET to date. Chapter 3 concludes after outlining all the available extension points that are built in.

Chapter 4 gives further insight into views. After outlining the key abstractions in the default view engine, it pulls the reader along to essential concepts such as layouts, partial views, and building your own validation and HTML helpers.

Chapter 5 goes deeper than you will ever need into routing. Although most projects will not need this amount of advanced routing, we explore the topic thoroughly. We cover the *why* and not just the *how* of crafting URLs. From designing a URL schema to adding dynamic routes, this chapter is a comprehensive guide to the most flexible routes you will need.

Chapter 6 explores the many ways to customize and extend the ASP.NET MVC Framework. It starts with custom route handlers and moves to when, why, and how to create your own controller factory. Two Inversion of Control containers are covered in the controller factory section: Windsor and StructureMap. Because most nontrivial applications will want to use a custom controller factory, this section is covered thoroughly. Next the chapter moves through the ways to extend the controller with action invokers and filters. After a custom view engine and using the new T4 templates, the reader will have the full picture of the available extension points.

Chapter 7 communicates ways to scale the architecture for more complex sites. The first is solving the problem of large controller actions and how to move multiple, ill-placed responsibilities out of the controller. View helpers are also covered in more detail as well as techniques for segmenting large views into a number of cohesive smaller ones. The chapter also covers larger issues encountered with action filters.

Chapter 8 offers ways to leverage existing ASP.NET features in an ASP.NET MVC application. The text covers how to use existing server controls, then moves to caching, both output caching and using request level caching provided by `HttpContext.Items`. It then moves through tracing, health monitoring, site maps, personalization, localization, linq, cookies, session state, and configuration. Because ASP.NET MVC is an add-on to ASP.NET and not a replacement, this chapter ensures the reader understands where all these existing features fit.

Chapter 9 has been one of the most popular chapters in the early access program because now, in mid-2009, AJAX is a hot topic. We first lay down our opinionated view on AJAX and then outline the most common uses and techniques for it starting with simple HTML replacement. The chapter covers implementing a REST API with controllers as well as some of the third-party libraries and controls available for AJAX. The chapter also outlines ways to make controller actions automatically support AJAX.

Chapter 10 covers hosting and deployment. Though not as sexy of a topic as AJAX, it is critical to understand how to deploy applications built on this framework to IIS5/6/7/7.5. All versions are covered in detail as well as the implications of using extensions, wildcard mappings, and URL rewriting. After covering XCopy deployment, the chapter delivers techniques for managing production and development environment settings. The chapter closes out with an autodeployment example that is similar to how CodeCampServer is autodeployed in the wild.

Chapter 11 explores MonoRail and Ruby on Rails as a comparison and benchmark against ASP.NET MVC. It starts out with MonoRail and covers validation, data access with ActiveRecord, as well as the view engine choices. Rails follows closely on its heels with "The Rails Way," ActiveRecord and ActionPack. The purpose of the chapter is to give the reader some familiarity with competing MVC frameworks because good ideas come from everywhere.

Chapter 12 uses the controversial title, "Best Practices." We outline the context that these practices support. We outline best practices for controllers, views, routes, and testing. Each topic has very opinionated recommendations borne from real-world usage of ASP.NET MVC in this type of application.

Chapter 13 provides four comprehensive recipes that can be easily implemented on your project. One of the larger chapters, it starts with using jQuery for an autocomplete text box and then moves on to how to implement automatic client-side data validation. Data access with NHibernate is the next recipe and provides a full vertical slice implementation for calling data access backed by NHibernate from controllers. It outlines how to map and configure NHibernate as well as some basic mapping and querying techniques. The chapter wraps up with a full Spark view engine implementation for those who don't like the tag format of Web Forms.

Code conventions and downloads

All source code in listings or in text is in a `fixed-width font like this` to separate it from ordinary text. Code annotations accompany many of the listings, highlighting important concepts. In some cases, numbered bullets link to explanations that follow the listing.

The source code for the examples in this book is available online from the publisher's website at http://www.manning.com/ASP.NETMVCinAction.

Author Online

The purchase of *ASP.NET MVC in Action* includes free access to a private web forum run by Manning Publications, where you can make comments about the book, ask technical questions, and receive help from the author and from other users. To access the forum and subscribe to it, point your web browser to http://www.manning.com/ASP.NETMVCinAction.

This page provides information about how to get on the forum once you're registered, what kind of help is available, and the rules of conduct on the forum. Manning's commitment to our readers is to provide a venue where a meaningful dialogue between individual readers and between readers and the authors can take place. It's not a commitment to any specific amount of participation on the part of the authors, whose contribution to the book's forum remains voluntary (and unpaid). We suggest you try asking them some challenging questions, lest their interest stray!

The Author Online forum and the archives of previous discussions will be accessible from the publisher's website as long as the book is in print.

about the authors

JEFFREY PALERMO is the CTO of Headspring Systems. Jeffrey specializes in Agile management coaching and helps companies double the productivity of software teams. He is instrumental in the Austin software community as a member of AgileAustin and a director of the Austin .NET User Group. Jeffrey has been recognized by Microsoft as a "Microsoft Most Valuable Professional" (MVP) in Solutions Architecture for five years and participates in the ASPInsiders group, which advises the ASP. NET team on future releases. He is also certified as a MCSD.NET and ScrumMaster. Jeffrey has spoken and facilitated at industry conferences such as VSLive, DevTeach, the Microsoft MVP Summit, various ALT.NET conferences, and Microsoft Tech Ed. He also speaks to user groups around the country as part of the INETA Speakers' Bureau. His web sites are headspringsystems.com and jeffreypalermo.com. He is a graduate of Texas A&M University, an Eagle Scout, and an Iraq war veteran. Jeffrey is the founder of the Code-CampServer open-source project and a cofounder of the MvcContrib project.

Jeffrey Palermo is responsible for the popular Party with Palermo events that precede major Microsoft-focused conferences. Started in June of 2005, Party with Palermo has grown in popularity and size. Typical events host hundreds of people for free drinks and food and door prizes. It is the perfect way to hook up with friends and colleagues before the conference week begins. You can see past and upcoming parties at http://party-withpalermo.com where the website has run on ASP.NET MVC since October 2007.

BEN SCHEIRMAN is a software developer specializing in .NET. He has worked extensively on the web on various platforms and languages. Ben is a Microsoft MVP, Microsoft ASP Insider, and Certified ScrumMaster. When not programming, Ben enjoys speaking, blogging, spending time with his wife and five wonderful children, or voiding warranties on his latest gadgets. Ben is a Principal Consultant with Sogeti in Houston, Texas. Read his blog online at http://flux88.com.

JIMMY BOGARD is a Principal Consultant at Headspring Systems. He is an agile software developer with six years of professional development experience. He has delivered solutions from conception to production for many clients. The solutions delivered by Jimmy range from shrink-wrapped products to enterprise ecommerce applications for Fortune 100 customers. He is also a Microsoft Certified Application Developer (MCAD) and is an active member in the .NET community, lead-

ing open-source projects, giving technical presentations and facilitating technical book clubs. Currently, Jimmy is the lead developer on the NBehave project, a Behavior-Driven Development framework for .NET, AutoMapper, a convention-based object-to-object mapper and the facilitator of the Austin Domain-Driven Design Book Club. Jimmy is a member of the ASPInsiders group, and received the "Microsoft Most Valuable Professional" (MVP) award for ASP.NET in 2009.

About the technical reviewers

JEREMY SKINNER lives in the UK and works as a software developer. Most of his work involves writing web applications using ASP.NET and C#. He is involved with several open-source projects including MvcContrib, Fluent Validation, and Fluent Linq to Sql.

Jeremy has been invaluable to this book project by reviewing each paragraph of text, each figure, and code example. He found and corrected numerous errors, and this book would not be a good book without him. He is capable of being an author himself, and we fully expect full books out of him in the future. Jeremy's experience with the ASP.NET MVC framework as well as popular third-party frameworks such as Castle has made him a strong reviewer. His blog can be found at http://www.jeremyskinner.co.uk/.

FREEDOM DUMLAO is a software engineer working primarily in .NET. He has a blog at http://weblogs.asp.net/FreedomDumlao/. Freedom reviewed the first drafts of each chapter and made critical suggestions for improvement. His perspective was very valuable to the quality of the book.

about the cover illustration

The figure on the cover of *ASP.NET MVC in Action* is captioned "L'Habitant de Versailles" which means a resident of the town of Versailles. Today, Versailles is a suburb of Paris with a population of over 90,000, but in the past it was famous both as the capital city of France for a number of years in the 17th and 18th centuries and for the Palace of Versailles around which the city grew.

The illustration is taken from a 19th century edition of Sylvain Maréchal's four-volume compendium of regional dress customs published in France. Each illustration is finely drawn and colored by hand. The rich variety of Maréchal's collection reminds us vividly of how culturally apart the world's towns and regions were just 200 years ago. Isolated from each other, people spoke different dialects and languages. In the streets or in the countryside, it was easy to identify where they lived and what their trade or station in life was just by what they were wearing.

Dress codes have changed since then and the diversity by region, so rich at the time, has faded away. It is now hard to tell apart the inhabitants of different continents, let alone different towns or regions. Perhaps we have traded cultural diversity for a more varied personal life—certainly for a more varied and fast-paced technological life.

At a time when it is hard to tell one computer book from another, Manning celebrates the inventiveness and initiative of the computer business with book covers based on the rich diversity of regional life of two centuries ago, brought back to life by Maréchal's pictures.

Getting started with the ASP.NET MVC Framework

This chapter covers

- Running the starter project
- Progressing through Hello World examples
- Routing basics
- Unit testing basics

Depending on how long you've been building web applications on the Microsoft platform, you'll relate to some or all of the following pain. In the 1990s, developers built interactive websites using executable programs that ran on a server. These programs (Common Gateway Interface [CGI] was a common technology at the time) accepted a web request and were responsible for creating an HTML response. Templating was ad hoc, and the programs were difficult to write, debug, and test. In the late 1990s, Microsoft, after a brief stint with HTX templates and IDC connectors, introduced Active Server Pages, or *ASP*. ASP brought templating to web applications.

The server page was an HTML document with dynamic script mixed in. Although this was a big step forward from the alternatives, the world soon saw massive server pages with code indecipherable from the markup.

In early 2002, along came ASP.NET and the Web Forms Framework. Web Forms were a complete shift for ASP developers, partly because they moved most program logic into a class file (called a code-behind) and replaced the HTML markup with dynamic server controls written in an XML syntax. Although performance increased, and the debugging experience improved, new problems arose.

The new server-side postback event lifecycle caused newsgroups to explode with activity as confused developers searched for that *magic* event in which to add those two simple lines of code necessary to make the page work as needed. ViewState, although good in theory, broke down as the application scaled with complexity. Simple pages surpassed 100KB in size, as the entire state of the application had to be stored in the output of every generated page. Development best practices were ignored as tools like Visual Studio encouraged data access concerns like SQL queries to be embedded within view logic. Perhaps the greatest sin of the Web Forms Framework was the tight coupling to everything in the System.Web namespace. There was no hope of unit testing any code in the code-behind file, and today we see Page_Load methods that take several trees to print. Although early versions of Web Forms had some drawbacks, ASP.NET and the larger .NET Framework have made huge inroads into the web application market. Today we see major websites such as CallawayGolf.com, Dell.com, Newsweek.com, WhiteHouse.gov, and Match.com all running on ASP.NET. The platform has proven itself in the marketplace, and when combined with IIS running on Windows, ASP.NET can easily support complex web applications running in large data centers. The ASP.NET MVC Framework leverages the success of ASP.NET and Web Forms to propel ASP.NET forward as a leader in the web application development space.

The ASP.NET MVC Framework has been introduced to simplify the complex parts of Web Forms application development while retaining the power and flexibility of the ASP.NET pipeline. The ASP.NET infrastructure and request pipeline, introduced in .NET 1.0, stay the same, and ASP.NET MVC provides support for developing ASP.NET applications using the Model-View-Controller web presentation pattern. The concerns of the data model, the application logic, and data presentation are cleanly separated, with the application logic kept in a class separated from hard dependencies on how the data will be presented. Server pages have become simple views, which are nothing more than HTML templates waiting to be populated with objects (models) passed in by the controller. The postback event lifecycle is no more, and ViewState is no longer necessary. In this chapter, we'll walk through your first lines of code built on top of the ASP.NET MVC Framework. After this primer, you'll be ready for more advanced topics.

In this chapter, and throughout the book, we assume that the reader has knowledge of ASP.NET. If you're new to ASP.NET, please familiarize yourself with the ASP.NET request pipeline as well as the .NET runtime. Throughout this chapter, we'll take you through creating an ASP.NET MVC Framework web application project, creating your

> ### Integrating with or migrating from ASP.NET Web Forms applications
>
> Can we create screens that leverage the ASP.NET MVC Framework while others continue to work using Web Forms? Of course we can. They can run side by side until the entire application is MVC. Using the MVC framework is not an all-or-nothing proposition. There are many, many ASP.NET applications in production using Web Forms. If a software team wants to migrate the application from Web Forms to ASP.NET MVC, it's possible to do a phased migration and run the two side by side in the same App-Domain. ASP.NET MVC does not replace core ASP.NET libraries or functionality. Rather, it builds on top of existing ASP.NET capabilities. The `UrlRoutingModule` that we registered in the web.config file causes an incoming URL to be evaluated against the existing routes. If a matching route is not found, ASP.NET will continue on and use Web Forms to fill the request, so it's pretty simple to mix and match features during a migration or for the purpose of application extension.
>
> Although Web Forms is not going away any time soon, we believe that controllers, actions, and views will be the preferred way to write ASP.NET applications going into the future. Although Microsoft will continue to support both options (and active development on the next version of Web Forms continues), we believe that the ASP.NET MVC Framework will be favored over Web Forms much like we see C# favored over VB in documentation, industry conferences, and technical books.

first *routes*, *controllers*, and *views*. We'll comb through the default application and explain each part. Then we'll extend it, and you'll create your first controller and view. First, let's explore the MVC pattern and the default application template provided with the framework.

1.1   Picking apart the default application

In this section, we'll explain what the MVC pattern is and create our first ASP.NET MVC Web Application. We'll focus first on the controller because in the Model-View-Controller triad, the controller is in charge and decides what model objects to use and what views to render. The controller is in charge of coordination and executes first when the web request comes in to the application. The controller is responsible for deciding what response is appropriate for the request.

The Model-View-Controller pattern is not new. A core tenet of the MVC pattern is to separate control logic from the view, or a screen. A view is only responsible for rendering the user interface. By separating domain logic and decoupling data access and other calls from the view, the UI can stay the same even while logic and data access changes within the application. Figure 1.1 shows a simple diagram of the MVC triad. Note that the controller has a direct relationship with the view and the model, but the model does not need to know about the controller or the view. The web request will be handled by the controller, and the controller will decide which model objects to use and which view objects to render.

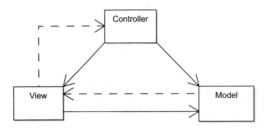

Figure 1.1 A simple diagram depicting the relationship between the Model, View, and Controller. The solid lines indicate a direct association, and the dashed lines indicate an indirect association (graphic and description used with permission from Wikipedia).

To begin, we'll open up Visual Studio 2008 SP1 and create our project. The edition of Visual Studio 2008 makes a difference. Although there are some workarounds to using the ASP.NET MVC Framework without SP1, System.Web.Abstractions.dll and System.Web.Routing.dll are in the GAC (global assembly cache) as of SP1. You can use Visual Studio 2008 Professional, a Team Edition SKU, or Visual Web Developer Express SP1. Note that the ASP.NET MVC Framework builds on top of Web Application Projects, and although it's possible to make it work with websites, the development experience is optimized for use with Web Application Projects.

NOTE You must already have Visual Studio 2008 SP1 or Visual Web Developer 2008 SP1, .NET 3.5 SP1, and the ASP.NET MVC Framework installed to proceed. The MVC framework is an independent release that builds upon .NET 3.5 Service Pack 1. The examples in this book will use Visual Studio 2008 SP1, but you can find information on using the free Visual Web Developer Express 2008 SP1 on the ASP.NET MVC website: http://www.asp.net/mvc/.

We'll begin in Visual Studio 2008 Professional SP1 by creating a new ASP.NET MVC Web Application project. When you pull up the New Project dialog, make sure you have .NET Framework 3.5 selected. If you have .NET Framework 3.0 or 2.0 selected, Visual Studio will filter the list, and you'll not see the project template for ASP.NET MVC Web Application. Now that you understand the basics of the pattern and how to install the MVC framework, we'll dive into our first project.

1.1.1 *Creating the project*

Creating your first ASP.NET MVC Web Application project will be one of the simplest things you do in this chapter. In Visual Studio 2008, when you have .NET Framework 3.5 selected as the target framework, you'll see a new project template named ASP.NET MVC Web Application. Choose this project template. The new project dialog will look like that shown in figure 1.2.

We're going to be working with a C# ASP.NET MVC Web Application project. You have two options for creating the project. When you click OK, the IDE will ask you about creating a test project. Decide if you'd like it done for you or if you'd rather create the unit test project yourself. For this example, we'll choose the ASP.NET MVC Web Application with the test project. Figure 1.3 shows the solution structure of the default Visual Studio template. Since this is not a beginners' book, we'll skip the hand-holding and go straight into the project.

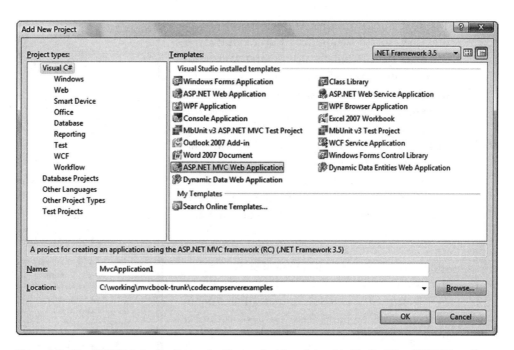

Figure 1.2   The MVC Web Application project is a project template added to the C# and VB.NET sections of the New Project dialog. It's only available when you have .NET Framework 3.5 selected as the target framework.

NOTE   More ASP.NET MVC starter kits and sample applications are available from the community on the ASP.NET website. At the time of writing, http://www.asp.net/community/projects/ and http://www.asp.net/mvc/ have several starter kits and sample applications for starting ASP.NET MVC projects (as well as ASP.NET Web Forms starter kits). The options include

- Kigg Starter Kit—a Digg-like application
- Contact Manager Sample Application
- Storefront Starter Kit

Although the starter kits are quite basic, you should also check out more complete starter kits like those found at http://CommunityForMvc.net. This site contains a bare-bones template as well as one complete with MvcContrib, StructureMap, NHibernate, NUnit, NAnt, AutoMapper, Tarantino, Naak, NBehave, Rhino Mocks, WatiN, Gallio, Castle, 7zip, and more.

If you're new to .NET development in general, you should first become familiar with Microsoft's default template. Then use a more robust starter kit or sample application provided by the community to have a better jumping-off point. When you have mastered the framework, think about contributing your own starter kits.

The first thing to notice is that in contrast to the very sparse structure of a default Web Forms project template, the default MVC template creates several folders: Content, Controllers, Models, Scripts, and Views. These folders represent part of the MVC application development conventions, which, if adhered to, can make the experience of developing with the MVC framework a breeze.

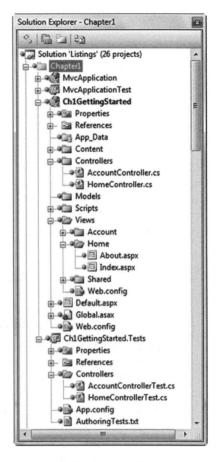

For now, the most important of these folders to become familiar with are the three which have been named after their MVC pattern counterparts (the Model, View, and Controller folders). As you'd expect, the purpose of each of these folders is to provide logical separation of the three MVC concerns, as well as to tap into a nice feature of Visual Studio that will automatically namespace any class created within a folder with that folder's name.

The Controllers folder is probably the least interesting. The folder should contain only classes which are to be used as controllers, or base classes and interfaces that controllers might inherit from. The Views folder is special because it will contain code that will probably be the most familiar to Web Forms developers. The Views folder contains the aspx (views), ascx (partial views), and master pages used to present the data. Typically you'll have a folder inside the Views folder for each controller

Figure 1.3 The default structure for a web application project using the ASP.NET MVC Framework uses conventions for the placement of files.

which will contain views intended to be used specifically by that controller, as well as a Shared folder to contain shared views.

The Happy Path

ASP.NET MVC developers (and developers using other convention-centric frameworks) will often mention the Happy Path. This refers to the notion that following the MVC framework's conventions will make the developer's experience both enjoyable and relatively painless. The MVC framework does not require you to adhere to any particular convention, but the farther you stray from the Happy Path the greater the effort will be required by the developer. The MvcContrib project enhances the path, and you'll certainly find ways to enhance it in your system. Staying on the path gains you a great deal in consistency.

For most nontrivial projects, you probably won't place your models in the Models folder. Generally speaking it's a best practice to keep your domain model in a separate project so that other applications can use it without taking a dependency on your MVC application. We recommend that you put only presentation concerns in the Web Application project.

In the default project, you may be familiar with the `Default.aspx` file that is provided for you, and we'll discuss shortly why it is there. First, we must understand the concept of a *route*.

1.1.2 *Your first routes*

Routes will be discussed in great detail in chapter 5; however, you should be aware of some route basics to move through this section. Although Web Forms mandated a strict convention for URLs, the MVC framework provides a mechanism to allow developers to handcraft URLs, and have them map automatically to an object in the system that can handle the incoming web request. Routing was added to ASP.NET in the .NET Framework 3.5 Service Pack 1 release, and is available to all ASP.NET applications. The `Global.asax.cs` file contains basic routes that are provided with the MVC Web Application project to help you get started. Before continuing, we should define a route.

A route is the complete definition for how to dispatch a web request to a controller, usually using the `System.Web.Mvc.MvcRouteHandler`. In the past we have had little control over message dispatching without resorting to external tools like ISAPI filters or carefully crafted `HttpModules` for URL rewriting. With Web Forms, the URL of the web request was tightly coupled to the location of the page handling the request. If the page was named `Foo.aspx` in a folder named `Samples`, the URL was sure to be something like `http://MvcContrib.org/Samples/Foo.aspx`. Many teams have resorted to URL rewriting to wrangle some control over the URLs and how they are produced. With the ASP.NET MVC Framework, and ASP.NET 3.5 SP1 in general, routes are first-class citizens that can be managed directly in the web application. We start with defining how we want our URLs structured. The project template gives us a few routes to start, as shown in listing 1.1.

Listing 1.1 Default routes for a new project

```
using System.Web;
using System.Web.Mvc;
using System.Web.Routing;

namespace Ch1GettingStarted
{
    public class MvcApplication : HttpApplication
    {
        public static void RegisterRoutes(RouteCollection routes)
        {
            routes.IgnoreRoute("{resource}.axd/{*pathInfo}");

            routes.MapRoute(
                "Default",                          ◁— Route name
                "{controller}/{action}/{id}",       ◁— URL with parameters
```

```
                new {controller = "Home", action = "Index", id = ""}      ◄─┐
                );
        }                                                         Parameter defaults │

    protected void Application_Start ()
    {
        RegisterRoutes(RouteTable.Routes);
    }
  }
}
```

Routes must be defined before any request can be received by the application, so the project template adds the routes to the Application_Start method in the Global. asax.cs file. Later in the book, you'll see that we do not leave the routes in this location except for the most trivial of web applications.

NOTE   We'll follow long-standing best practices of *separation of concerns (SoC)* and the *single responsibility principle,* or *SRP,* by moving the routes to a dedicated location separated by an interface. We'll go further into these principles later, but, in short, the responsibility (or concern) of the Application_Start method is to kick off operations that must happen at the beginning of the application's life. The responsible approach is to avoid performing every bit of work that must happen on start. Any operations that must happen when the application starts should reside in separate classes and merely be called in the appropriate order in the Application_Start method.

Note that the URL portion of the route is simply a matching mechanism for the request. If the URL matches a particular route, then we specify what controller should handle the request and what action method should execute. You can create as many routes as you like, but one route is provided for you. This route has the template, {controller}/ {action}/{id}.

The route with the template {controller}/{action}/{id} is a generic one and can be used for many, many different web requests. Tokens are denoted by the inclusion of {braces}, and the word enclosed in braces matches a value the MVC framework understands. The most common values that we'll be interested in are controller and action. The controller route value is a special value that the System.Web.Mvc. MvcHandler class uses to call into the IControllerFactory interface. This is also the route we'll be using for the rest of the chapter, so we'll be content with a URL in the form of http://MvcContrib.org/controller- name/actionname. The basic route handler is an instance of IRoute- Handler named MvcRouteHandler. We have complete control and could provide our own implementation of IRouteHandler if we wished, but we'll save that for a later chapter.

Before we spin up our first controller, let's examine what is different about the web.config file in an MVC Web Application project. The differences are easy to spot.

Just look for "routing" or "MVC." One difference we see is that a new `IHttpModule` is registered in the config file. We see the `UrlRoutingModule` in listing 1.2.

Listing 1.2   Unique addition to the web.config file

```
<add name="UrlRoutingModule" type="System.Web.Routing.UrlRoutingModule,
    System.Web.Routing, Version=3.5.0.0, Culture=neutral,
    PublicKeyToken=31BF3856AD364E35" />
```

The `UrlRoutingModule` evaluates a request and checks if it matches a route that is stored in the `RouteTable`. If the route matches, it overrides the default handler (`IHttpHandler`) for the request so that the MVC framework handles the request. We're going to examine our first controller as a means to handle a route for the URL /home. In the next section you'll see how all the pieces of the starter project fit together.

1.1.3   Running with the starter project

We're going to move through the starter project quickly looking at each piece of provided code. Each serves as an example of how to fit code together when writing an application with the presentation layer powered by the ASP.NET MVC Framework. Before looking at code, run the web application by pressing CTRL + F5, and you should see a screen that resembles figure 1.4.

The starter project includes some navigation, a Log On, and content. The CSS provides simple formatting

Figure 1.4   The starter project comes with a basic layout and CSS.

on top of XHTML. Notice the URL in the address bar is /. "/home" also will bring up the same page since our route specifies "home" as the default controller. This URL does not have an extension, so if you're planning on running your application on IIS 6, you must either add a wildcard mapping or install an ISAPI filter that provides this functionality. Deployment to IIS 6 will be covered in more detail in chapter 10.

Since you're familiar with the ASP.NET request pipeline, we'll briefly move through how this request makes its way to an ASP.NET MVC controller. The following outlines how the request moves through ASP.NET, to the controller, and through the view:

1   Request comes in to /Home.
2   IIS determines the request should be handled by ASP.NET.
3   ASP.NET gives all `HttpModules` a chance to modify the request.
4   The `UrlRoutingModule` determines that the URL matches a route configured in the application.

5 The `UrlRoutingModule` gets the appropriate `IHttpHandler` from the `IRoute-Handler` that is used in the matching route (most often, `MvcRouteHandler`) as the handler for the request.

6 The `MvcRouteHandler` constructs and returns `MvcHandler`.

7 The `MvcHandler`, which implements `IHttpHandler`, executes `ProcessRequest`.

8 The `MvcHandler` uses `IControllerFactory` to obtain an instance of `IController` using the "controller" to route data from the route `{controller}/{action}/{id}`.

9 The `HomeController` is found, and its `Execute` method is invoked.

10 The `HomeController` invokes the `Index` action.

11 The `Index` action adds objects to the `ViewData` dictionary.

12 The `HomeController` invokes the `ActionResult` returned from the action, which renders a view.

13 The `Index` view in the Views folder displays the objects in `ViewData`.

14 The view, derived from `System.Web.Mvc.ViewPage`, executes its `Process-Request` method.

15 ASP.NET renders the response to the browser.

These steps represent the simplified life of a request handled by the ASP.NET MVC Framework. If you're curious about the details, you can browse the source code at http://www.codeplex.com/aspnet. The 15 steps are sufficient for understanding how to write code based on the ASP.NET MVC Framework, and most of the time you'll need to pay attention only to the controller and the view. You have already seen the route used in the starter project. Let's look at the `HomeController`, shown in listing 1.3.

Listing 1.3 The `HomeController`

```
using System.Web.Mvc;

namespace Ch1GettingStarted.Controllers
{
    [HandleError]
    public class HomeController : Controller        ❶
    {
        public ActionResult Index()
        {
            ViewData ["Message"] = "Welcome to ASP.NET MVC!";        ❷

            return View();
        }
        public ActionResult About()
        {
            return View();
        }
    }
}
```

❶ Default action for controller
❷ Return default view for action

Another action method

Notice how simple the controller is. There is not much generated code to wade through, and each action method returns an object derived from `ActionResult`. This controller derives from System.Web.Mvc.Controller ❶. You'll probably find this base class adequate, but there are others to choose from in the MvcContrib project, and as time goes on, the community will likely make many more available. It also may be a good practice to create your own *layer supertype* to use in your application.

Inside each action method, you'll typically put some objects into a dictionary called ViewData ❷. This dictionary will be passed to the view upon rendering. The controller can provide any objects the view requires in this ViewData dictionary; the primary object the view will render should be assigned to the ViewData's Model property. This can be done automatically by passing the object into the controller's View() method. In the starter project, the objects are simple strings, but in your application, you'll use more complex objects like those in figure 1.5.

Each default action returns the result of the View() method, which returns a System.Web.Mvc. ViewResult object. This ActionResult subclass will likely be a common result given that your applications will have many screens. In some cases, you may use the other ActionResult types as shown in figure 1.5. Your controller action can return any type. The Controller base class will call ToString() on your object and return that string in a ContentResult object. Next, let's look at the view shown in listing 1.4, which can be found in the project in the following path: /Views/Home/Index.aspx.

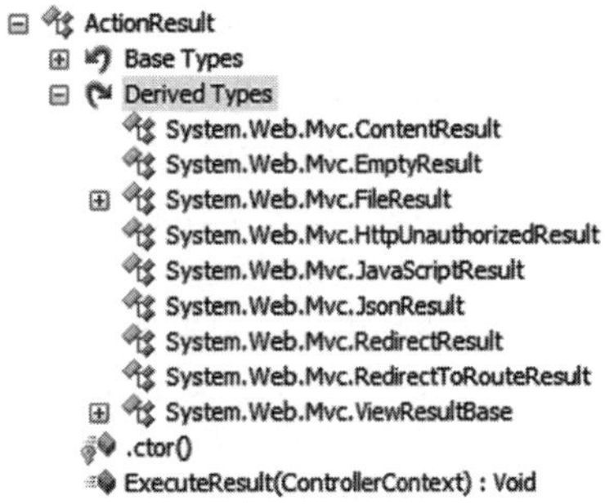

Figure 1.5 Classes that derive from ActionResult. This screenshot is from Red Gate's .Net Reflector.

Listing 1.4 A simple view

```
<%@ Page Language="C#" MasterPageFile="~/Views/Shared/Site.Master"
Inherits="System.Web.Mvc.ViewPage" %>

<asp:Content ID="indexTitle" ContentPlaceHolderID="TitleContent"
➥     runat="server">
  Home Page
</asp:Content>

<asp:Content ID="indexContent" ContentPlaceHolderID="MainContent"
➥     runat="server">
  <h2><%= Html.Encode(ViewData ["Message"]) %></h2>
  <p>
    To learn more about ASP.NET MVC visit
    <a href="http://asp.net/mvc" title="ASP.NET MVC
        Website">http://asp.net/mvc</a>.
  </p>
</asp:Content>
```

The view shown in listing 1.4 is the one rendered in the browser screenshot shown in figure 1.4. With the MVC framework, markup files do not use a code-behind file. Since the view uses the Web Forms templating engine, you could use it, but by default just a simple markup file is generated.

This view uses a master page, as you can see in the `MasterPageFile` attribute in the `Page` directive. The master can be specified by the controller for compatibility with many view engines, but some view engines support the view specifying the layout, which is the case with the Web Forms view engine, the default view engine that ships with the MVC framework.

NOTE: A `ViewResult` leverages the `IViewEngine` interface, which is an abstraction that allows the usage of any mechanism for rendering a view. View engines will be covered in more depth later, but some alternatives can be found in the MvcContrib open source project.

In the body of this view, the server-side tags are pulling objects out of `ViewData` and rendering them in line with HTML. The responsibility of the view is to take objects in `ViewData` and render them for consumption by the user. The view does not decide what to render, only how to render. The controller has already decided what needs to be rendered.

In listing 1.5, examine the code of the layout. You immediately see that it's a plain master page, not much different from those found in Web Forms. The difference is that master pages in MVC projects do not need to use code-behind files.

Listing 1.5 The starter project master page

```
<%@ Master Language="C#" Inherits="System.Web.Mvc.ViewMasterPage" %>

<!DOCTYPE html PUBLIC "-//W3C//DTD XHTML 1.0 Strict//EN" "http://www.w3.org/
    TR/xhtml1/DTD/xhtml1-strict.dtd">
<html xmlns="http://www.w3.org/1999/xhtml">
<head runat="server">
  <meta http-equiv="Content-Type" content="text/html; charset=iso-8859-1"/>
  <title><asp:ContentPlaceHolder ID="TitleContent" runat="server" />
  </title>
  <link href="../../Content/Site.css" rel="stylesheet" type="text/css" />
</head>
<body>
  <div class="page">
    <div id="header">
      <div id="title">
        <h1>My MVC Application</h1>
      </div>
      <div id="logindisplay">
        <% Html.RenderPartial("LogOnUserControl"); %>          ⟵┐ Render
      </div>                                                         another view
      <div id="menucontainer">

        <ul id="menu">
          <li><%= Html.ActionLink("Home", "Index", "Home")%></li>     ⟵┐
          <li><%= Html.ActionLink("About", "About", "Home")%></li>     │
        </ul>                                                          │
      </div>                                                           │
    </div>                                                    Render hyperlinks
    <div id="main">
      <asp:ContentPlaceHolder ID="MainContent" runat="server" />
```

```
            <div id="footer">
            </div>
        </div>
    </div>
</body>
</html>
```

The master page here is in charge of navigation. It uses *view helpers* (Html.Action-Link in this case) to render the links. View helpers are available for most common dynamic needs and for all form elements. More view helpers are available in Mvc-Contrib, and third-party component vendors will not be far behind in offering commercial view helpers.

Now that you have seen how the code in the starter project fits together, let's see how to test the controller code. View code will still need to be tested with a tool like Selenium, Watir, or WatiN, but controller code can easily be test-driven since it's decoupled from the view and the ASP.NET runtime. When you start a new MVC project, a dialog will ask you which unit testing framework you'd like to use.

If you're using Visual Studio 2008 Professional then *Visual Studio Unit Test* will already be in the list and selected. Most common unit testing frameworks have templates that show up in the list when they are installed. For now we'll look at using MSTest (Visual Studio Unit Test), but we recommend using NUnit. If you're just starting out in automated testing, any mainstream framework will do. Listing 1.6 shows an MSTest test method included in the default test project template.

Listing 1.6 The unit test for the Index action

```
using System.Web.Mvc;
using Ch1GettingStarted.Controllers;
using Microsoft.VisualStudio.TestTools.UnitTesting;

namespace Ch1GettingStarted.Tests.Controllers
{
    [TestClass]
    public class HomeControllerTest
    {
        [TestMethod]
        public void Index()
        {
            HomeController controller = new HomeController();

            ViewResult result = controller.Index() as ViewResult;

            ViewDataDictionary viewData = result.ViewData;
            Assert.AreEqual("Welcome to ASP.NET MVC!",viewData["Message"]);
        }
    }
}
```

Believe it or not, we have walked through the complete ASP.NET starter project, and you now know the basics of the new framework. Obviously, we'll be moving into more complex topics throughout this book, and if any topic along the way does not sink in completely, please crack open Visual Studio and poke around while reading. Working with the code directly, along with reading this text, will give you a solid understanding of this technology. In fact, now is a great time to download the code samples for this book and open your IDE default application.

1.2   *Your first ASP.NET MVC controller from scratch*

Look at listing 1.7 to understand how a web request is processed by the controller. Note the only requirement is to implement the `IController` interface.

> **Listing 1.7   Our first controller**

```
using System;
using System.Web.Mvc;
using System.Web.Routing;

namespace MvcApplication.Controllers
{
    public class HelloWorld1Controller : IController        ❶
    {
        public void Execute(RequestContext requestContext)
        {
            requestContext.HttpContext.Response.Write(
                "<h1>Hello World1</h1>");
        }
    }
}
```

As with everything in the ASP.NET MVC Framework, there is very little the developer must do to create custom functionality. In the case of the controller, the only—I will say it again—the only requirement is that the class implement the `IController` interface ❶. This interface only requires that you implement a single method: `Execute`. How you handle the request is entirely up to you. In the controller in listing 1.7, we're intentionally violating all principles of sensible programming as well as the *Law of Demeter* in order to get the message "Hello World" written out to the screen as quickly as possible. In this case, I've chosen not to make any use of a view. Rather, I'm formulating incomplete HTML markup and directing it to the response stream. We'll run the sample and note the output in figure 1.6. In the code solution that comes with the book, you can find `HelloWorld1ControllerTester` that illustrates how you'd unit test a simple controller like this.

Figure 1.6   Our web application running in the browser. Note the simple URL and the absence of .aspx.

Listing 1.7 shows the absolute and complete power you have when creating a controller class. It's very important to have complete control; however, most of the time, we're working in a handful of scenarios that repeat over and over. For these scenarios, the product provides a base class that gives extra functionality. The base class for these common controllers is System.Web.Mvc.Controller. It implements the Execute method for us and uses the route values to call different *action* methods depending on the URL and the route defaults.

NOTE   System.Web.Mvc.Controller is only one option to choose as a base class for your controllers. As mentioned earlier, it's often appropriate to create your own *layer supertype* for all of your controllers. This type can inherit from System.Web.Mvc.Controller, implement IController, or derive from any other controller base class.

Our first use of the Controller base class will need only one action method, and we'll go with the convention for the default action and call it Index. Observe in listing 1.8 what our controller looks like while we leverage the Controller base class. This base class implements the IController interface for us and provides the capability of invoking action methods based on the current Route.

Listing 1.8   Using the Controller base class

```
using System.Web.Mvc;

namespace MvcApplication.Controllers
{
    public class HelloWorld2Controller : Controller      ◁——  Inherit from
    {                                                           Controller
        public string Index()
        {
            return "<h1>Hello World2</h1>";
        }
    }
}
```

The public Index action method is all that is necessary for this controller to be web-callable. Simple content action methods need not return ActionResult. Returning any other type will result in that object being rendered as content to the response stream.

If we point our browser to /HelloWorld2, we'll see that our controller sends the same response to the browser as shown in figure 1.7:

Figure 1.7   The web page has the same output as before. The end result is the same even though the controller implementation has evolved.

Now that we know how to craft a controller, we'll explore our first view.

1.3 Our first view

Recall that the ASP.NET MVC Framework uses a convention for locating views. The convention is to find a .aspx file in a directory tree that matches /Views/controller-name/actionname.aspx. In our next example, we'll modify our controller by calling a method on the Controller base class called View(). We'll set the model, which is a string with the text "Hello World", to an entry in the ViewDataDictionary object on the ViewData property of the Controller base class. This ViewDataDictionary instance will be forwarded to the view. Although ViewData is a ViewDataDictionary we recommend you depend only on the IDictionary<string, object> interface if you're replacing the view engine. View engines will be discussed in more detail in chapter 4. In listing 1.9, we see that our action returns ActionResult instead of string. After an action method returns, the ActionResult executes to perform the appropriate behavior, which is rendering a view in this case. Examine listing 1.9 for the current implementation of our controller. ViewData contains the object that will be forwarded on to the view. The View() method also supports passing a single object to the view that is then accessible via ViewData.Model, which we'll explore later.

> **Listing 1.9 Using a view to render the model**

```
using System.Web.Mvc;

namespace MvcApplication.Controllers
{
    public class HelloWorld3Controller : Controller
    {
        public ActionResult Index()
        {
            ViewData.Add("text", "Hello World3");    ◁⎯┐ Add objects
            return View();                                  │ to ViewData
        }
    }
}
```

If you're following along with this example, you'll want to create a HelloWorld3 folder inside /Views in your project as shown in figure 1.8.

Next, add a view to the project inside /Views/Helloworld3. You can use the New Item dialog for the project and select the MVC View Page; a quicker way is to use the context menu (right click) off of the action and select Add View… as shown in figure 1.9. This tool will create a view with the proper name inside the proper folder. Your project should now look similar to figure 1.8. Our new view, Index.aspx, resides in the HelloWorld3 folder.

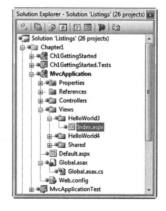

Figure 1.8 The proper location of the HelloWorld3 folder is inside the /Views folder. The default view factory uses this convention. You can override this behavior if you wish.

```
public class HelloWorld3Cor                                    ler
{
    public ActionResult In
    {
        ViewData.Add("text
        return View();
    }
}
```

**Figure 1.9 Adding the view to
our project via the context menu**

Our markup within the view will be very simple. After all, this application is so trivial that all it has to do is output "Hello World3" to the screen in big text. We'll use the <% server-side operators to pull out our model (which is a string) from the `ViewData` dictionary and render it to the screen. Listing 1.10 has our markup for the view. The base class is `System.Web.Mvc.ViewPage`. This is a very important difference from Web Forms.

Listing 1.10 Accessing `ViewData` from within the view

```
<%@ Page Language="C#" Inherits="System.Web.Mvc.ViewPage" %>
<!DOCTYPE html PUBLIC "-//W3C//DTD XHTML 1.0 Transitional//EN"
"http://www.w3.org/TR/xhtml1/DTD/xhtml1-transitional.dtd">

<html xmlns="http://www.w3.org/1999/xhtml" >
<head runat="server">
  <title></title>
</head>
<body>
  <div>
    <h1><%=ViewData ["text"]%></h1>
  </div>
</body>
</html>
```

The flow from our controller to our view is simple. The controller designates one or many objects to be forwarded to the view, then optionally specifies the name of the view. The MVC framework will locate the view, instantiate it, push in the `ViewData`, and have the view render itself to the response stream. The `ViewPage` base class fully supports rendering, but `ViewState`, postbacks, and the server-side postback events no longer happen. Rendering events still fire since `ViewPage` derives from `System.Web.UI.Page`.

The view's only responsibility is to transform objects passed to it into HTML. This is a key part of the SoC, a key best practice that Microsoft is focusing on with this product. The controller does not know how the view is doing the formatting. The only point of coupling is that the controller names the view, either implicitly with the name of the action, or explicitly with the `View()` method. It does not matter that the `System.Web.Mvc.WebFormViewEngine` is executing. The same controller could function quite well with an NVelocity view (supported in MvcContrib) since the controller's only coupling to the view is the view name. For now, we'll forward "Hello World3" to the view, and figure 1.10 shows the rendered page. This example has shown how to get a simple case working, but there are maintenance concerns you should be aware of while building an application with this framework.

Figure 1.10   The output is the same as previous examples, except now we have a full HTML page and not an HTML fragment.

1.4   *Ensuring the application is maintainable*

You might have cringed when you saw that the domain model object was being pushed into an `IDictionary` with a `string` key as the way to identify the object in the view. .NET has conditioned us to want everything to be strongly typed, so string identifiers are sometimes viewed as a negative. That point is subjective and controversial, and you have several options depending on your preferences.

NOTE   Using a dictionary to pass objects between different parts of an application (typically called a *property bag*) allows the various parts of the application to be loosely coupled. The downside is that objects coming out of the property bag may need to be cast before being used.

The use of an `IDictionary<string, object>` for `ViewData` is the default mechanism in the `Controller` base class. As the number of objects forwarded to the view increase, it's easy to create helpers in the view to avoid casting operations everywhere. However, many controller actions will forward only one object to the view, and for those cases, we can make use of the `ViewData.Model` property as well as strongly typed views. For our next example, we'll make a small change to our controller and view to enable a strongly typed reference.

Listing 1.11 shows our controller discarding the use of the `IDictionary<string, object>` and passing the domain model object directly to the `View()` method. This works well for many scenarios and it scales to large applications with the use of a view model, which is a presentation object specifically crafted for use in a single view. For composed views using `ViewData` as a dictionary may be necessary, but partial views, covered in chapter 4, can also provide for composed views.

NOTE   In listing 1.11 we have to cast our string "Hello World4" to an object when we pass it to the `View()` method. This is because one of the overloads of `View()` takes a single string as a parameter, which is used to specify a particular view to be rendered.

> **Listing 1.11   Passing in the presentation model to the `View` method**

```
using System.Web.Mvc;

namespace MvcApplication.Controllers
```

```
{
  public class HelloWorld4Controller : Controller
  {
    public ActionResult Index()
    {
      return View((object)"Hello World4");    ◁──┐ Cast so correct
    }                                              overload called
  }
}
```

Notice that we have a `Model` property (a shortcut to `ViewData.Model`) available that is the type declared as the generic parameter for `ViewPage<T>` in the `Inherits` tag. In listing 1.12 we have chosen `System.Web.Mvc.ViewPage<string>`. The generic base class allows us to strongly type the `ViewData.Model` property because the `ViewData` property is of type `ViewDataDictionary<T>`, and the `Model` property is of type `T`.

Listing 1.12 Strongly typed view with master page

```
<%@ Page Language="C#" Inherits="System.Web.Mvc.ViewPage<string>"
MasterPageFile="~/Views/Shared/HelloWorld.Master"%>
<%@ Import Namespace="MvcApplication.Controllers"%>

<asp:Content ID="Content2" ContentPlaceHolderID="Main" runat="server">

  <h1><%=Model%>! I'm strongly typed in a layout!</h1>

</asp:Content>
```

In this example, the view has chosen the master page, but as we've said before, you can also choose the master inside the controller action. It's up to you, but not all view engines support the view specifying the master, so if there is a chance you may want to change view engines later, you may want to consider specifying the master in the controller. The downside to this is that you increase the tightness of coupling to the views.

Master pages function the same as in Web Forms for templating, but the server-side postback and `ViewState` mechanisms are irrelevant. Rendering is the only responsibility of the view and the master page. Listing 1.13 shows our master page, which outlines the structure for the page. The layout declares `System.Web.Mvc.View-MasterPage` as the base type.

Listing 1.13 The layout for our view

```
<%@ Master Language="C#" AutoEventWireup="true"
  Inherits="System.Web.Mvc.ViewMasterPage" %>

<!DOCTYPE html PUBLIC "-//W3C//DTD XHTML 1.0 Transitional//EN"
"http://www.w3.org/TR/xhtml1/DTD/xhtml1-transitional.dtd">

<html xmlns="http://www.w3.org/1999/xhtml" >
<head runat="server">
  <title>Hello!!</title>
  <asp:ContentPlaceHolder ID="head" runat="server">
  </asp:ContentPlaceHolder>
</head>
```

```
<body>
  <div style="border: solid 4px red">
    <asp:ContentPlaceHolder ID="Main" runat="server">

    </asp:ContentPlaceHolder>
  </div>
</body>
</html>
```

If we run the project (CTRL + F5) and point our browser to /HelloWorld4, we see our strongly typed view and master page in action. To make it stand out, we have given it a strong border as shown in figure 1.11. Most views that we'll work with in this book will use the ViewPage<T> base class to enable a strongly typed Model property and the easy usage of view models, which will be covered in chapter 2.

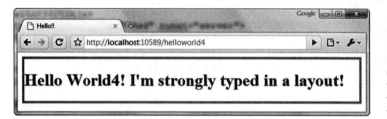

Figure 1.11 This is our final view, complete with layout, strong typing, and a little CSS to spice it up.

Congratulations! You have created your first controller, and it handles its responsibility perfectly. From this point forward, we won't cover every small step of developing with the MVC framework. If you're reading this book, you should already be well versed in ASP.NET, so we'll be covering only the items that are new with the ASP.NET MVC Framework. We'll be using best practices and advanced software development techniques throughout the examples. The first important practice we'll cover is unit testing. Because the MVC framework allows us to keep our controllers separate from the views, we can now easily test the controlling logic. We consider testing an important part of getting started with the MVC framework, so we'll touch on it now and keep a strong emphasis on testing throughout this book. Although we won't print every unit test in the book, you can find more unit tests in the examples for this book, which can be downloaded from the publisher's website (www.manning.com/ASP.NETMVCinAction).

1.5   *Testing controller classes*

For this section you'll need the unit testing framework NUnit installed. It can be found at http://www.nunit.org, and is free. After installing the latest version, you should open the NUnit GUI and select: Tools > Options > Visual Studio (on the left) and check the box that says Visual Studio Integration. This will make it easier to work with NUnit from within Visual Studio.

Now return to the unit test project we created earlier. You'll need to remove the references to MSTest, and add a reference to NUnit. We have created a class named HelloWorld4ControllerTester to house the unit tests that verify the controller functions correctly. See in figure 1.12 that we're grouping controller unit test fixtures in a Controllers folder. As you browse through the code listings, you'll notice that we have created stubs for several classes that the controller needs to function. This unit test example is the simplest one we'll see in this book. Listing 1.14 depicts the NUnit test fixture for HelloWorld4Controller.

Listing 1.14 Unit test fixture with NUnit

```csharp
using System.Web.Mvc;
using MvcApplication.Controllers;
using NUnit.Framework;
using NUnit.Framework.SyntaxHelpers;

namespace MvcApplicationTest.Controllers
{
  [TestFixture]
  public class HelloWorld4ControllerTester
  {
    [Test]
    public void IndexShouldRenderViewWithStringViewData()
    {
      var controller = new HelloWorld4Controller();         ❶
      var viewResult = (ViewResult) controller.Index();        ❷

      Assert.That(viewResult.ViewName, Is.EqualTo(""));          ❸
      Assert.That(viewResult.ViewData.Model, Is.EqualTo("Hello World4"));
    }
  }
}
```

Let's examine our simple unit test inside Hello-World4ControllerTester. Our test is Index-ShouldRenderViewWithStringViewData. We create an instance of the class under test, HelloWorld4Controller ❶. We then call our Index method ❷ capturing the ActionResult returned. Our test expects it to be a ViewResult instance, so we cast it as such. If the code returns the wrong type, our test will fail appropriately. At the end of the test, we easily assert our expectations ❸. Unit tests normally follow an *arrange, act, assert* flow, and this test is a perfect example of that. This was a very simple unit test, and chapter 3 will cover unit testing controllers in more depth. Figure 1.13 shows the test being run with UnitRun from JetBrains. UnitRun is also a feature of ReSharper.

Figure 1.12 In your unit test project, after adding a reference to nunit.framework.dll, you're ready to add a test fixture.

Creating automated unit tests for all code and running these tests with every build of the software will help ensure that as the application scales with complexity, the

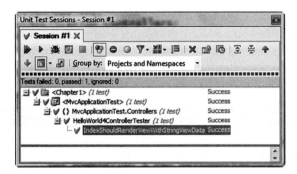

Figure 1.13   When we run this unit test using JetBrains ReSharper, it passes as we expect.

software continues to be maintainable. Typically, as an application grows, it becomes more difficult to manage. An automated test suite helps counter that natural tendency for entropy. Fortunately, it's easy to test controllers with the MVC framework. In fact, the team at Microsoft used test-driven development (TDD) while developing the framework.

NOTE Along with the MVC framework, Microsoft has wrapped some of the ASP.NET code and provided abstract classes to some of the key APIs such as `HttpResponseBase`, `HttpRequestBase`, and most importantly, `Http-ContextBase`. A Google search will reveal how many people have had trouble testing against `HttpContext` because of its sealed and static members. Providing abstract classes for these key APIs loosens the coupling to them, increasing testability.

We have mentioned unit testing several times in the text, and it's important to understand the connection to TDD. Test-driven development is a development style where unit tests (and other tests) are created before code that make the tests pass is written. In this chapter we have not adhered strictly to the TDD process, in an attempt to focus on key areas of the MVC framework without adding the mental overhead of a new development process.

It's a good practice to ensure that as you're writing your unit tests, they do not call out to any database or web service. This helps keep the testing portion of your build running fast, and ensures maintainability by not adding a dependency to an external system that is not guaranteed to not change. It's reasonable to run a build containing 2000 automated tests in 5 seconds; if many of your unit tests involve a database, your build will likely take much longer. Other tests that integrate with external things like a database are still valuable, but they can take several seconds each in some cases, so you want to concentrate on keeping controller tests at the unit level. To help with this, you can stub out (or "mock") controller dependencies.

1.6   *Summary*

We have now seen how easy it is to get started with the ASP.NET MVC Framework, and for the rest of this book, the examples will not be so trivial. You now know how to add a route to the application and that the route defines what controller and action should be invoked for a given URL. Once the controller is invoked, an action method is in charge of determining what should be passed to the view for the given request. The view takes the objects passed and formats the objects using a view template. The view does not make any decisions about the objects passed but merely formats them for display. This separation of concerns contributes to a more maintainable application than what we have seen with Web Forms.

For most of this book, we'll be using CodeCampServer in our examples. Along with being included in the downloads for this book, CodeCampServer can be found at http://CodeCampServer.org. It's an ASP.NET MVC Framework application that can host a conference for a user group. It uses a decoupled *Onion Architecture*, domain-driven design, the ASP.NET MVC Framework, and NHibernate to show how a real enterprise application would look. It has a complete build process with NAnt, which is monitored by a build server such as CruiseControl.Net or JetBrains TeamCity. The entire application is meant as a living example of how to write a real application with the ASP.NET MVC Framework. Since its inception, more volunteers have joined the project, and now it's a full community effort. It will live on well past the life of this book, so the copy of the code you receive with this book is a snapshot in time. We invite you to join the project as it continues to progress.

We'll use this real-world application in our examples going forward. What this means is that you'll need to be up to speed with the concepts and patterns discussed. As an author team, we have decided that we could provide more value with advanced, real-world examples that might cause the reader to have to do a bit of research than we could by over-simplifying the examples. We're choosing not to compromise on software design, even if it makes the book a bit more difficult to write. The first topic we cover in depth is the Model portion of Model-View-Controller in the next chapter.

The model in depth

This chapter covers

- Guidance for designing the model
- Exploring a real-world domain model
- Using a presentation
- Tips for working with model objects

Without a model, software is not interesting. A *model* in the English language is just like a *model* in software: a representation of the real thing. In software, we represent the real world by using objects that are named after concepts we deal with every day. These objects have attributes and behaviors similar to those found in the real world. In this chapter, we'll explore a model for a system that helps to manage a small conference, like a *Code Camp*. The model enables the application to provide an interesting service. Without the model, the application provides no value. We place great importance on creating a rich model with which our controllers can work.

The style of modeling we'll use in this book is *domain-driven design* (DDD), as conveyed by Eric Evans in his book, *Domain-Driven Design: Tackling Complexity in the Heart of Software*. Covering the topic in depth is a book in itself; we'll tackle a small primer, which should enable you to follow the software examples in the rest of this book. After the DDD primer, we'll discuss how to best use the domain model; then we'll move through how to use a presentation model to keep controllers and views simple. We'll keep a keen eye on SoC, and we'll ensure that every class has a single, well-defined responsibility. Before digging deep, we need a good understanding of the basics of DDD.

2.1 Understanding the basics of domain-driven design

Developers can use different methods to model software. The method we prefer is domain-driven design, which looks at the business domain targeted by the software and models objects to represent the appropriate concepts. We refer to the domain model as the object graph that represents the business domain of the software. If the software lives in the online e-commerce space, we would expect to find objects such as `Order`, `Customer`, `Product`, etc. These are not just *data-transfer objects* either. They are rich objects with properties and methods that mimic behavior in that business space. Popular in .NET development, the `DataSet` object would not be appropriate in a domain model because the `DataSet` is a relational representation of database tables. Whereas the `DataSet` is a model focused on the data relationships and persistence, a domain model is focused more on behavior and responsibility.

In our fictitious e-commerce application, when retrieving order history for a customer, we would want to retrieve an array or collection of `Order` objects, not a `DataSet` of order data. The heavy focus on the demarcation of behavior and the encapsulated view of data is key in DDD. If you are unfamiliar with domain-driven design, you may want to review some of the following references. Reviewing these publications is not necessary for the purpose of this book, but they will help you as you develop software in your career. From this point forward we'll defer to these resources for more detail on domain models, aggregates, aggregate roots, repositories, entities, and value objects. When discussing each of these concepts, we'll talk only briefly about their purpose and then move on. The next section is an overview of the core domain model for this book.

References for learning more

Domain-Driven Design: Tackling Complexity in the Heart of Software by Eric Evans—The most complete reference for DDD. Evans can be credited for making this collection of patterns known. He applies his own experience as he names patterns that work together to simplify complex software. Addison-Wesley Professional (2003).

Domain Driven Design Quickly by Abel Avram Floyd Marinescu—A 104-page book designed to be a more concise guide to DDD than Evans' book. This e-book is summarized mainly from Evans' book. Lulu Press, Inc. (2007).

Applying Domain-Driven Design and Patterns: With Examples in C# and .NET by Jimmy Nilsson—The author takes the reader through real, complete examples and applies DDD patterns along with test-driven development (TDD) and O/R mapping. Addison-Wesley Professional (2006).

http://domaindrivendesign.org/—An evolving, information website maintained by Eric Evans, Jimmy Nilsson, and Ying Hu.

2.2   *Domain model for this book*

Throughout the rest of this book, our examples will be centered on the open source project, CodeCampServer. Authors of this book started the project, and it is being extended at the time of publishing by a strong network of contributors. This software can serve as the official website for a software conference, often called a *Code Camp*. The domain model is centered on the concepts present when managing a Code Camp. Since *Code Camp* is a common name (also common is *TechFest* or *BarCamp*), our central object is Conference. In figure 2.1, you see the complete domain model for the application, and we'll work with different pieces in the examples following in the chapter and the rest of the book.

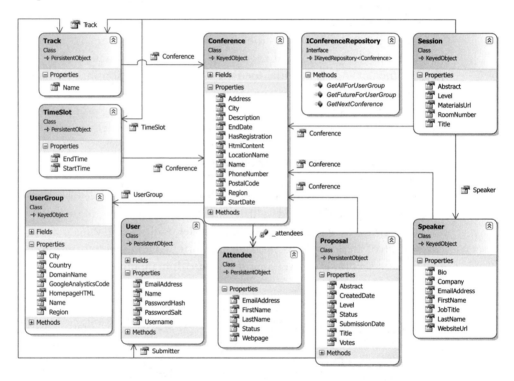

Figure 2.1   Partial domain model for CodeCampServer, which will serve as the basis of future examples in this book.

2.2.1   *Key entities and value objects*

Figure 2.1 shows some of the entities and value objects in play within our domain model. The entities are the key objects in our domain model, such as Conference, Session, Track, and TimeSlot. With so many types in the diagram, you probably wonder what is special about these classes and what makes them entities. The reason these are entities is that they have the concept of an identity, a property which can be examined to determine uniqueness. The reason we give these objects an identifier is that these can stand on their own, and we can speak about these objects without other supporting concepts. It would make sense to list a collection of any of these objects. Entities can stand on their own, and we can reason about them in a collection or as a single object.

Value objects don't make sense on their own without the supporting context of an entity to which they belong. Two value objects in our domain model are `Session Level` and `Conference Address`. Also many properties of entities are value objects. Let's discuss `Level` and what context is required for it to make any sense.

A `Level` has a value that indicates the difficulty level of the session. It does not have an identifier. `Level` belongs completely to the `Session` class. Without `Session`, `Level` would have no context and would have no meaning. The purpose of `Level` is to denote the information that helps attendees of the conference choose what sessions may be appropriate. Being a value object, `Level` is defined by its properties and methods and has no identifier. It would not make sense to list out a collection or array of `Level` instances because without the `Session`, it has no meaning or purpose. Its relationship with other entities gives it meaning. The `Session` it belongs to and the difficulty level information it includes give it the context to convey meaning in the application, and when some other code needs the session's `Level`, it must ask the `Session` instance for the `Level`. The `Session` object will hand back this object. Like `Level`, other types without identifiers are value objects. Value objects are not glamorous and even describing them can be boring. The arrangement of entities and value objects into larger structures can be interesting.

Entities and value objects are useful in separating responsibilities in a domain model, but there is more. If we need to load a `Conference` entity for the Austin .NET User Group Code Camp, what does that mean? We see that our `Conference` object can have many `Sessions`, and that each `Session` has a `Speaker`. Going further, a `Speaker` has a `WebsiteUrl` property. `Tracks`, `Sessions`, and `Attendees` all have a relationship with a `Conference`. When we need to deal with a `Conference` object, must we have all associated objects in memory for any operation to make sense? The answer is no. In DDD, we divide our domain model into aggregates.

2.2.2 Aggregates

Aggregates are groups of objects that work and live together. We group them along natural operational lines, and one entity serves as the *aggregate root*. The aggregate root serves as the entry point and the hub of operations for all objects in the aggregate. An aggregate can have many objects, or it can just be a single entity, but the aggregate root is always an entity since it must be able to stand on its own, and only entities can stand on their own. In figure 2.2, we see some of the aggregates for Code-CampServer, with the `Conference` aggregate in the center.

The aggregate root is the `Conference` class, and another member of the `Conference` aggregate is `Attendee`. This is not the complete `Conference` aggregate, but it demonstrates some conventions of the aggregate pattern. It may seem trivial that we classify this object in the `Conference` aggregate, but specifying ownership is valuable.

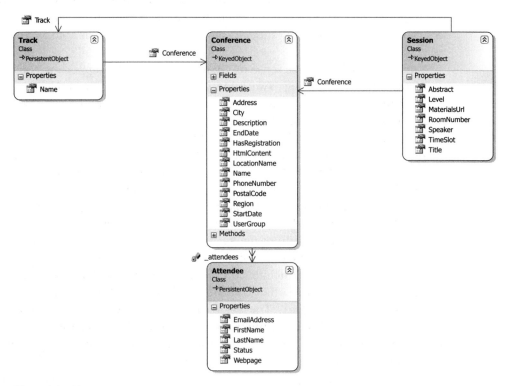

Figure 2.2   The `Conference` aggregate

We have specified that the `Conference` type owns the types in the `Conference` aggregate. Objects in other aggregates are not allowed to have a durable relationship with the nonroot objects in the `Conference` aggregate.

NOTE   `Session` holds a reference to `Track`, which is another aggregate root. Types in an aggregate are allowed to hold references to other aggregate roots only, not to other nonroot types in a different aggregate. For instance, even if only five `Attendees` could attend a session, `Session` would not be allowed to have a reference to the several `Attendee` instances because `Attendee` is a nonroot type in the `Conference` aggregate. In short, if a type belongs to an aggregate, types in other aggregates must not hold a durable reference.

The separation into aggregates enables the application to work with domain objects easily. If we did not draw aggregate boundaries, the entire domain model could easily devolve into a ball of spaghetti references. Conceivably, we wouldn't be able to use any objects without the entire object graph loaded into memory. Aggregate boundaries help us to define how much of the domain model is necessary for an interesting operation. For instance, if we want to show conference information on a screen with the location, directions, sessions, and speakers, we don't need to load the entire object graph. We only need the Conference aggregate and the other aggregate roots that are necessary. In fact, if we need only the start and end dates for the conference, we would not even have to load the entire Conference aggregate. Now that we are discussing how much of the object graph to load, you might wonder why we haven't yet discussed persistence to a database.

2.2.3   *Persistence for the domain model*

For this book, persistence is just not that interesting. Sure, we can imagine how we might load and save these objects from and to a relational database, xml files, web services, and so on, but when designing a domain model, persistence concerns are mostly orthogonal to the model. For most business applications, we'll have to durably save the state of the application somehow, but the domain model should not have to care whether that persistence is to XML files, a relational database, an object database, or if the entire state of the application is just kept around in memory.

NOTE   Persistence is interesting and necessary for real applications. We are not discussing specific data access techniques because that topic is orthogonal to the ASP.NET MVC Framework. The MVC framework is a presentation layer concern, and it can work with many data access strategies. Your back-end data access decisions do not change if you use the ASP.NET MVC Framework instead of Web Forms, Windows Forms, WPF, Silverlight, or even a console UI.

Regardless of the persistence mechanism, the domain model includes a concept for loading and saving object state. Notice how we are not talking about loading and saving data. In the domain model, we are concerned about objects, not data. We need to load object state and persist object state. We do that using *repository* types. In domain-driven design, we dedicate a repository to each aggregate, and the repository is responsible for loading and saving object state. The repository performs the operations on the aggregate root only. In the case of the Conference aggregate, we'll work with a type called IConferenceRepository. In figure 2.3, we see the repository whose responsibility it is to perform persistence operations on the Conference aggregate.

For more examples, we have a repository for each aggregate in our domain model. Some of them are listed here:

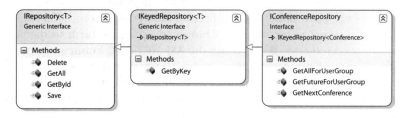

Figure 2.3   IConferenceRepository—all persistence operations on the aggregate root

- *IConferenceRepository*—Persistence operations on the `Conference` aggregate
- *ISessionRepository*—Persistence operations on the `Session` aggregate
- *ITimeSlotRepository*—Persistence operations on the `TimeSlot` aggregate
- *ITrackRepository*—Persistence operations on the `Session Track` aggregate

Let's examine the `Conference` aggregate once again as it relates to persistence. Suppose that when managing a Code Camp with this application we add several attendees. In the application we would add `Attendee` instances to our `Conference` instance and then pass our `Conference` to the `Save()` method of `IConferenceRepository`. The repository would be responsible for saving the `Attendee` instances as well because these objects live within the `Conference` aggregate. The repository's responsibility is to manage persistence for the `Conference` aggregate, which means every object in the aggregate.

You are probably wondering what mechanism we are using for persistence because we still have not mentioned it. With this book, you can download the full source code and examine the classes that implement our repository interfaces, but for the purpose of exploring the ASP.NET MVC Framework, we find it irrelevant and a distraction to explore the data access code, and we'll keep this book's focus on the presentation layer, which is where the ASP.NET MVC Framework lives. The repository interfaces will provide the objects we need to work with for all the examples in this book, and the controller classes will depend on these repository interfaces as well as other logical service types. Since data access and a screen controller have completely different concerns, a screen controller in this book will never concern itself with how any sort of data access is performed, or that data access is happening at all. A screen controller will call methods on dependencies, which will often be repositories, and when calling the `Save()` method on `IConferenceRepository`, the screen controller does not care whether the implementation saves the object in an in-memory cache, an XML file, or a relational database. The controller will merely call the repository and trust that what is behind the interface will work appropriately.

NOTE   No doubt you have seen some examples where controller actions directly contain data access code. With LINQ to SQL being new and growing in popularity, conference talks are featuring ASP.NET MVC Framework demos where a controller action performs a LINQ to SQL query. This works for small or short-lived applications, but it is inappropriate for long-lived business applications because of the coupling. For years, the industry has known that coupling presentation concerns with data access concerns is a recipe for disaster. These concepts gave birth to the well-known *data access layer*. When using the ASP.NET MVC Framework, a controller is part of the presentation layer. The best practice still stands to avoid putting data access in your presentation layer; any data access concern in a controller action creates technical debt that will put a tax on maintenance for the life of the application.

One benefit that we can capitalize on immediately when separating our data access layer from the presentation and business layers is unit testing. While unit testing our screen controllers, you will notice we frequently fake out the repository interfaces so that they return a canned list of objects as the context for a test. Unit testing controllers should never involve any persistence mechanism or exercise external dependencies. We'll cover the unit testing of controllers in much more detail in chapter 3, but in a unit test, the repository implementation will never come into play. A substitute object will always be provided for the interface.

At this point, we have enough information about our domain model to proceed, but the domain model is not the only type of model that we need. The domain model is important because it represents unique concepts in the real world. A conference can have many attendees, so that is how we model it. An attendee describes a person who is coming to the conference, and that is how we represent it in code. Now, what about a schedule listing? When listing the time slots, sessions, and speakers, how do we work with that in the presentation layer (in our screens)?

2.3 Presentation model

The domain model represents concepts as they truly are, but often a screen in our application needs a transformed representation of the domain model. For displaying a schedule of a conference, we need a flattened, or projected, model. This is the presentation model, a model that exists only for specific presentation needs. In the case of a schedule, we'll need to show the start time, end time, title, and speaker for every session. We can easily ask the repositories for the objects fully populated, and then we have all objects we need. However, if we place the responsibility on the screen controller for navigating the object graph and pulling all the appropriate pieces out, we are muddying the responsibilities of the controller. If the application is sufficiently trivial, we may let the controller take care of this, but that would be a judgment call for you to make. In CodeCampServer, our controllers will be quite thin. The controller is responsible for coordinating dependencies and forwarding objects for display on to the view. Controller code is code that is coupled to the framework being used for the UI. We want to get away from framework code as quickly as possible. Whose responsibility, then, is it to filter and arrange the conference schedule so it is in a shape suitable for display?

2.3.1 Presentation model responsibilities

This is where the presentation model shows its value. The presentation model is responsible for transforming the domain model into a representation that is useful for the presentation layer, namely, the controller and view. Whereas the domain model is an *n*-dimension object graph that accurately represents the real world, the presentation model takes these objects and projects them into a flatter model that can easily be represented on a graphical screen.

NOTE   The presentation model can be many things. Ultimately, it is an object model that serves a particular screen, not the entire domain. This object model can be populated in isolation, or it can take responsibility to populate itself when a domain object is passed into the constructor. The presentation model goes in the /Models folder in an ASP.NET MVC Framework application. The presentation model is part of the presentation layer and should not be referenced by the rest of the application. Typically a complex screen will require a presentation model object graph.

Let's revisit our conference listing example. It would not be appropriate for a controller to pass a Conference object to the view and hope the view knows how to traverse the object graphic in order to render the correct information. This is too much responsibility for the view. The controller needs an object that it can send to the view so that there is only one way for the view to render the object or structure of objects. If the view has a decision to make, we have introduced the possibility for a functional bug in the part of the code that is the most difficult to test. We want to pull all decisions back into the heart of the application where they can easily be tested. For this, we'll have ScheduleController use a new object in the presentation model called ScheduleForm. The controller will map a conference into a ScheduleForm instance by leveraging IScheduleMapper. See figure 2.4 for the ScheduleForm structure.

The ScheduleForm class, along with header information, can provide us with a collection of TimeSlotAssignmentForm objects, each of which are presentation objects and are easy to render. ScheduleForm also has a collection of TrackForm objects. These two collections will form the two axes of the table that the view is going to render for the schedule page. The view merely has to translate the graph of objects into a table. What makes a presentation object easier to render on a screen than a domain object?

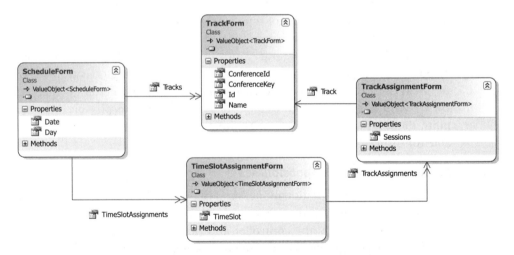

Figure 2.4   The presentation model contains classes specific to a particular screen. Logic that decides how to structure the domain model for presentation on a screen can be factored into presentation model's classes.

2.3.2 *Projecting from the domain model*

A presentation object is easier to render than a domain object because it discards the natural depth of a domain model object graph and provides a flattened, or projected, interface. In our view, we can ask the ScheduleForm for the two collections of objects that are the headers and rows of the schedule table when rendered to the screen. The presentation model is intentionally structured to naturally represent the presentation of the information. The goal of the presentation model is to match the view's desired structure closely. Figure 2.5 shows what the full structure looks like.

At the session level, SessionForm is not complicated. The SessionForm is responsible for representing a single cell in the schedule table on the screen. With track on the table header and time along the first column, sessions will be rendered in the appropriate track and time slot. The SessionForm has the properties that will be rendered so that the schedule makes sense.

NOTE The presentation model is not the only type of specialized model we could use. We have service models, storage models, security models, and messaging models. The common factor among these is that these object models lie at the extremities of the application and enable the application to interact with the outside world. The presentation model helps the presentation layer, which interacts with a human user. A messaging model would represent state and behavior necessary for messaging information to other systems asynchronously. It is conceivable that the UI could even send a message to the domain in a more complex system with large data entry screens.

The difference in these models is portability. Domain model objects are not portable. They are contained within the bounded context where they are useful. Presentation model objects are portable from the application layer up to the UI. A messaging model would be portable for serialization across MSMQ or similar transfer mechanisms. We would not send our domain objects directly in messages because we would end up coupling other systems to the shape and types of our domain model. Instead, the messaging model (call it whatever you like) represents the shape necessary to communicate with the external system or application layer.

The presentation model simplifies the domain model for rendering and helps make the numerous decisions that are necessary for rendering objects. If a controller or view were left with all these decisions, the likelihood of a defect would increase, and the amount of code in the controller or view would grow, causing maintainability to decrease. The presentation model is a key element of the presentation layer and should come into play any time a screen needs to work with an object that is not just an object but a deep object graph. For simple domain objects, or for merely displaying object header information, a presentation model object might not be necessary, but if you find yourself digging into an object graph in our view, pull back and consider introducing a presentation object. The unit tests are easy and quick, and the view becomes much simpler.

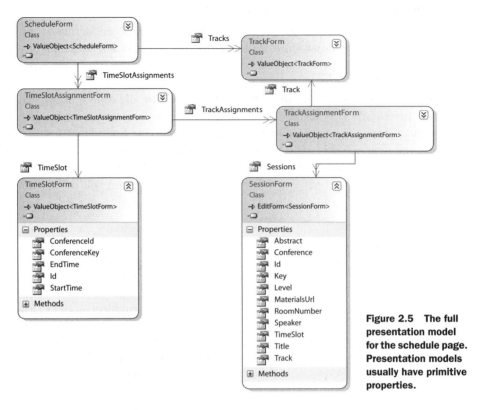

Figure 2.5   The full presentation model for the schedule page. Presentation models usually have primitive properties.

2.4   *Working with the model*

Congratulations! You now understand all you need to know to follow the rest of the examples in this book. Although you could study DDD for years, understanding this

---

About user stories

User stories are widely used by teams using Extreme Programming and other Agile methodologies. A user story is a placeholder for extensive conversation that takes place between the software customer and the software team. It is the widely accepted practice for a user story to contain a persona (or the type of user) who finds the functionality valuable. The user story describes what the persona wants to do and why. This format helps to keep the team focused on a task that is beneficial to a certain kind of user.

---

small Code Camp domain model is sufficient to master the techniques presented in the following chapters.

Now that we understand the model we'll be working with, let's put it together and use our Code Camp domain model. We'll start with a user story: "*As a community member, I want to navigate to http://codecampserver.org/austincodecamp2008/schedule so that I can see a schedule of the conference by day, time slots, and track.*"

2.4.1 Crafting the route

We know from the previous chapter how to create routes that will map a URL to a particular controller and action. In this case, we are breaking away from the simple {controller}/{action} route in favor of a URL that is obvious and intuitive. Furthermore, we are using a route API from MvcContrib inside of CodeCampServer. Chapter 5 will cover ASP.NET MVC routes in depth. This section focuses on how the model can integrate with the routes.

The part of the URL, *austincodecamp2008*, is actually the unique key that will identify which conference we are dealing with. In other words, for the next Code Camp, the URL might be *http://codecampserver.org/austincodecamp2009/schedule*, and so on. Since the first token in the URL is dynamic, we have a fairly interesting route, but not difficult to craft. The second token, *schedule* will denote the controller to use for this request. Now that we have examined each piece of the URL, take note of the entire route added to the RouteTable as shown in listing 2.1. This code is in the RouteConfigurator class.

> **Listing 2.1   A route that maps the desired URL to the proper controller and action**

```
MvcRoute.MappUrl("{conferenceKey}/{controller}/{action}")
    .WithDefaults(new {controller = "Conference", action = "index"})
    .WithConstraints(new
        {
            conferenceKey = new
                ConferenceKeyCannotBeAControllerNameConstraint(),
            controller = @"schedule|session|timeslot|track|attendee
                |conference|speaker|admin|proposal|user|sponsor"
        })
    .AddWithName("conferenceDefault", routes)
    .RouteHandler = new DomainNameRouteHandler();
```

This route has concerns other than ensuring the ScheduleController is invoked. The {conferenceKey}/{controller} portion is the most interesting for now. The constraints ensure that only our conference-centric controllers are available after the conference key. The framework will match the route with the URL and ensure the ScheduleController is executed with the Index action by default.

2.4.2 Crafting the controller action

We are very confident that the Index method of the ScheduleController will be invoked for this request, but we must have our controller in place so that we have a place to add the proper code. We'll create a ScheduleController class in Website/Controllers/ in our solution. We'll then inherit from the Controller base class and create an Index action method. In CodeCampServer, all controllers have a layer supertype (as defined by Martin Fowler in his book, *Patterns of Enterprise Application Architecture*) called SmartController. SmartController derives from Controller. In your own application, you might adopt your own controller supertype. The shell of the controller class should look similar to listing 2.2.

Listing 2.2   The shell of the `ScheduleController` class

```
namespace CodeCampServer.UI.Controllers
{
    public class ScheduleController : SmartController
    {
        public ViewResult Index(Conference conference)
        {
            return View();
        }
    }
}
```

This is the start of our controller class and action that will help display a conference schedule using a view named Index. We'll be leveraging an IModelBinder instance to bind the conference key from route data to a Conference object. Next we need to test-drive the logic that will map the conference into the presentation model that is appropriate to forward to the view.

2.4.3   *Test-driving the feature*

Logic in the application needs to have an automated test to verify that it works correctly. *TDD* is a technique that helps design loosely coupled, maintainable code while at the same time building up a complete regression suite of automated unit tests. We are going to test-drive the Index action method for our controller. We have added the action method first because we decided on the name when we created the route. To test-drive this functionality, you will need to create an NUnit test fixture in your unit test project. In our project, we'll call it ScheduleControllerTester.cs. Examine the full unit test in listing 2.3.

Listing 2.3   Unit test creates mock objects using Rhino Mocks, a .NET mocking library

```
using System.Web.Mvc;
using CodeCampServer.Core.Domain.Model;
using CodeCampServer.UI.Controllers;
using CodeCampServer.UI.Helpers.Mappers;
using CodeCampServer.UI.Models.Forms;
using NUnit.Framework;
using Rhino.Mocks;
using NBehave.Spec.NUnit;

namespace CodeCampServer.UnitTests.UI.Controllers
{
    [TestFixture]
    public class ScheduleControllerTester : TestBase
    {
        [Test]
        public void Should_map_schedule_and_display()
        {
            var conference = new Conference();
            var scheduleForms = new ScheduleForm[0];
```

```
            var mapper = S<IScheduleMapper>();
            mapper.Stub(x => x.Map(conference)).Return(scheduleForms);

            var controller = new ScheduleController(mapper);
            ViewResult result = controller.Index(conference);
            result.ViewName.ShouldEqual("");
            result.ViewData.Model.ShouldEqual(scheduleForms);
        }
    }
}
```

NOTE The `S` method is defined as return `MockRepository.Generate-Stub<T>(argumentsForConstructor);`. It resides on the base class as a shortcut. Because these examples are part of the larger CodeCampServer codebase, it will be valuable for you to explore the code included with this book.

It is important to realize that we are setting up a fake object that implements `IScheduleMapper`. We are passing this stub to the controller's constructor, and our controller will use it without knowing the difference. It is worth noting that the application uses an *IoC*, or *inversion of control*, container to manage dependencies. This means that we have a custom controller factory use our IoC container to create the controller complete with whatever dependencies are declared by the constructor. We'll cover controller factories in greater depth later in chapter 3, but realize that this is a best practice not just for controllers but for C# code in general. You can see the IoC container usage by opening the full solution delivered with this book. In general, a class should openly declare dependencies by requiring they be passed in through the constructor.

To complete this test, we call the `Index()` method with the `Conference` object, then assert that the view name and `ViewData.Model` are correct. We cannot compile at this point because the constructor we need does not exist. Let's add the constructor, run the test, and it will fail as expected in figure 2.6.

We'll now move back to our controller class, and write the interesting code until our unit test passes. The resulting controller code is shown in listing 2.4.

Listing 2.4 The complete controller class for showing a conference schedule

```
using System.Web.Mvc;
using CodeCampServer.Core.Domain.Model;
using CodeCampServer.UI.Helpers.Filters;
using CodeCampServer.UI.Helpers.Mappers;
using CodeCampServer.UI.Models.Forms;

namespace CodeCampServer.UI.Controllers
{
    [RequiresConferenceFilter]
    public class ScheduleController : SmartController
    {
        private readonly IScheduleMapper _mapper;          ❶
```

```
public ScheduleController(IScheduleMapper mapper)
{
    _mapper = mapper;
}

public ViewResult Index(Conference conference)
{
    ScheduleForm[] scheduleForms = _mapper.Map(conference);    ❷
    return View(scheduleForms);    ❸
}
}
}
```

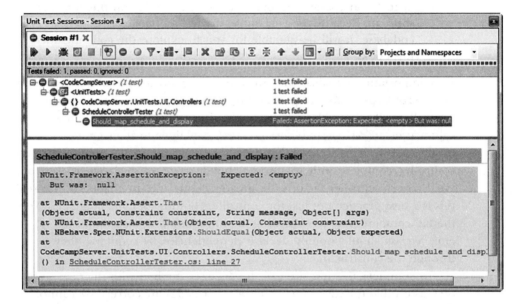

Figure 2.6   Running the unit test with JetBrains ReSharper shows the test failure, which is what we expect at this point.

The Rhino Mocks dynamic mock library

When performing automated testing on code libraries, developers and testers find it beneficial to simulate dependencies on which the code relies. By substituting a dependency, the code under test can be evaluated objectively and repeatedly. This technique delivers great results, but the code clutters the readability of the test and the code that results is bulky. This is where mocking frameworks like Rhino Mocks come in. Rhino Mocks can generate derived classes on the fly. This includes interface implementations as well as abstract class derivations. These dynamically created classes can return hard-code values or assert that a particular method is called with specific arguments. You can read more or download at http://www.ayende.com/projects/rhino-mocks.aspx. Oren Eini is the creator of Rhino Mocks, a vibrant open source project with many contributors.

The new code is the constructor and the guts of the action method. There does not appear to be much code, so can it possibly be correct? Is that really all the code that's necessary in the controller? Yes! Let's examine what's going on. First, we are saving our ISscheduleMapper in a private field ❶ so we can access it later. Remember that we do not care what object is passed into the constructor as long as it matches the type required. Next, we take the Conference passed into the Index method and use it to ask the ISscheduleMapper instance to "map" it into an array of ScheduleForm objects ❷. Once we are finished, we'll call View() on the Controller base class passing in our presentation object ❸. This will cause the Index view to be rendered with an array of ScheduleForm objects stored in the ViewData.Model property. To prove that the code we are writing is correct, let's go back and run our unit test to ensure it passes, as shown in figure 2.7.

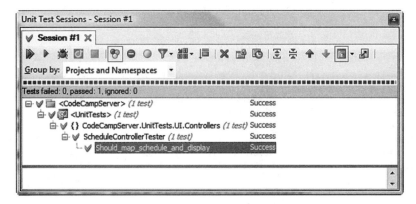

Figure 2.7 With the controller fully implemented, the unit test passes, and we can move on.

Now that you have expertly test-driven a controller action, all that's left is to finish off this feature with a view that takes the presentation object and formats it properly into HTML. In the controller we are creating a ScheduleForm array by passing in a Conference that the ISscheduleMapper will project into the shape necessary to render the screen. Although we won't publish the full code of the ScheduleMapper class here, it is useful to look at the structure of the ScheduleForm presentation object graph shown in figure 2.8. The supporting objects represent the time slots and tracks used to create the visual representation in the view. Using these objects, the view can easily render the schedule.

2.4.4 Finishing the view

We'll get into all the different ways to use views in chapter 4, but for now, we'll take the simple route and not make use of many view helpers. You will learn about view helpers later, but for this feature, we'll stick with simple HTML. Following convention, we'll create an MVC View Page in Website/Views/Schedule/. The rest of the work is just formatting, so we'll format the name of the conference in big letters at the top of the

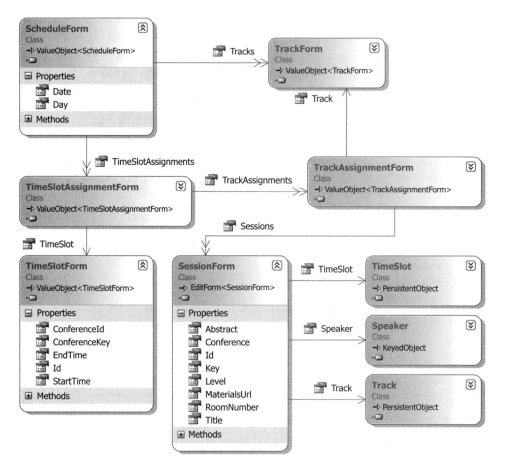

Figure 2.8   The complete `ScheduleForm` presentation model nicely encapsulates the presentation concern that would otherwise have cluttered our controller and view.

screen and then show the sessions in a table below. If you are curious about the layout used, browse through the solution delivered with the book. Examine listing 2.5 for the full source for `View.aspx`.

Listing 2.5   A view that formats our presentation object, `ScheduleForm`, as HTML

```
<%@ Page Language="C#"
    MasterPageFile="~/Views/Shared/Main.Master"
    AutoEventWireup="true"
    Inherits="CodeCampServer.UI.Helpers.ViewPage.
    ➥   BaseViewPage<ScheduleForm[]>" %>
```

```
<asp:Content ContentPlaceHolderID="Main" runat="server">
    <h2>Schedule</h2>                                          Output table
    <table class="schedule">                                   for conference
    <% foreach (var scheduleForm in Model) { %>        ◁──┘
        <tr class="headerrow">                  ◁── Header row
            <th class="day">                    ◁── Left column
                Day <%=scheduleForm.Day %>, <%=scheduleForm.Date %>
                </th>
            <% foreach (var track in scheduleForm.Tracks) { %>      ◁──┐
            <th>                                                        │
                <%=track.Name%>                        New column for each track
                <% Html.RenderPartial("EditTrackLink", track);%>
            </th>
            <% } %>                                           New row for
        </tr>                                         ◁──┘   each timeslot
        <% foreach (var timeSlotAssignment in
                scheduleForm.TimeSlotAssignments) { %>       Timeslot goes
        <tr class="timeslotrow">                      ◁──┘  in first column
            <td class="timeslot">
                <%=timeSlotAssignment.TimeSlot.GetName()%>
                <% Html.RenderPartial("EditTimeSlotLink",     ◁──┐
                    timeSlotAssignment.TimeSlot);%>            Render admin
            </td>                                             links using
            <% foreach (var trackAssignment in                partial
                    timeSlotAssignment.TrackAssignments) { %>
            <td>
                <% Html.RenderPartial("ScheduleSlot",   ◁──┐
                    trackAssignment.Sessions,ViewData);%>  Render sessions
            </td>                                           using partial
            <% } %>
        </tr>
        <% } %>
    <% } %>
    </table>
</asp:Content>
```

Note that we are using <%= operators to output properties of the presentation object. The code in listing 2.5 is such a mix of server-side code and markup that you might have trouble following it. When we discuss views in depth, we'll introduce techniques to simplify the view and extract even view logic into helpers. You can imagine what this view would look like if we attempted to pass the Conference object directly instead of a ScheduleForm object. To get the speaker name, the view would have to traverse three different object relationships and even perform lookup logic. It would be a mess. The view in listing 2.5 formats our presentation object and completes the current feature. If you run the application, you'll see a screen similar to figure 2.9.

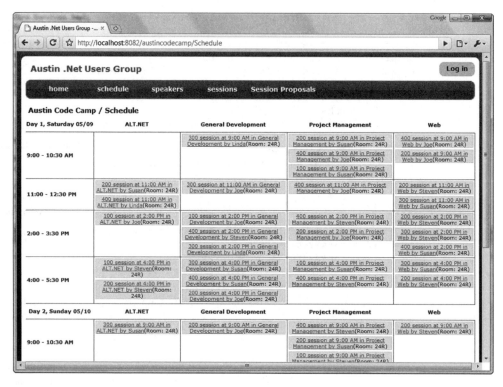

Figure 2.9   When we run the application, we see our controller and view work as intended. With a well-defined domain model and presentation model, the controller and view can become quite simple. Test data is used; the session names are not descriptive.

2.5   *Summary*

You have just completed a whirlwind tour of the *M* in *Model-View-Controller*. Key takeaways from this chapter are understanding both the importance of a rich domain model and when a presentation model makes controllers and view simpler. The domain model represents concepts as they exist in the real world. The names should be the same, the operations (methods) should be the same, and the relationships should mirror how the concepts are used in reality. With an intelligent domain model, the application has a solid core to build around.

Left to work with aggregates alone, the controller must take the responsibility for extracting information out of the object graph for the view to render. This makes the controller more complicated and harder to test. Complexity and difficult testability both result in more costly maintenance. This is where the presentation model comes in. Use presentation model objects to project a deep domain object graph into a flattened view that is easy for a view to render. Creating these presentation objects is a snap for a controller, and when used properly, test-driving controller logic becomes easy and predictable.

With a proper model in place, the controller and view are straightforward. As you build your applications around the ASP.NET MVC Framework, do not forget the paramount importance of the model. *Model* comes first in the pattern name, and it should come first in your application. If you take shortcuts with the model, the controllers and views are going to be much more difficult to manage. The model is the core of each layer in the application. If the core is rotten, the entire application will soon smell quite bad. With the model now well understood, we'll turn our attention to controllers in chapter 3.

The controller in depth

This chapter covers

- Understanding controller anatomy
- Leveraging viewless controllers
- Testing controllers
- Using form and querystring values
- Binding action parameter
- Developing action filters

The focus of the Model-View-Controller pattern is the controller. With this pattern, every request is handled by a controller and rendered by a view. Without the controller, presentation and business logic would move to the view, as we have seen with Web Forms. With the ASP.NET MVC Framework, every request routes to a controller, which is simply a class that implements the IController interface. Microsoft provides the base class System.Web.Mvc.Controller to make creating a controller easy. The controller base class you choose is not crucial because most request processing goes into executing the ActionResult, which is the type that each *action* returns.

An action is a method that handles a particular request. This method can take no parameters or many, but by the time the action method finishes executing, there ought to be one or many objects ready to be sent to the view, and the name of the view should be selected if the view does not follow the convention of having the same name as the action. Beyond that, the developer is in complete control regarding how to implement a controller and its actions. In chapter 1 we covered using the IController interface directly for controllers that need only one action. This chapter will explore controllers that use many actions and inherit from the System.Web.Mvc.Controller base class. The meat of the controller is the action.

3.1   *The controller action*

Any class that inherits from System.Web.Mvc.Controller can use action methods to serve web requests. An action method normally returns an ActionResult and can take zero or many arguments. Parameters are resolved into the action method by a combination of form values, the Route definition, and the querystring, in that order. The requirements for a method to be web-callable as an action method are well documented on http://www.asp.net/mvc. The method

- Must be public
- Cannot be a static method
- Cannot be an extension method
- Cannot be a constructor, getter, or setter
- Cannot have open generic types
- Is not a method of the Controller base class
- Is not a method of the ControllerBase base class
- Cannot contain ref or out parameters

An action has a clear purpose and a single responsibility. That responsibility is to accept arguments, if any, coordinate with relevant dependencies, push objects into ViewData, and choose a view to render.

Action methods should not be performing functions such as data access or file I/O. Action methods exist to perform presentation coordination for a screen/page. Any supporting logic should be factored into appropriate classes. If you see an action method that does not fit on one screen without scrolling, consider how many responsibilities it has. You will end up with more maintainable software by factoring much of the logic into supporting service classes or presentation model classes. If you think of the whole application's layering, you should be able to take away all the screens, that is, views and controllers, without losing system functionality. In other words, if users upload a batch file to your web app, and the processing of the contents of the batch file is inside an action method, that logic is in the wrong place. As soon as that controller goes away, the application cannot process batch files. This example is a good rule of thumb for determining if the action is trying to do too much.

NOTE   In this book, we focus on complex, long-lasting web applications. In line with that, we do not make compromises to optimize the speed of writing the application. Software engineering is full of trade-offs, and software construction techniques are no exception. If you need a small web application, you can probably get away with putting all the logic in the controller action, but realize that you're trading off long-term maintainability for short-term coding speed. If the application will have a long life, this is a bad trade-off. The examples in this book are factored for long life and easy maintenance, so you will notice interfaces employed to separate concerns.

In listing 3.1 we see a simple controller with a single action. This is a trivial example, and we will tackle more complex scenarios later. We begin by ensuring that the action method is `public` and returns `ActionResult`. If the method is not `public`, it will not be called. At this point, we can push some objects into `ViewData` and call the `View()` method with the name of the view that should render. That is the meat and potatoes of what it means to be an action method.

> **Listing 3.1   The `SimpleController` decides on `ViewData` and renders a view**

```
using System.Web.Mvc;

namespace MvcInAction.Controllers
{
    public class SimpleController : Controller
    {
        public ActionResult Hello()
        {
            ViewData.Add("greeting", "Hello Readers!");
            return View();
        }
    }
}
```

The most important point to remember is that the controller action adds objects to the `ViewData` and calls for the rendering of a view by name. A popular convention is to keep the view name the same as the action name for simplicity. If the view name matches the action name, there is no need to specify it when calling `return View()`. `ViewData` is a `IDictionary<string, object>` at its core. The type is `System.Web.Mvc.ViewDataDictionary`, but we only need to worry about the interface. MvcContrib contains a group of extension methods called `ViewDataExtensions` which make `ViewData` easier to work with within a controller as well as a view. The extensions don't take away any functionality; they add functionality. You will see use of these extensions sprinkled throughout this book.

Action methods can return any object type, including void. If the type derives from `System.Web.Mvc.ActionResult`, that result will be executed. If any other type is returned, the framework will call the `ToString()` method on it and return a `Content-Result`. The following listed types are the available derivations of `ActionResult`:

1 `ContentResult`—Represents a text result

2 `EmptyResult`—Represents no result

3 `FileResult`—Represents a downloadable file (abstract class)

4 `FileContentResult`—Represents a downloadable file (with the binary content)

5 `FilePathResult`—Represents a downloadable file (with a path)

6 `FileStreamResult`—Represents a downloadable file (with a file stream)

7 `HttpUnauthorizedResult`—Represents the result of an unauthorized HTTP request

8 `JavaScriptResult`—Represents a JavaScript script

9 `JsonResult`—Represents a JavaScript Object Notation (JSON) result that can be used in an AJAX application

10 `RedirectResult`—Represents a redirection to a new URL

11 `RedirectToRouteResult`—Represents a result that performs a redirection given a route values dictionary

12 `PartialViewResult`—Base class used to send a partial view to the response

13 `ViewResult`—Represents HTML and markup

14 `ViewResultBase`—Base class used to supply the model to the view and then render the view to the response

15 `XmlResult`—Action result that serializes the specified object into XML and outputs it to the response stream (provided by the MvcContrib library)

Each of these types has a corresponding helper method on the `Controller` base class that can be used to easily construct the type and return it. Although most actions will return a `ViewResult` or some other type of result, a controller action is not required to have a view associated with it.

3.2 *Simple controllers do not need a view*

Most of the examples in this book use a view to render objects to an HTML screen; however, if you want the behavior but not the display, you would do well to use a controller without a view. Suppose we wanted to support some alternative URLs for Code-CampServer. In an installation of CodeCampServer, we can have many conferences listed. Some conferences are past and some future. Suppose we wanted an easy URL to pull up the next Code Camp. Let's say this URL would be: `http://www.codecamp-server.org/nextconference`. We would start by defining a special route because this is a special case. This route uses the default API included in the ASP.NET MVC Framework. Both chapter 2 and the CodeCampServer source code make use of the route API wrappers found in MvcContrib. You can configure routes in many ways, so we are showing a variety of techniques, which we explain in depth in chapter 5. The route for our simple controller as defined in listing 3.2 is a simple route for the purposes of this example. It uses the included API from ASP.NET 3.5 Service Pack 1, which includes the routing capability. As covered in chapter 5, when you progress to more control over routes, you will need a richer API, such as the one used by CodeCampServer, or you can create your own wrapper.

Listing 3.2 Adding a route to redirect with a special controller action

```
RouteTable.Routes.MapRoute("next", "nextconference",
                    new
                        {
                            controller = "redirect",        ❶
                            action = "nextconference"        ❷
                        });
```

We want the ASP.NET MVC Framework to route this URL to a controller named Redi-rectController ❶. The default action will be NextConference ❷. Listing 3.3 shows the full source for the RedirectController. Note that there is no need to call the View() method because we do not have or need a view.

Listing 3.3 A view is unnecessary when performing a redirect.

```
using System.Web.Mvc;
using CodeCampServer.Core.Domain;
using CodeCampServer.Core.Domain.Model;

namespace MvcInAction.Controllers
{
    public class RedirectController : Controller
    {
        private readonly IConferenceRepository _repository;

        public RedirectController(IConferenceRepository
            conferenceRepository)
        {
            _repository = conferenceRepository;
        }
                                                              Return derived type
        public RedirectToRouteResult NextConference()    ◁──┘ of ActionResult
        {
            Conference conference = _repository.GetNextConference();

            return RedirectToAction("index", "conference",
                            new {conferenceKey = conference.Key});
        }
    }
}
```

As we walk through the NextConference action, we notice that we are coordinating dependencies to get the job done. Figure 3.1 illustrates the controller and its dependencies.

The IConferenceRepository instance knows how to retrieve the appropriate conference that is next on the schedule. After we have the conference that is next, we can redirect to the URL that will route to the ConferenceController, which knows how to work with a single conference. We will discuss the design of this controller shortly, but notice that the dependency, IConferenceRepository, is passed in through the constructor. What is *dependency injection* (DI)? It's a fancy term for passing objects into a constructor or public setters. The default controller factory supplied with the ASP.NET MVC Framework does not know how to resolve constructor dependencies of controllers, but there are several IControllerFactory implementations available in the MvcContrib

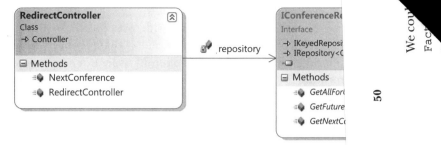

Figure 3.1 The `RedirectController` depends on one interface. It d
in its constructor which makes dependency injection easier.

open source project. For this example, we use the `StructureMapControllerFactory` source copied from MvcContrib. We register the controller factory with a single line of code as shown in listing 3.4.

Listing 3.4   Using an MvcContrib controller factory enables IoC support.

```
ControllerBuilder.Current.SetControllerFactory(          ⟵  Initialize ControllerFactory
    new StructureMapControllerFactory());                    in Global.asax

public class StructureMapControllerFactory : DefaultControllerFactory
{
    protected override IController GetControllerInstance(
        Type controllerType)
    {
        return (IController) ObjectFactory.GetInstance(controllerType);
    }
}
```

The inversion of control principle and DI

Normally when code executes other code, there is a linear flow of creation and execution. For instance, if I have a class that depends on another class, I will create that class with the `"new"` operator, then execute the class by calling a method. If I used inversion of control (IoC), I would still call methods on the class, but I would require an instance of the class passed into my constructor. In this manner, I yield control of locating or creating my dependency to the calling code. DI is the act of injecting a dependency into a class that depends on it. Often used interchangeably, IoC and DI yield loosely coupled code and are often used with interfaces. With interfaces, classes declare dependencies as interfaces in the constructor arguments. Calling code then locates appropriate classes and passes them in when constructing the class.

IoC containers come into play to assist with managing this technique when used through an application. There are plenty of IoC containers to choose from, but the favorites at this time seem to be StructureMap and Castle Windsor found at http://structuremap.sourceforge.net and http://www.castleproject.org/container/index.html respectively.

...d just as easily have used the `WindsorControllerFactory`, `SpringController-Factory`, or `UnityControllerFactory`, all supplied with MvcContrib. Using an IoC container to construct the controller allows us to externalize dependency configuration. You're probably wondering how to test this controller that does not have a view because we are doing a redirect directly in the controller. Regardless of the IoC container used, testing is still the same.

3.3   *Testing controllers*

The focus of this section is testing controllers. Of the different types of automated testing, we are concerned with only one type at this point: unit testing. Unit tests run fast because they do not call out of process. In a unit test, dependencies are simulated so the only production code running is the controller code. For this to be possible the controllers have to be well designed. A well-designed controller

- Is loosely coupled with its dependencies
- Uses dependencies but is not in charge of locating or creating those dependencies
- Has clear responsibilities and only handles logic relevant to serving a web request

A well-designed controller does not do file I/O, database access, web service calls, and thread management. The controller may very well call a dependency that performs these functions, but the controller itself should be responsible only for interaction with the dependency, not for performing the fine-grained work. This is very important to testing because good design and testing go hand in hand. It's very difficult to test poorly designed code.

NOTE   Writing automated tests for all code in a code base is a best practice. It provides great feedback when the test suite is run multiple times per day. If you're not doing it now, you should start immediately. Several popular, high quality frameworks for automated testing available include NUnit and MbUnit. At the time of writing, NBehave, MSTest, and xUnit are also available, but they are not as widely adopted as NUnit or MbUnit. All are free (with the exception of MSTest, which requires the purchase of Visual Studio) and they simplify testing code.

In this section, we will walk through testing our viewless `RedirectController`.

3.3.1   *Testing the RedirectController*

The `RedirectController` must find the next conference and issue a redirect to another URL so that a single conference can be displayed on the screen. This controller must find the conference and ask for a redirect to the action that can take it from there. The ASP.NET MVC Framework provides a redirect mechanism that makes it unnecessary to use `Response.Redirect()`, which is more difficult to test. The action method in question returns an object that has public properties, which can be evaluated in a test. The action result contains an `Execute` method that performs the redirect, but the controller action merely returns an object. This is important for the easy testing of controller actions. In listing 3.5, we set up a unit test for this code along with fake implementations of the dependencies on which the RedirectController relies.

Listing 3.5 RedirectControllerTester: ensuring we redirect to the correct URL

```
using System;
using System.Web.Mvc;
using CodeCampServer.Core.Domain;
using CodeCampServer.Core.Domain.Model;
using NUnit.Framework;
using NUnit.Framework.SyntaxHelpers;

namespace MvcInAction.Controllers.UnitTests
{
    [TestFixture]                                        Exercise class
    public class RedirectControllerTester                 under test
    {
        [Test]
        public void ShouldRedirectToTheNextConference()    Create using
        {                                                    simulated
            var conferenceToFind =                         dependencies
                new Conference{Key = "thekey", Name = "name"};
            var repository = new
                ConferenceRepositoryStub(conferenceToFind);

            var controller = new RedirectController(repository);   ◁

            RedirectToRouteResult result = controller.NextConference();   ◁

            Assert.That(result.RouteValues["controller"],
                Is.EqualTo("conference"));
            Assert.That(result.RouteValues["action"],           Assert
                Is.EqualTo("index"));                           correct
            Assert.That(result.RouteValues["conferenceKey"],    results
                Is.EqualTo("thekey"));
        }

        private class ConferenceRepositoryStub : IConferenceRepository   ❶
        {
            private readonly Conference _conference;

            public ConferenceRepositoryStub(Conference conference)
            {
                _conference = conference;
            }

            public Conference GetNextConference()
            {
                return _conference;
            }

            public Conference[] GetAllForUserGroup(UserGroup usergroup)
            {
                throw new NotImplementedException();
            }

            public Conference[] GetFutureForUserGroup(UserGroup usergroup)
            {
```

```
            throw new NotImplementedException();
        }

        public Conference GetById(Guid id)
        {
            throw new NotImplementedException();
        }

        public void Save(Conference entity)
        {
            throw new NotImplementedException();
        }

        public Conference[] GetAll()
        {
            throw new NotImplementedException();
        }

        public void Delete(Conference entity)
        {
            throw new NotImplementedException();
        }

        public Conference GetByKey(string key)
        {
            throw new NotImplementedException();
        }
    }
  }
}
```

Notice that most of the code listing is test double code, and not the Redirect-Controller test itself. We have to stub out an IConferenceRepository implementation ❶ because calling that interface inside the controller action provides the next conference. How it performs that search is beyond the scope of this chapter and is irrelevant to the controller. When glancing at this test, you probably think that it's too complex for a single unit test. We will see shortly how to reduce the amount of code in the unit test fixture. Reducing code starts with making dependencies explicit.

3.3.2   *Making dependencies explicit*

There are only three real lines of code in the RedirectController. The controllers should all be thin, and this is a good example. The logic for finding the correct Conference object is a data access issue, and does not belong in the controller, so it's factored into a repository object. Only logic related to presenting information to the user belongs in the controller. In this case, the user experiences a redirect. This controller demonstrates proper separation of concerns, and it's easily unit tested because it's only involved with a single responsibility. We are able to simulate dependencies using test doubles.

In Figure 3.2, you see the unit test passing because we were able to properly simulate this controller's dependencies and verify that given the dependencies, the controller will do its job correctly.

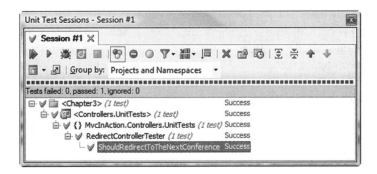

Figure 3.2
Redirect test passing

3.3.3 *Using test doubles, such as stubs and mocks*

As far as the controller is concerned, its caller is passing in an implementation of the necessary interface. This interface is a dependency, and the controller makes use of it in an action method. How the dependency is passed in or what class implements the interface is irrelevant. At runtime, a production class will be passed into the controller, but at the time of unit testing, we use stand-in objects, or test doubles, to simulate the behavior of the dependencies. There are different types of simulated objects, and some of the definitions overlap. There are entire books written about testing and how to separate code for testing using fakes, stubs, and mocks, and if you're interested in exploring the subject further, we highly recommend reading Michael Feather's *Working Effectively with Legacy Code*. In short, the terms *fake* and *test double* are generic terms for a nonproduction implementation of an interface or derived class that stands in for the real thing. Stubs are classes that return hard-code information solely for the purpose of being called. The ConferenceRepositoryStub shown in listing 3.5 is an example of a stub. A mock is a recorder that remembers being called so that we can assert the behavior later on. It remembers arguments passed in and other details depending on what capability has been programmed into it.

One downside to using hand-coded stubs and mocks is that you have many lines of code just to satisfy an interface implementation that may have six methods. This is not the only option, however. A favorite library for automating the creation of mocks and stubs is *Rhino Mocks*, originally written by Oren Eini. Rhino Mocks drastically reduces the number of lines of code in a unit test fixture by streamlining the creating of test doubles. If code is designed so that all dependencies are injected into the constructor, as shown in listing 3.6, unit testing becomes easy and soon becomes a repetitive pattern of faking dependencies and writing assertions. Over time, if you employ this technique, you will see a marked improvement in the quality of your code.

Listing 3.6 Controllers can define dependencies in the constructor.

```
public RedirectController(IConferenceRepository conferenceRepository)
{
    _repository = conferenceRepository;
}
```

Remember how many lines of code we wrote for a stubbed implementation of IConferenceRepository? Now, examine listing 3.7 and notice how short this code listing is in comparison. Rhino Mocks supports setting up dynamic stubs as well as dynamic mocks. The lines with Stub(...) are used so that a stubbing method or property always returns a given object. By using the Rhino Mocks library, we can provide dependency simulations quickly for easy unit testing.

Listing 3.7   Using Rhino Mocks to streamline code necessary for fakes

```
using System.Web.Mvc;
using CodeCampServer.Core.Domain;
using CodeCampServer.Core.Domain.Model;
using NUnit.Framework;
using NUnit.Framework.SyntaxHelpers;
using Rhino.Mocks;

namespace MvcInAction.Controllers.UnitTests
{
    [TestFixture]
    public class RedirectControllerTesterWithRhino
    {
        [Test]
        public void ShouldRedirectToTheNextConference()
        {
            var conferenceToFind = new Conference          ◁── Return a specific
            {                                                    conference
                Key = "thekey", Name = "name"
            };                                             ◁── Stub using
                                                               Rhino Mocks
            var repository =
                MockRepository.GenerateStub<IConferenceRepository>();

            repository.Stub(r =>
                r.GetNextConference()).Return(conferenceToFind);

            var controller = new RedirectController(repository);
            RedirectToRouteResult result = controller.NextConference();

            Assert.That(result.RouteValues["controller"],
                Is.EqualTo("conference"));                 ◁── Assert
            Assert.That(result.RouteValues["action"],          correct
                Is.EqualTo("index"));                          results
            Assert.That(result.RouteValues["conferenceKey"],
                Is.EqualTo("thekey"));
        }
    }
}
```

A dynamic mocking library like Rhino Mocks is not appropriate in every unit testing scenario. The usage in listing 3.7 is the bread-and-butter scenario that reduces the amount of setup code inside unit tests. More complex needs can quickly stress the Rhino Mocks API and become hard to read. Although Rhino Mocks supports almost everything you could want to do, the readability of the tests is important to maintain. When you need to assert method parameters of dependencies or do something special, do not be afraid to push Rhino Mocks to the side and leverage a concrete mock or stub to keep the test readable.

3.3.4 *Elements of a good controller unit test*

If you're just getting started with unit testing you might run into common pitfalls and stub your toe. Again, this is not meant to be an entire course on testing. There are already comprehensive books on that, such as *The Art of Unit Testing* by Roy Osherove. This book specifically addresses writing unit tests for controller classes. We focus heavily on testing controller classes because test-driving the controllers ensures they are well designed. It's nearly impossible to test-drive code that ends up with a bad design.

NOTE   Poorly designed code tends to be untestable, so observable untestability is a very objective gauge of poorly designed code. A good controller unit test runs fast. We are talking 2000 unit tests all running within 10 seconds. How is that possible? .NET code runs fast, and if you're running unit tests, you're waiting only for the processor and RAM. Unit tests run code only within the AppDomain, so we do not have to deal with crossing AppDomain or Process boundaries. You can quickly sabotage this fast test performance if you break a fundamental rule of unit testing, and that is allowing out-of-process calls. Out-of-process calls are orders of magnitude slower than in-process calls, and your test performance will suffer. Ensure that you're faking out all controller dependencies, and your test will continue to run fast.

You also want your unit tests to be self-sufficient and isolated. You might see repeated code and think you need to refactor your unit tests. Resist this temptation and create only test helpers for the cross-cutting concerns. The DRY principle (Don't Repeat Yourself) does not apply to test code as much as to production code. Rather, keeping test cases isolated and self-contained reduces the change burden when the production code needs to change. It's also more readable if you can scan a unit test and see the context all in one method.

The tests should also be repeatable. That means no shared global variables for the test result state, and no shared state between tests in general. Keep a unit test isolated in every way, and it will be repeatable, order-independent, and stable.

Pay attention to pain. If your tests become painful to maintain, there's something wrong. The tests should enable development, not slow it down. If you start to think that you could move faster without writing the tests, look for technique errors or bad design in the production code. Get a peer to review the code. Correctly managed design and tests enable sustained speed of development whereas poor testing techniques cause development to slow down to a point where testing is abandoned. At that point, it's back to painstaking, time-intensive manual testing. With that critical practice safely stowed in our tool belt, let's explore actions in more detail.

3.4   *Simple actions and views*

To demonstrate how a controller can do interesting things without a view, our previous controller, RedirectController, did not use a view. A controller can work independently from a view. More interesting (and common), though, is a controller that pushes objects into ViewData and then returns a ViewResult with a named view to render. The only coupling between the controller and a view is the view name declared in the call to return View().

Views can be simple or complex, and complex views can require many objects to be passed in as view data. Simple views, likewise, often require only a single object or no object at all. In listing 3.8, we see an action in the CodeCampServer project that is responsible for fulfilling a request to display the registration form. This screen needs to display header information about the Conference and then a list of text boxes to collect an attendee registration. The URL that would be routed to this action would be http://CodeCampServer.org/AustinCodeCamp09/Attendee/New. Because the routes in CodeCampServer specify the first segment named conferenceKey, the ASP.NET MVC Framework will extract this portion of the URL and add it to RouteData to make it available to model binders. The argument will be used to resolve the action parameter, conference, and the action code in listing 3.8 will be able to use it when preparing to render the view.

Listing 3.8   Action passes information so the view can render a data entry screen

```
public ViewResult New(Conference conference)
{
    var model = new AttendeeForm {ConferenceID = conference.Id};
    return View("Edit", model);
}
```

Figure 3.3   The Edit view can be used for a new attendee or existing attendee.

When views containing forms, like the one in figure 3.3, are involved, the potential for interactive web applications makes us think about how to pass arguments from the browser back in to a controller. One of the fundamental data transactions of the web is the *form post*.

3.5   *Working with form values*

An HTML page that has a `<form method="POST"/>` tag will generate a `POST` back to the same URL, unless an alternate action is specified. When a page is posted to a URL, all form fields are translated into a form values collection. For instance, if the page contains `<input type="text" name="FirstName"/>`, user entries in that text box will be entered into the form collection and available to the server code that handles the request. With the ASP.NET MVC Framework, form values are routed automatically into the controller action. The action parameters are matched to values in the form collection by name. In figure 3.2, we see a page containing a form with text boxes that collect attendee registration information for CodeCampServer. Each of these text boxes has a unique name used to match action parameters.

Looking at listing 3.9, we see one option for receiving the form post. Notice the names of the parameters on this method. The parameter `conferenceKey` is still there and will be matched to the appropriate part of the route. Next are `firstName`, `lastName`, and so on. The ASP.NET MVC Framework will search to match parameters to this method. The matching mechanism matches by name. Because `firstName` exists in the form collection, the value will be passed into this method along with the other parameters. The end result is that all the attendee registration information is translated into action parameters and passed in. As developers, we don't have to do a thing to extract the appropriate information from the form collection on the request. We must only ensure the names of the action parameters match up with the names posted to the URL.

> **Listing 3.9   Form values are automatically passed to the action**

```
public ActionResult Save(string conferenceKey, string firstName,
                         string lastName, string email,
                         string webpage)
{                    ┌─ Method body
                  <──┘  omitted
}
```

Already, you're probably wondering about conflicts. What happens if a form or querystring value is named `conferenceKey`? Which value will be used? The ASP.NET MVC Framework matches action parameters in the following order:

1 Form values
2 Route arguments
3 Querystring parameters

Parameters on an action method are always matched by name in the order given. If there is a duplicate, the first one found wins, and subsequent duplicates are ignored. If there is a valid reason to have a form value and route argument named the same, your code will have to handle extracting the route values explicitly using `RouteData.GetRequiredString("key")`. In our sample in listing 3.9, all the parameters are of type `string`. Because web requests are processed in string form, we will need some mechanism to parse them into more complex types. We will cover this in depth in the section on *model binders*.

NOTE   Because the form values are processed first, there are certain form parameter names you should not use (they will likely cause unexpected behavior if you do) such as `action` and `controller`.

Already we begin to see the value proposition of the ASP.NET MVC Framework, and we understand why folks also enjoy Ruby on Rails and MonoRail. These frameworks abstract away repetitive plumbing code like mapping query strings and form parameters to variables and leave only the interesting code to be written. We have seen how form and route values are mapped into action methods. Next we will examine doing the same with querystring values.

3.6   *Processing querystring parameters*

Querystrings are mapped into a controller action in a fashion similar to form values—by name matching. If the ASP.NET MVC Framework does not find a matching value in the form collection, it will then search the querystring for a parameter that matches. Upon finding the matching value, it will pass it through the appropriate action parameter. In this way, we can alter our URLs to provide a dynamic environment within a single controller action.

In listing 3.10, this controller is going to pass along the greeting to the view as the `ViewData.Model`. A URL similar to `~/hello?greeting=Hello+Jeffrey` would cause the page to output "Hello Jeffrey" on the screen. If the querystring value is missing, the parameter will be null. Since `System.String` is a nullable type, we have no problem here.

> **Listing 3.10   Querystring parameters are passed to the action just like form values.**

```
using System.Web.Mvc;

namespace MvcInAction.Controllers
{
    public class HelloController : Controller
    {
        public ActionResult Index(string greeting)
        {
            ViewData.Model = greeting;
            return View();
        }
    }
}
```

NOTE The ASP.NET MVC Framework matches querystring values based completely on name. The order is unimportant. As an exercise, pull down the code for this chapter and change the order of the action parameters. The behavior of the application will be unaffected. Similarly, change the order of the querystring parameters. No change. The name of the parameter is what matters.

So far, all of our action parameters have been strings. In practice, we need to be able to use a diverse set of types in our application. We will tackle that next. Two main concerns exist when binding from the form, route, and querystring. The first is to match the value based on key. The next is to parse it into the correct object. With string action parameters, there is no parsing because string is the native type. Now let's investigate how to parse more complex types.

3.7 *Binding more complex objects in action parameters*

As soon as we get away from Hello World applications, we are faced with complex types, and we need to be able to accept them in action parameter lists. In listing 3.9, we saw an action method signature that accepted a form posting as a series of string parameters. A better binding method uses a form object, such as the AttendeeForm shown in listing 3.11. This class is from CodeCampServer, which leverages a value object supertype from the Tarantino project, ValueObject<T>. In your code, this may be irrelevant.

> **Listing 3.11   A dedicated form object can encapsulate the data of a form post.**

```
public class AttendeeForm : ValueObject<AttendeeForm>
{
    public virtual Guid ConferenceID { get; set; }
    public virtual string FirstName { get; set; }
    public virtual string LastName { get; set; }
    public virtual string EmailAddress { get; set; }
    public virtual string Webpage { get; set; }
}
public ActionResult Save(AttendeeForm form){}          ◁——┐ Resulting action
                                                            method signature
```

The mechanism in charge of matching action parameters and pulling them in from the request is the IModelBinder interface. Out of the box, the class that matches .NET Framework types, simple or nested, is the System.Web.Mvc.DefaultModelBinder class. The DefaultModelBinder class can bind any type with a .NET TypeConverter, such as Int32, DateTime, Guid, etc. It can also match

- Arrays
- Collections
- Dictionaries
- Complex objects containing any of these types

The built-in binding capabilities are powerful, and they work for all the primitive types, both on their own and when nested within complex types. We still need the capability to bind our own custom types, such as the Conference type in CodeCampServer. For this, we will need to implement our own IModelBinder instance. In listing 3.12, we see a controller action that requires a custom type as well as a custom model binder. The listing handles an HTTP request that has a parameter named conference, which contains the conference key.

Listing 3.12   Using a custom model binder to take control over binding custom types

```
public class BindConferenceController : Controller
{
    public object Index(Conference conference)
    {
        return conference.Name;
    }
}

using System.Web.Mvc;
using CodeCampServer.Core.Domain;
using CodeCampServer.Core.Domain.Model;

namespace MvcInAction
{
    public class ConferenceModelBinder : DefaultModelBinder      <──┐
    {
        private readonly IConferenceRepository _repository;

        public ConferenceModelBinder(IConferenceRepository repository)   <──┐
        {
            _repository = repository;
        }

        public override object BindModel(
            ControllerContext controllerContext,
            ModelBindingContext bindingContext)
        {
            ValueProviderResult providerResult =
                bindingContext.ValueProvider[bindingContext.ModelName];

            Conference conference =
                _repository.GetByKey(providerResult.AttemptedValue);

            return conference;
        }
    }
}
```

Binder has dependencies

Inherit from Default ModelBinder

Find Conference by key

Find value matching name

One more step is needed to hook in this custom model binder. When the application starts up, we need to register our model binder with the ASP.NET MVC Framework. We can do that easily in the Global.asax.cs file. Listing 3.13 shows the one line of code necessary to register our custom model binder. Here you see that we are passing in a stub for the IConferenceRepository. In your application, you would probably resolve the model binder with an IoC container or a factory.

Listing 3.13 Register our custom model binder when the web application starts.

```
ModelBinders.Binders.Add(typeof (Conference),
                    new ConferenceModelBinder(
                    new ConferenceRepositoryStub()));
```

It's a good idea to use meaningful types in controller actions. If the action parameters are all strings, ints, and Guids, the action methods will be cluttered with lookup code while the controller struggles to convert a string to a better object. By leveraging the model binder mechanism, we can externalize this lookup and mapping code so that the controller actions can concentrate on making "what" decisions about how the screen will behave. This results in smaller action methods and more maintainable controllers. When you browse through CodeCampServer, look at the types passed into action methods. Rarely are they .NET primitive types.

The resolution of action parameters coupled with model binders makes it easy to craft an action method that takes in information from a web request. We can use the form values, route values, and the querystring to make the action behavior more dynamic. Again, notice how effortless it is to consume this request data. We do not have to write any repetitive code to pull these values in. Rather, the ASP.NET MVC Framework finds the correct parameter and maps it to the action parameter. Our custom model binders take it from there and convert the values to our custom types where necessary. Now that we have objects coming into our action, we will examine how we push objects out to the view.

3.8   *Options for passing ViewData*

The System.Web.Mvc.Controller base class has a ViewData property, which is essentially a dictionary. You can use it as is or leverage extension methods in MvcContrib for a richer API on top of the IDictionary<string, object> type. ViewData has a Model property that is a first-class citizen in the view. The primary object passed to the view should go in this property. When more objects are necessary, add them to the dictionary and retrieve them in the view by key name.

We have several options for passing view data from a controller action to a view. After you start creating your own types for view data, the options increase well beyond those presented here. The first option, and the default mechanism you might use at first, is to use the built-in View() method parameter. Listing 3.14 demonstrates this. By passing in the object directly to the View() method, the framework will automatically assign it to ViewData.Model.

Listing 3.14 Calling the View() method on the Controller base class

```
public ActionResult ViewDataModel(Conference conference)
{
    return View(conference);
}
```

The default mechanism for adding additional objects to a dictionary is to assign each object a key. ViewData is no different; however, with MvcContrib, we have an option available that allows us to forgo string keys for access to all objects in ViewData. Using ViewDataExtensions, we can add an object into ViewData without giving it a key. These extensions will implicitly use the type of the variable as the key in the dictionary, and the following code can be used in the view to retrieve the Conference added in listing 3.15: ViewData.Get<Conference>();. No casting, no dictionary keys. Now you have strong typing on many objects. The only constraint is that you can add only one Conference to ViewData. If you need to add multiple objects of the same type, you can fall back and assign a unique key to each one.

> **Listing 3.15   Passing a single object directly to the View method**

```
public ActionResult MultipleObjectsInViewData(Conference conference, string
    someOtherVariable)
{                                                    Using MvcContrib
    ViewData.Add(new Conference());  ⟵──────         ViewDataExtensions
    ViewData.Model = someOtherVariable;
    return View();
}
```

For some scenarios, a single object may be sufficient for the view to render. In others, you will need several objects. In our opinion, because IDictionary is very flexible, it's appropriate for most uses. The extension methods from MvcContrib enhance the experience even more, and together, we recommend their use in most scenarios. Set the primary object to ViewData.Model and put the others in the dictionary. While binding objects into action methods and passing objects to ViewData, we often need to insert code in unique places and even share this code among controllers. Filters provide a way to do this.

3.9   *Filters*

The function of a filter in ASP.NET MVC is similar to its function in the real world. Using filters, we can filter out requests or modify the data that gets through. The notion of a filter applies when using the System.Web.Mvc.Controller base class, which, in our experience, is most of the time.

Four interfaces combine to provide filtering support as a controller is executing:

- *IActionFilter*—Before and after hooks when an action is executing
- *IResultFilter*—Before and after hooks when an action result is executing
- *IAuthorizationFilter*—Hooks when ASP.NET is authorizing the current user
- *IExceptionFilter*—Hooks when an exception occurs during the execution of a controller

The Controller base class implements all these interfaces, so to hook into any of these extensibility points, all you have to do is override the appropriate method in your controller. Overriding controller lifecycle methods is not the engaging part of filters, however. The interesting part is how with filter attributes, you can reuse filters on many controllers and even pick and choose which filters should apply to which actions. These filter attributes can be applied on the action method or on the controller class definition (which will cause them to apply to all actions in the controller). Filter attributes supplied by the ASP.NET MVC Framework include

- `System.Web.Mvc.ActionFilterAttribute`
- `System.Web.Mvc.OutputCacheAttribute`
- `System.Web.Mvc.HandleErrorAttribute`
- `System.Web.Mvc.AuthorizeAttribute`
- `System.Web.Mvc.ValidateAntiForgeryTokenAttribute`
- `System.Web.Mvc.ValidateInputAttribute`

Implementing one of the filter interfaces is the easiest way to intercept the execution of the controller. It's not the only way to interrupt, or prevent, the execution of a web request. The controller also has a notion of an *action method selector*. The action method selector is in charge of selecting which action method to execute. By decorating action methods with the following attributes, you can alter the default mechanism for action method selection:

- *System.Web.Mvc.AcceptVerbsAttribute*—Limits action selection to requests of the specified HTTP verb type
- *System.Web.Mvc.NonActionAttribute*—Prevents action method from being selected

To affect the selection of an action method for execution, you can create your own derivations of `ActionMethodSelectorAttribute`. Probably the most useful selector is the `AcceptVerbsAttribute`, where you can limit an action to the "POST" verb so that "GET" requests do not modify server state. It's most important to understand the order of execution of the controller, when many filters are layered on. In listing 3.16, we see a controller that has many filters. You can view the code of `LoggingAction-FilterX` in the code that accompanies the book. This class implements each filter interface listed previously and writes to the response on each hook method. The result is the order of operations shown in figure 3.4.

Listing 3.16 Demonstrating many ways filters can be applied to a controller

```
using System.Web.Mvc;

namespace MvcInAction.Controllers
{
    [LoggingActionFilterA(LogMessage = "controller, index 1", Order = 0)]
    [LoggingActionFilterB(LogMessage = "controller, index 2", Order = 1)]
    public class FilterExampleController : Controller
    {
        [LoggingActionFilterA(LogMessage = "action, index 1", Order = 0)]
        [LoggingActionFilterB(LogMessage = "action, index 2", Order = 1)]
        public ActionResult Index()
        {
            Response.Write("Action body executing<br/>");
```

```
            return Content("Action internals<br/>");
        }
    }
}
```

`LoggingActionFilterA` and `LoggingAction-FilterB` implement all four of the filter interfaces and output text to the response stream at each hook point. The `Order` property on the attributes controls the order, and we see that the controller always has the first and last word when hooking filter points.

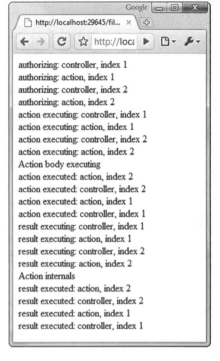

Figure 3.4   The output shows the order of execution of filters when many are applied at both the controller and action level.

3.10   *Summary*

Controllers are the center of an MVC presentation layer. Controllers handle all the coordination between the Model and the View. Without the controller, we must find another place for this presentation logic. In the ASP.NET MVC Framework, logic is separated into controllers and actions. Actions can accept parameters and can call for the rendering of a view. Actions are not required to have a view, but they commonly do. When using a view, we have several methods for passing view data, and the preferred method is to use an object that best suits your needs. Keep in mind that the default way might not be best for your situation.

Action parameters are matched by name first from the form, then the route, and then querystring. Order is unimportant. If one of the responsibilities of the controller is to perform some task for every action, consider an action filter. In fact, if this task is applicable for many controllers, consider creating a layer supertype that applies this filter. When you're starting a new application based on the ASP.NET MVC Framework, consider creating a layer supertype right from the start. Chances are, the need to make some functionality available to all controllers through inheritance will surface, and it will save you time if you have accumulated many controllers. Of course, YAGNI (You aren't going to need it) applies here, so evaluate your scenario and choose wisely. We often find a layer supertype comes into play at some point. The variable is *when*.

Wielded without caution, controllers have the potential of becoming just as large and convoluted as `Page_Load` methods in Web Forms. Armed with test-driven development and a disciplined approach to separation of concerns, you will ensure the maintainability of your presentation layer. With controller techniques under our belt, we need to fully understand the options for formatting output to the screen using views. This is the topic of chapter 4.

The view in depth

This chapter covers
- Rendering views
- Techniques for working with ViewData
- Error reporting
- Handling complexity

Views have long been abused in the Microsoft web application space. In Classic ASP, and in IDC/HTX before that, the view was the primary programming tool for the Microsoft-centric developer. Using the Server Page pattern, developers used IDC and ASP pages as transaction scripts to perform a single operation and render a screen. Each page has logic, behavior, and a UI. ASP.NET 1.0 sought to separate logic from the UI rendering to make applications easier to maintain and extend, because having logic intermixed with screen rendering had often proved to be an unworkable solution for many teams. Although it certainly was possible for teams to separate the concerns in their applications, Microsoft had provided no guidance on how to do so, and most samples and demo applications encouraged the intermingling of concerns.

ASP.NET set the foundation for how a Windows web server would handle web requests. The framework has proven highly scalable and robust. Web Forms, one part of the .NET framework, has faced maintainability challenges. Although Web Forms allowed scores of VB6 programmers to make the transition from Windows applications to web applications, these developers did not fall into the "pit of success." The code-behind idea did, in fact, separate logic from UI rendering, but in practice, and coupled with guidance available in the industry, the logic ended up merely separated in a file instead of abstracted into new concepts. Web Forms continued the Server Page pattern started in IDC and carried through Classic ASP. The ASP.NET MVC Framework attempts to provide developers with an alternative to the Web Forms Server Page pattern. In this chapter, we'll see how simple a view can be and how to handle complex views. We'll cover techniques for working with `ViewData`, view helpers, form validation, and other complex issues. Before diving into a specific topic, let's look at the major differences between ASP.NET MVC views and Web Forms.

4.1   *How ASP.NET MVC views differ from Web Forms*

ASP.NET MVC views and Web Forms views can exist side by side, so it is possible to do a phased port from Web Forms to ASP.NET MVC. Web Forms serve a much bigger purpose in the application than MVC views. By the time your code executes in a Web Form `Page_Load`, the framework has already

- Selected the Web Form to execute
- Constructed the Web Form and all its design-time controls
- Processed any `ViewState` received

With a Web Form, your code runs as the page is executing. There are plenty of ways to get into the pipeline before the page starts executing, but they are not obvious or easy. A Web Form is built upon the concept of a *control*, which is the building block of the page. Controls can have child controls, and `System.Web.UI.Page` derives from `System.Web.UI.Control`. A control's purpose is to be responsible for the behavior and rendering of what will ultimately become an HTML element on the page. During the heyday of browser wars and incompatibility, controls were able to render different markup based on the browser receiving the page. This was a useful feature in 2002 and 2003. With Internet Explorer 7 and FireFox 2+ now responsible for more than half of the markup rendering, most web users are employing a more standards-compliant web browser than in 2002; the need to render different markup to different browsers has diminished.

ASP.NET MVC Views take back control of HTML markup. Although it is possible to use the rendering capabilities of some existing controls, the guidance with MVC Views is to lay out the HTML by hand and use server delimiters to make parts of the view dynamic. MVC Views leverage the Web Forms rendering engine but jettison the postback logic, `ViewState`, and control hierarchy. An MVC view renders top to bottom and then goes away. It also has much less responsibility than a Web Form. The view accepts objects in its `ViewData` dictionary and transforms those objects into a response suitable for the web. That is it. No decision logic, no permissions, no database access, no web service calls, just rendering. MVC views do not use a code-behind file, but you can retain a code-behind while migrating from Web Forms if necessary. This ability comes from the fact that `System.Web.Mvc.ViewPage` derives from `System.Web.UI.Page`.

If you are porting an application from Web Forms to ASP.NET MVC and you have not rigorously factored logic into many supporting classes, you will find yourself moving much of your code-behind logic into a controller. You will also probably find that much of the logic does not belong in a controller. You will most certainly need to develop additional classes to absorb logic that has inappropriately lived in a Web Form code-behind file. We'll begin by exploring the folder structure for views and some of the basics.

4.2 Folder structure and view basics

Views employ conventions for naming and placement. Although these are overridable, we find that the default structure and naming work well for many small and midsize projects. For larger projects, the architecture needs to be modular, so it then becomes necessary for views to live with the parent module.

In figure 4.1, we see the solution explorer for CodeCampServer. The Views folder inside the web application is the home for folders that match controller names. Inside each folder, named for the parent controller, are individual views that may or may not match a controller action's name.

The ASP.NET MVC Framework will work hard to locate a view to use for rendering. The framework will search each registered view engine before giving up with an exception. Out-of-the-box, ASP.NET MVC comes with a single view engine, `WebFormViewEngine`. This default view engine has several paths where views can reside, and views can be named with either the .aspx or .ascx extension. In listing 4.1, we see some of the code from the ASP.NET MVC Framework itself showing where the framework looks for views.

Figure 4.1 Default folder structure demonstrating convention for organizing views. The dots you see next to each file are part of the VisualSVN plugin. CodeCampServer uses Subversion for source control.

Listing 4.1 In the constructor of `WebFormViewEngine`, the default paths are set.

```
public WebFormViewEngine () {
    MasterLocationFormats = new[] {
        "~/Views/{1}/{0}.master",
        "~/Views/Shared/{0}.master"
    };

    ViewLocationFormats = new[] {
        "~/Views/{1}/{0}.aspx",
```

```
    "~/Views/{1}/{0}.ascx",
    "~/Views/Shared/{0}.aspx",
    "~/Views/Shared/{0}.ascx"
};

PartialViewLocationFormats = ViewLocationFormats;
}
```

If you need your view to live elsewhere, you can extend the framework to provide a custom location. What happens if your view is not found? To demonstrate the answer, I have defined a controller that returns a `ViewResult`, but I have purposely left out the view. See how, in figure 4.2, the ASP.NET MVC Framework throws an exception listing the specific places searched just to find that view.

A view is an instance of the `System.Web.Mvc.IView` interface. You can see the definition of this interface in listing 4.2.

Listing 4.2   The `IView` interface has a single `Render` operation.

```
public interface IView {
    void Render(ViewContext viewContext, TextWriter writer);
}
```

The only type of view included with the MVC framework is `System.Web.Mvc.WebFormView`. This class leverages the Web Forms infrastructure to perform rendering. Let's examine the order of events that occur when a particular view is rendered.

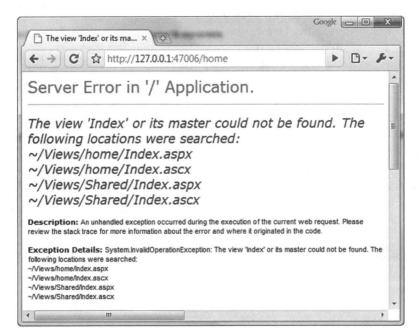

Figure 4.2   When looking for a view, the framework searches four paths before giving up.

1 The `ViewResult` returned from an action method executes.

2 The `ViewResult` uses the `ViewEngineCollection` to find the view.

3 The `ViewEngineCollection` gives each registered `IViewEngine` a chance to resolve the view. The order is determined by the order of the view engines within the collection.

4 The `ViewResult` creates a `ViewContext` using the `ControllerContext`, view name, `ViewData`, and `TempData`.

5 The `ViewResult` calls `Render()` on the `IView` passing in the `ViewContext` and the response stream.

6 If the `IView` instance derives from `WebFormView`, the following steps occur.

7 The `WebFormView` uses `IBuildManager` to create a `ViewPage` or `ViewUser-Control` from a virtual path.

8 The `WebFormView` sets the `MasterLocation` on the `ViewPage`, sets the `ViewData` and calls `RenderView()` passing in the `ViewContext`.

9 The `ViewPage` stores the `ViewContext`, initializes `HtmlHelper`, `AjaxHelper`, and `UrlHelper`, then delegates to `base.ProcessRequest()`, with which you are already familiar because it is the primary method on `IHttpHandler`.

From the time an action method returns a `ViewResult` to the time the existing response pipeline executes, you, as the developer, have several places to customize the behavior of the rendering process. The following interfaces are extensibility points where you can insert your own logic and alter the default behavior once an action method has returned:

- `IView`
- `IViewDataContainer`
- `IViewEngine`
- `IViewLocationCache`

A widely used extension point is `IViewEngine` because that is the extension point required to integrate other view engines like NVelocity, Brail, or Spark. It is also quite easy to derive a class from `WebFormViewEngine` and merely override the `FileExists()` method or `CreateView()` method. Refer to chapter 6 for more information about view engines.

4.3   *Overview of view basics*

As we said before, views are responsible for rendering objects for consumption by a user. Decision logic should be limited, if not eliminated from views in order to ensure maintainability; we'll focus on how views are organized and leveraged to render a screen. We'll assume decision logic is retained in the controller, domain objects, and supporting presentation objects.

At first glance, it may seem that the view is not doing much, and that is correct. Intentionally, a view's responsibility should be limited. Inherently, views are more brittle than other types of code because to verify the correctness of a view, one has to run the application and physically look at the screen to ensure it is correct. Even with automated tools like Selenium and Wati(r/N), you often have to wait because these types of tests take a long time to run (measured in seconds, not milliseconds). There are ways to independently test views, but we have found the return on the large investment to be less than ideal. Our approach to views is to limit decision logic by factoring any necessary logic out into other objects. The views become simple HTML markup with variable tokens. When working with views, the basic topics include view engines, master pages, `ViewData`, and partials. We'll begin with view engines.

4.3.1   *Examining the IViewEngine abstraction*

`System.Web.Mvc.IViewEngine` is the interface responsible for locating a view or a partial view. The full definition is in listing 4.3.

> **Listing 4.3   `IViewEngine` defines the contract used to locate views and partials.**

```
public interface IViewEngine {
    ViewEngineResult FindPartialView(ControllerContext controllerContext,
        string partialViewName, bool useCache);
    ViewEngineResult FindView(ControllerContext controllerContext,
        string viewName, string masterName, bool useCache);
    void ReleaseView(ControllerContext controllerContext, IView view);
}
```

Regardless of whether a view or a partial is found, each method returns a `View-EngineResult`, which contains the `IView` instance as well as an `IEnumerable<string>` that contains the paths searched in order to locate the view. This interface is all that is necessary to

- Change the default directory where views live
- Change the default names of views
- Amend the searched locations
- Add a new file extension for valid views
- Adapt a third-party view engine

The ASP.NET MVC Framework provides one view engine right out of the box, `Web-FormViewEngine`. This is the view engine supported by the file templates registered with Visual Studio and works with .aspx and .ascx views. We can expect most of the market to stick with this view engine because it is familiar and supported by tools such as Visual Studio and JetBrains ReSharper. When you want to leverage an alternate view engine, register the second view engine in an HTTP Module or in the Global.asax.cs file as shown in listing 4.4.

> **Listing 4.4   Registering our view engine in Global.asax.cs**

```
protected void Application_Start()
{
```

```
    RegisterRoutes(RouteTable.Routes);
    ViewEngines.Engines.Add(new MyViewEngine());        ❶
}

public class MyViewEngine : IViewEngine
{
    public ViewEngineResult FindPartialView(ControllerContext
        controllerContext, string partialViewName, bool useCache)
    {
        return new ViewEngineResult (new string[0]);    ⟵— Find a partial view
    }

    public ViewEngineResult FindView(ControllerContext controllerContext,
        string viewName, string masterName, bool useCache)
    {
        return new ViewEngineResult (new string[0]);    ⟵— Find a view
    }

    public void ReleaseView(ControllerContext controllerContext,
        IView view)
    {
                    ⟵⌐  No need to implement
    }               │   ReleaseView
}
```

We have created a naïve implementation of IViewEngine for the purposes of this example. In the Global.asax.cs file, we use one line of code to add this new view engine to the collection ❶. When the view name cannot be found by the WebForm-ViewEngine, MyViewEngine will get a chance to find the view. Now that we understand the mechanics of locating and invoking a view, let's explore master pages.

4.3.2 Understanding master pages in the ASP.NET MVC Framework

Layout is a fundamental element of screen design. A layout is known as a master page in ASP.NET, but the term precedes master pages. ASP.NET MVC carries master pages forward as one way to componentize the view necessary for a single screen. Just as with Web Forms, view master pages can be nested. In fact, System.Web.Mvc.ViewMaster-Page derives from System.Web.UI.MasterPage; it has all the same capabilities. When using ASP.NET MVC, you use master pages in a manner similar to Web Forms. You specify the screen frame with specific sections marked as placeholders for content specific to the screen. Web applications typically have a common page border and color scheme. The master page is the perfect place to put the common elements as well as style sheets and site-wide JavaScript libraries such as jQuery. Figure 4.3 shows the portion of the screen that is specific to the page shown. The area not shadowed is rendered from the master page.

A view engine is in complete control of handling master pages: view engine handles. A view engine could allow only a single master page, but the IViewEngine interface allows a view engine to support many, each named with a string name. For instance, the FindView method accepts masterName as an argument. With this key, the view engine can locate a master page. Although it is possible to mix views within an

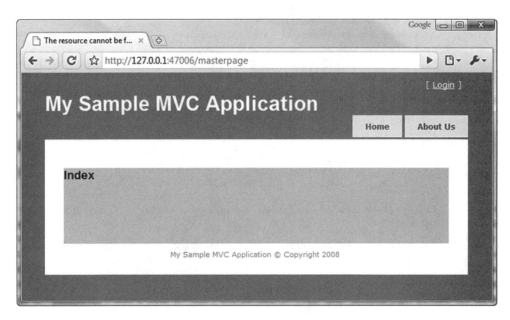

Figure 4.3   The master page represents the area around the shadowed section.

application, and even to mix views on a single page with different partial views from different view engines, the master page chosen must be of the same view engine as the view to be found and rendered. Although a single screen could have a master page of SiteLayout, with a view of Edit, and partials of First and Second, the partials can be of any type of view, but the SiteLayout and Edit must be from the same view engine. Remember: if you are transitioning to a different view engine, you can use two master pages, but you will have to duplicate the markup so that during the transition you have the same master page coded in both view engine formats.

Because the WebFormViewEngine leverages master pages from Web Forms, the experience should be familiar to current ASP.NET developers. The difference is that view master pages have no postback capabilities or server-side form posting. They should be used for common markup for screen borders and navigation. Each .aspx view can declare a master page directly, or the controller action can specify it. If the view specifies a master page, but the controller action also specifies one, the action wins, and the view's selection is overridden. This is behavior specific to the WebFormViewEngine. Each view engine is free to implement arbitrary rules on precedence or requirements.

Listing 4.5 is a simple master page, and we see it rendering objects in ViewData the same way as with a regular view. All markup is the same. The only difference is that we use the ContentPlaceHolder control to designate where the view should be placed. In a master page, you can use any of the normal or custom view helpers you may have at your disposal.

Listing 4.5   A layout using `WebFormViewEngine`

```
<%@ Master Language="C#" AutoEventWireup="true"
    Inherits="System.Web.Mvc.ViewMasterPage" %>
<%@ Import Namespace="System.Web.Mvc.Html"%>

<!DOCTYPE html PUBLIC "-//W3C//DTD XHTML 1.0 Strict//EN" "http://www.w3.org/
    TR/xhtml1/DTD/xhtml1-strict.dtd">
<html xmlns="http://www.w3.org/1999/xhtml">
<head runat="server">
    <meta http-equiv="Content-Type" content="text/html; charset=iso-8859-1"
    />
    <title><%= Html.Encode(ViewData ["Title"])%></title>
    <link href="../../Content/Site.css" rel="stylesheet" type="text/css" />
</head>

<body>
    <div class="page">
        <div id="header">
            <div id="title">
                <h1>My Second Sample MVC Application</h1>
            </div>

            <div id="menucontainer">

                <ul id="menu">
                    <li><%=Html.ActionLink("Home", "Index", "Home")%></li>
                    <li><%=Html.ActionLink("About Us","About","Home")%>
                    </li>
                </ul>

            </div>
        </div>

        <div id="main">
            <asp:ContentPlaceHolder ID="MainContent" runat="server" />

            <div id="footer">
                My Sample MVC Application &copy; Copyright 2008
            </div>
        </div>
    </div>
</body>
</html>
```

To help you understand how views are selected and how you can modularize them, we'll explore the common object structure that all views use to get objects to render.

4.3.3   *Using ViewData to send objects to a view*

ViewData is the bag of state (sometimes referred to as a *property bag*) that is passed to a view. A view should get all the information it needs from ViewData, which is implemented as a dictionary. It contains key/value pairs as well as some special properties, like Model. The controller is responsible for filling the ViewData dictionary with objects, but action filters can add to the dictionary as well. In fact, ViewData is a property on System.Web.Mvc.ControllerBase, so anywhere you can access the controller you can access `ViewData`. As the view is executing, it pulls objects from `ViewData` during the rendering process.

In chapter 1, you saw a simple use of `ViewData`, so we won't repeat that here. In any nontrivial application, your view will be composed of a master page, a main view, and many partials—possibly nested partials. It will help to know how `ViewData` is segmented among the views. For instance, it is important to consider a partial view that might be used by several other views. If the partial view needs an object in `ViewData`, whose responsibility is it to put the object into the dictionary? The following is an example that illustrates just what happens in this complex scenario. Examine the source of the controller in listing 4.6, the Index.aspx view in listing 4.7, Partial.aspx in listing 4.8 and NestedPartial.aspx in listing 4.9.

Listing 4.6   The controller puts objects into `ViewData`.

```
using System.Web.Mvc;

namespace ViewSamples.Controllers
{
    public class ViewDataController : Controller
    {
        public ActionResult Index()
        {
            ViewData.Add("one", "onevalue");          ⟵  Add objects
            ViewData.Add("two", "twovalue");              to ViewData
            ViewData.Add("three", "threevalue");      ⟵  Render default
            return View(3);                               view with model
        }
    }
}
```

Listing 4.7   Accessing `ViewData` from the view

```
<%@ Page Language="C#" AutoEventWireup="true"
    Inherits="System.Web.Mvc.ViewPage<object>" %>
<%@ Import Namespace="System.Web.Mvc.Html"%>
<!DOCTYPE html PUBLIC "-//W3C//DTD XHTML 1.0 Transitional//EN"
    "http://www.w3.org/TR/xhtml1/DTD/xhtml1-transitional.dtd">
<html xmlns="http://www.w3.org/1999/xhtml" >
<head runat="server">
    <title></title>
</head>
<body>
    <div>
        This view:    <%=GetType().Name %>
        Model:        <%=ViewData.Model %><br />
        Model Type:   <%=ViewData.Model.GetType().Name %>
        ViewDataDictionary hashcode: <%=ViewData.GetHashCode()%>
        <br />
        <%foreach (KeyValuePair<string, object> pair in ViewData){%>
            View data <%=pair.Key%> : <%=pair.Value %><br />
        <% } %>
```

```
        <hr />
        PARTIAL
        <%Html.RenderPartial("partial"); %>

        <hr />
        NESTED PARTIAL PASSING IN MODEL
        <%Html.RenderPartial("nestedpartial", 89); %>

        <hr />
        NESTED PARTIAL PASSING IN MODEL AND VIEWDATA
        <%Html.RenderPartial("nestedpartial", 89,
            new ViewDataDictionary {{"first", "1"} , {"second", "2"}}); %>

        <hr />
        NESTED PARTIAL PASSING IN VIEWDATA
        <%
            var dictionary = new ViewDataDictionary {{"first", "value"}};
            dictionary.Model = 100;
            Html.RenderPartial("nestedpartial", dictionary);
        %>
    </div>
</body>
</html>
```

Listing 4.8 Partial.aspx is loaded as a partial and loads a partial itself.

```
<%@ Page Language="C#" AutoEventWireup="true"
    Inherits="System.Web.Mvc.ViewPage<object>" %>
<%@ Import Namespace="System.Web.Mvc.Html"%>
<div style="border:solid 5px Lime">
    This view:  <%=GetType().Name %>
    Model:      <%=ViewData.Model %><br />
    Model Type: <%=ViewData.Model.GetType().Name %>
    ViewDataDictionary hashcode: <%=ViewData.GetHashCode() %>
    <br />
    <%foreach (KeyValuePair<string, object> pair in ViewData){%>
        View data <%=pair.Key%> : <%=pair.Value %><br />
    <% } %>
    <hr />
    <%Html.RenderPartial("nestedpartial"); %>
</div>
```

Listing 4.9 NestedPartial.aspx is loaded two views deep.

```
<%@ Page Language="C#" AutoEventWireup="true"
    Inherits="System.Web.Mvc.ViewPage<object>" %>
<div style="border:solid 5px Red">
    This view:  <%=GetType().Name %>
    Model:      <%=ViewData.Model %><br />
    Model Type: <%=ViewData.Model.GetType().Name %>
    ViewDataDictionary hashcode: <%=ViewData.GetHashCode() %>
    <br />
    <%foreach (KeyValuePair<string, object> pair in ViewData){%>
        View data <%=pair.Key%> : <%=pair.Value %><br />
    <% } %>
</div>
```

Notice the values that are added in the controller in listing 4.6. We have three key/value pairs and an object set to the Model property (by virtue of passing in "3" to the View method). It is important to know that when a view renders a partial, the partial will get the same ViewData objects; anything passed from the controller will also make it to any partial and any master page (not shown here). This is because ViewData is a member of ControllerBase, and ControllerBase is part of System.Web.Mvc.Controller-Context. System.Web.Mvc.ViewContext derives from ControllerContext, so it has everything ControllerContext has and more.

We also see in listing 4.7 that while rendering a partial, a view can decide to override the ViewData passed into the partial. Even though each view will have access to the same objects in the ViewData dictionary, the instance of ViewDataDictionary is different for each one. Multiple views do not share instances of ViewDataDictionary. We cannot expect to use ViewData as a mechanism for a partial to pass an object back to the parent view. In fact, views should be isolated and should not try to communicate with one another.

Views are functional, and once they begin rendering, they should expect to have all the information necessary to complete rendering. Note the hash code values printed with the data when rendering /viewdata/index in a browser. The output is shown in figure 4.4. We see that the hash code values are different, even for the multiple instances of the nested partial view. Shared state and global variables can cause maintainability problems; each view receives a fresh instance of ViewData to avoid these issues.

You can see from figure 4.4 that ViewData is the central object that is passed to a view. A view relies completely on ViewData to get the information it needs to render. The view can choose to pass on all or some of the same objects to partial views, and the master page has access to the ViewData values as well. For proper segmentation, each view/master page/partial gets its own instance of ViewData even if the contents are identical. Partial views can be used to segment complex views into isolated sections that can be reused within multiple views. You should take special note of partials.

4.3.4 *Partial views can help decompose a complex screen*

In section 4.3.3, you saw a demonstration of nested views, but there is much more to know about partial views. First, a view is not partial based on its file extension. You can have partial views with either the .aspx or .ascx extension. The view engine does not care, and the view will render in the same fashion. What makes a view partial is how it is used. There are infinite uses for partial views. Conceptually, you could break your site into pieces and have each partial handle a section of your site. I will leave the exact layout up to you, but there are plenty of ways to determine which partial to render, and you can even choose what class makes the decision about what partial to use. You have already seen the scenario in which the view makes the decision about which partial to render. The following example puts the controller in control. Please examine listing 4.10 where the controller decides which partial to use by putting a View-Result into ViewData.

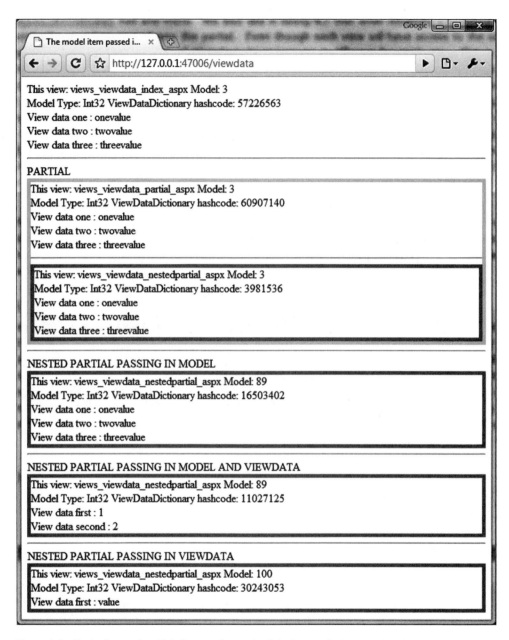

Figure 4.4   Each view and partial view receives a fresh instance of `ViewData`.

Listing 4.10   `RenderViewController` **puts a pointer to a partial view into** `viewdata`.

```
using System.Web.Mvc;

namespace ViewSamples.Controllers
{
    public class RenderViewController : Controller
```

```
    {
        public ViewResult Index()
        {
            ViewResult partialResult = View("next");      ❶
            return View(partialResult);
        }
    }
}
```

In listing 4.10 the controller is deciding which partial view to use. The controller passes a ViewResult to the view inside the ViewData's Model property ❶. The view, in listing 4.11, is a strongly typed view expecting a ViewResult, and it executes the View-Result passing in the ViewContext. Although this is a contrived example, it shows that there is flexibility in who makes the decision about which partial view to use. Most often, a view will decide which partial view to use because the responsibility for rendering belongs to the view, not the controller. In cases where data or user input changes a section of the screen, it may be appropriate for the controller to handle the logic and decide. As with everything in software, it depends on your application.

Listing 4.11 shows a view that renders any view passed to it.

Listing 4.11   Index.aspx is a view that renders any partial passed to it.

```
<%@ Page Language="C#" AutoEventWireup="true"
    Inherits="System.Web.Mvc.ViewPage<ViewResult>" %>
<%@ Import Namespace="System.Web.Mvc"%>
<!DOCTYPE html PUBLIC "-//W3C//DTD XHTML 1.0 Transitional//EN"
    "http://www.w3.org/TR/xhtml1/DTD/xhtml1-transitional.dtd">
<html xmlns="http://www.w3.org/1999/xhtml" >
<head runat="server">
    <title></title>
</head>
<body>
    <div>
        <%=GetType().Name %>
        <br />
        <% ViewData.Model.ExecuteResult(ViewContext); %>
    </div>
</body>
</html>
```

Listing 4.12 shows the simple partial view that outputs the type name. In figure 4.5, the output of the rendered page shows that both of these views rendered in the correct order. If the controller had decided to pass a different partial, this output would be different.

Listing 4.12   Next.aspx is a simple partial view.

```
<%@ Page Language="C#" AutoEventWireup="true"
    Inherits="System.Web.Mvc.ViewPage<object>" %>
<div>
    <%=GetType().Name %><br />
</div>
```

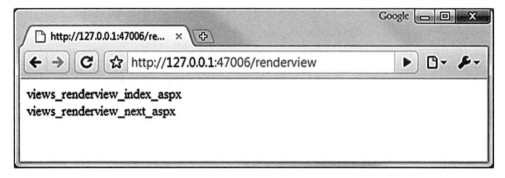

Figure 4.5 The output shows that the correct partial was rendered to the screen.

`ViewData`, views, master pages, `ViewEngines`, and partials are all important concepts in the view story of the ASP.NET MVC Framework. Now that we have covered the basics, the next section will explore view helpers, which are the building blocks of dynamic views developed with ASP.NET MVC.

4.4   *Leveraging the view to create dynamic screens*

We have already seen how controllers, views, and our model objects fit in, but there is more to formatting objects into HTML, posting forms, and creating dynamic web pages. Getting the objects to the view seems easy, but what is the best way to transform those objects into HTML? We could certainly build all HTML by hand, but we would end up with much of the markup being duplicated. View helpers take similar markup and handle the generation for us given a part of the view model. Form posting with model binding and validation make accepting user input a snap. This section explores all these topics.

In chapter 2, we saw how to use a domain model and even a presentation model. We saw how in some cases it works well to pass domain objects to the view, but in non-trivial applications, it becomes necessary to put a translation mechanism between our domain model and our UI toolkit. In smart client applications, we rely on the stateful-ness of the platform, and we want our domain model to be active at all times so that we can send events to it and consume quick responses. In a stateless application, we need to take care that our domain model does not become corrupted by the stateless paradigm of the web. The domain model does not need to know that it is living within a web application, a smart client, an autonomous process, or a test harness.

In the following examples, we'll keep the concerns separate and map from the domain model to the view model and back. This simulates real-world scenarios in enterprise applications.

4.4.1   *Rendering forms with view helpers and data binding*

The ASP.NET MVC Framework does not emphasize web controls as heavily as Web Forms. The concept is altogether different, and that concept is the view helper. There are numerous types of view helpers:

- *System.Web.Mvc.HtmlHelper<T>*—Used to help render HTML input elements
  - *Html.TextBox()*
  - *Html.CheckBox()*
  - Etc.
- *System.Web.Mvc.UrlHelper*—Used to generate URLs
  - *Url.Action()*
  - *Url.Content()*
  - *Url.RouteUrl()*
  - Etc.
- *System.Web.Mvc.AjaxHelper<T>*—Used to render links and form elements used in an AJAX request
  - *Ajax.ActionLink()*
  - *Ajax.BeginForm()*
  - Etc.

In this section, we concentrate on the HtmlHelper<T>. We are using strongly typed views almost everywhere, and the ViewData.Model type flows all the way through the helpers. Although we can use view helpers with any object, including our domain model, we are focused here on leveraging them with our view model.

When moving from complex objects to HTML and back, several things need to happen, such as HTML encoding, null checking, and formatting as a string. We easily think of HTML encoding because many of us have been bitten by HTML characters making their way into data, but why null checking? In listing 4.13, we have a Conference object with a start date. Because this property is a nullable date, we could potentially experience a NullReferenceException when we attempt to format it as a short date string. This raises the question of who is responsible for checking values for null and formatting as a string. Certainly the domain object is not responsible for this because it does not care that we have a web front end at all. This is where the *M* in *MVC* comes in: the *model*. No just any model, but the type of model that represents the shape necessary for our presentation layer. We can call it presentation model, form model, edit model, DTOs, view model, and so on, but these objects exist for the sole purpose of working well with a view. As an aside, the term *view model* is gaining popularity. In nontrivial applications, it is impractical to pass raw domain objects to views because views often need a clean, projected view of the domain. Listing 4.13 shows our sample domain object, the Conference.

Listing 4.13 The Conference object is abbreviated for this sample.

```
using System;

namespace ViewSamples.Models
{
    public class Conference
    {
        public virtual int Id { get; set; }
```

```
        public virtual string Name { get; set; }
        public virtual string Description { get; set; }
        public virtual DateTime? StartDate { get; set; }
        public virtual DateTime? EndDate { get; set; }
    }
}
```

At first we might be tempted to pass this simple object straight to the view, but the Date-Time? properties will cause problems. For instance, we need to choose a formatting for them such as ToShortDateString() or ToString(). The view would be forced to do null checking to keep the screen from blowing up when the properties are null. Views are difficult to unit test, so we want to keep them as thin as possible. Because the output of a view is a string passed to the response stream, we'll only use objects that are string-friendly; that is, objects that will never fail when ToString() is called on them. The ConferenceForm view model object is an example of this. Notice in listing 4.14 that all of the properties are strings. We'll have the dates properly formatted before this view model object is placed in view data. This way, the view need not consider the object, and it can format the information properly.

Listing 4.14   View model has simple properties and is dedicated to a single view.

```
namespace ViewSamples.Models
{
    public class ConferenceForm
    {
        public string Id { get; set; }
        public string Name { get; set; }
        public string Description { get; set; }
        public string StartDate { get; set; }
        public string EndDate { get; set; }
    }
}
```

We have an obvious gap now between our domain model Conference and the view model ConferenceForm. The controller action could be the place to map from the domain model to the view model, but our controller already has enough responsibility. In listing 4.15, see how the ConferenceController delegates to a mapper for this specific purpose. The mapper is pretty simple code, and only the interface is listed here.

Listing 4.15   ConferenceController uses a view model to enable easy binding.

```
using ViewSamples.Models;

namespace ViewSamples.Services
{
    public interface IConferenceMapper
    {
        ConferenceForm Map(Conference conference);
        Conference Map(ConferenceForm form);
    }
}

public class ConferenceController : Controller
```

```
{
    private readonly IConferenceMapper _mapper;
    private readonly IConferenceRepository _repository;
    private readonly IConferenceFormValidator _validator;

    public ConferenceController(IConferenceMapper mapper,
                                IConferenceRepository repository,
                                IConferenceFormValidator validator)
    {
        _mapper = mapper;
        _validator = validator;
        _repository = repository;
    }

    public ViewResult Edit(int conferenceId)
    {
        Conference conference = _repository.GetById(conferenceId);

        ConferenceForm form = _mapper.Map(conference);

        return View(form);
    }

    [AcceptVerbs(HttpVerbs.Post)]
    public ActionResult Edit(ConferenceForm form)
    {
        ModelStateDictionary dictionary = _validator.Validate(form);
        ModelState.Merge(dictionary);

        if (ModelState.IsValid)
        {
            Conference conference = _mapper.Map(form);

            _repository.Save(conference);
            return Redirect("/conference/current");
        }

        return View();
    }
}
}
```

Annotations:
- **Retrieve Conference from store** → `Conference conference = _repository.GetById(conferenceId);`
- **Map from Conference to ConferenceForm** → `ConferenceForm form = _mapper.Map(conference);`
- **Validate the form** → `ModelStateDictionary dictionary = _validator.Validate(form);`
- **Merge validation errors** → `ModelState.Merge(dictionary);`
- **Map ConferenceForm to Conference** → `Conference conference = _mapper.Map(form);`

Listing 4.16 contains the view that renders the input form. Notice how clean this view is. There is no conditional logic, no date formatting— it's clean. It is a strongly typed view around ConferenceForm, so ViewData.Model is the type we expect. In fact, the view helpers, such as the TextBox, will automatically bind from objects in ViewData. Our view has no code that specifically places a value inside of a TextBox, as is necessary when editing an existing conference.

Listing 4.16   New.aspx view binds to the view model to allow data entry.

```
<%@ Page Title="" Language="C#" MasterPageFile="~/Views/Shared/Site.Master"
    Inherits="System.Web.Mvc.ViewPage<ConferenceForm>" %>
<%@ Import Namespace="ViewSamples.Models"%>

<asp:Content ID="Content1" ContentPlaceHolderID="MainContent"
    runat="server">
    <h3><%=Html.ValidationSummary()%></h3>
    <p>
        Create new conference
```

```
    </p>
    <%using (Html.BeginForm()){%>
        <p>
            Name:<%=Html.TextBox ("Name")%>
            <%=Html.ValidationMessage("Name", "*")%>
        </p>
        <p>
            Description:<%=Html.TextBox ("Description")%>
            <%=Html.ValidationMessage("Description", "*")%>
        </p>
        <p>
            Start Date:<%=Html.TextBox ("StartDate")%>
            <%=Html.ValidationMessage("StartDate", "*")%>
        </p>
        <p>
            End Date:<%=Html.TextBox ("EndDate")%>
            <%=Html.ValidationMessage("EndDate", "*")%>
        </p>
        <input type="submit" value="Save" />
    <%}%>
</asp:Content>
```

In figure 4.6, we see the screen that displays when we navigate our browser to /conference/edit?conferenceId=XXXX. The controller uses the repository and the mapper to obtain a ConferenceForm view model object. Then the controller passes

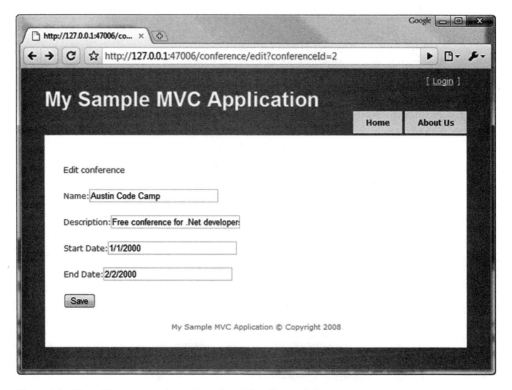

Figure 4.6 The edit screen renders a form for editing the conference.

the view model to the view, and the view renders an edit form with a `TextBox` for each property.

The framework knows how to bind directly from `ViewData.Model` to the HTML text boxes on this view. The fact that the model passed to this strongly typed view contained data was enough for the view helper to bind to the values. The built-in view helpers will work hard to find a value suitable for rendering. The following is the order in which the framework will look for values to bind to a view helper. The value will be bound if

1 The name is found in `ModelState`
2 The name is found as an explicit key in `ViewData`
3 The name is found as a property of `ViewData.Model`
4 The name is an expression interpretable, such as `Product.Name` or `Products[2].Name`

Rendering a screen is one of the easiest things to do in the MVC framework, but how do we post information back to the server so that our controller can save the conference? The next section tackles methods for taking this rendered form and posting it back to the server so that we can save modified information back to our data store.

4.4.2 *Posting HTML forms back to the server*

A web application is only a website without the posting of information. Saving information on the server makes the web interesting, and the ASP.NET MVC Framework delivers a compelling experience. In the following example, you will see that you can save a new conference without fishing around in the `Request` object or writing tedious mapping code. In listing 4.16, you saw a view that contains a form that will post back to the "edit" relative path. We used the `Html.BeginForm()` view helper to render the form tag, which renders the following: `<form action="/conference/edit" method="post">`.

With the form properly rendered, the page will post to the /conference/edit URL, which is exactly what we want. In listing 4.17 we see the `Edit` action method that receives the post. The single parameter this method receives is of type `Conference-Form`. Because the properties of this object are types that have built-in type converters, the ASP.NET MVC Framework is able to bind these properties without a custom `IModel-Binder` instance being registered. Take special notice that the controller does not have to dig into the form collection within the request object. If you have done ASP Classic programming or even advanced Web Forms development, you are familiar with working with form posts. The ASP.NET MVC Framework nearly eliminates the need to access `Request.Form` directly. Instead a form post can come in directly to an action method, and that method can work with it as it does any other object. In this case, we map it back to a `Conference` object, save it, and then redirect to another URL.

Listing 4.17 The save action binds the request and handles it.

```
[AcceptVerbs(HttpVerbs.Post)]                         ❶
public ActionResult Edit(ConferenceForm form)
```

```
{
    ModelStateDictionary dictionary = _validator.Validate(form);
    ModelState.Merge(dictionary);

    if (ModelState.IsValid)
    {
        Conference conference = _mapper.Map(form);
        _repository.Save(conference);
        return Redirect("/conference/current");
    }

    return View();
}
```

When using the same action name for a GET request as well as a POST request, we have to use an `ActionMethodSelectorAttribute` such as the `System.Web.Mvc.AcceptVerbsAttribute` ❶ to limit a single URL request to a single action. Without this attribute the controller class would not know which action method to select when handling the URL, /controller/edit. At this point we see how simple it is to craft a view with a form on it and post it back to the server. So far, we are only handling the happy path. If anything went wrong, we don't yet have the capability to handle it. In any real business application, we need the capability to validate user input and redirect the user back to the data entry form if something is left out or submitted in an invalid state. The next section dives into the validation capabilities included in ASP.NET MVC.

4.4.3   *Validation and error reporting*

The ASP.NET MVC Framework has a concept called `ModelState` which contains information about those objects in `ViewData` that are not valid. On almost every data entry screen, the user might enter data that is invalid for processing. In these cases, we want to redirect the user back to the data entry screen to give him an opportunity to correct the mistakes and try again. Let's quickly fast-forward to a case where our system would reject the saving of a conference. Our system needs to validate the user input and report any errors that occur. I will intentionally post invalid data, and figure 4.7 shows the resulting screen.

The built-in view helpers will match the keys in the `ModelStateDictionary` with the names of the form elements and tag them with a CSS class that calls attention to them on the screen. The ASP.NET MVC Framework uses three CSS classes to report form validation errors:

- *input-validation-error*—On the <input> tag
- *field-validation-error*—On the <span> tag of Html.ValidationMessage()
- *validation-summary-errors*—On the <ul> tag of the Html.Validation-Summary()

At the top of the screen, we have a validation summary, and we have an individual message that describes the problem. This validation summary will take any errors in the `ModelStateDictionary` and format them as an unordered list. These errors can

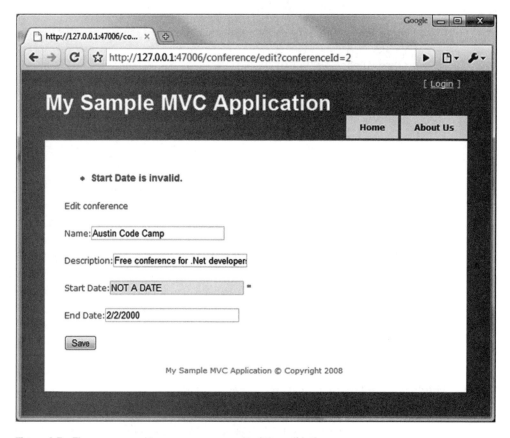

Figure 4.7   The screen reports an error as a result of the validation.

get into the ModelState dictionary in several places. In this case, our custom UI validator performed the validation and added a ModelState object to the dictionary. The
ASP.NET MVC Framework will also add an error to ModelState when it encounters an
error binding an action parameter. You are free to add errors inside the controller
action, in action filters and anywhere you have access to the controller object. In our
case, and in complex business applications, you want to keep validation away from
your controller because the business rules can become quite detailed. In fact, implementing a small business rules engine quickly pays dividends in maintainability. Listing 4.18 shows our IConferenceFormValidator interface and the implementing class.

Listing 4.18   Validating the view model object posted from the form.

```
public interface IConferenceFormValidator
{
    ModelStateDictionary Validate(ConferenceForm form);
}

public class ConferenceFormValidator : IConferenceFormValidator
```

```
{
    public ModelStateDictionary Validate(ConferenceForm form)
    {
        var dictionary = new ModelStateDictionary ();
        ValidateStartDate(form, dictionary);
        return dictionary;
    }

    private void ValidateStartDate(ConferenceForm form,
                            ModelStateDictionary dictionary)
    {
        DateTime result;                                       ⟵  Check if start
        if (!DateTime.TryParse(form.StartDate, out result))    ⟵  date valid
        {
            var state = new ModelState ();
            state.Value = new ValueProviderResult(form.StartDate,
                form.StartDate,                                    Create
                CultureInfo.InvariantCulture);                     ModelState
            state.Errors.Add("Start Date is invalid.");            entry

            dictionary.Add("StartDate", state);   ⟵  Add ModelState
        }                                            entry
    }
}
```

Although we validate only one property, you will want to implement full validation to check all the necessary properties. Even with a single property, validation can consume twenty lines of code. Imagine how large this class would be if we had to validate thirty fields! The need for a business rules engine comes on quickly.

This view model and mapping implementation is just one way to do it. Another excellent way to do binding is through an object mapper tool that specializes in mapping objects to objects. By following the conventions of the AutoMapper library, found at http://automapper.codeplex.com/, you can reduce tedious mapping code.

NOTE   The ASP.NET MVC Framework also provides support for System.ComponentModel.IDataErrorInfo. If your view model implements this interface, it can integrate seamlessly with IModelBinder and ModelState. Unfortunately, this requires the view model to handle the validation. We have seen the need to separate validation logic from the view model itself; therefore, only consider implementing this interface on the most trivial of ASP.NET MVC web applications.

Another great way to accomplish data entry validation is to use the validation classes from the Castle Project (http://www.castleproject.org/) in the Castle.Components. Validator namespace. The Castle validators have a complete array of attributes that describe the validation to be performed. This leads to a declarative way to specify validation, and it removes the need for lots of imperative coding in each view model object.

While reading through the example, you have probably wondered why each field requires so much markup just for a label, input box, and validation message. The following section shows us how we can reduce the markup required in the form by extending HtmlHelper.

4.4.4   *Extending HtmlHelper*

If you have seen any presentations with the ASP.NET MVC Framework, you probably have noticed the volume of string identifiers used in the views. With a bit of work we can drastically reduce the amount required to render the same view while reducing the risk of a typo causing a functional bug in one of our screens. The view in listing 4.19 uses a custom view helper that we'll explore shortly.

> **Listing 4.19   By using a custom view helper, we can eliminate many string literals.**

```
<%@ Page Title="" Language="C#" MasterPageFile="~/Views/Shared/Site.Master"
    Inherits="System.Web.Mvc.ViewPage<ConferenceForm>" %>
<%@ Import Namespace="ViewSamples.Views.Conference"%>
<%@ Import Namespace="ViewSamples.Models"%>

<asp:Content ID="Content1" ContentPlaceHolderID="MainContent"
    runat="server">
    <h3><%=Html.ValidationSummary()%></h3>
    <p>
        Edit conference
    </p>
    <%using (Html.BeginForm()){%>
    <%=Html.Hidden(x=>x.Id) %>
    <p><%=Html.TextBox (x=>x.Name)%></p>
    <p><%=Html.TextBox (x=>x.Description)%></p>
    <p><%=Html.TextBox (x=>x.StartDate)%></p>
    <p><%=Html.TextBox (x=>x.EndDate)%></p>
    <input type="submit" value="Save" />
    <%}%>
</asp:Content>
```

Notice how little markup is required to render the same edit screen as we saw before. By using .NET 3.5 LINQ Expressions and a strongly typed view, we can describe the property we wish to display and bind without coupling to the name using a string literal. We leverage view model binding, specific error reporting, and seamless form post binding all without string literals cluttering the view. Reducing the number of repetitive string literals is a good idea, but you may be wondering what is necessary to use this type of technique when creating a custom view helper.

The `HtmlHelper` class itself does not contain any view helpers. You cannot render a text box, a check box, or a button with the `HtmlHelper` class alone. All view helpers are implemented as extension methods off of the `HtmlHelper` class in a class called `InputExtensions`. The above example uses a custom view helper implemented as an extension method. This custom view helper

- Renders a label with the property text
- Renders the textbox with the appropriate ID, name, and value
- Renders a validation message span tag ready for form validation

The custom view helper is invoked by calling `Html.TextBox (x=>x.Name)` where `x.Name` is a property of `ConferenceForm`. It is represented as a lambda expression, which is part of the LINQ extensions in .NET 3.5. The code for this view helper is in listing 4.20. This is advanced code, and it is not necessary for basic use of ASP.NET MVC, but extensions like this are useful in applications with many, many screens.

Listing 4.20   A custom view helper that enables easy view code

```
using System;
using System.Linq.Expressions;
using System.Reflection;
using System.Web.Mvc;
using System.Web.Mvc.Html;

namespace ViewSamples.Views.Conference
{
    public static class HtmlHelperExtensions
    {
        public static string Hidden<T>(
            this HtmlHelper<T> helper, Expression<Func<T, object>> expr)
            where T : class
        {
            MemberInfo property = GetMemberInfo(expr);        ❶
            string propertyName = property.Name;
            Func<T, object> func = expr.Compile();

            object propertyValue = func.Invoke(helper.ViewData.Model);
            return helper.Hidden(propertyName, propertyValue);
        }

        public static string TextBox<T>(this HtmlHelper<T> helper,
                                        Expression<Func<T, object>> expr)
            where T : class
        {
            MemberInfo property = GetMemberInfo(expr);
            string propertyName = property.Name;
            Func<T, object> func = expr.Compile();

            object propertyValue = func.Invoke(helper.ViewData.Model);
            string textBoxString =
                helper.TextBox(propertyName, propertyValue);     ❷

            return string.Format(
                "<label for=\"{0}\">{1}: </label>{2} {3}",
                propertyName, propertyName, textBoxString,
                helper.ValidationMessage(expr));
        }

        public static string ValidationMessage<T>(
            this HtmlHelper<T> helper, Expression<Func<T, object>> expr)
            where T : class
        {
            MemberInfo property = GetMemberInfo(expr);
            string propertyName = property.Name;
            return helper.ValidationMessage(propertyName, "*");   ❸
        }

        public static MemberInfo GetMemberInfo<T>(
            Expression<Func<T, object>> expr)
```

Get property from expression ❶

Get value from view model

```
    {
        if (expr.Body.GetType() == typeof (UnaryExpression))
            return ((MemberExpression)
                (((UnaryExpression) expr.Body).Operand)).Member;

        return ((MemberExpression) expr.Body).Member;
    }

  }
}
```

Notice that the view helper reuses the `TextBox` view helper that already comes with the ASP.NET MVC Framework ❷. This ensures that the built-in binding and error CSS class labeling logic are also included when this view helper renders. You can see that this view helper examines the expression passed in and uses the property name as the name for the form elements ❶ as well as the validation message if an error occurs ❸. This automatically matches up keys, and when combined with the validation logic shown in listing 4.17, no string literals are necessary anywhere. All keys are kept in sync, and this makes for a trivial data entry programming task.

4.5   *Summary*

Views have changed significantly from early web technologies, through Web Forms and now with ASP.NET MVC views. The most obvious change is that views have become simpler. When realizing that a view should have the responsibility only for rendering, we find that much logic can be factored out to other classes.

   In this chapter, we have seen how to create views of various types and work with layouts and partial views. We have explored the intricacies of `ViewData` and the mechanics of view engines and the sequence of events that happen when rendering a view. Our deep dive into views concluded with a complex scenario with all the pieces coming together to provide a complete data entry scenario that included binding, validation, error reporting, and a custom view helper that enabled the elimination of string literals in the view. With the basics in place, we'll now dive into routing, which is a major topic itself. Up to this point, we have used the default route of {controller}/{action}/{id}. Chapter 5 explores routing in greater detail.

Routing

This chapter covers

- Routing as a solution to URL issues
- Designing a URL schema
- Using routing in ASP.NET MVC
- Route testing
- Using routing in Web Forms applications

Routing is all about the URL and how we use it as an external input to the applications that we build. The URL has led a short but troubled life and the HTTP URL is currently being tragically misused by current web technologies. As the web began to change from being a collection of hyperlinked static documents into dynamically created pages and applications, the URL has been kidnapped by web technologies and undergone terrible changes. The URL is in trouble and as the web becomes more dynamic we, as software developers, can rescue it to bring back the simple, logical, readable, and beautiful resource locator that it was meant to be.

Rescuing the URL means controlling those that control applications. Although routing is not core to all implementations of the MVC pattern, it is often implemented as a convenient way to add an extra level of separation between external inputs and the controllers and actions which make up an application. The code required to implement routing using the ASP.NET MVC Framework is reasonably trivial but the thought behind designing a schema of URLs for an application can raise many issues. In this chapter, we'll go over the concept of routes and their relationship with MVC applications. We'll also briefly cover how they apply to Web Forms projects. We'll examine how to design a URL schema for an application, and then apply the concepts to create routes for Code Camp Server, our sample application. Because routes are the *front door* of your web application, we'll discover how to test routes to ensure they are working as intended. Now that you have an idea of how important routing is, we can start with the basics.

5.1 What are routes?

The history of the URL can be traced back to the very first web servers, where it was primarily used to point directly to documents in a folder structure. This URL would have been typical of an early URL and it's reasonably well structured and descriptive:

```
http://example.com/plants/roses.html
```

It seems to be pointing to information on roses and the domain also seems to have a logical hierarchy. But hold on, what is that .html extension on the end of the URL? This is where things started to go wrong for our friend the URL. Of course .html is a file extension because the web server is mapping the path in the URL directly to a folder of files on the disk of the web server. The category is being created by having a folder called *plants* containing all documents about plants.

The key thing here is that the file extension of .html is probably redundant in this context, as the content type is being specified by the `Content-Type` header returned as part of the HTTP response. An example HTTP header is shown in listing 5.1.

> ### Listing 5.1 HTTP headers returned for a .html file

```
C:\> curl -I http://example.com/index.html

HTTP/1.1 200 OK
Date: Thu, 10 Jan 2008 09:03:29 GMT
Server: Apache/2.2.3 (CentOS)
Last-Modified: Tue, 15 Nov 2005 13:24:10 GMT
ETag: "280100-1b6-80bfd280"
Accept-Ranges: bytes
Content-Length: 438
Connection: close
Content-Type: text/html; charset=UTF-8
```

5.1.1 What's that curl command?

The `curl` command shown in listing 5.1 is a Unix command that allows you to issue an HTTP GET request for a URL and return the output. The `-I` switch tells it to display the HTTP response headers. This and other Unix commands are available on Windows via the Cygwin shell for Windows (http://cygwin.com).

The response returned contained a `Content-Type` header set to `text/html; charset=UTF8`, which specifies both a MIME type for the content and the character encoding. The file extension has no meaning in this situation.

> **File extensions are not all bad!**
>
> Reading this chapter so far, you might think that all file extensions are bad, but this is not the case. Knowing when information would be useful to the user is key to understanding when to use a file extension. Is it useful for the user to know that HTML has been generated from an .aspx source file? No, the MIME type is sufficient to influence how that content is displayed, so no extension should be shown. However, if a Word document is being served it would be good practice to include a .doc extension in addition to setting the correct MIME type, as that will be useful when the file is downloaded to the user's PC.

Mapping the path part of a URL directly to a disk folder is at the root of the problems that we face today. As dynamic web technologies have developed, .html files that contain information changed to be .aspx files containing source code. Suddenly the URL is not pointing to a document but to source code which fetches information from a database, and the filename must be generic as one source file can fetch any information it wants: what a mess!

Consider the following URL:

```
http://microsoft.com/downloads/details.aspx?FamilyID=9ae91ebe-3385-447c-8a30-
    081805b2f90b&displaylang=en
```

The file path is /download/details.aspx, which is a reasonable attempt to be descriptive with the source code name, but as it's a generic page which fetches the actual download details from a database, the file name can't possibly contain the important information that the URL should contain. Even worse, an unreadable GUID is used to identify the actual download and at this point the URL has lost all meaning.

This is a perfect opportunity to create a beautiful URL. Decouple the source code file name from the URL and it can become a resource locator again with the resource being a download package for Internet Explorer. The user never needs to know that this resource is served by a page called *details.aspx*. The result would look like this:

```
http://microsoft.com/downloads/windows-internet-explorer-7-for-windows-xp-sp2
```

This is clearly an improvement but we are making an assumption that the description of the item is unique. Ideally, in the design of an application, we could make some human-readable information like the title or description unique to support the URL schema. If this were not possible, we could implement another technique to end up with something like the following URL:

```
http://microsoft.com/downloads/windows-internet-explorer-7-for-windows-xp-
    sp2/1987429874
```

In this final example, both a description of the download and a unique identifier are used. When the application comes to process this URL, the description *can* be ignored and the download looked up on the unique identifier. You might want to enforce agreement between the two segments for search engine optimization. Having multiple URLs pointing to the same logical resource yields poor results for search engines. Let's see how we can apply these ideas to create better URLs.

5.1.2   *Taking back control of the URL with routing*

For years, the server platform has dictated portions of the URL, such as the *.aspx* at the end. This problem has been around since the beginning of the dynamic web and affects almost all current web technologies, so you should not be surprised that many solutions to the problem have been developed. Although ASP.NET *does* offer options for URL rewriting,[1] many ASP.NET developers ignore them. URL rewriting is discussed again in chapter 10.

Many web technologies such as PHP and Perl, hosted on the Apache web server, solve this problem by using mod_rewrite.[2] Python and Ruby developers have taken to the MVC frameworks and both Django and Rails have their own sophisticated routing mechanisms.

A routing system in any MVC framework manages the decoupling of the URL from the application logic. It must manage this in both directions so that it can

- Map URLs to a controller/action and any additional parameters
- Construct URLs which match the URL schema from a controller, action, and additional parameters

This is more commonly referred to as *inbound* routing (figure 5.1) and *outbound* routing (figure 5.2). Inbound routing describes the URL invocation of a controller action; outbound routing describes the framework generating URLs for links and other elements on your site.

When the routing system performs both of these tasks, the URL schema can be truly independent of the application logic. As long as it's never bypassed when constructing links in a view, the URL schema should be trivial to change independent of the application logic. Now let's take a look at how to build a meaningful URL schema for our application.

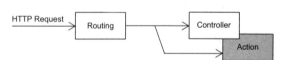

Figure 5.1   Inbound routing refers to taking an HTTP request (a URL) and mapping it to a controller and action.

Figure 5.2   Outbound routing generates appropriate URLs from a given set of route data (usually controller and action).

---

[1]   URL Rewriting in ASP.NET—http://msdn2.microsoft.com/en-us/library/ms972974.aspx

[2]   Apache Module mod_rewrite—http://httpd.apache.org/docs/2.2/mod/mod_rewrite.html

5.2   *Designing a URL schema*

As a professional developer, you would not start coding a new project before mapping out what the application will do and how it will look. The same should apply for the URL schema of an application. Although it's hard to provide a definitive guide on designing URL schema (every website and application is different) we'll discuss general guidelines with an example or two thrown in along the way.

Here is a list of simple guidelines:

- Make simple, clean URLs.
- Make hackable URLs.
- Allow URL parameters to clash.
- Keep URLs short.
- Avoid exposing database IDs wherever possible.
- Consider adding unnecessary information.

These guidelines will not all apply to every application you create. You should run through a process similar to this before deciding on your final application URL schema.

5.2.1   *Make simple, clean URLs*

When designing a URL schema, the most important thing to remember is that you should step back from your application and consider it from the point of view of your end user. Ignore the technical architecture you will need to implement the URLs. Remember that by using routing, your URLs can be completely decoupled from your underlying implementation. The simpler and cleaner a permalink is, the more usable a site becomes.

> **Permalinks and deep linking**
>
> Over the past few years permalinks have gained popularity, and it's important to consider them when designing a URL schema. A permalink is simply an unchanging direct link to a resource within a website or application. For example, on a blog the URL to an individual post would usually be a permalink such as `http://example.com/blog/post-1/hello-world`.

Let's take the example of our events management sample application. In a Web Forms world we might have ended up with a URL something like this:

`http://example.com/eventmanagement/events_by_month.aspx?year=2008&month=4`

Using a routing system it's possible to create a cleaner URL like this:

`http://example.com/events/2008/04`

This gives us the advantage of having an unambiguous hierarchical format for the date in the URL, which raises an interesting point. What would happen if we omitted that 04 in the URL? What would you (as a user) expect? This is described as *hacking* the URL.

5.2.2 *Make hackable URLs*

When designing a URL schema, it's worth considering how a URL could be manipulated or "hacked" by the end user in order to change the data displayed. In the following example URL, it might reasonably be assumed that removing the parameter 04 from the URL might present all events occurring in 2008.

```
http://example.com/events/2008
```

By the same logic this could be expanded into the more comprehensive list of routes shown in table 5.1.

Table 5.1   Partial URL schema for the events management application

URL	Description
http://example.com/events	Displays all events
http://example.com/events/<year>	Displays all events in a specific year
http://example.com/events/<year>/<month>	Displays all events in a specific month
http://example.com/events/<year>/<month>/<date>	Displays all events on a specific single day

Being this flexible with your URL schema is great but it can lead to having an enormous number of potential URLs in your application. When you build your application views you should always give appropriate navigation; remember it may not be necessary to include a link to every possible URL combination on every page. It's all right for some things to be a happy surprise when a user tries to hack a URL and for it to work!

> **Slash or dash?**
>
> It's a general convention that if a slash is used to separate parameters, the URL should be valid if parameters are omitted. If the URL /events/2008/04/01/ is presented to users, they could reasonably assume that removing the last "day" parameter could increase the scope of the data shown by the URL. If this is not what is desired in your URL schema, consider using dashes instead of slashes as /events/2008-04-01/ would not suggest the same hackability.

The ability to hack URLs gives power back to the users. With dates this is very easy to express, but what about linking to named resources?

5.2.3 *Allow URL parameters to clash*

Let's expand the routes and allow events to be listed by category. The most usable URL from the user's point of view would probably be something like this:

```
http://example.com/events/meeting
```

But now we have a problem! We already have a route that matches /events/ <something> used to list the events on a particular year, month, or day and how are we now going to try to use /events/<something> to match a category as well? Our second route segment can now mean something entirely different; it *clashes* with the existing route. If the routing system is given this URL, should it treat that parameter as a category or a date? Luckily, the routing system in ASP.NET MVC allows us to apply conditions. The syntax for this can be seen in section 5.3.3 but for now it's sufficient to say that we can use regular expressions to make sure that routes only match certain patterns for a parameter. This means that we could have a single route that allows a request like /events/2009-01-01 to be passed to an action that shows events by date and a request like /events/asp-net-mvc-in-action to be passed to an action that shows events by category. These URLs should "clash" with each other but they don't because we have made them distinct based on what characters will be contained in the URL.

This starts to restrict our model design, however. It will now be necessary to constrain event categories so that category names made entirely of numbers are not allowed. You'll have to decide if in your application this is a reasonable concession to make for such a clean URL schema.

The next principle we'll learn about is URL size. For URLs, size matters, and smaller is better.

5.2.4 Keep URLs short

Permalinks are passed around millions of times every day through email, instant messenger, micromessaging services such as SMS and Twitter, and even in conversation. Obviously for a URL to be spoken (and subsequently remembered!), it must be simple, short, and clean. Even when transmitting a permalink electronically this is important, as many URLs are broken due to line breaks in emails.

Short URLs are nice; however you shouldn't sacrifice readability for the sake of brevity. Remember that when a link to your application is shared, it's probably going to have only the limited context provided by whoever is sharing it. By having a clear, meaningful URL that is still succinct you can provide additional context that may be the difference between the link being ignored or clicked.

The next guideline is both the most useful in terms of maintaining clarity, and the most violated, thanks to the default routes in the ASP.NET MVC Framework.

5.2.5 Avoid exposing database IDs wherever possible

When designing the permalink to an individual event, the key requirement is that the URL should uniquely identify the event. We obviously already have a unique identifier for every object that comes out of a database in the form of a primary key. This is usually some sort of integer, autonumbered from 1, so it might seem obvious that the URL schema should include the database ID.

```
http://example.com/events/87
```

Unfortunately, the number 87 means nothing to anyone except the database administrator, and wherever possible you should avoid using database-generated IDs in URLs. This doesn't mean you cannot use integer values in a URL where relevant, but try to make them meaningful.

In the `Conference` model of Code Camp Server, there are two possible properties which are suitable for the permalink identifier that are not database generated: `Name` and `Key`. `Name` could be made to be unique without too much trouble but will probably include spaces, apostrophes, or other punctuation, so `Key` seems like a more logical choice as a short unique text string for an event.

```
http://example.com/events/houstonTechFest2008
```

Sometimes creating a meaningful identifier for a model adds benefits only for the URL and has no value apart from that. In cases like this, you should ask yourself if having a clean permalink is important enough to justify additional complexity not only on the technical implementation of the model, but also in the UI, as you will usually have to ask a user to supply a meaningful identifier for the resource.

This is a great technique, but what if you don't have a nice unique name for the resource? What if you need to allow duplicate names and the only unique identifier is the database ID? This next trick will show you how to utilize both a unique identifier *and* a textual description to create a URL that is both unique and readable.

5.2.6 *Consider adding unnecessary information*

If you must use a database ID in a URL, consider adding additional information which has no purpose other than to make the URL readable. Look at the URL for a specific session in our events application. The `Title` property is not necessarily going to be unique, and it's probably not practical to have people add a text identifier for a session. If we add the word *session* just for readability, the URL might look something like

```
http://example.com/houstonTechFest2008/session-87
```

This isn't good enough, though, as it gives no indication what the session is about; let's add another superfluous parameter to it. The addition has no purpose other than description. It will not be used at all while processing the controller action. The final URL could look like

```
http://example.com/houstonTechFest2008/session-87/an-introduction-to-mvc
```

Much more descriptive, and the `session-87` parameter is still there so we can look up the session by database ID. Of course we'd have to convert the session name to a more URL-friendly format, but this would be trivial.

The routing principles covered in this section will guide you through your choice of URLs in your application. Decide on a URL schema before going live on a site, as URLs are the entry point into your application. If you have links out there in the wild and you change your URLs, you risk breaking these links and losing referral traffic from other sites. You also lose any reputation for your URLs from the search engines.

Search engine optimization (SEO)

It's worth mentioning the value of a well-designed URL when it comes to optimizing your site for the search engines. It's widely accepted that placing relevant keywords in a URL has a direct effect on search engine ranking, so bear the following tips in mind when you are designing your URL schema.

1. Use descriptive, simple, commonly used words for your controllers and actions. Try to be as relevant as possible and use keywords which you would like to apply to the page you are creating.

2. Replace all spaces (which are encoded to an ugly %20 in a URL) to dashes (-) when including text parameters in a route.

3. Strip out all nonessential punctuation and unnecessary text from string parameters.

4. Where possible, include additional, meaningful information in the URL. Additional information like titles and descriptions provide context and search terms to search engines that can improve the site's relevancy for search terms.

Now that you've learned what kind of routes you'll use, let's create some with ASP.NET MVC.

5.3   *Implementing routes in ASP.NET MVC*

When you first create a new ASP.NET MVC project, two default routes are created with the project template (shown in listing 5.2). They are defined in `Global.asax.cs`. These routes cover

- An ignore route to take certain URLs out of the ASP.NET MVC pipeline
- A generic dynamic route covering a standard /controller/action/id route

Listing 5.2   Default routes

```
public class MvcApplication : HttpApplication
{
    public static void RegisterRoutes(RouteCollection routes)
    {
        routes.IgnoreRoute("{resource}.axd/{*pathInfo}");        ❶

        routes.MapRoute(
            "Default",                              ❷
            "{controller}/{action}/{id}",           ❸

            new { controller = "Home", action = "Index", id = "" }    ❹
        );

    }

    protected void Application_Start()
    {
        RegisterRoutes(RouteTable.Routes);
    }
}
```

REST and RESTful architectures

A style of architecture called REST (or RESTful architecture) is a recent trend in web development. REST stands for *representational state transfer*. The name may not be very approachable, but the idea behind it absolutely is.

REST is based on the principle that every notable "thing" in an application should be an addressable *resource*. Resources can be accessed via a single, common URI, and a simple set of operations is available to those resources. This is where REST gets interesting. Using lesser-known HTTP verbs like PUT and DELETE in addition to the ubiquitous GET and POST, we can create an architecture where the URL points to the resource (the "thing" in question) and the HTTP verb can signify the method (what to do with the "thing"). For example, if we use the URI /speakers/5, with the verb GET, this would show the speaker (in HTML if it were viewed in a web browser). Other operations might be as shown in this chart:

URL	VERB	ACTION
/sessions	GET	List all sessions
/sessions	POST	Add a new session
/sessions/5	GET	Show session with id 5
/sessions/5	PUT	Update session with id 5
/sessions/5	DELETE	DELETE session with id 5
/sessions/5/comments	GET	List comments for session with id 5

REST isn't useful just as an architecture for rendering web pages. It's also a means of creating reusable services. These same URLs can provide data for an AJAX call or a completely separate application. In some ways, REST is a backlash against the more complicated SOAP-based web services.

If you are coming from Ruby on Rails and are smitten with its built-in REST support, you'll be disappointed to find that ASP.NET MVC has no built-in support for REST. However, due to the extensibility provided by the framework, it's not difficult to achieve a RESTful architecture. MvcContrib has an implementation called SimplyRestful that contains a usable REST implementation. Look it up if you are interested in REST.

In listing 5.2, the first operation is an IgnoreRoute ❶. We don't want Trace.axd, WebResource.axd, and other existing ASP.NET handlers routed through the MVC framework, so the route {resource}.axd/{*pathInfo} ensures any request coming in with an extension of .axd will not be served by ASP.NET MVC.

The second operation defines our first route. Routes are defined by calling MapRoute on a RouteCollection, which adds a Route object to the collection. So, what comprises a route? A route has a name ❷, a URL pattern ❸, default values ❹, and constraints. The latter two are optional, but you will most likely use default values in your routes. The route in listing 5.2 is named *Default*, has a URL pattern of {controller}/{action}/{id}, and a default value dictionary that identifies the default controller and action. These default values are specified in an anonymous type, which is new in .NET 3.5.

If we pick apart this route, we can easily see its components: the first segment of the URL will be treated as the *controller*, the second segment as the *action*, and the third segment as the *id*. Notice how these values are surrounded in curly braces. When a URL comes in with the following format, what do you think the values will be for controller, action, and id?

http://example.com/users/edit/5

Figure 5.3 shows how the values are pulled out of the URL. Remember, this is only the default route template. You are free to change this for your own applications.

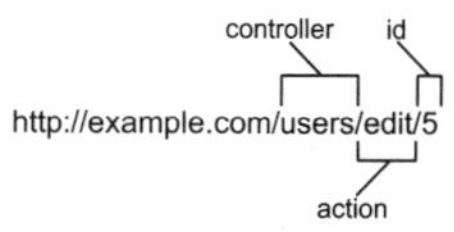

Figure 5.3 Decomposing a URL into route values using the default route of {controller}/{action}/{id}

Name	Value
Controller	"users"
Action	"edit"
Id	"5"

Table 5.2 The route values are set to the values extracted from the URL

The route values, shown in table 5.2, are all strings. The controller will be extracted out of this URL as *users*. The "Controller" part of the class name is implied by convention; thus the controller class created will be UsersController. As you can probably already tell, routes are not case sensitive. The action describes the name of the method to call on our controller. In ASP.NET MVC, an action is defined as a public method on a controller that returns an ActionResult. By convention the framework will attempt to find a method on the specified controller that matches the name supplied for action. If none is found it will also look for a method that has the ActionNameAttribute applied with the specified action. The remaining values defined in a route are pumped into the action method as parameters, or left in the Request.Params collection if no method parameters match.

Notice that the id is also a string; however if your action parameter is defined as an integer, a conversion will be done for you.

Listing 5.3 shows the action method that will be invoked as a result of the URL in figure 5.3.

Listing 5.3 An action method matching http://example.com/users/edit/5

```
public class UsersController : Controller
{
```

```
    public ActionResult Edit(int id)
    {
        return View();
    }
}
```

What happens if we omit the id or action from our URL? What will the URL http: /
/example.com/users match? To understand this we have to look at the route
defaults. In our basic route defined in listing 5.2, we can see that our defaults are
defined as

```
new { controller = "Home", action = "Index", id = "" }
```

This allows the value of "Index" to be assumed when the value for action is omitted in
a request that matches this route. You can assign a default value for any parameter in
your route.

We can see that the default routes are designed to give a reasonable level of functionality for an average application but in almost any real world application you want
to design and customize a new URL schema. In the next section we'll design a URL
schema using custom static and dynamic routes.

5.3.1   *URL schema for an online store*

Now we are going to implement a route collection for a sample website. The site is a
simple store stocking widgets for sale. Since the routes for Code Camp Server are a bit
more complex, we'll first examine a slightly simpler case and continue our examples
with Code Camp Server later in the chapter. Using the guidelines covered in this
chapter we have designed a URL schema shown in table 5.3.

Table 5.3   The URL schema for sample widget store

	URL	Description
1	http://example.com/	Home page, redirects to the widget catalog list
2	http://example.com/privacy	Displays a static page containing site privacy policy
3	http://example.com/<widget code>	Shows a product detail page for the relevant <widget code>
4	http://example.com/<widget code>/buy	Adds the relevant widget to the shopping basket
5	http://example.com/basket	Shows the current user's shopping basket
6	http://example.com/checkout	Starts the checkout process for the current user

There is a new kind of URL in there that we have not yet discussed. The URL in
route 4 is not designed to be seen by the user. It's linked via form posts. After the
action has processed, it immediately redirects and the URL is never seen on the
address bar. In cases like this it is still important for the URL to be consistent with
the other routes defined in the application. How do we add a route?

5.3.2 *Adding a custom static route*

Finally it's time to start implementing the routes that we have designed. We'll tackle the static routes first as shown in table 5.4. Route 1 in our schema is handled by our route defaults, so we can leave that one exactly as is.

Table 5.4 Static routes

	URL	Description
1	http://example.com/	Home page, redirects to the widget catalog list
2	http://example.com/privacy	Static page containing site privacy policy

The first route that we'll implement is number 2 which is a purely static route linking http://example.com/privacy to the `privacy` action of the `Help` controller. Let's look at it in listing 5.4.

Listing 5.4 A static route

```
routes.MapRoute("privacy_policy", "privacy", new {controller = "Help", action
    = "Privacy"});
```

The route in listing 5.4 does nothing more than map a completely static URL to an action and controller. Effectively it maps http://example.com/privacy to the `Privacy` action of the `Help` controller.

NOTE *Route priorities* The order in which routes are added to the route table determines the order in which they will be searched when looking for a match. This means routes should be listed in source code from highest priority with the most specific conditions down to lowest priority or a catch-all route.

This is a common place for routing bugs to appear. Watch out for them!

Static routes are useful when there are a small number of URLs that deviate from the general rule. If a route contains information relevant to the data being displayed on the page, look at dynamic routes.

5.3.3 *Adding a custom dynamic route*

Four dynamic routes are added in this section (shown in table 5.5); we'll consider them two at a time.

Table 5.5 Dynamic routes

	URL	Description
1	http://example.com/<widget code>	Shows a product detail page for the relevant <widget code>
2	http://example.com/<widget code>/buy	Adds the relevant widget to the shopping basket

Table 5.5   Dynamic routes (*continued*)

	URL	Description
3	http://example.com/basket	Shows the current user's shopping basket
4	http://example.com/checkout	Starts the checkout process for the current user

Listing 5.5 implements routes 3 and 4. The route sits directly off the root of the domain, just as the privacy route did. It does not simply accept any and all values. Instead, it makes use of a route constraint. By convention, if we place a string value here it will be treated as a regular expression. We can create our own custom constraints by implementing `IRouteConstraint`, as we'll see later in this chapter. A request will only match a route if the URL pattern matches *and* all route constraints pass.

Listing 5.5   Implementation of routes 3 and 4

```
routes.MapRoute("widgets", "{widgetCode}/{action}",
          new {controller = "Catalog", action = "Show"},
          new {widgetCode = @"WDG[0-9]{4}"});          ❶
```

TIP   If you are planning to host an ASP.NET MVC application on IIS6, mapping issues will cause the default routing rules not to work. For a quick fix, simply change the URLs used to have an extension such as `{controller}.mvc/{action}/{id}`. Chapter 10 presents more detail on this.

The `Constraints` parameter in `MapRoute` takes a dictionary in the form of an anonymous type which can contain a property for each named parameter in the route. In listing 5.5 we are ensuring that the request will only match if the `{widgetCode}` parameter starts with `WDG` followed by exactly 4 digits ❶. Listing 5.6 shows a controller that can handle a request that matches the route in listing 5.5.

Listing 5.6   The controller action handling the dynamic routes

```
public ActionResult Show(string widgetCode)
{                                              Find widget by
    var widget = GetWidget(widgetCode);    ⊲── widget code

    if(widget == null)
    {                                          Return 404 if
        Response.StatusCode = 404;         ⊲── widget not found
        return View("404");
    }
    else
    {                                          Render view
        return View(widget);               ⊲── for widget
    }
}
```

Listing 5.5 shows the action implementation in the controller for the route in listing 5.4. Although it's simplified from a real world application, it's straightforward until we get to the case of the widget not being found. That's a problem. The widget does not exist and yet we have already assured the routing engine that we would take care of this request. As the widget is now being referred to by a direct resource locator, the HTTP specification says that if that resource does not exist, we should return *HTTP 404 not found*. Luckily, this is no problem and we can just change the status code in the Response and render the same 404 view that we have created for the catch-all route. (We'll cover catch-all routes later in this chapter.)

NOTE You may have noticed in the previous example that we appear to have directly manipulated the HttpResponse, but this is not the case. The Controller base class provides us with a shortcut property to an instance of HttpResponseBase. This instance acts as a façade to the actual Http-Response, but allows you to easily use a mock if necessary to maintain testability. For an even cleaner testing experience, consider using a custom ActionResult.

TIP It's good practice to make constants for regular expressions used in routes as they are often used to create several routes.

Finally, we can add routes 5 and 6 from the schema. These routes are almost static routes but they have been implemented with a parameter and a route constraint to keep the total number of routes low. There are two main reasons for this. First, each request must scan the route table to do the matching, so performance can be a concern for large sets of routes. Second, the more routes you have, the higher the risk of route priority bugs appearing. Having few route rules is easier to maintain. The regular expression used for validation in listing 5.7 is simply to stop unknown actions from being passed to the controller.

> **Listing 5.7 Shopping basket and checkout rules**

```
routes.MapRoute("catalog", "{action}",
                new{controller="Catalog"},
                new{action=@"basket|checkout"});
```

We've now added static and dynamic routes to serve up content for various URLs in our site. What happens if a request comes in and doesn't match any requests? In this event, an exception is thrown, which is hardly what you'd want in a real application. For exceptions, we can use catch-all routes.

5.3.4 Catch-all routes

The final route we'll add to the sample application is a catch-all route to match any URL not yet matched by another rule. The purpose of this route is to display our HTTP 404 error message. Global catch-all routes, like the one in listing 5.8, will catch anything, and as such should be the *last* routes defined.

NOTE   The standard ASP.NET custom errors section is still useful. For example if a URL matches your standard {controller}/{action} route, but the controller doesn't exist, the framework will render the 404 page registered in that section. If a URL comes in and doesn't match any route, we'll get an exception stating, "The incoming request does not match any route." Catch-all routes can help give you even more control in these situations.

Listing 5.8   The catch-all route

```
routes.MapRoute("catch-all", "{*catchall}", new {controller = "Error",
    action = "NotFound"});
```

The value "catchall" gives a name to the information that the catch-all route picked up. You can retrieve this value by providing an action parameter with the same name.

The action code for the 404 error can be seen in listing 5.9.

Listing 5.9   The controller action for the HTTP 404 custom error

```
public class ErrorController : Controller
{
    public ActionResult Notfound()
    {
        Response.StatusCode = 404;
        return View("404");
    }
}
```

Catch-all routes can be used for other scenarios as well. If you wanted to match a certain string first, and then have everything else past the URL captured, you add the catch-all parameter to the end of the route definition. We saw this earlier: routes.IgnoreRoute("{resource}.axd/{*pathInfo}") will capture anything after the first segment. Another interesting use for a catch-all route is for dynamic hierarchies, such as product categories. When you reach the limits of the routing system, create a catch-all route and do it yourself.

The example in listing 5.8 is a true catch-all route and will literally match any URL that has not been caught by the higher priority rules. It's valid to have other catch-all parameters used in regular routes such as /events/{*info} which would catch every URL starting with /events/. Be cautious using these catch-all parameters as they will include *any* other text on the URL, including slashes and period characters. It's a good idea to use a regular expression parameter wherever possible so you remain in control of the data being passed into your controller action rather than just grabbing everything.

At this point, the default {controller}/{action}/{id} route can be removed as we have completely customized the routes to match our URL schema. You might choose to keep it around to serve as a default way to access your other controllers.

We have now customized the URL schema for our website. We have done this with complete control over our URLs, and without modifying where we keep our controllers and actions. This means that any ASP.NET MVC developer can come and look at

> **Internet Explorer's "friendly" HTTP error messages**
>
> If you are using Internet Explorer to develop and browse your application, be careful that you are not seeing Internet Explorer's "friendly" error messages when developing these custom 404 errors, as IE will replace your custom page with its own. To avoid this, go into Tools > Internet Options and untick "Show friendly HTTP error messages" under browsing options on the Advanced tab. Your custom 404 page should appear. Don't forget, though, that users of your application using Internet Explorer may not see your custom error pages.

our application and know exactly where everything is. This is a powerful concept. Next, we'll discover how to use the routing system from *within* our application.

5.4　*Using the routing system to generate URLs*

Nobody likes broken links. And since it's so easy to change the URL routes for your entire site, what happens if you directly use those URLs from within your application (for example, linking from one page to another)? If you changed one of your routes, these URLs could be broken. Of course the decision to change URLs does not come lightly; it's generally believed that you can harm your reputation in the eyes of major search engines if your site contains broken links. Assuming that you may have no choice but to change your routes, you'll need a better way to deal with URLs in your applications.

Instead, whenever we need a URL in our site, we'll ask the framework to give it to us, rather than hard-coding it. We'll need to specify a combination of controller, action, and parameters. The ActionLink method does the rest. It's a method on the HtmlHelper class included with the MVC framework which generates a full HTML <a> element with the correct URL inserted to match a route specified from the object parameters passed in.

```
<%= Html.ActionLink("WDG0001", "show", "catalog", new { widgetCode =
    "WDG0001" }, null) %>
```

This example generates a link to the show action on the catalog controller with an extra parameter specified for widgetCode. The output from this is shown next.

```
<a href="/WDG0001">WDG0001</a>
```

Similarly, if you use the HtmlHelper class' BeginForm method to build your form tags, it will generate your URL for you. As you saw in the last section, the controller and action may not be the only parameters that are involved in defining a route. Sometimes additional parameters are needed to match a route.

Occasionally it's useful to be able to pass parameters to an action that has not been specified as part of the route.

```
<%= Html.ActionLink("WDG0002 (French)", "show", "catalog",
    new { widgetCode = "WDG0002", language = "fr" }, null) %>
```

This example shows that passing additional parameters is as simple as adding extra members to the object passed to ActionLink. The link generated by this code is shown next. If the parameter matches something in the route, it will become part of the URL. Otherwise it will be appended to the query string, as you can see in this example:

```
<a href="/WDG0002?language=fr">WDG0002 (French)</a>
```

When using `ActionLink`, your route will be determined for you, based on the first matching route defined in the route collection. Most often this will be sufficient, but if you want to request a specific route, you can use `RouteLink`. `RouteLink` accepts a parameter to identify the route requested, like this:

```
<%= Html.RouteLink("WDG003", "special-widget-route",
    new { widgetCode = "WDG003" }, null) %>
```

This will look for a route with the name *special-widget-route*. Most often you will not need to use this technique unless the URL generated by routing is not the desired one. Try to solve the issue by altering route ordering or with route constraints. Use `RouteLink` as a last resort.

Sometimes you need to obtain a URL, but not for the purposes of a link or form. This often happens when you are writing AJAX code, and the request URL needs to be set. The `UrlHelper` class can generate URLs directly, and in fact the `UrlHelper` is used by the `ActionLink` methods and others. Here is an example:

```
<%= Url.Action("show", "catalog",
    new { widgetCode="WDG0002", language="fr" }) %>
```

This will return the same URL as above, but without any surrounding tags.

5.5   *Creating routes for Code Camp Server*

Now that we are armed with the techniques for building routes for an application, let's apply this to Code Camp Server. Table 5.6 shows the desired URLs for the application. It's important to list all of the desired entry points to your website. We'll use this as a basis for route testing later.

Table 5.6   Desired URLs for Code Camp Server

Example	URL	Purpose
1	/	Redirect to current conference
2	/<conferenceKey>	See the details for the conference specified
3	/<conferenceKey>/edit	Edit the conference (admin only)
4	/<conferenceKey>/speakers	See the list of speakers for the conference
5	/<conferenceKey>/speakers/<id>/<personKey>	See the details of a speaker
6	/<conferenceKey>/sessions	See the list of sessions
7	/<conferenceKey>/sessions/new	Create a new session (admin only)

Table 5.6   Desired URLs for Code Camp Server *(continued)*

Example	URL	Purpose
8	/<conferenceKey>/sessions/<id>/<sessionKey>	See the details of a session
9	/<conferenceKey>/schedule	See the schedule of the conference
10	/<conferenceKey>/attendees	See who's coming
11	/<conferenceKey>/attendees/new	Create a new attendee
12	/<conferenceKey>/attendees/<id>/<personKey>	See the details of an attendee
13	/login	Log in to the site
14	/conference/list	List the conferences on the site (admin only)
15	/conference/new	Create a new conference (admin only)

This is a pretty exhaustive list of the URLs that we would like to have for our conference application. You can see that some of these do not follow the pattern that we are given by default (`{controller}/{action}/{id}`), so we have to customize.

Listing 5.10 defines the route that will handle requests at the root of our site. As you can see, we rely on the defaults to determine what controller and action to route to.

Listing 5.10   Default values help define which controller/action is invoked for site root

```
public static void RegisterRoutes(RouteCollection routes)
{
    routes.IgnoreRoute("{resource}.axd/{*pathInfo}");
    routes.MapRoute("root", "",
        new {controller = "Conference", action = "Current"});
}
```

In listing 5.11 we want to match a route where the first (and only) segment is the word *login*. Because this is a static route, we should define it before other dynamic routes. This way it is matched before a different, dynamic route matches it.

Listing 5.11   Defining a static route before other dynamic routes

```
public static void RegisterRoutes(RouteCollection routes)
{
    routes.IgnoreRoute("{resource}.axd/{*pathInfo}");

    routes.MapRoute("root", "",
        new {controller = "Conference", action = "Current"});

    routes.MapRoute("login", "login",
        new { controller = "Account", action = "Login" });
}
```

The second and third URL in our list are intended for an action on the conference controller. We do not explicitly set the controller name in this URL, so we'll have to set a default value for it. Listing 5.12 shows this.

Listing 5.12   Routes for satisfying examples 3 and 4

```
public static void RegisterRoutes(RouteCollection routes)
{
    routes.IgnoreRoute("{resource}.axd/{*pathInfo}");

    routes.MapRoute("root", "",
        new {controller = "Conference", action = "Current"});

    routes.MapRoute("login", "login",
        new { controller = "Account", action = "Login" });

    routes.MapRoute("conference", "{conferenceKey}/{action}",
        new {controller = "Conference", action = "Index"});
}
```

Looks as if this will work for examples 3 and 4, but it will incorrectly match the following routes. We'll treat rules 5 through 12 as static routes, which means they should be defined above the route we just added. Listing 5.13 shows these new routes.

Listing 5.13   Static routes for sessions, speakers, attendees, and more

```
public static void RegisterRoutes(RouteCollection routes)
{
    routes.IgnoreRoute("{resource}.axd/{*pathInfo}");
    routes.MapRoute("root", "",
                new {controller = "Conference", action = "Current"});
    routes.MapRoute("login", "login",
                new { controller = "Account", action = "Login" });
    routes.MapRoute("sessions", "{conferenceKey}/sessions/{action}",
                new {controller = "Sessions", action = "index"});
    routes.MapRoute("attendees", "{conferenceKey}/attendees/{action}",
                new { controller = "Attendees", action = "index" });
    routes.MapRoute("speakers", "{conferenceKey}/speakers/{action}",
                new {controller = "Speakers", action = "Index"});

    routes.MapRoute("schedule", "{conferenceKey}/schedule/{action}",
                new {controller = "Schedule", action = "Index"});
    routes.MapRoute("conference", "{conferenceKey}/{action}",
                new {controller = "Conference", action = "Index"});
}
```

The new routes (bolded) define the general routes for sessions, attendees, speakers, and the schedule. These are similar enough that you might already be looking to combine them with a single, dynamic route. We'll visit that later in the chapter.

These routes also will not match the SEO-friendly routes we wanted, namely examples 5, 8, and 12. Listing 5.14 contains the definitions for these. Notice how the listing uses constraints on the {id} segment so that it will not incorrectly match as an action on another route. Because these routes are more specific, we'll need to add them before the more general (but very similar) routes.

Listing 5.14   Providing SEO-friendly routes that take extra information

```
public static void RegisterRoutes(RouteCollection routes)
{
    routes.IgnoreRoute("{resource}.axd/{*pathInfo}");
```

```
routes.MapRoute("root", "",
    new {controller = "Conference", action = "Current"});

routes.MapRoute("login", "login",
    new { Controller = "Account", Action = "Login" });

routes.MapRoute("single_session",
                "{conferenceKey}/sessions/{id}/{sessionKey}",
                new {controller = "Sessions", action = "show"},
                new {id = @"\d+"});

routes.MapRoute("sessions", "{conferenceKey}/sessions/{action}",
                new {controller = "Sessions", action = "index"});

routes.MapRoute("single_attendee",
                "{conferenceKey}/attendees/{id}/{personKey}",
                new { controller = "Attendees", action = "show" });

routes.MapRoute("attendees", "{conferenceKey}/attendees/{action}",
                new { controller = "Attendees", action = "index" });

routes.MapRoute(null, "{conferenceKey}/speakers/{id}/{personKey}",
                new {controller = "Speakers", action = "Show"},
                new {id = @"\d+"});

routes.MapRoute("speakers", "{conferenceKey}/speakers/{action}",
                new {controller = "Speakers", action = "Index"});

routes.MapRoute("schedule", "{conferenceKey}/schedule/{action}",
                new {controller = "Schedule", action = "Index"});

routes.MapRoute("conference", "{conferenceKey}/{action}",
                new {controller = "Conference", action = "Index"});
}
```

The bolded routes now allow our SEO-friendly URLs for sessions, speakers, and attendees. This allows nice URLs such as http://example.com/sessions/129/introduction-to-asp-net-mvc. The constraint is a simple regular expression that matches one or more integers.

We have now addressed each URL in our table of desired URLs (table 5.6). Now it's time to write unit tests to ensure that these routes work as intended. This will also ensure that future routes will not break our URL structure.

5.6   *Testing route behavior*

When compared with the rest of the ASP.NET MVC Framework, testing routes is not easy or intuitive. Although ASP.NET MVC has advanced the functions interfaces and abstract base classes, many elements still must be mocked out before route testing is possible. Luckily, MvcContrib has a nice, fluent route testing API, which we can use to make testing these routes easier. But before we look at that, listing 5.15 demonstrates how you would test a route with NUnit and Rhino Mocks.

Listing 5.15   Testing routes can be a pain.

```
using System.Web;
using System.Web.Routing;
using NUnit.Framework;
using NUnit.Framework.SyntaxHelpers;
```

```
using Rhino.Mocks;

namespace CodeCampServerRoutes.Tests
{
    [TestFixture]
    public class NaiveRouteTester
    {
        [Test]
        public void root_matches_conference_controller_and_current_action()
        {
            const string url = "~/";
            var request = MockRepository.GenerateStub<HttpRequestBase>();
            request.Stub(x => x.AppRelativeCurrentExecutionFilePath)
                .Return(url).Repeat.Any();
            request.Stub(x => x.PathInfo)
                .Return(string.Empty).Repeat.Any();

            var context = MockRepository.GenerateStub<HttpContextBase>();
            context.Stub(x => x.Request).Return(request).Repeat.Any();

            RouteTable.Routes.Clear();
            MvcApplication.RegisterRoutes(RouteTable.Routes);
            var routeData = RouteTable.Routes.GetRouteData(context);

            Assert.That(routeData.Values["controller"],
                Is.EqualTo("Conference"));
            Assert.That(routeData.Values["action"], Is.EqualTo("Current"));
        }
    }
}
```

If all of our route tests looked like that, nobody would even bother. Those specific stubs on `HttpContextBase` and `HttpRequestBase` were not lucky guesses. It took a peek inside of Reflector to find out exactly what to mock. This is not how a testable framework should behave! Luckily, we do not have to deal with this if we are smart. MvcContrib's fluent route testing API makes this a lot easier. Listing 5.16 is the same test, using MvcContrib:

Listing 5.16 Much better route testing with MvcContrib's TestHelper project

```
using System.Web.Routing;
using CodeCampServerRoutes.Controllers;
using MvcContrib.TestHelper;
using NUnit.Framework;

namespace CodeCampServerRoutes.Tests
{
    [TestFixture]
    public class FluentRouteTester
    {
        [Test]
        public void root_matches_conference_controller_and_current_action()
        {
            MvcApplication.RegisterRoutes(RouteTable.Routes);
            "~/".ShouldMapTo<ConferenceController>(x => x.Current());      ❶
```

```
            }
        }
}
```

This is all done with the magic and power of extension methods and lambda expressions.

You can't get away so easily! What kind of magic are you talking about?

Inside of MvcContrib there is an extension method on the `string` class that builds up a `RouteData` instance based on the parameters in the URL. The `RouteData` class has an extension method on it to assert that the route values match a controller and action ❶. You can see from the example that the controller comes from the generic type argument to the `ShouldMapTo<TController>()` method. The action is then specified with a lambda expression. The expression is parsed to pull out the method call (the action) and any arguments passed to it.

The arguments are matched with the route values. See the code for yourself here: http://code.google.com/p/mvccontrib/source/browse/trunk/src/MvcContrib.Test-Helper/MvcContrib.TestHelper/Extensions/RouteTestingExtensions.cs.

Now it's time to apply this to our Code Camp Server routing rules and make sure that we have covered the desired cases. We do that in listing 5.17.

Listing 5.17 Testing Code Camp Server routes

```
using System.Web.Routing;
using CodeCampServerRoutes.Controllers;
using MvcContrib.TestHelper;
using NUnit.Framework;

namespace CodeCampServerRoutes.Tests
{
    [TestFixture]
    public class RouteTester
    {
        [SetUp]
        public void SetUp()
        {
            RouteTable.Routes.Clear();
            MvcApplication.RegisterRoutes(RouteTable.Routes);
        }

        [Test]
        public void incoming_routes()
        {
            "~/".ShouldMapTo<ConferenceController>(x => x.Current());

            "~/boiseCodeCamp".ShouldMapTo<ConferenceController>(
                x => x.Index("boiseCodeCamp"));

            "~/boiseCodeCamp/edit".ShouldMapTo<ConferenceController>(
                x => x.Edit("boiseCodeCamp"));

            "~/portlandTechFest/speakers".ShouldMapTo<SpeakersController>(
                x => x.Index("portlandTechFest"));

            "~/portlandTechFest/speakers/12/barney-rubble"
                .ShouldMapTo<SpeakersController>(
```

```
            x => x.Show("portlandTechFest", 12));

        "~/michigandayofdotnet/sessions"
            .ShouldMapTo<SessionsController>(
            x => x.Index("michigandayofdotnet"));

        "~/michigandayofdotnet/sessions/82/learning-nunit"
            .ShouldMapTo<SessionsController>(
            x => x.Show("michigandayofdotnet", 82));

        "~/houstonTechFest/schedule".ShouldMapTo<ScheduleController>(
            x => x.Index("houstonTechFest"));

        "~/austinCodeCamp/attendees".ShouldMapTo<AttendeesController>(
            x => x.Index("austinCodeCamp"));

        "~/austinCodeCamp/attendees/new"
            .ShouldMapTo<AttendeesController>(
            x => x.New("austinCodeCamp"));

        "~/austinCodeCamp/attendees/123/bob-johnson"
            .ShouldMapTo<AttendeesController>(
            x => x.Show("austinCodeCamp", 123));

        "~/login".ShouldMapTo<AccountController>(x => x.Login());

        "~/conference/new".ShouldMapTo<ConferenceController>(
            x => x.New());
        }
    }
}
```

NOTE You should probably separate out your tests into logical test methods. I have combined them for the sake of brevity in the example.

After running this example, we see that all of our routes are working properly (the output may look slightly different depending on your testing framework and runner):

```
------ Test started: Assembly: CodeCampServerRoutes.Tests.dll ------

1 passed, 0 failed, 0 skipped, took 2.03 seconds.
```

Remember earlier when we noticed an opportunity to make those other routes more dynamic? This would avoid duplication in the route rules and hopefully make them easier to understand. Armed with tests to back us up, we can now attempt to combine these routes.

We can probably match these all with a single route along the lines of {conferenceKey}/{controller}/{action}; however this route would prevent the preceding one ({conferenceKey}/{action}) from matching the routes on Conference-Controller. It's clear that we'll have to leverage route constraints to get the URLs we want.

If we add the {conferenceKey}/{action} route first, then all we need to do is make it not match when the second segment—{action}—is equal to one of the other controller names. This can be accomplished fairly easily with regular expressions. Listing 5.18 shows the modified route.

Listing 5.18 Constraining the route so it will not be so greedy

```
routes.MapRoute("conference", "{conferenceKey}/{action}",
      new { controller = "Conference", action = "Index" },
      new { conferenceKey = "(?!conference|account).*",
          action = "(?!speakers|schedule|sessions|sttendees).*" });
```
Don't match conference or account

Don't match other controllers

This route will no longer match any route that has one of the values specified in the action constraint. This will allow us to match the request in a later route, which we have defined in listing 5.19.

Listing 5.19 Matching our other controllers with a single route

```
routes.MapRoute("other_controllers",
     "{conferenceKey}/{controller}/{action}",
        new {action="index"},
        new { conferenceKey = "(?!conference|account).*" });
```

This route must also contain the conferenceKey constraint, so that the final route (which is the default route provided in ASP.NET MVC applications) will match URLs that have *Conference* or *Account* in the first segment.

Now that we're done with the change, we'll run the tests again to make sure we didn't break anything.

```
------ Test started: Assembly: CodeCampServerRoutes.Tests.dll ------

1 passed, 0 failed, 0 skipped, took 1.97 seconds.
```

Excellent! Only by having unit tests can we be this confident this fast that we didn't break anything.

There is an important facet of route testing that we have paid little attention to so far: *outbound routing*. As defined earlier, outbound routing refers to the URLs that are generated by the Framework, given a set of route values. Look to projects like Mvc-Contrib to eventually provide helpers for this type of route testing in the future. At the time of writing, no examples of outbound route testing were available.

Now that you've seen two complete examples of realistic routing schemas, you are prepared to start creating routes for your own applications. You have also seen some helpful unit testing extensions to make unit testing inbound routes *much* easier. We haven't yet mentioned that all of this routing goodness is available to Web Forms projects as well!

5.7 *Using routing with existing ASP.NET projects*

The URL problems discussed at the start of this chapter (URLs tied directly to files on disk, no ability to embed dynamic content in the URL itself, and so on) can affect all websites/applications and although you may not be in a position to adopt a full MVC pattern for an application, you should still care about your application's URL usability. System.Web.Routing is a separate assembly released as part of .NET 3.5 SP1, and as you might guess, it's available for use in Web Forms as well.

Luckily, by importing the `UrlRoutingModule` from the `System.Web.Routing` assembly, we can use the routing mechanism from the MVC framework in existing ASP.NET Web Forms applications. To get started, open an existing ASP.NET Web Forms project and add the lines from listing 5.20 (and 5.21 for IIS 7) in to the `assemblies` and `httpModules` sections in your web.config.

Listing 5.20   Configuration for the `UrlRoutingModule`

```
<assemblies>
   <add assembly="System.Web.Routing, Version=3.5.0.0, Culture=neutral,
     PublicKeyToken=31BF3856AD364E35" />
   ...
</assemblies>

...                        For IIS6 or IIS7
<httpModules>      ◁───┘   classic mode
   <add name="UrlRoutingModule" type="System.Web.Routing.UrlRoutingModule,
     System.Web.Routing,    Version=3.5.0.0, Culture=neutral,
     PublicKeyToken=31BF3856AD364E35"/>
   ...
</httpModules>

...
```

Listing 5.21   Configuration for IIS 7 integrated mode

```
<system.webServer>
  <handlers>
    <add name="UrlRoutingHandler" preCondition="integratedMode" verb="*"
       path="UrlRouting.axd"
       type="System.Web.HttpForbiddenHandler, System.Web, Version=2.0.0.0,
         Culture=neutral,
         PublicKeyToken=b03f5f7f11d50a3a" />
   ...
  </handlers>
  ...
  <modules>
    <remove name="UrlRoutingModule" />
    <add name="UrlRoutingModule" type="System.Web.Routing.UrlRoutingModule,
      System.Web.Routing,
      Version=3.5.0.0, Culture=neutral,
      PublicKeyToken=31BF3856AD364E35"/>
   ...
  </modules>
</system.webServer>
```

Next, we need to define a custom route handler that will—you guessed it—handle the route! You may have a custom route handler for each route, or you might choose to make it more dynamic. It's entirely up to you.

Defining the route is similar to methods we've seen earlier, except that there are no controllers and actions to specify. Instead you just specify a page. A sample route for Web Forms might look like this:

```
RouteTable.Routes.Add("ProductsRoute", new Route
    (
        "products/apparel",
        new CustomRouteHandler("~/Products/ProductsByCategory.aspx",
            "category=18")
    ));
```

The custom route handler simply needs to build the page. Here is a bare-bones handler that will work:

```
public class CustomRouteHandler : IRouteHandler
{
    public CustomRouteHandler(string virtualPath, string queryString)
    {
        this.VirtualPath = virtualPath;
        this.QueryString = queryString;
    }

    public string VirtualPath { get; private set; }
    public string QueryString { get; private set; }

    public IHttpHandler GetHttpHandler(RequestContext
        requestContext)
    {
        requestContext.HttpContext.RewritePath(
            String.Format("{0}?{1}", VirtualPath, QueryString));

        var page = BuildManager.CreateInstanceFromVirtualPath
            (VirtualPath, typeof(Page)) as IHttpHandler;
        return page;
    }
}
```

Now, requests for */products/apparel* will end up being served by the URL in the example.

NOTE   When using `UrlRoutingModule` to add routing capabilities to your Web Forms application, you are essentially "directing traffic" around parts of the normal ASP.NET request processing pipeline. This means that the normal URL-based authorization features of ASP.NET will be circumvented, and even if users don't have access to a particular page, they can view it if the `CustomRouteHandler` does not implement authorization checking or the route is not listed in the authorization rules in the `web.config`. Although the complete implementation is outside the scope of this text, you can use the `UrlAuthorizationModule.Check-UrlAccessForPrincipal()` method to verify a user has access to a particular resource.

5.8   *Summary*

In this chapter we have seen how the routing module in the ASP.NET MVC Framework gives us virtually unlimited flexibility when designing routing schemas able to implement both static and dynamic routes. Best of all, the code needed to achieve this is relatively insignificant.

Designing a URL schema for an application is the most challenging thing we have covered in this chapter and there is never a definitive answer to what routes should be implemented. Although the code needed to generate routes and URLs from routes is simple, the process of designing that schema is not. Ultimately every application is different. Some will be perfectly happy with the default routes created by the project template, whereas others will have complex, custom route definition spanning multiple C# classes.

We saw that the order in which routes are defined determines the order they are searched when a request is received and that you must carefully consider the effects of adding new routes to the application. As more routes are defined, the risk of breaking existing URLs increases. Your insurance against this problem is route testing. Although route testing can be cumbersome, helpers like the fluent route testing API in MvcContrib can certainly help.

The most important thing to note from this chapter is that there should be no application written with the ASP.NET MVC Framework that is limited in its URL by the technical choices made by source code layout, and that can only be a good thing! Separation of the URL schema from the underlying code architecture gives ultimate flexibility and allows you to focus on what would make sense for the user on the URL rather than what the layout of your source code requires.

We'd like to offer a special note of thanks to Dave Verwer, who wrote the initial version of this chapter. In the next chapter, we'll see how to customize and extend the ASP.NET MVC Framework.

Customizing and extending the ASP.NET MVC Framework

This chapter covers

- Customizing route handlers
- Creating your own controller factory
- Extending the controller
- Decorating controller actions for additional behavior
- Building and using custom view engines

One of the greatest aspects of ASP.NET MVC is its flexibility. The majority of the framework is built upon interfaces and abstract base classes, which enables unit testing of components in isolation. This also gives us the ability to substitute our own implementations of these features. ASP.NET MVC comes with functional default implementations, but sometimes these don't meet our needs. Sometimes we don't agree with the choices that Microsoft bakes in, and by customizing these components we are free to make our own choices.

In this chapter we'll cover some of the extension points of the ASP.NET MVC Framework. We'll surround their use with examples and mention the purpose of each one. By the end of the chapter, you will be familiar with most of the extensible components of ASP.NET MVC and how to apply them.

First we'll examine URL routing. We'll take a look at how it functions and then explore how to enhance it to behave differently.

6.1   Extending URL routing

The `UrlRoutingModule` is an implementation of `IHttpModule` and represents the entry point into the ASP.NET MVC Framework. This module examines each request, builds up the `RouteData` for the request, finds an appropriate `IRouteHandler` for the given route matched, and finally redirects the request to the `IRouteHandler`'s `IHttpHandler`. Make sense?

In chapter 5 we discovered how routing works. Our default route looked like listing 6.1. The `MapRoute` method is actually a simplified way of specifying routes. The same route can be specified more explicitly, as is shown in listing 6.2.

Listing 6.1   A simple way of specifying routes

```
routes.MapRoute("default", "{controller}/{action}/{id}",
    new { Controller="home", Action="index", id=""});
```

Listing 6.2   A more detailed way of specifying routes

```
routes.Add(new Route("{controller}/{action}/{id}",
    new RouteValueDictionary(new { Controller = "home", Action = "index",
    id = "" }), new MvcRouteHandler()));
```

That third argument in listing 6.2 is telling the framework which `IRouteHandler` to use for this route. We are using the built-in `MvcRouteHandler` that ships with the framework. By default we are using this class when using the `MapRoute` method. We can change this to be a custom route handler and take control in interesting ways. An `IRouteHandler` is responsible for creating an appropriate `IHttpHandler` to handle the request given the details of the request. This is a good place to change the way routing works, or perhaps to gain control extremely early in the request pipeline. The `MvcRouteHandler` simply constructs an `MvcHandler` to handle a request, passing it a `RequestContext`, which contains the `RouteData` and an `HttpContextBase`.

A quick example will help illustrate the need for a custom route handler. When starting to define your routes, you'll sometimes run across errors. Let's assume you have defined the route shown in listing 6.3.

Listing 6.3   Adding another route

```
routes.MapRoute("conferenceKey", "{conferenceKey}/{action}",
    new { Controller = "Conference", Action="index" });
```

Here we've added a new custom route at the top position that will accept URLs like /HoustonCodeCamp2008/register, use the conference controller, and call the register action on it, passing in the conferenceKey as a parameter to the action, as shown in listing 6.4.

Listing 6.4   A controller action that handles the new route

```
public class ConferenceController : Controller
{
    public ActionResult Register(string conferenceKey)
    {
        return View();
    }
}
```

This is a good example of a custom route that makes your URLs more readable.

Now let's assume that we have another controller called Home. HomeController has an Index action to show the start page, as shown in listing 6.5.

Listing 6.5   A controller action to respond to the default route

```
public class HomeController : Controller
{
    public ActionResult Index()
    {
        return View();
    }
}
```

We'd like the URL for the action in listing 6.4 to look like /home/index. If we try this URL, we'll get a 404 error as shown in figure 6.1. Why?

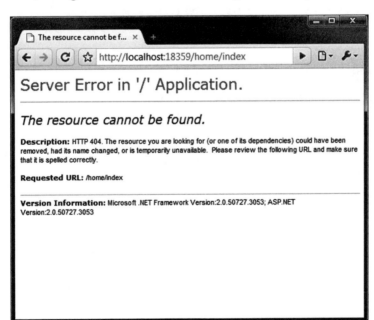

Figure 6.1   This message doesn't tell us much about what's wrong. An action couldn't be found on the controller, but which one?

The problem is not apparent from that error message. We certainly have a controller called HomeController, and it has an action method called Index. If you dig deep into the routes you can deduce that this URL was picked up by the first route, {conferenceKey}/{action}, which was not what we intended. We should be able to quickly indentify a routing mismatch, so that we can fix it speedily.

With lots of custom routes, it is easy for a URL to be caught by the wrong route. Wouldn't it be nice if we had a diagnostics tool to display which routes are being matched (and used) for quickly catching these types of errors?

What we'd like to do is have an extra querystring parameter that we can tack on if we want to see the route information. The current route information is stored in an object called RouteData, available to us in the IRouteHandler interface. The route handler is also first to get control of the request, so it is a great place to intercept and alter the behavior for any route, as shown in listing 6.6.

Listing 6.6   A custom route handler creates an associated IHttpHandler.

```
public class CustomRouteHandler : IRouteHandler
{
    public IHttpHandler GetHttpHandler(RequestContext requestContext)
    {
        if(HasQueryStringKey("routeInfo",                          ❶
                            requestContext.HttpContext.Request))
        {
            OutputRouteDiagnostics(requestContext.RouteData,
                                requestContext.HttpContext);
        }

        var handler = new CustomMvcHandler(requestContext);
        return handler;
    }

    private bool HasQueryStringKey(string keyToTest,
        HttpRequestBase request)
    {
        return Regex.IsMatch(request.Url.Query,
            string.Format(@"^\?{0}$", keyToTest));
    }
}
```

A route handler's normal responsibility is to construct and hand off the IHttpHandler that will handle this request. By default, this is MvcHandler. In our CustomRouteHandler we first check to see if the querystring parameter is present ❶ (we do this with a simple regular expression on the URL query section). The OutputRouteDiagnostics method is shown in listing 6.7.

Listing 6.7   Rendering route diagnostic information to the response stream

```
private void OutputRouteDiagnostics(RouteData routeData, HttpContextBase
    context)
{
```

```
var response = context.Response;
response.Write(
    @"<style>body {font-family: Arial;}
            table th {background-color: #359; color: #fff;}
      </style>
      <h1>Route Data:</h1>
      <table border='1' cellspacing='0' cellpadding='3'>          Create an
      <tr><th>Key</th><th>Value</th></tr>");          ◁─── HTML table
foreach (var pair in routeData.Values)
{
    response.Write(string.Format("<tr><td>{0}</td><td>{1}</td></tr>",
      pair.Key, pair.Value));
}

response.Write(
    @"</table>
      <h1>Routes:</h1>
      <table border='1' cellspacing='0' cellpadding='3'>          Display
          <tr><th></th><th>Route</th></tr>");          ◁─── the routes
bool foundRouteUsed = false;
foreach(Route r in RouteTable.Routes)
{
    response.Write("<tr><td>");                                   Green
    bool matches = r.GetRouteData(context) != null;          if matching,
    string backgroundColor = matches ? "#bfb" : "#fbb";          red otherwise
    if(matches && !foundRouteUsed)          ◁───
    {                        Chevron (») next
                             to route selected
        response.Write("&raquo;");          ◁───
        foundRouteUsed = true;
    }
    response.Write(string.Format(
        "</td><td style='font-family: Courier New;
            background-color:{0}'>{1}</td></tr>",
        backgroundColor, r.Url));
}

response.End();
}
```

This method outputs two tables, one for the current route data, and one for the routes in the system. Each route will return null for `GetRouteData` if the route doesn't match the current request. The table is then colored to show which routes matched, and a little arrow indicates which route is in use for the current URL. The response is ended to prevent any further rendering.

To finalize this change, we have to alter the current routes to use our new handler, as shown in listing 6.8.

Listing 6.8 Assigning routes to our custom route handler

```
RouteTable.Routes.Add(
    new Route("{conferenceKey}/{action}",
        new RouteValueDictionary( new { Controller="Conference" }),
        new CustomRouteHandler()));
```

```
RouteTable.Routes.Add(
    new Route("{controller}/{action}/{id}",
        new RouteValueDictionary(
            new { Controller="Home", Action="Index", id="" }),
        new CustomRouteHandler()));
```

The end result (shown in figure 6.2) is incredibly helpful. Let's use the /home/index URL (that resulted in a 404 in figure 6.1) but this time we'll add ?routeInfo to the querystring. We can see in the route data table that the value home was picked up as a conference key. The route table confirms that the conference key route was picked up first, since it matched.

Now you can immediately tell that the current route used is not the one we intended. We can also tell whether or not other routes match this request by the color of the cell. If you're reading the print version of this book this might not be apparent, but if you run the sample application you'll see that both rows are green. We now quickly identify the issue as a routing problem and can fix it accordingly. In this case, if we add constraints to the first route such that conferenceKey isn't the same as one of our controllers, the problem is resolved. *Remember that order matters! The first route matched is the one used.*

Of course you wouldn't want this information to be visible in a deployed application, so use it only to aid your development. You could also build a switch that changes the routes to the CustomRouteHandler if you're in debug mode, which would be a more automated solution. I'll leave this as an exercise for the reader.

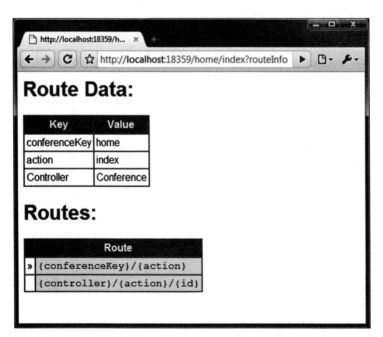

Figure 6.2 Appending the querystring parameter ?routeInfo to our URL gives us detailed information about the current request's route. We can see now that the wrong route was chosen.

NOTE   This example was inspired by Phil Haack's route debugger that he posted on his blog when the ASP.NET MVC Framework was in Preview 2. It is a great example of what you can do with the information provided to you by the routing system. You can see his original example of here:

http://haacked.com/archive/2008/03/13/url-routing-debugger.aspx

Another potential use of a custom route handler would be to append a specific identifier to the querystring automatically. This could be useful in scenarios where you rely on cookie-less sessions or have a company identifier that limits what is displayed on the screen (your authors have interfaced with such a framework). An `IHttpHandler` that would satisfy this requirement might look like listing 6.9:

Listing 6.9   An `MvcHandler` that can enforce querystring parameters

```
public class EnsureCompanyKeyHandler : MvcHandler
{
    public EnsureCompanyKeyHandler(RequestContext requestContext)
        : base(requestContext)
    {
    }

    protected override void ProcessRequest(HttpContextBase context)
    {
        var controller =
            (string)RequestContext.RouteData.Values["controller"];
        var company = context.Request.QueryString["company"];

        if (controller != "login" && company == null)      ❶
        {
            context.Response.Redirect("~/login");      ◁─┐ Force user
        }                                                 │ to login
        else
        {
            base.ProcessRequest(context);
        }
    }
}
```

In this example, every request must have a company key ❶, and the `Process-Request` method will not continue unless the URL contains one. Since we have guaranteed that every request will contain the company key, why don't we pass this on to our controllers automatically? That is an interesting question, and is the subject of the next section.

6.2   *Creating your own ControllerFactory*

Controllers are the core of any Model-View-Controller framework. The flexibility (or inflexibility) of a framework in this regard can make it ultimately useful (or not). Microsoft shipped the MVC framework with an `IController` interface and the abstract base class: `Controller`. `Controller` makes many decisions for us, and controllers that derive from it are automatically instantiated by the framework.

The ability to take control of controller instantiation gives us the flexibility to pass in arguments to the Controller's constructor or even create different implementations of IController. We'll start with the controller factory for passing in arguments, continuing the example from the previous section.

6.2.1   *The ControllerFactory implementation*

Let's assume that we want all our controllers to be given the specific company object (based on the company key) from the database. Listing 6.10 shows our base controller class.

Listing 6.10   A base controller that requires specific constructor arguments

```
public abstract class CompanyControllerBase : Controller
{
    private readonly Company _company;
    protected Company Company
    {
        get { return _company; }
    }
    protected CompanyControllerBase(Company company)     ⟵ No default
    {                                                      constructor exists
        _company = company;
    }
}
```

By making our only constructor take the Company object in as a parameter, we are enforcing all derived classes to also accept this as a constructor argument.

In this example, we will have a Company class, uniquely identified by a friendly identifier companyKey. The companyKey would be something like "MSFT" or "AAPL." To get the company object, assume that we can utilize an ICompanyService (which takes care of data access and caching for us).

This controller base could be extended as shown in listing 6.11:

Listing 6.11   CompanyControllerBase subclasses require a nondefault constructor

```
public class EmployeeController : CompanyControllerBase
{
    public EmployeeController(Company company) : base(company)
    {
    }

    public ActionResult List()
    {
        return View(Company.Employees);
    }
}
```

If we try to run this code and access the list action, we'll get an error and shown in figure 6.3.

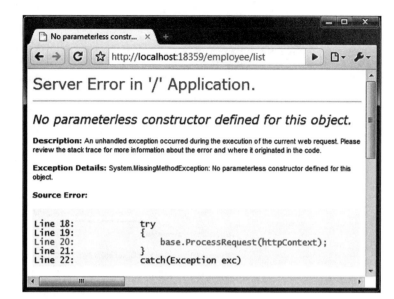

Figure 6.3 By default, controllers cannot be created without a no-arg constructor.

We need to assume control over building the controller to fix this. If we examine the stack trace closely, we can see which object is trying to build our controller class, as shown in figure 6.4:

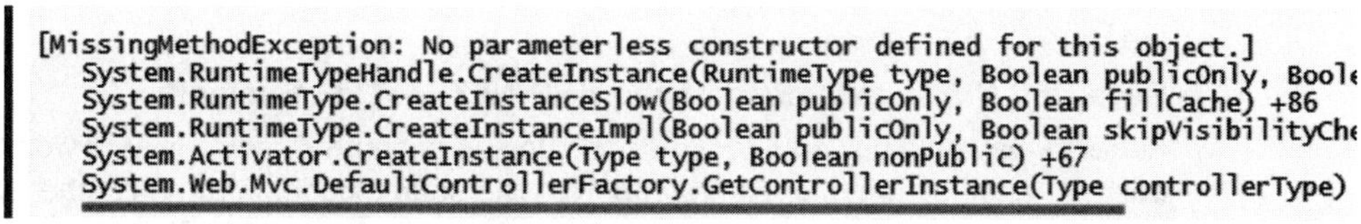

```
[MissingMethodException: No parameterless constructor defined for this object.]
   System.RuntimeTypeHandle.CreateInstance(RuntimeType type, Boolean publicOnly, Boole
   System.RuntimeType.CreateInstanceSlow(Boolean publicOnly, Boolean fillCache) +86
   System.RuntimeType.CreateInstanceImpl(Boolean publicOnly, Boolean skipVisibilityChe
   System.Activator.CreateInstance(Type type, Boolean nonPublic) +67
   System.Web.Mvc.DefaultControllerFactory.GetControllerInstance(Type controllerType)
```

Figure 6.4 Examination of the stack trace shows us the culprit.

Reflector comes to the rescue here. Using Reflector, we can pry open the assembly and take a look at what `DefaultControllerFactory` is doing that causes the error, as shown in figure 6.5.

As you can see in figure 6.5, `Activator.CreateInstance` is being used to create the controller. This *requires* a parameter-less constructor. If we could somehow tell the `ControllerBuilder` to let us create the controller, we could pass in the company object ourselves. Well, guess what? We can.

The `ControllerBuilder` is a singleton class that allows you to specify which `IControllerFactory` to use when instantiating controllers. To wire up your custom `IControllerFactory`, type the following code in the `Application_Start` event:

```
ControllerBuilder.Current.SetControllerFactory(
    typeof(CompanyControllerFactory));
```

The `CompanyControllerFactory` is our custom class. Like most extension points in the ASP.NET MVC Framework, it is based on an interface, as shown in listing 6.12.

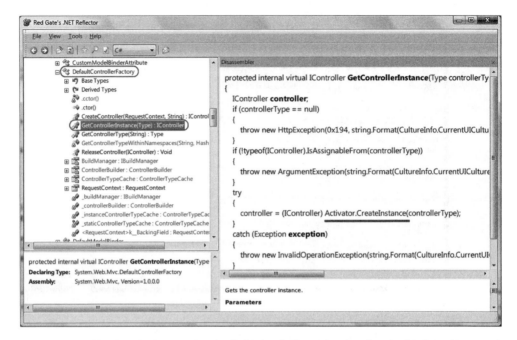

Figure 6.5   Digging into the framework using Reflector. Reflector is a free download at http://www.red-gate.com/reflector.

Browsing the source code of the ASP.NET MVC Framework

Reflector can be a powerful tool, as you can see in figure 6.5; however, it won't retain original variable names or comments from the source code. Fortunately the ASP.NET team released the source code for this framework (under the MS-PL license), and you can download it to browse around and see how it is implemented. Often there are helpful comments that can give you insights and aid your learning of the framework.

It is unfortunate that we even *need* to see the source to understand how to extend the framework, but thankfully the source is available to us.

You can download the source code directly from http://asp.net/mvc. Alternatively, you can use the Microsoft Reference Symbol Servers to automatically step into and debug code built into the framework. That's right, you can actually debug .NET Framework code! In May 2009 the ASP.NET MVC source code was added to this reference. For more details, visit the Microsoft Reference Source Code Center at http://refer-encesource.microsoft.com/ .

Listing 6.12   `ControllerFactory` to build `CompanyController`-based controllers

```
public class CompanyControllerFactory : IControllerFactory
{
    private readonly ICompanyService _companyService;
```

```
public CompanyControllerFactory() :
    this(ServiceLocator.Resolve<ICompanyService>())
{
}

public CompanyControllerFactory(ICompanyService companyService)     ❶
{
    _companyService = companyService;
}

public IController CreateController(RequestContext context,
    Type controllerType)
{
    if (controllerType.IsSubclassOf(typeof (CompanyControllerBase)))
    {
        string companyKey =
          context.HttpContext.Request.QueryString["company"];          ❷

        Company company = _companyService.FindCompany(companyKey);      ❸

        if (company == null)                                            ❹
            context.HttpContext.Response.Redirect("~/login");

        return (IController) Activator.CreateInstance(      ❺
            controllerType, company);
    }

    return (IController) Activator.CreateInstance(controllerType);      ❻
}

public IController CreateController(RequestContext context,
    string controllerName)
{
    string fullControllerName = "MvcApplication.Controllers."
                                 + controllerName + "Controller";
    var controllerType = Type.GetType(fullControllerName, false, true);
    return CreateController(context, controllerType);

}

public void ReleaseController(IController controller)
{
    if(controller is IDisposable)
        ((IDisposable)controller).Dispose();
}
}
```

The CompanyControllerFactory utilizes the ICompanyService to retrieve the company based on the company key ❸, which we can guarantee exists in the querystring ❷. If the company key was valid and a company object was returned, we would pass this in the constructor to the controller in question ❺ and we'd be done. If the specified company does not exist then the user will be redirected to the login page ❹.

Obviously your LoginController must *not* inherit from CompanyControllerBase or you'll be in an infinite redirect loop. Any controller class that doesn't inherit from the base class will be built assuming no constructor arguments ❻.

You might have noticed that the ControllerFactory itself accepted an ICompanyService in its constructor ❶. This is called IoC (or dependency injection), and it is a technique used often to decouple systems and make them more testable. IoC containers are tools that allow you to declare your dependencies, and request to resolve them at runtime. If you aren't familiar with IoC, read up on http://martinfowler.com/articles/injection.html. We'll utilize this technique in our next example.

NOTE   The `CompanyControllerFactory` has two constructors, one that accepts an instance of `ICompanyService` and one that does not. We can use the detailed constructor for testing, and the framework will use the default constructor. When you cannot control the creation of the class, but you still want to allow your dependencies to be injected, you can use the Service Locator pattern, as we have here. A .NET implementation of Service Locator is available at http://www.codeplex.com/CommonServiceLocator. It works in conjunction with a number of popular DI frameworks. You will learn more about dependency injection later in this chapter.

6.2.2   *Leveraging IoC for your controllers*

Earlier we added support for injecting a single custom object into the controllers to make our lives easier. That technique, although useful for this scenario, breaks down once you add a second type of object, then a third, and so on. If we leverage an IoC container, our controllers will be more flexibile.

Within a week of the first CTP of ASP.NET MVC, community members added support for "The Big 3" inversion of control containers: Spring.NET, Castle Windsor, and StructureMap. (They are called *The Big 3* because they were the three most widely used at the time.) Since then, others such as Unity have been implemented. Let's take a look at how a couple of these are implemented.

A CASTLE WINDSOR CONTROLLERFACTORY

The Castle Project is a collection of useful frameworks and components used to build applications. Castle Windsor is just a small part of this project. You can configure Windsor to store the types of objects you want to build either in an XML configuration file or in a code file. I prefer to configure it with code, because it is far less verbose, and you get the added benefit of IntelliSense.

To add Windsor to your application, download the binaries from http://castle-project.org and reference these assemblies in your project:

- Castle.Core
- Castle.MicroKernel
- Castle.DynamicProxy2
- Castle.Windsor

For this example, let's assume that we have a controller that lists sessions for a conference. Our `SessionsController` will take an implementation of `IConferenceRepository` to get the conference in question, as shown in listing 6.13.

Listing 6.13 A controller that has a dependency listed in the constructor

```
public class SessionsController : Controller
{
    private readonly IConferenceRepository _conferenceRepository;

    public SessionsController(                              Dependencies passed
         IConferenceRepository conferenceRepository)        through constructor
    {
        _conferenceRepository = conferenceRepository;
    }

    public ActionResult Index(string conferenceKey)
    {
        var conf = _conferenceRepository.GetConference(conferenceKey);
        var sessions = conf.GetSessions();
        return View(sessions);
    }

}
```

NOTE When we ask for dependencies in the constructor, we call it *constructor injection*. There is another technique called *property injection* but it is not as apparent that these components are *required* for the object to do its job. Windsor can do both, but constructor injection is recommended.

In Windsor, you store objects (or types) in a *container*. These can be requested later by type (or by interface) and Windsor will do the dirty work of arranging the dependency chain to build up a fully constructed object and hand it to you. So if your dependency has dependencies, and those have more dependencies, Windsor wires it all up for you. The first thing we need to do is register all the types we are going to use in the container. For starters, all of the controllers need to be added, because Windsor will be building them for us. Listing 6.14 shows this in detail.

Listing 6.14 Initializing Windsor

```
private void InitializeWindsor()              Called by
{                                             Application_Start
    _container = new WindsorContainer();

                                                            Ensure
    _container.AddComponentLifeStyle<SessionsController>(   controllers
                             LifestyleType.Transient);      are Transient

    _container
       .AddComponent<IConferenceRepository, ConferenceRepository>();

}                                             Add other components
```

It can be tedious to manually add each controller, so you might consider using the Windsor registration extension methods in MvcContrib, or consider adding a snippet like this to automatically add all of your controllers:

```
var assemblyTypes = typeof(SessionsController).Assembly.GetTypes();
foreach(var controllerType in
    assemblyTypes.Where(t=>typeof(IController).IsAssignableFrom(t)))
```

```
{
    container.AddComponentLifeStyle(controllerType.Name.ToLower(),
        controllerType, LifestyleType.Transient);
}
```

Now that Windsor is wired up, we need to create a simple controller factory that will use Windsor to build our controllers, as shown in listing 6.15.

Listing 6.15   A simplified controller factory for Windsor

```
using System;
using System.Web;
using System.Web.Mvc;
using System.Web.Routing;
using Castle.MicroKernel;
using Castle.Windsor;

public class MyWindsorControllerFactory : IControllerFactory
{
    private readonly IWindsorContainer _container;

    public MyWindsorControllerFactory(IWindsorContainer container)
    {
        _container = container;
    }

    public IController CreateController(RequestContext requestContext,
        string controllerName)
    {
        try
        {
            controllerName = controllerName.ToLower() + "controller";   ❶
            var controller =
                _container.Resolve<IController>(controllerName);        ❷
            return controller;
        }
        catch (ComponentNotFoundException)
        {
            throw new HttpException(
                404, "The controller was not found");                  ❸
        }
    }

    public void ReleaseController(IController controller)               ❹
    {
        _container.Release(controller);
    }
}
```

The class implements the `IControllerFactory` interface, which requires two methods: `CreateController` and `ReleaseController`. Each of these is trivial; we simply ask the container to *resolve* our type ❷. The name needs to be lowercase and suffixed with "controller" ❶ in order for the key to match what we entered in listing 6.13. If the component is not found in the container, an exception will be thrown. We don't want our users seeing a nasty exception if they type in a bad URL. In this instance, a 404 (Not

Found) error code should be thrown back to the browser ❸. Finally, the `ReleaseCon-troller` method ❹ asks Windsor to dispose of the controller.

Now that we have a controller factory, how do we tell the framework to use it? Place the following code at the bottom of the `InitializeWindsor` method:

```
ControllerBuilder.Current.SetControllerFactory(new
    MyWindsorControllerFactory(_container));
```

From this point on, all our controllers will be built using our new controller factory. This example works, but a more full-featured version is available in MvcContrib along with a handful of others. One of these is the `StructureMapControllerFactory`, which we will examine next.

A STRUCTUREMAP CONTROLLER FACTORY

For this example we will simply leverage the existing work within MvcContrib. You can find the latest releases at http://mvccontrib.org. Better yet, download the source and build it yourself. Reading the source is an excellent learning tool. Assuming you now have the MvcContrib binaries, copy the following files into your project:

- StructureMap.dll
- MvcContrib.dll
- MvcContrib.StructureMap.dll

In StructureMap, you don't have to add the controllers to the container. You can simply request the object, and its dependencies will be fulfilled. Registering other dependencies is as easy as this:

```
StructureMapConfiguration.ForRequestedType<IConferenceRepository>()
    .TheDefaultIsConcreteType<ConferenceRepository>();
```

Next is setting the controller factory to the `StructureMapControllerFactory`, which by now should be obvious:

```
ControllerBuilder.Current.SetControllerFactory(
    new StructureMapControllerFactory());
```

That's all there is to it. We can now access the controller from listing 6.12, and the dependency will be satisfied by StructureMap. I have barely scratched the surface of what Windsor and StructureMap can do, but we can easily see how they satisfy controller dependencies.

Now that you've seen two complete IoC controller factories, others are straightforward. Any IoC controller factory will be so similar that you won't even notice which one you're using. Just declare your dependencies as constructor arguments and everything works. The only thing that changes is the configuration to register the dependencies and the code to manage the container. Understanding and leveraging an IoC container is a great way to decouple your applications and embrace testability.

We've taken a look at how to customize the creation of controllers. Next, we'll see how to gain additional behavior by extending the `Controller` class, given to us by the framework.

6.3   *Extending the controller*

Creating a replacement implementation for `Controller` is straightforward. The only requirement is that you implement the `IController` interface, which has one required method: `Execute`. This gives the implementer ultimate control when deciding how a controller should behave. Microsoft ships with a functional default implementation, but if you need something drastically different, you can roll your own.

You'll rarely have to start from scratch and implement `IController` directly. A lot of work is required to translate a single `Execute` method into something useful. If you don't care for the way actions are invoked, or perhaps don't like the `ActionResult` way of returning objects, you might roll your own `IController` implementation. For more basic modifications you can simply inherit from `Controller` and override the desired method to add or alter behavior.

The `Controller` class, which derives from `ControllerBase`, provides these virtual methods that you can override and handle in inherited classes:

- *ExecuteCore*—The entry point. Everything starts here.
- *HandleUnknownAction*—Called when action cannot be found.
- *OnAuthorization*—Occurs when an authorization filter runs.
- *OnActionExecuting*—Occurs before an action is executed.
- *OnActionExecuted*—Occurs after an action is executed.
- *OnResultExecuting*—Occurs before an `ActionResult` is executed.
- *OnResultExecuted*—Occurs after an `ActionResult` is executed.
- *OnException*—Occurs if an action throws an exception.

In addition, you can override and alter the built-in `ActionResult` helper methods, namely:

- *Content*—Returns a `ContentResult` with the literal content passed in.
- *File*—Returns a `FileResult` with appropriate response headers.
- *JavaScript*—Returns a `JavaScriptResult` that contains JavaScript to be executed on the client.
- *Json*—Returns a `JsonResult` with a JSON serialized object.
- *PartialView*—Returns a `PartialViewResult` that renders a partial.
- *Redirect*—Returns a `RedirectResult` with the given URL.
- *RedirectToAction*—Returns a `RedirectToRouteResult` that redirects to the given action.
- *RedirectToRoute*—Returns a `RedirectToRouteResult` that redirects to the given route.
- *View*—Returns a `ViewResult` object corresponding to the view.

These extension points allow you to intercept and alter behavior at many levels, at each step in the controller pipeline. Next is an example that will show this in action.

6.3.1   *Creating a FormattableController*

Ruby on Rails has a feature that allows actions to be rendered in a variety of formats. A request for /products would render an HTML page to be displayed by the browser. A similar request of /products.xml would call the same action; however the result would be formatted as an XML document. JSON could also be requested with /products.json. This allows you to easily reuse actions for use in AJAX requests, or allows your customers to use your URLs as an API for your application. We are going to walk through creating a controller called FormattableController with this feature.

NOTE   When the formattable controller feature was first introduced in Ruby on Rails, it was designed to help advance the RESTful nature of that framework. (We learned a little bit about REST in chapter 5.) This technique can help support a RESTful architecture by providing different representations for our models.

We added the formattable feature to ASP.NET MVC by subclassing Controller. Let's take AttendeesController from Code Camp Server as an example. We want the Index action to render an HTML document, an XML document, or a JSON object with the attendee data that is passed to the view.

We'll start with the basic action. This returns predefined data; however the real application would probably get items from the database, as shown in listing 6.16.

> **Listing 6.16   A simple action that returns Attendees to the view**

```
public ActionResult Index()
{
    var attendees = new[] {
        new Attendee { Name="Fred Flinstone",
            City = "Bedrock", Comments = "yabba dabba doo",
            Registered = DateTime.Parse("Mar 03 1942")},
        new Attendee { Name="Charlie Chaplin",
            City="Manhattan", Comments=".....",
            Registered=DateTime.Parse("Jul 18 1918")},
        new Attendee { Name="John Smith",
            City="Tulsa, OK", Comments="howdy",
            Registered=DateTime.Parse("Apr 7 1999")}
    };

    return View(attendees);
}
```

This action renders a simple list of attendees, as you can see in figure 6.6. The result contains an entire HTML document, with the content portion formatted as a table according to our view template.

What if we wanted to allow a separate application to retrieve the current list of attendees from our site? It would be easier for that application to consume XML or JSON instead of screen-scraping the HTML for the needed data.

Let's create a new route that understands formats.

Figure 6.6   Our action renders a simple HTML table with the attendee listing.

```
//global.asax
routes.MapRoute("Format", "{controller}/{action}.{format}/{id}",
    new {id = ""});
```

This route will match /attendees/index.xml. When this happens, we will have a route value called format that we can use in the controllers. Armed with this, we can create a base class that can handle the various formats that we allow. Listing 6.17 shows our new base controller in detail.

Listing 6.17   A base controller that understands formats

```
public abstract class FormattableController : Controller
{
    private static readonly string[] ValidFormats =
        new[] {"xml", "html", "json"};
    protected string Format { get; set; }

    protected override void OnActionExecuting(                         ❶
                          ActionExecutingContext filterContext)
    {
        base.OnActionExecuting(filterContext);

        var routeValues = filterContext.RouteData.Values;
        var formatKey = "format";
        if(routeValues.ContainsKey(formatKey))
        {
            string requestedFormat =
                routeValues[formatKey].ToString().ToLower();
            if (Array.Exists(ValidFormats, x => x == requestedFormat))   ❷
            {
                Format = requestedFormat;
```

```
                return;
            }
        }

        Format = "html";
    }
}
```

In this class we override the `OnActionExecuting` method ❶ to intercept the call and check to see if we have a format specified in the route values. We also ensure that the format matches one of the formats that we intend to handle ❷. The `FormatResult` method (listing 6.18) will be called from the actions instead of the other `Action-Result` methods.

Listing 6.18   The `FormatResult` method returns the correct `ActionResult`

```
protected ActionResult FormatResult(object viewModel)
{
    switch(Format)
    {
        case "html" : return View(viewModel);
        case "xml": return new XmlResult(viewModel);        ❶
        case "json": return Json(viewModel);                ❷
        default:
            throw new FormatException(
                string.Format("Cannot handle the requested format '{0}'",
                Format));
    }
}
```

For each supported type, we simply return the correct `ActionResult` derivative that handles the type. The `XmlResult` class comes from MvcContrib ❶, which serializes the object into XML. The `Json` method returns a `JsonResult` ❷ and automatically serializes the object into JSON format. If there were other formats, we could add them to this class and return the appropriate `ActionResult` instance.

Now we can inherit the `AttendeesController` from `FormattableController` and change the return call from listing 6.16 to utilize the new `FormatResult` method. Listing 6.19 demonstrates these changes (in bold).

Listing 6.19   Changing the base class using the new `FormattableController`

```
public class AttendeesController : FormattableController
{
    public ActionResult Index()
    {
        var attendees = new[] {
            new Attendee { Name="Fred Flinstone",
                City = "Bedrock", Comments = "yabba dabba doo",
                Registered = DateTime.Parse("Mar 03 1942")},
            new Attendee { Name="Charlie Chaplin",
                City="Manhattan", Comments=".....",
                Registered=DateTime.Parse("Jul 18 1918")},
```

```
        new Attendee { Name="John Smith",
            City="Tulsa, OK", Comments="howdy",
            Registered=DateTime.Parse("Apr 7 1999")}
    };

    return FormatResult(attendees);
}
}
```

We can try the same URL again to make sure the HTML result still renders (and it does). We can also try /attendees/index.xml (figure 6.7) and /attendees/index.json (figure 6.8) to verify the new formats work!

Figure 6.7   Requesting with an .xml extension gives us an XML document with the data.

NOTE   *What is JSON?*   JSON is a format that is easily consumed via JavaScript. If you are not familiar with the JSON format, refer to chapter 9 for details.

Our simple example demonstrated some of the extension points available to controllers. Next up, we will see how to apply functionality to a single action across many controllers. These extension points are called *action filters*.

6.3.2   *Working with action filters*

Action filters are typically attributes that you can decorate on an action (or controller) that execute before the action is called. Because action filters are backed by interfaces, you can implement them as simple classes as well. Just as we wrote code to capture the format for a request, we can write action filters that handle the events thrown by the controller. Examples of built-in action filters are the following:

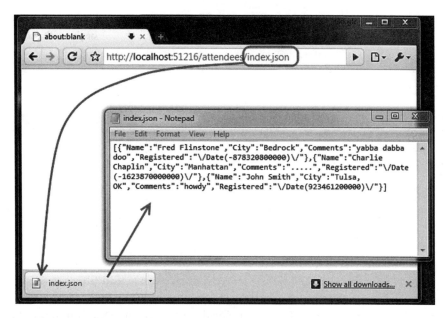

Figure 6.8   Requesting with a .json extension yields a JSON object.

- *[Authorize]*—Allows you to secure an action to a set of roles/users
- *[HandleError]*—Captures exceptions thrown and allows you to display friendly error pages
- *[OutputCache]*—Caches the output of the action for future requests
- *[AcceptVerbs]*—Limits the HTTP verbs that are allowed to call the action

Creating your own action filters is easy. You simply inherit from ActionFilterAttribute and override the methods provided.

Let's create a simple action filter. In a login page, you usually want to utilize SSL to protect the user's credentials from being sent in plaintext across a network. Often sites will *require* certain URLs to be accessed with SSL. We can accomplish this with a simple action filter that redirects to the SSL URL. You can set the Result property on the ActionExecutingContext or use the HttpContext directly. Listing 6.20 has the action filter, while its usage is shown in listing 6.21.

Listing 6.20   A custom action filter to require SSL for an action

```
[AttributeUsage(AttributeTargets.Method | AttributeTargets.Class)]
public class RequireSSLAttribute : ActionFilterAttribute
{
    public override void OnActionExecuting(
        ActionExecutingContext filterContext)
    {
        var requestUri = filterContext.HttpContext.Request.Url;
        if(requestUri.Scheme == "http")
        {
```

```
        string url = requestUri.ToString()          │ Ensure URL
                .Replace("http://", "https://");     │ begins with https

        filterContext.HttpContext.Response.Redirect(url);
    }
  }
}
```

Listing 6.21   Using the `RequireSSL` action filter

```
[RequireSSL]
public class LoginController : Controller
{
    public ActionResult Index()
    {
        return View();
    }
}
```

The action filter is placed on the class element when you want all actions in the controller to have the attribute. To be selective, place the action filter on the methods in question. Now, a request for /login will result in an HTTP 302 redirect to the equivalent https:// URL. The HTTP headers for this example are shown in figure 6.9.

Figure 6.9   Requesting /login from http:// with a `RequireSSL` action filter yields a redirect to https://.

Action filters provide an easy way to share common functionality across controllers without bloating a controller base class with unrelated functionality.

NOTE   The action filter classes are created by the `ControllerActionInvoker` calling the `ReflectedActionDescriptor`, which constructs the filter using a default (no-arg) constructor. To inject dependencies in your action filters, you have a couple of options. You can use the Service Locator pattern, as we saw earlier, or you can write your own `IActionInvoker` (or derive from `ControllerActionInvoker`) that understands how to request the filters from the container. With Windsor (or other IoC frameworks) you register an implementation for `IActionInvoker` in the container and it will be set (via property injection) on all controller instances. For most people, using a service locator will be a quicker solution.

Now that we have seen how to extend controllers, we can examine how to customize the way views are rendered.

6.4   *Creating a custom view engine*

Most of the samples in this section use the default, `WebFormViewEngine`. Indeed it is usually a smart choice for benefits it provides:

- Familiar experience
- Strongly typed
- IntelliSense
- Compiled form

Why would you want anything else? At times the strong typing and code block syntax can get in your way. Visual Studio statement completion and autocode formatting tend to make code blocks inside views look awkward. In C# we prefer curly braces on their own line. In a view, it is easier to read if the open curly brace is on the same line. In Visual Studio 2008 you cannot have two separate rules for code formatting. What you choose for your code will also affect your views.

In addition, the `WebFormViewEngine` templates contain excessive line noise to accomplish something simple (we'll see a great example in a bit). Often views can be expressed much more concisely with a template syntax like NVelocity. Those who have used the Castle Monorail framework might also prefer Brail as a template language. Both of these exist (along with others) in MvcContrib.

NOTE   *NVelocity* NVelocity is a port of the Apache Velocity project. You can read more about NVelocity at http://nvelocity.sourceforge.net.

Brail Brail is a template language that uses Boo, which is a dynamic CLS-compliant language for .NET. Read more about Brail at the Monorail website here: http://www.castleproject.org/MonoRail/documentation/trunk/viewengines/brail/index.html.

Details about Boo are located at http://boo.codehaus.org.

Consider the code in listing 6.22.

Listing 6.22   A `WebFormViewEngine` user control to display login info

```
<%@ Control Language="C#" Inherits="System.Web.Mvc.ViewUserControl" %>
<%
    if (Request.IsAuthenticated) {
%>
```

```
        Welcome <b><%= Html.Encode(Page.User.Identity.Name) %></b>!
        [ <%= Html.ActionLink("Log Off", "LogOff", "Account") %> ]
<%
    }
    else
    {
%>
        [ <%= Html.ActionLink("Log On", "LogOn", "Account") %> ]
<%
    }
%>
```

This is taken from the default project template LoginUserControl.ascx, which is located in the Shared folder. There is lots of "gunk" here (to appease the compiler) that takes away from the actual content being displayed. Now look at the same thing, implemented with NVelocity (listing 6.23).

> **Listing 6.23   Showing the same login status with NVelocity syntax**

```
#if($isAuthenticated)
  Welcome <b>$html.encode($httpcontext.user.identity.name)</b>!
  [ $html.actionlink("Log Off", "LogOff", "Account") ]
#else
  [ $html.actionlink("Log On", "LogOn", "Account") ]
#end
```

This is much easier to write and read, but NVelocity has drawbacks. One drawback is the limited number of helper methods available on the view. Most helper methods are extension methods on `HtmlHelper`, so they don't come automatically. MvcContrib contains a facility for adding new `HtmlHelper` extension types to get around this limitation. In addition, NVelocity does not automatically have Visual Studio integration for IntelliSense, compile-time checking of views, or refactoring. If these drawbacks are too significant to ignore, you can revert to the `WebFormViewEngine`. If you like easy-to-write/read, concise view code, then read on. We'll discover how to write a trivial (and quite naïve) view engine.

There are two main components of a view engine. The `IViewEngine` implementation finds and builds an appropriate `IView` implementation. The latter usually does the heavy lifting. Our `SimpleViewEngine` will simply find the template on disk (the template could be from anywhere) and construct a `SimpleView` to return. The `SimpleView` will interpret the template, along with `ViewData`, and emit the result to the response stream, as shown in listing 6.24.

> **Listing 6.24   A simple `IViewEngine` implementation**

```
public class SimpleViewEngine : IViewEngine
{
    public ViewEngineResult FindPartialView(
        ControllerContext controllerContext, string partialViewName,
        bool useCache)
    {
```

```
            return FindView(controllerContext, partialViewName);
    }
    public ViewEngineResult FindView(ControllerContext controllerContext,
        string viewName, string masterName, bool useCache)
    {
        return FindView(controllerContext, viewName);
    }
    private ViewEngineResult FindView(ControllerContext controllerContext,
        string partialViewName)
    {
        var controllerName = controllerContext.Controller.GetType().Name
            .Replace("Controller", "");
        var server = controllerContext.HttpContext.Server;
        var extension = "st";

        string pathPattern = string.Format("~/Views/{{0}}/{0}.{1}",
                                            partialViewName, extension);
        var paths = new[] {
                            string.Format(pathPattern, controllerName),
                            string.Format(pathPattern, "Shared")
                          };
        foreach(var path in paths)
        {
            if(File.Exists(server.MapPath(path)))
                return new ViewEngineResult(
                    new SimpleView(server.MapPath(path)), this);
        }

        return new ViewEngineResult(paths);
    }
    public void ReleaseView(ControllerContext controllerContext,
        IView view)
    {
        if(view is IDisposable)
            ((IDisposable)view).Dispose();
    }
}
```

◁ Same logic for partial views

◁ Construct view locations

◁ Build SimpleView and return

◁ Report where we looked

The responsibility of the view engine is to locate the view (we chose to look on disk) and construct an appropriate view instance for return. The view we created is shown in listing 6.25.

Listing 6.25   A simple view

```
public class SimpleView : IView
{
    private readonly string _file;

    public SimpleView(string file)
    {
        _file = file;
    }

    public void Render(ViewContext viewContext, TextWriter writer)
    {
```

```
    Regex propertyPattern = new Regex(@"\$\[(?<property>[^\]]+)\]");    ◁─┐
    string fileContents = File.ReadAllText(_file);
    foreach(Match match in propertyPattern.Matches(fileContents))
    {
        var property = match.Groups["property"].Value;
        var value = viewContext.ViewData[property].ToString();
        fileContents = fileContents.Replace(match.Value, value);
    }                                                          Matches
    writer.Write(fileContents);                              $[variable]
    }                                                           format
}
```

We configure our view engine in the `Application_Start` event like this:

```
ViewEngines.Engines.Add(new SimpleViewEngine());
```

NOTE Notice that `Engines` is a collection, so you can have multiple view engines in the same application. The collection has order, so the first view engine to find a matching view will be rendered.

Our naïve view simply finds properties in the template with the format `$[property-Name]`. Each of these is matched with an element in `ViewData` and replaced on the view. Finally the result is written to the `TextWriter`. This view engine is not very usable, because we don't have any conditional branching, loops, child templates, or support for complex types. It does show the basic steps required for any custom view engine implementation. A sample view is shown in listing 6.26, and the rendered output is displayed in figure 6.10.

Listing 6.26   A simple template (index.st)

```
<html>
<head>
</head>
<body>
    <h1>Awesome view!</h1>
    <p>$[Message]</p>
    <p>This was rendered at $[Time]</p>
</body>
</html>
```

One other aspect of our example is flawed —the way we are sending the content to the `TextWriter`. We do it all in one chunk. To take advantage of buffering it is important to render the content *as you process it.* This adds significant complexity to the rendering logic. For the sake of brevity we have shown a simplified version here.

Having flexibility to choose different view engines is a wonderful property of the ASP.NET MVC Framework. Leveraging a view engine that fits your development

Figure 6.10   **A rendered template based on the simple view engine**

style and leads to less friction will help you be more productive as a developer. One major area of ASP.NET MVC customization remains: customizing some of the Visual Studio tooling around the framework.

6.5 Customizing Visual Studio for ASP.NET MVC

As you saw earlier, specific tooling within Visual Studio makes building ASP.NET MVC applications faster. We will look at two quick ways of customizing these tools.

6.5.1 Creating custom T4 templates

If you right-click on an action, you'll see an option to open the Add View dialog, shown in figure 6.11. In this dialog, you can choose the name of the view, the view model type, and the master page. If you select a strongly typed view, you have the option of choosing an automatic view template. The options are Empty, List, Create, Details, and Delete. Figure 6.11 shows us selecting Create for our view content and `Conference` for our view model.

The options in the View Content dropdown list are T4 templates that are located in

```
C:\Program Files\Microsoft Visual Studio 9.0\Common7\IDE\ItemTemplates\
CSharp\Web\MVC\CodeTemplates\AddView
```

NOTE T4 templates are a little-known feature of Visual Studio. They are code generation template processors built into Visual Studio. T4 templates allow you to customize how files are generated using a familiar syntax.

If we press Add, we're given a complete form, generated for us by Visual Studio using the default template. Our view now looks like listing 6.27.

Figure 6.11 The Add View dialog allows you to autogenerate scaffolding for your model.

Listing 6.27 The autogenerated `Create` view based on the `Conference` object

```
<h2>Details</h2>

<%= Html.ValidationSummary("Create was unsuccessful. Please correct the
➡    errors and try again.") %>

<% using (Html.BeginForm()) {%>

    <fieldset>
        <legend>Fields</legend>
        <p>
            <label for="Name">Name:</label>
            <%= Html.TextBox("Name") %>
            <%= Html.ValidationMessage("Name", "*") %>
        </p>
        <p>
            <label for="Description">Description:</label>
            <%= Html.TextBox("Description") %>
            <%= Html.ValidationMessage("Description", "*") %>
        </p>
        <p>
            <label for="StartDate">StartDate:</label>
            <%= Html.TextBox("StartDate") %>
            <%= Html.ValidationMessage("StartDate", "*") %>
        </p>
        <p>
            <label for="EndDate">EndDate:</label>
            <%= Html.TextBox("EndDate") %>
            <%= Html.ValidationMessage("EndDate", "*") %>
        </p>
        <p>
            <input type="submit" value="Create" />
        </p>
    </fieldset>

<% } %>

<div>
    <%=Html.ActionLink("Back to List", "Index") %>
</div>
```

As you can see, lots of code is generated for us. It contains a basic form, with fields corresponding to the object, complete with validation, Submit button, and back link. This can get us started building the application quickly. Of course this is just a starting point, and you're free to customize it from here. This template is static, and you can create a different, application-specific template for the `Create` view.

Add a folder in your project called CodeTemplates. Into this folder, copy the contents of the default template folder. You can create subfolders corresponding to the different types of templates (figure 6.12).

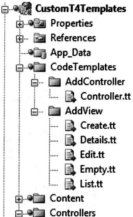

Figure 6.12 Copy the templates into your project under a CodeTemplates folder to customize them.

These templates will be effective for the current project only. You are free to alter the templates here for your project. You can also add more items to this list. Adding another .tt file in this folder will enable it for selection in the Add View dialog, as show in figure 6.13.

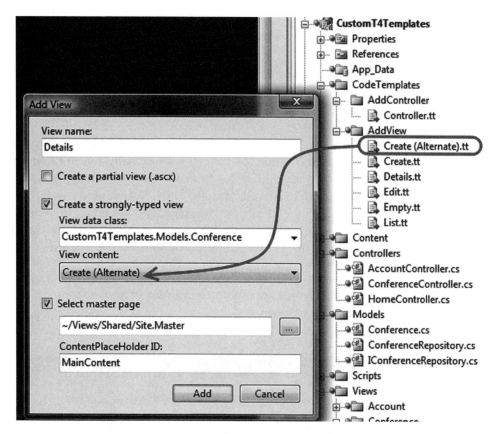

Figure 6.13   **Adding new template files in the Add View folder enables them for selection in the Add View dialog.**

The templates themselves are fairly complex. Here is an excerpt from the `Controller.tt` template:

```
<#@ template language="C#" HostSpecific="True" #>
<#@ output extension="cs" #>
<#
MvcTextTemplateHost mvcHost = (MvcTextTemplateHost)(Host);
#>
using System;
using System.Collections.Generic;
using System.Linq;
using System.Web;
using System.Web.Mvc;
```

```
using System.Web.Mvc.Ajax;

namespace <#= mvcHost.NameSpace #>
{
    public class <#= mvcHost.ItemName #> : Controller
    {
        //
        // GET: /<#= mvcHost.ControllerRootName #>/

    ...... more ....
```

As you can see, code blocks are denoted by <# #> blocks. Each template has a Host property that contains basic context information. For MVC templates, this is actually of type MvcTextTemplateHost, so we can see here that the template is casting the Host property and storing it in a variable called mvcHost for use later in the template.

T4 templates can be a little intimidating but you can do a lot of things with them. If you are interested in customizing the templates, download Visual T4 Editor for Visual Studio 2008 Community Edition (free) from Clarius Consulting. This will give you syntax highlighting, which is really helpful when you find yourself writing code that writes code! The tool can be downloaded at http://www.visualt4.com/downloads.html. To learn more about T4 template syntax and the ASP.NET MVC integration, check out http://blogs.msdn.com/webdevtools/archive/2009/01/29/t4-templates-a-quick-start-guide-for-asp-net-mvc-developers.aspx.

6.5.2 *Adding a custom test project template to the new project wizard*

When you first create an ASP.NET MVC project, you're eventually greeted with the dialog shown in figure 6.14:

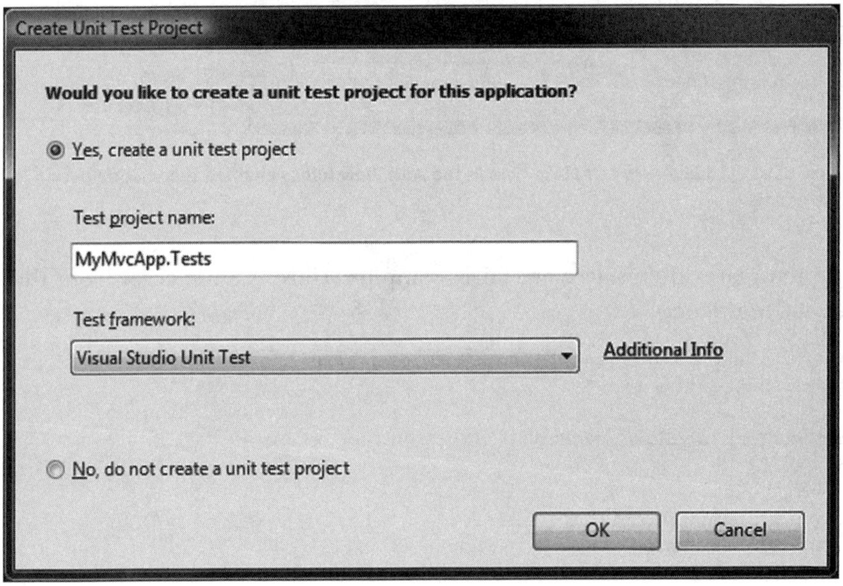

Figure 6.14 When you create a new project, you are asked if you want to create a unit test project.

Unfortunately, the only available test framework that is provided out of the box is the Visual Studio Unit Test framework. Developers who are experienced with testing will no doubt prefer NUnit, MbUnit, or xUnit.NET. There is hope! You can add your framework of choice to this dialog box (and simultaneously implement a custom project template).

The first step is to create a project that represents what you want when you create new ASP.NET MVC applications with the test project included. Make sure all third-party references (such as NUnit, Rhino Mocks) are set to Copy Local. Then go to File > Export Template. Follow the wizard here, which will result in a single zip file. Copy this zip file to

```
C:\Program Files\Microsoft Visual Studio\9.0\Common7\IDE\ProjectTemplates\CSharp\Test
```

(If you're running on a 64-bit machine, then adjust the path to `C:\Program Files (x86)` accordingly). Now that you've got the template in the right place, close all instances of Visual Studio, open up the Visual Studio 2008 Command Prompt (as Administrator if UAC is enabled), and run

```
devenv /installvstemplates
```

This will take a few seconds. Now that you have a project template installed into Visual Studio, open `regedit` and navigate to

```
HKEY_LOCAL_MACHINE\Software\Microsoft\VisualStudio\9.0\MVC\
    TestProjectTemplates
```

Here you'll find the default Visual Studio Unit Test key. To create a custom entry, make a new key here, and add the following `String` values:

- *Package*—Leave blank unless you have a custom Visual Studio package GUID to register here.
- *Path*—Usually `CSharp\Test`.
- *TestFrameworkName*—The name that you want to appear in the Unit Test Framework dropdown.
- *AdditionalInfo*—A URL that provides the user more information about your framework or template. When the user clicks on Additional Info, the browser will navigate to this URL.
- *Template*—The name of the zip file that contains the template.

Figure 6.15 shows a new template installed in this location.

NOTE On 64-bit machines–like the one we are using–the registry path is slightly different (...`SOFTWARE\Wow6432Node\Microsoft`...). In addition, the Program Files path is actually `C:\Program Files (x86)\`. Be sure to adjust accordingly for your system as shown in figure 6.15.

With all of this in place, we can launch Visual Studio, create a new ASP.NET MVC Web Application project, and be greeted with the message shown in figure 6.16.

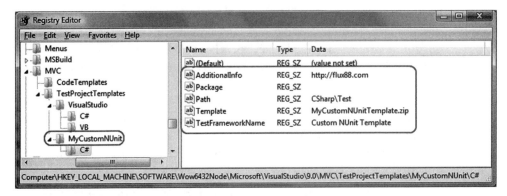

Figure 6.15   Adding a registry entry for a new custom test project template. Note that this registry path is for 64-bit machines.

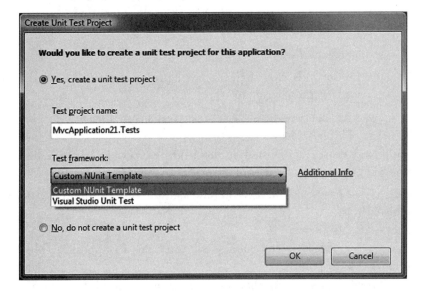

Figure 6.16   Our new test template is now available in the Create Unit Test Project dialog box.

6.6   *Summary*

In this chapter, you have seen some of the extension points in the ASP.NET MVC Framework. You learned how to create a custom IRouteHandler, to add behavior surrounding the life of MVC requests. You learned how to create custom base controllers to encapsulate and reuse functionality. You also learned how to leverage dependency injection and custom controller factories for building these controllers. To accommodate cross-controller concerns, you learned how to use attributes to decorate actions with custom behaviors. We implemented a naïve view engine to demonstrate the moving parts, and also discovered how to customize Visual Studio to evolve with you as you adopt new styles for developing applications.

Hopefully you noticed how easy it was to extend the framework. Because most objects that you interact with are either interfaces or abstract base classes, the framework allows you to completely (or almost completely) substitute behavior for your own. At this level of flexibility the ASP.NET MVC Framework shines. Running parallel to the ASP.NET MVC project is the open source project called MvcContrib (http://mvccontrib.org). This is the playground for customizations and extensions that people find useful. Your authors recommend that you examine MvcContrib regularly for extensions that might be useful to you (and contribute back if they would be useful to others!).

The next chapter will use some of these extension points and cover tools and techniques for letting the framework scale in the face of complex web applications.

Scaling the architecture
for complex sites

7

This chapter covers

- Taming large controller actions
- Leveraging view helpers
- Using partials
- Creating components
- Applying action filters
- Organizing controllers into areas

Most applications we write grow beyond their originally intended use. Often we see quick-and-dirty, low-quality demos graduate directly to production. These applications have to be maintained, and likely by you (or me). Complexity is inevitable, but we can follow good design principles to keep the applications maintainable.

How can we ensure that we are creating maintainable solutions in the face of complexity? One key principle to follow is the single responsibility principle (SRP). This principle states that a piece of code should only have one reason to change. In this chapter we will visit some of the areas that often grow out of control in sites of any measurable size. The first is controller actions.

7.1   *Taming large controller actions*

We're all guilty of it. Given a place to put our code, we do just that: put code in a file. And it grows. *And grows.* Pretty soon we're staring at single methods that span the entire viewable region. For starters, we should be able to read the entire action on a single screen. No, I don't mean wrap the offending code in a #region block and hide it. (Yes, your authors have seen this too). We need to identify the areas that belong in other classes and extract them.

An example will surely help. In the context of Code Camp Server, let's say you wanted to provide a facility for first-time installers to set up their administrator accounts automatically. The workflow would be like figure 7.1.

The first time a user installs Code Camp Server, no users will be present in the system. So when they request /admin and it redirects to /login, we can provide a better first-time install experience by allowing the user to create an admin account.

The login action checks to see if any users have been set up in the system. If not, then it prompts the user to create a new administrator account. When the user submits this form, it submits to the CreateAdminAccount action. Now of course we don't want random blokes to submit fake HTTP POSTS to this action, so we protect it by verifying that there are still no users in the system before proceeding.

With a general idea of what we want, we open up LoginController.cs and write the action shown in listing 7.1:

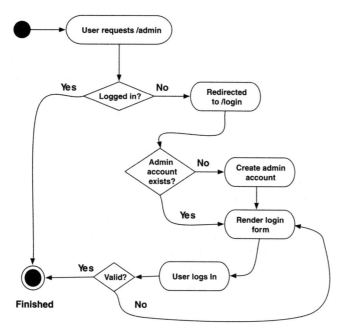

Figure 7.1
Workflow for creating the first administrator account

Listing 7.1   The `CreateAdminAccount` action

```
public ActionResult CreateAdminAccount(string firstName, string
    lastName, string email, string password, string passwordConfirm)
{
    if (GetNumberOfUsers() > 0)        ❶
    {
        throw new SecurityException(@"This action is only valid when
            there are no registered users in the system.");
    }

    if (string.IsNullOrEmpty(email)                  ❷
        || string.IsNullOrEmpty(password))
    {
        TempData["error"] = "Email and Password are required.";
        return RedirectToAction("index");
    }

    if (password != passwordConfirm)        ❸
    {
        TempData["error"] = "Passwords must match";
        return RedirectToAction("index");
    }

    Person admin = new Person(firstName, lastName, "");
    admin.PasswordSalt = _crypto.CreateSalt();
    admin.Password = _crypto.HashPassword(password,
        admin.PasswordSalt);                              ❹
    admin.IsAdministrator = true;

    _personRepository.Save(admin);

    return RedirectToAction("index");
}
```

That's a lot of code for one method. First it's checking to verify that there are still no users in the system ❶ (to prevent this action from being called once users have been defined). Then it's validating the presence of the fields ❷ and that the password and confirmation password match ❸. Finally the admin account is created and saved to the database ❹. In this code the authentication cookie is not being set, so it is assumed that the user would have to fill out the *actual* login form after this action was completed. (Please excuse our lack of attention to usability in this example.)

How can we get this controller under control? (Sorry for the pun.) For starters we can identify that we have three calls to return `RedirectToAction("index")`. No matter what, the user will end up at the index view. We also have a section for validation, where we want to return an error message to the view. Finally, we have the section that creates and saves the `Person` object and marks the `Person` as an administrator.

If we were to extract most of this functionality into another class that has the distinct responsibility of creating an admin account, we could simplify this code. Verifying that the user count is still zero is not really a responsibility of this new create-an-admin class, and thus it should remain a part of the controller. The rest relates directly to creating an admin account, so we can extract this into a method on another class: `CreateAdminAccountTask`. The name of the class indicates its function exactly. The responsibility of any given class should be painfully obvious. If not, your class is probably either named inappropriately or is not fully decomposed into logical units. Listing 7.2 illustrates a refactoring of the code.

The single responsibility principle

The guiding principle behind this refactoring is the SRP. Basically, SRP states that a class should have one and only one responsibility. Another way to look at it is that a class should only have one reason to change. If you find that a class has potential to be changed for nonrelated reasons, the class is probably doing too much. A common violation of SRP is mixing data access with business logic. For example, a Customer probably shouldn't have a `Save()` method.

SRP is a core concept of good object-oriented design, and its application can help your code become more maintainable. SRP is sometimes referred to as *separation of concerns* (SoC). You can read more about SRP/SoC from Bob Martin's excellent article on the subject:

http://www.objectmentor.com/resources/articles/srp.pdf

Listing 7.2   The updated `CreateAdminAccount` action

```
public class LoginController
{
    /* snip */

    ICreateAdminTask _createAdminTask;        <—— Injected via the
                                                   constructor
    /* snip */

    public ActionResult CreateAdminAccount(string firstName,
        string lastName, string email, string password,
        string passwordConfirm)
    {
        if (GetNumberOfUsers() > 0)
        {
            throw new SecurityException(@"This action is only valid
                when there are no registered users in the system.");
        }

        _createAdminTask.Execute(firstName, lastName, email, password,
            passwordConfirm);

        if (!_createAdminTask.Success)
        {
            TempData["error"] = _createAdminTask.ErrorMessage;
            return RedirectToAction("index");
        }

        TempData["message"] =
            "Your admin account was created successfully.";
        return RedirectToAction("index", "home");
    }
}
```

Here we have introduced a new interface (defined in listing 7.3) which is responsible for creating the admin account. This interface encapsulates the validation and operation for our sequence of code. It provides a clear separation of responsibility and a mechanism for returning success/failure along with error messages. The implementation is left as an exercise for the reader.

Listing 7.3   The `ICreateAdminTask` interface

```
public interface ICreateAdminTask
{
    void Execute(string firstName, string lastName, string email, string
        password, string passwordConfirm);
    string ErrorMessage { get; }
    bool Success {get;}
}
```

We have cleaned up the controller and introduced a new, focused interface responsible for performing the task. Both controller and task class remain fully testable. It is important to keep your controllers small, and keep responsibilities clearly defined. This helps tame your controllers. When your controllers seem to be getting unwieldy, look for

- Data access code that could be pushed into a repository.
- Model construction code that could be moved to a custom `ModelBinder`.
- Many repository calls that might be consolidated into a single application service.
- Complex or repetitive validation that could be done inside the domain entity (or a separate class, such as our `ICreateAdminTask` class in listing 7.3).
- Too many exit points. In listing 7.1 we noticed the duplication of the `return RedirectToAction()` calls. Removing duplication is good, but the removal also improved the readability of the code. Having too many exit points from any function is a design smell in general, and that clearly applies to controllers as well.

Now that you've seen how to tackle controller complexity, what about complex views? Surely views can be made more maintainable as well.

7.2   *Whipping views into shape*

When building HTML, your views can get complex. With view helpers, you can simplify your views and reduce duplication and complexity. For larger views, segmenting the view into *partials* can simplify the view, and provide more options for rendering with AJAX. Finally, *components* can be created to completely encapsulate the data retrieval and rendering of a partial.

7.2.1   *Using and creating view helpers*

When you build your first link to an action with dynamic parameters, you'll notice the visual complexity of the code.

```
<a href='/sessions/view/<%= ViewData["id"] %>'>
    <%= ViewData["name"] %>
</a>
```

Yuck. Mixing code blocks within strings is a sure way to give anyone a headache. This is both cumbersome to read and to write, so Microsoft gave us helper methods early on. Here is the same link, written using the Link Helpers:

```
<%= Html.ActionLink((string)ViewData["name"], "view", "sessions",
    new { id = (int)ViewData["id"] }, null) %>
```

This is much easier to write, and has the added effect of adapting to changing routes; but it is still hard to tell exactly what each parameter means, so we prefer another format, using lambda expressions:

```
<%= Html.ActionLink<SessionsController>(c=>c.View((int)ViewData["id"]),
➥   (string)ViewData["name"]) %>
```

This representation makes it a bit more obvious which controller and action are being used. Having type-safe lambda expressions also allows us to refactor. Refactoring tools will detect lambda expressions and include them in refactoring changes. Don't underestimate the power of this.

NOTE *ActionLink<T>* Microsoft decided against including the lambda expression syntax of ActionLink() in the framework. Microsoft did not feel comfortable supporting a method with known performance issues for high-volume sites. The technique has been refined over time and ought to be in ASP.NET MVC version 2. This helper method and others are available in the ASP.NET MVC Futures assembly–Microsoft.Web.Mvc. This is available on CodePlex at http://codeplex.com/aspnet.

Microsoft ships a handful of view helpers for creating forms, HTML tags, and a few other things. There will be a number of opportunities for additional view helpers in your applications that are specific to your domain. If you were Amazon.com, you might create a helper method to create the product rating widget, like this:

```
<%= Html.ProductRatingWidget(product) %>
```

In Code Camp Server, let's say that we want to have speaker links formatted a specific way (where they link to the speaker profile and possibly have a mouse-over popup of a picture and bio).

To create the new view helper, we'll create an extension method in a static class. The class's namespace must be referenced using the `<%@ Import Namespace=… %>` directive at the top of the view or globally imported in the web.config file. Listing 7.4 shows a view helper for building speaker links. View helpers can extend HtmlHelper, UrlHelper, or others. In this example, we are extending ViewPage.

Listing 7.4 A view helper for building speaker links easily

```
public static class CodeCampServerHelpers
{
    public static string SpeakerLink(this ViewPage page,
        Speaker speaker)
    {
        string linkHtml = new HtmlHelper(page.ViewContext)
```

```
        .ActionLink<SpeakerController>(
        c => c.View(speaker.SpeakerKey), speaker.GetName());

    return string.Format("<span class='speaker-link'>{0}</span>",
        linkHtml);
    }
}
```

This gives us a clean and easy way to represent links to speakers within any Code Camp Server view. It is used like this:

```
<%= this.SpeakerLink(speaker) %>
```

It may seem trivial, but the benefit is twofold: readability of your views, and the ability to change the visual representation in one place. The more concise view helper in this example has much less visual weight.

Another great example of a quick and easy view helper is generating script and CSS references. These aren't hard to write by hand, but it's nice to have the path calculated for you. Usage is simple, and listing 7.5 shows a full example:

```
<%= Html.Stylesheet("master.css") %>
<%= Html.ScriptInclude("jquery.js") %>
```

This will be rendered as

```
<link type="text/css" rel="stylesheet" href="/content/css/site.css" />
<script type="text/javascript" src="/content/js/jquery.js"></script>
```

Listing 7.5 Implementations of CSS and JavaScript view helpers

```
public static string Stylesheet(this HtmlHelper html, string cssFile)
{
    string cssPath = cssFile.Contains("~") ? cssFile :
        "~/content/css/" + cssFile;
    string url = ResolveUrl(html, cssPath); /* defined below */
    return string.Format(@"<link type=\"text/css\"
        rel=\"stylesheet\" href=\"{0}\" />\n", url);
}

public static string ScriptInclude(this HtmlHelper html, string jsFile)
{
    string jsPath = jsFile.Contains("~") ? jsFile :
        "~/content/js/" + jsFile;
    string url = ResolveUrl(html, jsPath); /* defined below */
    return string.Format(@"<script type=\"text/javascript\"
        src=\"{0}\" ></script>\n", url);
}

public static string ResolveUrl(this HtmlHelper html,
    string relativeUrl)
{
    if (relativeUrl == null)
        return null;

    if (! relativeUrl.StartsWith("~"))
        return relativeUrl;
```

```
    var basePath =
        html.ViewContext.HttpContext.Request.ApplicationPath;
    string url = basePath + relativeUrl.Substring(1);
    return url.Replace("//", "/");
}
```

The Stylesheet() helper assumes that your CSS files are located in the /content/css directory, but you can specify a relative path such as ~/content/css/some/other/folder/style.css, and it will work as well. The ScriptInclude() helper does the same, but assumes your scripts are located in the /content/js directory.

The possibilities for view helpers are endless. Most of the ones you will create will be specific to your application. Others will be applicable to many applications. When you are displaying date/time values, for instance, you might want them to be displayed relative to the current time. A label that says "Posted 2 days ago" rather than "Posted on 9/15/2009" is much friendlier to the user.

> **Rob Conery's Law**
> When you have an "if" statement in the view, make a helper!

View helpers are good when the required markup is relatively limited. When the required HTML is more complex, view helpers generally become cumbersome and difficult to manage. To alleviate the pain of creating complex HTML within a C# code file, we can turn to using *partials*.

7.2.2 Creating partials

Often views have sections of relatively self-contained segments of HTML. You can tighten your views by separating these segments into *partials*. In the same way you break a large section of C# code into methods, you extract partials from a complex view to simplify it. With the WebFormViewEngine, these partials are called ViewUser-Controls, but ViewPage works just as well as a partial. Like view helpers, ViewUserControls help reduce the visual weight of a view. In addition, they help compartmentalize the output. This turns out to be a benefit in rendering partial HTML fragments during AJAX requests as well. We will see an example of this later in this section.

In Code Camp Server, there is a list of sponsors on the right side of every page. We can build a ViewUserControl to handle this segment of the page. ViewUserControls, by default, share ViewData with the parent view. You can pass in a specific value for the view user control's strongly typed view data if you prefer. Listing 7.6 shows the sponsor list ViewUserControl.

> **Listing 7.6 A ViewUserControl for listing sponsors**

```
<%@ Control Language="C#" Inherits="System.Web.Mvc.ViewUserControl" %>
<%@ Import Namespace="MvcContrib" %>

<ul class="sponsors">
```

```
<% foreach (var sponsorLevel in Enum.GetValues(typeof(SponsorLevel))) { %>
    <li>
        <h2><%= sponsorLevel %> Sponsors</h2>
        <ul>
        <% foreach (var sponsor in
            ViewData.Get<IEnumerable<Sponsor>>(sponsorLevel.ToString())){ %>
            <li><%= sponsor.Name %></li>
        <% } %>
        </ul>
    </li>
<% } %>
</ul>
```

Sponsor levels are defined as

```
public enum SponsorLevel
{
    Platinum,
    Gold,
    Silver
}
```

The list loops over the three different levels of sponsors and outputs the sponsors in each one. Notice we are using an extension method on `ViewDataDictionary` from MvcContrib to provide us with friendly syntax for getting strongly typed objects out of the bag. See more examples of this in chapter 4.

Of course we need to load the data for this `ViewUserControl` in the controller; otherwise it won't have any data to render! We have to ensure that the controller for this action preloads the sponsors whenever we want to render this user control. Such an action is shown in listing 7.7.

Listing 7.7   Preloading sponsors for the view component

```
public ActionResult Index()
{
    Conference conference = GetConference();
    Sponsor[] sponsors = GetSponsorsFor(conference);
    ViewData.Add("conference", conference);

    foreach (var level in Enum.GetNames(typeof(SponsorLevel)))
    {
        string sponsorLevel = level;
        ViewData.Add(sponsorLevel,                          Load the
            conference.Sponsors.Where(                      sponsors in
                s => s.Level.ToString() == sponsorLevel));  ViewData
    }

    return View();
}
```

Our controller action loads up the data necessary to render the entire view. This includes any partials like our sponsor view user control. The `Index.aspx` view renders the partial:

```
<div class="sponsor-list">
    <% Html.RenderPartial("_sponsors"); %>
</div>
```

The resulting page looks like figure 7.2.

In this example our user control shared view data with the main view. We could instead use a strongly typed `ViewUserControl` by passing the model directly into the `RenderPartial` method:

```
<%= Html.RenderPartial("_sponsors",
    ViewData.Get<IEnumerable<Sponsor>>("Platinum")) %>
```

Using this technique the view user control will be constrained to the view data that you pass in to it (via the `Model` property). You also have to ensure that you declare the type of view data in the `@Control` directive, like so:

```
<%@ Control Language="C#"
    Inherits="System.Web.Mvc.ViewUserControl<IEnumerable<Sponsor>>" %>
```

> ### What's with the underscore?
> You may have noticed that we named the partial "*_sponsors*". This name refers to the user control _sponsors.ascx. The underscore is a convention borrowed from Rails that allows you to quickly differentiate between full HTML views and partial ones. Also, because our partial templates have a different extension than normal views, view names can collide (i.e., sponsors.aspx vs. sponsors.ascx). Adopting the underscore convention addresses this problem, but otherwise has no semantic meaning in ASP.NET MVC.

You can probably imagine that if you have many partials and each needs its own specific view data, your controller actions can be encumbered by the loading of

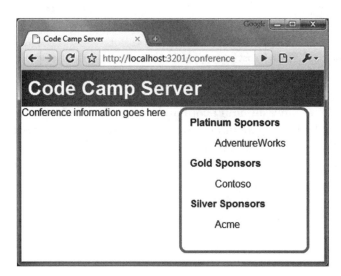

Figure 7.2   The sponsors are loaded into `ViewData` by the controller action; the partial displays it.

seemingly unrelated data. You'd be right. Imagine if every action for every controller in our application needed to load these sponsors and other data. This becomes serious duplication that we should notice right away. It also adds to the noise of the action method, clouding the responsibility. Figure 7.3 shows a 10-foot glance at a controller action whose meaning is being lost in surrounding noise.

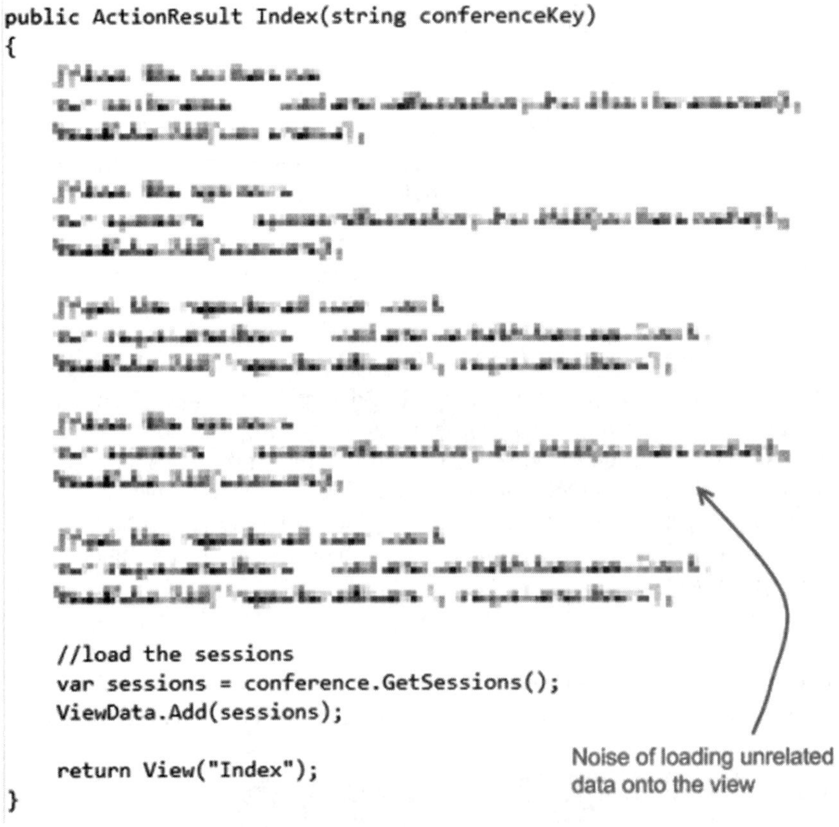

```
public ActionResult Index(string conferenceKey)
{



    //load the sessions
    var sessions = conference.GetSessions();
    ViewData.Add(sessions);

    return View("Index");
}
```

Noise of loading unrelated data onto the view

Figure 7.3 The purpose of the action is lost when loading all the required data for a view.

You'll probably notice that this data needs to be loaded into view data for every action on this controller. We certainly shouldn't copy and paste this code in each place, but even different, but similar-looking method calls can get repetitive. If the code truly runs for every action of the controller, we can move this common code to the OnActionExecuting event that we learned about in the last chapter. Listing 7.8 demonstrates this.

Listing 7.8 Handling common functionality for all actions of a controller

```
public void ConferenceController : Controller
{
    /* snip */

    protected override OnActionExecuting(
```

```
        ActionExecutingContext context)
    {
        Conference conference = GetConference();
        Sponsors[] sponsors = GetSponsorsFor(conference);
        ViewData.Add(sponsors);
    }
}
```

Now `ViewData` will contain the sponsors for the current conference for every action on this controller. You can also accomplish this in a base controller class, in order to have this code executed for every controller that inherits from it.

Another direction you might take is to allow the partial to be in control of loading its own data. This is helpful for scenarios when you want to package up a reusable view segment that can be used on many views. It is accomplished through a helper method called `RenderAction` in combination with partial views. These are sometimes referred to as *components*.

7.2.3 Creating components

Components are the result of packaging up a controller, an action, and a view segment all in one piece. It turns out components are supported by ASP.NET MVC by using an extension method on `HtmlHelper` called `RenderAction`. It takes as parameters the controller and action that you want to render. You can render any action on any controller, but you'll probably want to use this in conjunction with an action that renders a partial view. In other words, the rendered view should be a user control, not a full page.

NOTE: `Html.RenderAction` is located in the MVC Futures assembly, `Micro-soft.Web.Mvc`.

With this approach, the controller will simulate another full request (this time with different route data), almost as if it was requested directly through a browser. The component will have its own entire request pipeline, load its own data, and pass it on to its own view. Since it is completely usable outside the containing view, these are easily packaged up and reused among many views. Listing 7.9 demonstrates rendering a partial view.

Listing 7.9 An action rendering a partial view for sponsors

```
public class SponsorsController : Controller
{
    /* snip */
    public ActionResult ListPartial(string conferenceKey)
    {
        var conference =
            _conferenceRepository.GetConference(conferenceKey);
        foreach (var level in
            Enum.GetNames(typeof(SponsorLevel))) {
            string sponsorLevel = level;
            ViewData.Add(sponsorLevel,
```

```
        conference.Sponsors.Where(
        s => s.Level.ToString() == sponsorLevel));
    }

    return View("_sponsors");
    }
}
```

In this action we get all of the sponsors for the conference, add them to ViewData, then render our partial. We named it ListPartial to be clear that this action renders a partial view. Note that we are using the same partial view that was outlined in listing 7.5. This partial view will now get rendered and inserted inside the parent view:

```
<% Html.RenderAction<SponsorsController>(x=>x.ListPartial(conferenceKey)); %>
```

If you aren't familiar with lambda expressions, then take a couple of minutes to soak it in. Basically we are telling the method that we want it to call the ListPartial() action on the SponsorsController class. This is like passing a delegate to the method, but much cleaner to read (and write). We're also getting the current conference from the main view's ViewData, which is needed to execute the Index() action.

Lambda expressions aid in refactoring

Don't underestimate the value of lambda expressions in your views. These are compiled along with the rest of your code, so if you rename an action, for example, this code will break at compile time. Contrast this with code in your ASPX that references classes and methods with strings. You won't find those errors until runtime. Having strongly typed view data references also aids in refactoring. Using a tool like JetBrains ReSharper (http://www.jetbrains.com/resharper) will allow you to refactor code and have it reach out to all of the views that use it as well. Very powerful, indeed.

Partial actions can help you segment the loading and displaying of disparate data required to render a complete page. One caveat is that to have all this magic happen this technique simulates another web request from the beginning of the lifecycle. If you have deeply nested components you might notice performance hits. For this reason we suggest you avoid it. Make your controllers more focused and easier to develop and maintain.

In listing 7.9, we showed an action that was specifically crafted for our partial use. Sometimes it is useful to reuse actions that already load the data we need. If we change the method signature we might be able to accommodate both. Listing 7.10 shows an action that serves both partial and full requests.

Listing 7.10   A controller action that services partial views as well as full views

```
public ActionResult List(string conferenceKey, bool? partial)      ❶
{
    var conference = _conferenceRepository.GetConference(conferenceKey);

    foreach (var level in Enum.GetNames(typeof(SponsorLevel)))
    {
```

```
            string sponsorLevel = level;
            ViewData.Add(sponsorLevel, conference.Sponsors.Where(
                s => s.Level.ToString() == sponsorLevel));
        }
        string viewName = "list";
        if (partial == true)
            viewName = "_sponsors";

        return View(viewName);
    }
```

Here we declared an action parameter for an optional boolean parameter, partial ❶.
Because this parameter is *nullable*, existing calls to this action work (unless you use the
lambda helpers, in which case you need to pass nulls in). If partial is true, then it renders a partial view; otherwise it renders the default view. Now we've reused our action
to support partial requests as well! Sometimes this is appropriate, other times not. When
you find code with more than one responsibility in the case of a partial result, you probably need a separate action.

  Using these methods you can keep your controller actions and the associated views
organized. One method we used was overriding the OnActionExecuting event to pre-
load data. What if we needed this data to be used for actions in other controllers? For
that matter, just about any code that we write in an OnActionExecuting handler could
be reused in other controllers. To accomplish that reuse, we can leverage action filters.

> **This sounds like Rails Components**
>
> This method of repurposing the request with different route values was included in
> early version of Ruby on Rails called Components. In a subsequent version, Compo-
> nents were removed from the Rails Core. You could opt in and continue to use them
> as a separate gem/plugin; however the Rails team didn't condone their use. Why?
> Some would argue performance, but the main reason is that it turns the MVC pattern
> on its head. Instead of your controllers being in control, you're relinquishing some of
> that control to the view. It's good to learn from other communities and notice how a
> pattern can be abused. In ASP.NET MVC, RenderAction can definitely be abused,
> but can also be an elegant solution for complex views.

7.3　*Using action filters to load common data*

Chapter 6 introduced you to action filters. We can leverage action filters to provide
common logic that can be executed across many controllers. Listing 7.11 shows an
action filter that loads sponsors into ViewData.

Listing 7.11　A custom action filter for preloading common data

```
public class RequireSponsorsAttribute : ActionFilterAttribute
{
    private readonly IConferenceRepository _conferenceRepository;

    public RequireSponsorsAttribute()
```

```
    {                                                  Cannot utilize constructor injection
        _conferenceRepository =
            ServiceLocator.Resolve<IConferenceRepository>();
    }

    public override void OnActionExecuting(            Get conference
        ActionExecutingContext filterContext)         from route value
    {
        Conference conf = GetConference(filterContext.RouteData);

        if (conf == null)                              Ensure conference
            return;                                    exists

        var controller = filterContext.Controller;

        foreach(var level in
            new [] { "Platinum", "Gold", "Silver" })
        {
            var sponsorLevel =
                (SponsorLevel)Enum.Parse(typeof(SponsorLevel), level);

            controller.ViewData.Add(level,
                conf.Sponsors.Where(s => s.Level == sponsorLevel));

        }
    }

    private Conference GetConference(RouteData routeData)
    {
        string conferenceKey = routeData.Values["conferenceKey"] as string;
        if (conferenceKey == null)
            return null;

        return _conferenceRepository.GetConference(conferenceKey);
    }
}
```

Usage is simple. You decorate an action method with the new attribute, and it will be executed when the action is invoked:

```
[RequireSponsors]
public ActionResult Index(string conferenceKey)
{
    return View();
}
```

You can also apply the attribute at the class level, if you want the behavior to occur for all actions in the controller.

As you can see, to create a custom action filter, you inherit from ActionFilter-Attribute and override the methods for which you need to provide functionality. Unfortunately, the framework instantiates these attributes for us when the App-Domain starts, so we must rely on a Service Locator pattern to fetch dependencies. We could also choose to implement our own IActionInvoker if we wanted to integrate more deeply with an IoC container.

The use of action filters is expressive. They are also incredibly easy to reuse among other controllers in your application or even packaged in their own assembly to be used on multiple projects.

How is code in the action filter called?

It may seem strange that the behavior defined in the attribute is called when the action is invoked. At runtime the method is not called directly; it is passed to the `Controller-ActionInvoker`, which reads the action filters that are present on the controller and action. This is a nice extension point in the framework, as you are allowed to substitute your own `IActionInvoker` if you want to customize the semantics.

During unit tests, you will be calling action methods directly. None of the behavior defined in the action filters will be executed. Thus, you should treat your tests as if the action filters *were* executed (for example, load any data into `ViewData` that would have been loaded by an action filter). For things like `[Authorize]` or `[AcceptVerbs(HttpVerbs.POST)]` you can easily test the existence of the attribute with reflection. Here is a class that can help you simplify the reflection code required to get attributes.

```
public static class ReflectionExtensions
{
    public static TAttribute GetAttribute<TAttribute>(
        this MemberInfo member) where TAttribute : Attribute
    {
        var attributes = member.GetCustomAttributes(typeof (TAttribute),
            true);
        if (attributes != null && attributes.Length > 0)
            return (TAttribute)attributes[0];
        return null;
    }

    public static bool HasAttribute<TAttribute>(
        this MemberInfo member) where TAttribute : Attribute
    {
        return member.GetAttribute<TAttribute>() != null;
    }
}
```

Usage is simple:

```
type.GetMethod("Index").HasAttribute<AcceptVerbsAttribute>()...
```

7.4 Organizing controllers into areas

Organizing controllers into hierarchies can help rein in complex sets of controllers by grouping them into logical areas. One way to accomplish this is through custom routing rules, as we saw in chapter 5. Managing this can become complex, and your route rules can become brittle.

How many controllers do you think you'd have if you were Amazon.com? What about Facebook? In any complex web application, it's easy to imagine having 50 controllers along with 50 folders for their respective views. Clearly this would be a mess.

We can borrow a feature from Castle MonoRail to solve this. In MonoRail there is a concept of *areas*. An area is like a namespace for your controllers. Within an area, everything must be unique. Additionally areas provide a directory for your controllers and views. This allows you to segment your controllers and views into logical pieces that make sense to your application. If you were building Dell.com, you'd probably want an area for shopping and an area for customer support. You might even want a separate area for forums. Each of these might have its own `HomeController`, and areas will allow this to happen.

As of writing, this feature has not made it into the ASP.NET MVC Framework, but we can add it ourselves without too much trouble through the extensibility points of ASP.NET MVC. We will leverage the `WebFormViewEngine` as our starting point, as all we want to do is change where it looks for views.

7.4.1   Capturing the area for a request

The first step is to add a required "area" route parameter to our route definitions. We won't give it a default value. This will force your URLs to contain an area. Listing 7.12 shows the definition.

> **Listing 7.12   Adding area to the route definition**

```
routes.MapRoute("AreaRoute",
    "{area}/{controller}/{action}/{id}",
    new { controller = "Home", action = "Index", id = "" }
);
```

Next we'll create a custom view engine for locating views.

7.4.2   Creating a view engine with support for areas

By default the `WebFormViewEngine` looks for views in ~/views/controllername/viewname.aspx, and so on. When a view isn't found, view engine returns a `ViewEngineResult` object that contains a list of the locations searched. This is why you see an informative error message when a view isn't found. Figure 7.4 shows an example of this.

In our view engine, we will have to continue to provide this functionality. This means that although this seems like the simple task of telling the `WebFormViewEngine` to look somewhere else, we also have to override the methods that return the `ViewEngineResult`. Listing 7.13 outlines our custom view engine.

> **Listing 7.13   A custom view engine for handling areas**

```
public class AreaWebFormsViewEngine : WebFormViewEngine
{
    public AreaWebFormsViewEngine()
    {
        ViewLocationFormats = new[]
                              {
                                  "~/views/{2}/{1}/{0}.aspx",
                                  "~/views/{2}/{1}/{0}.ascx",
                                  "~/views/Shared/{1}/{0}.aspx",
                                  "~/views/Shared/{1}/{0}.ascx",
                              };

        MasterLocationFormats = new[]
```

```
                                          {
                                              "~/views/{1}/{0}.master",
                                              "~/views/Shared/{0}.master",
                                              "~/views/{2}/{1}/{0}.master",
                                              "~/views/{2}/Shared/{0}.master",
                                          };
        }
        public override ViewEngineResult FindPartialView(
            ControllerContext controllerContext,
            string partialViewName, bool useCache)
        {
            //snip
        }
        public override ViewEngineResult FindView(
            ControllerContext controllerContext,
            string viewName, string masterName, bool useCache)
        {
            //snip
        }
    }
```

In our constructor, we redefine the `ViewLocationFormats` and `MasterLocationFormats` arrays to accommodate an extra parameter (area). The view locations use standard string formatting placeholders. The first placeholder, {0}, denotes the action name. The second placeholder, {1}, is the controller name and the final placeholder, {2}, is the area name (if specified). The formatting of these strings happens

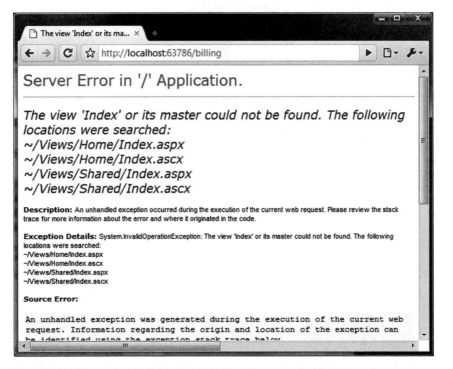

Figure 7.4   When a view isn't found, a list of locations searched is displayed.

in the `FindPartialView` and `FindView` methods, so we must override these as well. Listing 7.14 shows this code.

Listing 7.14   `FindPartialView` and `FindView` methods for a custom view engine

```
public override ViewEngineResult FindPartialView(
    ControllerContext controllerContext,
    string partialViewName, bool useCache)
{
    if(HasArea(controllerContext))                    ←┐  Only handle
    {                                                     routes with areas
        string[] searchedLocations;

        string viewPath = FindViewWithArea(controllerContext,
            partialViewName,                              ┐  Try and
            ViewLocationFormats,                             find view
            out searchedLocations);                       ┘

        if(viewPath == null)
            return new ViewEngineResult(searchedLocations);

        var view = CreatePartialView(controllerContext, viewPath);
        return new ViewEngineResult(view, this);
    }

    return base.FindPartialView(controllerContext, partialViewName,
        useCache);
}

public override ViewEngineResult FindView(             ┐  FindView also
    ControllerContext controllerContext,                  handles master
    string viewName, string masterName, bool useCache)  ←┘  pages
{
    if (HasArea(controllerContext))
    {
        string[] searchedLoations;
        string viewPath = FindViewWithArea(controllerContext, viewName,
            ViewLocationFormats, out searchedLoations);
        if(viewPath == null)
            return new ViewEngineResult(searchedLoations);

        string masterPath = "";
        if(! string.IsNullOrEmpty(masterName))
            masterPath = FindViewWithArea(controllerContext,
                masterName,                               ┐  Find master
                MasterLocationFormats,                       page
                out searchedLoations);                    ┘

        var view = CreateView(controllerContext, viewPath, masterPath);
        return new ViewEngineResult(view, this);
    }

    return base.FindView(controllerContext, viewName, masterName,
        useCache);
}
```

These methods are fairly similar; however the `FindView` method also has to deal with the concept of a master page. If the route data contains an area, we call the

FindViewWithArea method. If this method doesn't return a valid path, we return a ViewEngineResult that contains a list of searched locations. If the view *was* found, we call the CreateView method (provided by the base class) and return it. The HasArea and FindViewWithArea methods are defined in listing 7.15.

Listing 7.15 Helper methods for our custom view engine

```
private string FindViewWithArea(ControllerContext controllerContext,
    string viewName, IEnumerable<string> locationFormats,
    out string[] searchedLocations)
{
    searchedLocations = new string[0];         ◄── Default value for 'out' parameter
    string controller =
        controllerContext.RouteData.GetRequiredString("controller");
    string area = controllerContext.RouteData.GetRequiredString("area");

    var searched = new List<string>();          ◄── Track each location
    foreach (var locationFormat in locationFormats)
    {
        string viewLocation = string.Format(locationFormat,    ◄── Format each string
            viewName, controller, area);
        searched.Add(viewLocation);
        if(FileExists(controllerContext, viewLocation))
        {
            return viewLocation;
        }
    }
    searchedLocations = searched.ToArray();      ◄── Return complete location list
    return null;
}

private bool HasArea(ControllerContext controllerContext)
{
    return controllerContext.RouteData.Values.ContainsKey("area");
}
```

7.4.3 Tying it all together

Because our controllers will now reside in a subfolder of the Controllers folder, we have to register the additional controller namespaces:

```
ControllerBuilder.Current.DefaultNamespaces.Add(
    "AreasSample.Controllers.Billing");
```

This is required because the default ControllerBuilder does not want to reflect over the entire assembly looking for the controller when matching a route to a specific controller. By default, the controllers are searched only in the namespace YourApp.Controllers. You have to add a new line for each defined area in your application. Note that with these new namespaces added, it is possible to have multiple HomeController classes. We also have to replace the default view engine, like so:

```
ViewEngines.Engines.Clear();
ViewEngines.Engines.Add(new AreaWebFormsViewEngine());
```

These can be placed next to your route definitions in `Application_Start`.

Now it's time to see it all working. In the Controllers folder, we create a new subfolder called Billing (the area name) and place a controller in it. We also create a similar Billing folder for our views. Figure 7.5 shows the Visual Studio solution structure.

Now we can run our project, navigate to http://localhost/billing/home/about and see it working as shown in figure 7.6.

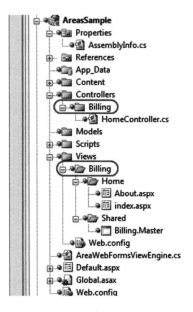

Figure 7.5   Organizing controllers and views into an area subfolder called Billing

7.5   Summary

In this chapter we covered a number of techniques to help your application adapt to complexity. We talked about the single responsibility principle and how you can apply it to controllers to keep them small and focused. We talked about centralizing the loading of

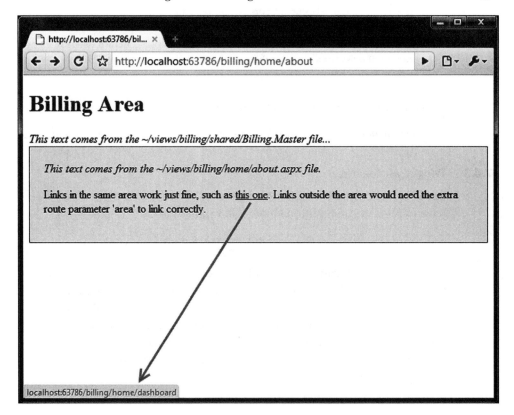

Figure 7.6   Seeing our finished result: a controller and action nested within a 'Billing' area

common view data into action filters. For views we learned that we can reduce clutter by creating view helpers. Finally we talked at length about how to create a custom view engine that supported controller hierarchies called *areas*. Each of these techniques can be applied to keep your applications' complexity under control.

In the next chapter, we'll take a look at the existing features of ASP.NET that we can still leverage in ASP.NET MVC.

Leveraging existing ASP.NET features 8

This chapter covers

- Exploring the ASP.NET server controls supported in ASP.NET MVC
- Using cache, cookies, and session
- Applying the tracing feature
- Setting up health monitoring
- Leveraging site maps
- Configuring membership, personalization, and localization

Many of us have invested heavily in ASP.NET. With ASP.NET MVC now available as an alternative to Web Forms, is all that knowledge useless? Do we have to relearn this platform entirely from scratch? You will be relieved to know that many of ASP.NET's platform features work the same way they always have. Even some Web Forms server controls work. In this chapter we'll cover what works in ASP.NET MVC and what does not. By the end of the chapter, you should feel comfortable leveraging your existing knowledge of ASP.NET to build robust websites with ASP.NET MVC.

8.1   *ASP.NET server controls*

As you just learned, some ASP.NET server controls work with ASP.NET MVC, but which ones? How can we determine if a control will work? To put it simply, any control that depends on `ViewState` or generates postbacks will not be helpful. Some controls will render, but they require a `<form runat="server">` which you might not want to add. Adding a server-side form tag will put hidden fields on the page for `ViewState` and event validation. The form will also POST to the same action you are on, which is sometimes unacceptable. In this section, we'll visit the `TextBox`, `Menu`, `TreeView`, and `Grid-View` and see how they function. Finally, we'll see some alternative options to the traditional server-side controls that you *can* leverage in your ASP.NET MVC applications.

NOTE   The code in this section is purely exploratory. Most of it contains hacks and other workarounds that go against the intended design of an MVC web application. The intent of this section is to see how far we can bend the framework without breaking it. Your authors would not recommend using these methods in a production application unless absolutely necessary.

8.1.1   *The TextBox*

The first control we'll examine is the `<asp:TextBox />`. It renders as an `<input />` HTML element. It requires a `<form runat="server">` tag to function, and will be given a generated ID (if it's placed in a container control such as a `MasterPage`). This is what we are trying to avoid! Because it's a form field, and the form is required to be `runat="server"`, its function is crippled. Figure 8.1 shows it in action, while figure 8.2 shows the resulting HTML.

We can see that the rendered HTML contains much we did not ask for. In addition, notice that the form tag has an `action` attribute that we did not specify. This will prevent the form from submitting to an action that we request.

We can apply a quick trick to avoid the server-side form requirement. In the `Page` class there is a method you can override called `VerifyRenderingInServerForm(Control control)`. If we override this method we can prevent the error that results when using a control outside of the server form. Because there is no code-behind, the only way to accomplish this is to add a server-side script block in your view directly, like this:

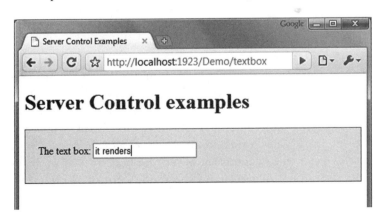

Figure 8.1   The `TextBox` renders correctly.

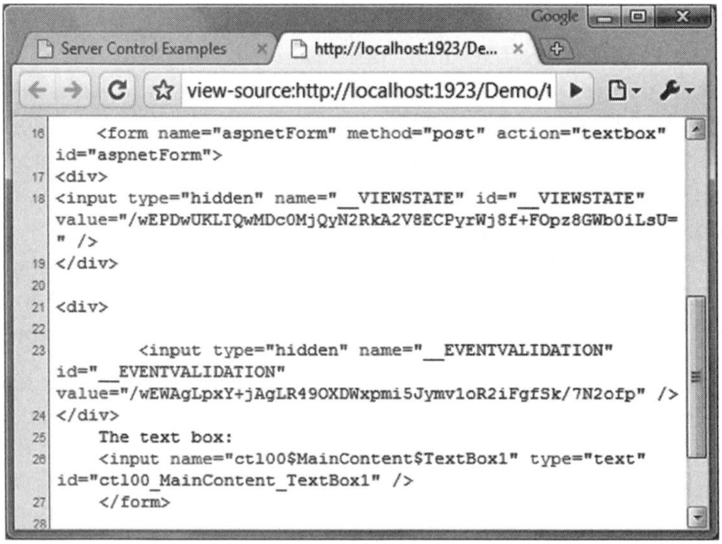

Figure 8.2
The resulting HTML for the TextBox is less than desirable.

```
<script language="C#" runat="server">
    public override void VerifyRenderingInServerForm(Control control)
    {
    }
</script>
```

Now you can use the TextBox (or any other control) in your own form tag, to avoid having the ViewState and EventValidation hidden fields generated for you.

Because a textbox in ASP.NET MVC is as simple as `<%= Html.TextBox("name") %>`, the TextBox server control offers no compelling functionality—only baggage—for your ASP.NET MVC views. ASP.NET controls are also only usable with the WebFormViewEngine. Other view engines cannot utilize them. Now that we've seen the TextBox, what about other controls?

8.1.2   *Other common controls*

We can see from our simple text box example that most ASP.NET Web Forms input controls have little to offer. However, some controls have semifunctional rendered output. One example is the `<asp:Menu />` control. It does not require postbacks if you specify a NavigateUrl for each of the MenuItems, and it does not *require* ViewState (though it does use it to store the last selected item). It simply renders HTML and JavaScript to allow elements to expand and hide on mouse events. Again, a server-side form tag is required and, unlike the TextBox, you should not remove it. Doing so will prevent the JavaScript that controls the hiding/showing of the items from being rendered. Also, Menu renders a nasty pile of HTML tables to display properly. We have come to expect this from Web Forms controls. We could choose to fix the poor markup with ASP.NET Control Adapters; however, the benefits will probably not be worth the trouble. Figure 8.3 demonstrates the menu control working on an MVC view. The rendered markup is shown in figure 8.4.

The `<asp:Menu />` control renders, and the JavaScript open/close behavior functions properly (as long as you have a server-side form tag). However, the links without a `NavigateUrl` property depend on the postback model of Web Forms. We could conjure up some JavaScript to alter this behavior; doing so would just add to the mess. Additionally, take a look at the rendered markup in figure 8.4. Hard-coded styles, deeply nested tables, and highly obtrusive JavaScript make this tiny menu render nothing short of a headache.

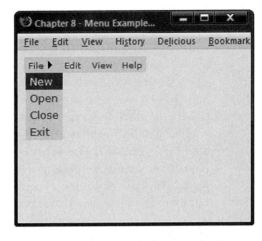

Figure 8.3   The menu control renders okay in Firefox and IE. Unfortunately it depends on a server-side form tag. JavaScript surgery would be needed to make it function properly. WebKit-based browsers (Chrome and Safari) have problems with the JavaScript used to pop open the menus.

NOTE   This type of markup is a constant reminder of why we want more control over our HTML! One of the original strengths of server controls is that they can modify the markup rendered based on a browser. This was of critical importance in 2002 when the popular browsers treated markup in a very different way. This varied rendering was more important than control over the markup. It was worth having to deal with generated markup and ClientIDs for the sake of cross-browser compatibility. Fast forward to 2009/2010. The major browsers now are on board with XHTML; the same markup works well in various browsers. Now, the architectural trade-offs are different. The need to compromise on messy markup no longer exists. In chapter 13, we'll see how to leverage client-side scripting in a clean manner. For now, let's continue on with our exploration of ASP.NET server controls.

```
<script src="/WebResource.axd?d=iypR5m18zfsh_maSixjPog2&amp;t=633329206614062500" type="text/javascript"></script>
    <a href="#menu1_SkipLink"><img alt="Skip Navigation Links" src="/WebResource.axd?d=s504Qa3CWHZuKYndWd05gw2&amp;t=633329206(
        <tr>
            <td onmouseover="Menu_HoverStatic(this)" onmouseout="Menu_Unhover(this)" onkeyup="Menu_Key(event)" id="menu1n0'
                <tr>
                    <td style="white-space:nowrap;"><a class="menu1_1 menu1_3" href="javascript:__doPostBack('menu!
                </tr>
                </table></td><td onmouseover="Menu_HoverStatic(this)" onmouseout="Menu_Unhover(this)" onkeyup="Menu_Key(event)'
                <tr>
                    <td style="white-space:nowrap;"><a class="menu1_1 menu1_3" href="javascript:__doPostBack('menu!
                </tr>
                </table></td><td style="width:3px;"></td><td onmouseover="Menu_HoverStatic(this)" onmouseout="Menu_Unhover(thi:
                <tr>
                    <td style="white-space:nowrap;"><a class="menu1_1 menu1_3" href="javascript:__doPostBack('menu!
                </tr>
                </table></td><td style="width:3px;"></td><td onmouseover="Menu_HoverStatic(this)" onmouseout="Menu_Unhover(thi:
                <tr>
                    <td style="white-space:nowrap;"><a class="menu1_1 menu1_3" href="javascript:__doPostBack('menu!
                </tr>
            </table></td>
        </tr>
</table><div id="menu1n0Items" class="menu1_0 menu1_7">
    <table border="0" cellpadding="0" cellspacing="0">
        <tr onmouseover="Menu_HoverDynamic(this)" onmouseout="Menu_Unhover(this)" onkeyup="Menu_Key(event)" id="menu1n
            <td><table class="menu1_6 menu1_11" cellpadding="0" cellspacing="0" border="0" width="100%">
                <tr>
```

Figure 8.4   The horrific markup that is rendered by the `Menu` control. Stay tuned for a better way.

It would be hard to live without these two controls: `<asp:TreeView />` and the `<asp:Calendar />`. The TreeView looks okay, but the nodes are postback links. The visual aspect works just fine, however. The calendar relies heavily on the postback model for navigation, so unfortunately it does not function in ASP.NET MVC except when viewing a single month. We still need tree views. We still need calendars. With ASP.NET MVC, we'll tend to use more client-side UI functionality, such as that found in jQuery UI, which has a rich JavaScript calendar and more.

I have so far neglected the big daddy of ASP.NET server controls. Yes, I am talking about the GridView. The GridView is an interesting case, because it has so many different forms. At its simplest, the GridView is just an HTML table. It's great for displaying tabular data. If we don't require any postback, then it should work, right? It does, but there are a few *gotchas* along the way.

8.1.3   *The GridView*

The first issue is that there is no declarative way to bind the GridView to data coming from ViewData. You can employ data binding code directly in the view markup, inside `<% %>` code blocks as listing 8.1 demonstrates. This type of code should send bad vibes up your spine, but the point is that it's possible.

> **Listing 8.1   Binding a GridView from the view itself**

```
<%
    grid1.DataSource = Model;
    grid1.DataBind();
%>
```

You also have the option of using the DataSource controls such as ObjectDataSource, SqlDataSource, and XmlDataSource. Of course, in doing this you have completely circumvented the MVC pattern and placed all of your data access directly in the view! Figure 8.5 illustrates the grid rendering properly.

Figure 8.5 shows our newly bound GridView in action. Unfortunately, that is all you get, because none of the advanced features of the GridView will work. No sorting, paging, editing, or selecting. Because of this, it's of limited utility, and will probably only aid you during prototyping and demos.

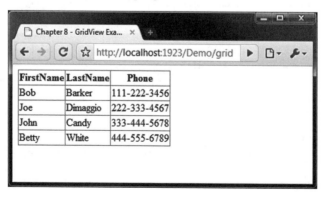

Figure 8.5
The GridView renders properly.

All is not lost, however. In ASP.NET MVC you can achieve the Holy Grail of an editable data grid, complete with sorting, paging, and editing, when you structure it in a different way.

8.1.4 Where do I get the good stuff?

The examples I have shown here might make ASP.NET MVC seem to taste sour. Before you spit it out and decide that you do not want to live without your `TreeView` and `Menu` controls, consider this: many thousands of samples online show how you can achieve the same functionality with a little bit of JavaScript and CSS. These are freely available solutions that many other platforms leverage. With ASP.NET MVC we can do the same, and with minimal friction in applying them. Often, these solutions are so simple they make the declarative ASP.NET controls look like sledgehammers. Here are a few references for platform-agnostic solutions to tree views, menus, and tabs using jQuery.

- jQuery Treeview example: http://jquery.bassistance.de/treeview/demo/
- jQuery Menu example: http://jdsharp.us/jQuery/plugins/jdMenu/
- jQuery Tabs example: http://stilbuero.de/jquery/tabs/

Although ASP.NET MVC does not gain much from server controls—as you have clearly seen in these examples—other aspects of ASP.NET function exactly as they did in Web Forms. We can leverage the ASP.NET platform in the same way as before. The first topic we'll investigate is *state management*.

8.2 State management

One of ASP.NET's strong points is state management. ASP.NET has excellent support for caching, cookies, and user sessions. In ASP.NET MVC we can leverage these as we have in the past. *State management* refers to the storage and retrieval of *state*. As we all know, the web is a stateless environment, so special techniques have to be used to retain data about the user's current state and recent activity. Session state and cookie storage address these concerns. Sometimes it's helpful to store per-user data that lives only for a single web request. Request storage is useful in these scenarios. Frequent trips to a back-end data store can yield horrible performance under heavy load. ASP.NET's built-in support for caching can help keep a popular application running efficiently. We'll examine the ASP.NET Cache first.

8.2.1 Caching

Caching is immensely important in today's web applications. A website of significant size or traffic can drastically reduce the amount of database access by effective use of caching. With ASP.NET we can also cache rendered HTML, which saves CPU resources on the server. Done properly, it's one of the best tools in your belt to cope with severe load. Done poorly, your efforts will be detrimental to your website's performance.

NOTE Caching tips and strategies are out of the scope of this book. Correctly applying caching strategies can be critical to website performance. We'll cover how caching is applied in ASP.NET MVC. If you want to read more about advanced caching, see Professional ASP.NET 3.5:

http://www.amazon.com/Professional-ASP-NET-3-5-VB-Programmer/dp/0470187573

In ASP.NET Web Forms, caching frequently accessed sets of data is accomplished by using the Cache object. This object has a hard dependency on HttpRuntime which impedes testing. For ASP.NET MVC, if we want to ensure testability, we cannot use this static reference. We can access the cache via ControllerContext.HttpContext. Cache, but this class is sealed, so we cannot create a mock object for use in tests. This inherent lack of testability is a remnant of the classic ASP.NET platform, which was not built with testability in mind. To cope with this, we can wrap the cache in our own interface. Listings 8.2 and 8.3 demonstrate this, while listing 8.4 shows the test.

Listing 8.2 Wrapping the cache in our own, testable interface

```
public interface ICache
{
    T Get<T>(string key);
    void Add(string key, object value);
    bool Exists(string key);
}

public class AspNetCache : ICache
{
    public T Get<T>(string key)
    {
        return (T)HttpContext.Current.Cache[key];
    }

    public void Add(string key, object value)
    {
        HttpContext.Current.Cache.Insert(key, value);
    }

    public bool Exists(string key)
    {
        return HttpContext.Current.Cache.Get(key) != null;
    }
}
```

Listing 8.3 Using the cache wrapper in our controllers

```
private ICache _cache;

public HomeController(ICache cache)
{
    _cache = cache;
}

public ActionResult CacheTest()
{
    const string key = "test";
```

```
    if(!_cache.Exists(key))
        _cache.Add(key, "value");

    var message = _cache.Get<string>(key);

    return Content(message);
}
```

Listing 8.4 Testing an action that accesses the cache

```
[Test]
public void CacheTest()
{
    var fakeCache = MockRepository.GenerateStub<ICache>();      Set up controller
    var controller = new HomeController(fakeCache);            with fake cache

    fakeCache.Stub(x => x.Exists("test")).Return(false);        Invoke action
                                                                on controller
    controller.CacheTest();

    fakeCache.AssertWasCalled(x => x.Add("test", "value"));     Assert
    fakeCache.AssertWasCalled(x => x.Get<string>("test"));      methods
}                                                               called on
                                                                cache
```

Wrapping the cache in our interface allowed us to write code decoupled from a specific implementation. It also aided us during testing. If we did not abstract this concept, our controller would remain untestable.

NOTE   It's generally not a recommended practice to specify your data caching strategy directly in your controllers. Application services can easily use this `ICache` interface in combination with a repository or service to hide this from you. Then your controller has a dependency only on the service, and its actions become much more concise. Always keep your controllers tight and focused.

As you might expect, cache dependencies (such as a file dependency or SQL 2005 table dependency) and all other features work just as they did in ASP.NET.

Output caching is another powerful feature of ASP.NET. It allows you to take the rendered HTML of a page or user control, cache it on the server, and return it directly for future requests. This not only eliminates the overhead in getting data, but also in rendering the page. Subsequent requests immediately return the cached HTML. In ASP.NET MVC, we have a slightly different construct for output caching. Listing 8.5 demonstrates how to enable output caching for a controller action.

Listing 8.5 Caching the result of an action for 100 seconds

```
[OutputCache(Duration=100, VaryByParam = "*")]           VaryByParam
public ActionResult CurrentTime()                        is required
{
    var now = DateTime.Now;
    ViewData["time"] = now.ToLongTimeString();
    return View();
}
```

Executing this action gives us the page shown in figure 8.6.

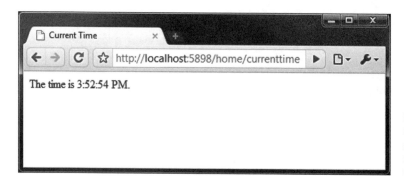

**Figure 8.6
Refreshing the page
gives us the same
result for up to 100
seconds.**

The HTML that makes up the page in figure 8.6 is cached on the server and returned
for subsequent request for up to 100 seconds (the duration we specified in the `Out-
putCache` attribute in listing 8.5). Of course we can vary the cache based on a number
of criteria, such as a specific HTTP Header value, or a query string value. All of the features that worked with output caching in Web Forms also work in ASP.NET MVC.

A limitation of the `OutputCache` attribute is that it only works at the action level. If
you render user controls on your main view with `Html.RenderAction("someAction")`
the cached version of that action will be used for the partial HTML snippet. This is an
excellent way of achieving page fragment caching. If instead you use `Html.Render-
Partial()`, the entire HTML document would have to be cached at the root action
level. StackOverflow.com is a great example of this. The home page has many pieces
of data on it, some of which are unique to the user logged in. See figure 8.7 for an
example. Under heavy load, it may make sense to output-cache the action for the
home page; however the per-user content should not be included in this cache. Here,

**Figure 8.7
StackOverflow.com
is a good example of
how you can use
output caching in
combination with
`Html.Render-
Action()` to
cache different
regions of the page.
On the home page,
some sections can
be cached globally,
and other sections
are rendered per
user.**

`Html.RenderAction` can be used for the per-user sections and the rest of the page can safely be cached.

Now that we have examined how to leverage ASP.NET cache in our apps, we can move on to session state.

8.2.2 Session state

In a web application, session state refers to temporary data (stored on the web server) that exists *per user.* An excellent example of this is a user's shopping cart. Each user gets his own shopping cart, which lives as long as the user is online. The data in the session typically expires after 30 minutes of inactivity.

Similar to `Cache`, `Session` depends deeply on `HttpContext`. Luckily, the ASP.NET MVC Framework has wrapped this object for us, in `HttpSessionStateBase`. This is an abstract base class that mirrors the public API of the real `HttpSessionState` class. We can now easily replace this with a mock object in our unit tests. Listing 8.6 contains an action that uses session state, and the respective test is shown in listing 8.7 with the use of the Rhino Mocks dynamic mocking library (note the calls to `Expect`).

Listing 8.6 An action that uses `Session`

```
public ActionResult ViewCart()
{
    const string key = "shopping_cart";
    if(Session[key] == null)
        Session.Add(key, new Cart());

    var cart = (Cart) Session[key];

    return View(cart);
}
```

Listing 8.7 Testing controllers that use `Session`

```
[Test]
public void SessionTest()
{
    var controller = new HomeController();

    var httpContext = MockRepository.GenerateStub<HttpContextBase>();
    var mockSession = MockRepository.GenerateMock<HttpSessionStateBase>();
    httpContext.Stub(x => x.Session)               Set up fake
        .Return(mockSession).Repeat.Any();         session

    const string key = "shopping_cart";
    mockSession.Expect(x => x[key]).Return(null);
    mockSession.Expect(x => x.Add(null, null)).IgnoreArguments();
    mockSession.Expect(x => x[key]).Return(new Cart());

    controller.ControllerContext =
        new ControllerContext(httpContext, new RouteData(), controller);

    controller.ViewCart();                    ⟵— Invoke the action

    mockSession.VerifyAllExpectations();         ⟵⎤ Verify expected
}                                                  ⎦ methods were called
```

Session is retrieved through the controller's `HttpContext` property (which in turn comes from `ControllerContext.HttpContext`), so we must create a stub for it to return our mocked session object. Sadly, the only way you would know this is by viewing the source or by using Reflector. Once we have the test double in place, we can set it up with canned data that the action method will actually use. The setting-up-the-fake-session code could be placed inside a test helper class so that you have a cleaner test. Something like this would be much nicer:

```
var controllerContext = new FakeControllerContext();
var mockSession = controllercontext.HttpContext.Session;

mockSession.Stub(...);
```

The other form of user-specific data storage lies in HTTP cookies, which we'll examine next.

8.2.3   *Cookies*

Cookies store tiny bits of information in the client's browser. They can be useful to track information, such as where a user has been. By default, the user's session ID is stored in a cookie. It's important to not entirely rely on the contents of a cookie. Cookies can be disabled by the user, and malicious users may even attempt to tamper with the data.

In ASP.NET Web Forms, you would add cookies like this:

```
Response.Cookies.Add( new HttpCookie("locale", "en-US") );
```

That API works going forward in ASP.NET MVC. The only difference is that the `Response` property of the controller is `HttpResponseBase`, rather than the sealed `HttpResponse` class in Web Forms. Testing actions that use cookies is similar to the method we used to test against the `Cache` or `Session` in previous sections.

8.2.4   *Request storage*

Sometimes you require data to be stored for a single web request only. Because individual requests are served by threads, it's tempting to put a `[ThreadStatic]` attribute on a piece of data and expect it to work. However, ASP.NET occasionally reuses threads for other requests, so this is a poor choice for ASP.NET if you want to avoid data mixing with requests from two separate users.

> **NHibernate Session-per-Request pattern**
>
> If you're familiar with NHibernate (http://nhibernate.org) you may be familiar with the Session-per-Request pattern. It refers to the lifecycle of the NHibernate `Session` object, and in web environments it is common to open the session at the beginning of the request, and close it at the end. Throughout the request, the current session is available in `HttpContext.Items`. There is an example of this in chapter 13 under the NHibernate recipe.

You access request storage through `HttpContext.Items`. It's guaranteed to be isolated from other concurrent requests. This works in ASP.NET MVC; however, the actual `HttpContext` property of the `Controller` class is of type `HttpContextBase`. This ensures that our controllers remain testable because you can mock `HttpContext-Base` easily.

We have examined each of the ways of storing and retrieving data in ASP.NET and how they work with MVC. Next, we'll investigate the tracing and debugging experience.

8.3 *Tracing and debugging*

Tracing and debugging work much as they do with Web Forms. The same techniques for placing breakpoints and stepping through code with Visual Studio apply. With tracing, however, there is a slightly different story.

Configuring tracing is done with the `web.config`. The configuration shown in listing 8.8 will enable tracing for an ASP.NET MVC application. The effect on the site is shown on figure 8.8.

> **Listing 8.8 Enabling tracing with the `web.config`**

```
<system.web>
        <trace enabled="true" pageOutput="true" localOnly="true" />
</system.web>
```

With that in place, we can browse our site and see the tracing information appended to the bottom.

You do not have to show the information at the bottom of every page. You can also see the trace information for each request using the `Trace.axd` handler, as seen in figure 8.9.

The only part of this story that does not function similarly to Web Forms is writing to the trace. There is no `Trace.Write()` in your controllers. We'll see why next.

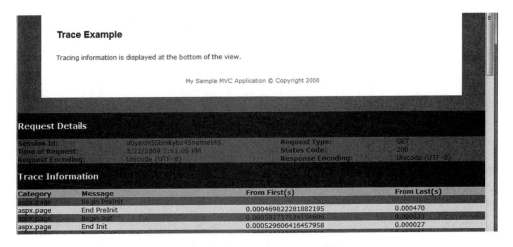

Figure 8.8 Tracing information appended to the bottom of our page

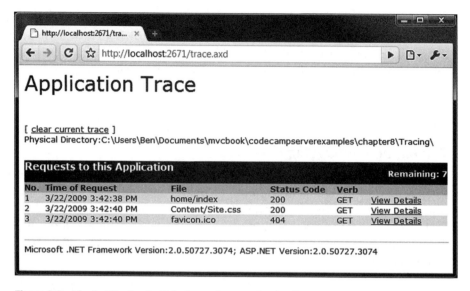

Figure 8.9   Viewing the tracing info for each request using the `Trace.axd` HttpHandler

8.3.1 *TraceContext*

When you called `Trace.Write()` in Web Forms, you were interacting with the `Trace-Context` class. This exists on your `ViewPage` in ASP.NET MVC; however, this is not where you would want to write tracing statements! By the time you have passed the baton over to the view, there is no logic there that you would need to trace. Instead, you would like to trace the logic embedded in our controllers.

You might try to leverage the `TraceContext` class in your controller; however, these statements won't ever make their way to the list of messages in the trace log (on your page or on Trace.axd). Instead, you can leverage `System.Diagnostics.Trace` and set up your own `TraceListeners` to inspect the activity in your controllers. Alternatively, you can leverage a more mature logging framework such as log4net or NLog:

- log4net: http://logging.apache.org/log4net/index.html
- NLog: http://www.nlog-project.org/

You debug ASP.NET MVC applications just as you would any .NET application. Tracing, however, does not offer as much for MVC. Instead, you can lean on the built-in `TraceListeners` in .NET, or utilize a good logging library like those mentioned earlier. Another aspect of error logging is called health monitoring.

8.3.2 *Health monitoring*

Health monitoring is related to tracing and debugging. ASP.NET 2.0 introduced a set of providers for reporting on events occurring in an ASP.NET application. The machine.config on your server (or local machine) defines some policies for reporting the health of your applications. You have probably noticed before that you receive an error in the computer's event log when an unhandled exception occurs in your ASP.NET applications. This is an example of one of those providers. Health monitoring continues to function in the same way in ASP.NET MVC.

8.4   *Implementing personalization and localization*

Often our applications need to display different information depending on the user. Sometimes this data is personal, such as your name or the customized look and feel of the site. Other times this might be displaying messages in a user's native language, depending on the locale on their browser.

ASP.NET personalization and localization work similarly in ASP.NET MVC, but we'll look at a couple of examples to highlight the difference in usage.

8.4.1   *Leveraging ASP.NET personalization*

ASP.NET personalization requires database objects to be created. You can create these on your database by running a Visual Studio 2008 command prompt and typing

```
C:\> aspnet_regsql -S <server> -E -A all
```

This will install database support for profiles, roles, membership, and personalization on the server specified. To define the type of data you want to store for your users, you have to define it in the web.config. Listing 8.9 shows a sample configuration.

Listing 8.9   Setting up the personalization properties

```
<system.web>
   ...
   <anonymousIdentification enabled="true"/>
   <profile>
      <properties>
         <add name="NickName" type="System.String" allowAnonymous="true" />
         <add name="Age" type="System.Int32" allowAnonymous="true"/>
      </properties>
      ...
   </profile>
   ...
</system.web>
```

We have identified two properties that we want to track for our users. In a Web Forms application, you would set these values to controls on your page, from directly accessing the profile API from your code-behind. The only difference in ASP.NET MVC is that we need to do this in our controller. When adding items to `ViewData`, we can choose between explicitly adding each property into `ViewData` directly, and passing the entire profile object. Your preference depends on how complex your profile properties are. Listing 8.10 shows a controller action that passes profile data to the view. The view is shown in listing 8.11, while the edit form is displayed in listing 8.12.

Listing 8.10   Passing the profile dictionary to the view

```
public class ProfileController : Controller
{
    public ActionResult My()
    {
        var profile = ControllerContext.HttpContext.Profile;
        return View(profile);
    }
}
```

Listing 8.11   Displaying profile data on the view

```
<h3>Your Profile:</h3>
Nick Name: <%= Model["NickName"] %><br />
Age: <%= Model["Age"] %><br />

<%= Html.ActionLink("Edit my Profile", "edit") %>
```

Listing 8.12   Editing the profile data

```
<h3>Edit my profile</h3>
<% using(Html.BeginForm("save", "profile")) {%>
    <label for="nickName">Nick Name:</label> <%= Html.TextBox("nickName")%>
    <br />
    <label for="age">Age:</label> <%= Html.TextBox("age") %><br />
    <input type="submit" value="save" />
<% } %>
```

Luckily, the `Profile` property is of type `ProfileBase`, and is an abstract base class. This means we can easily test actions that utilize profile data. Setting the profile data is basically the opposite operation: take form control values and put them on the profile dictionary.

8.4.2   *Leveraging ASP.NET localization*

With the power of the internet, the world can instantly become users of our sites. It would be naïve to believe that English would be sufficient for the entire world. In some cases, providing multilanguage/culture support can increase sales or reach and make your site much more popular (and profitable!).

.NET gave us resource files (`.resx`) that can house the translations for text or images that you would display on the screen. You would create a localized version of this resource file for each culture you wanted to support. In addition, localization controls how numbers are formatted on the screen, and whether the text reads left-to-right or right-to-left.

In .NET, there is the concept of global and local resources. Global resources are pieces of data that your entire site might need, such as the title of the site, whereas local resources refer to the content specific to one page of your site. In ASP.NET MVC, this means that your views will be able to reference local resources, but your controllers will have access only to global resources.

Let's start with an example. We have taken the ASP.NET MVC starter template and added a global resources directory (right-click, add ASP.NET folder, `App_Global_Resources`). We have also added a resource file called `Site. resx`. Figure 8.10 shows the solution and figure 8.11 shows the resources we have created.

As you can see in figure 8.11, we have pulled out some of the text you will find on the sample project. We have also changed the default `HomeController` to pull these resource strings out, depending on the current culture. Listing 8.13 demonstrates this.

We have used a simple helper method to make it easier to pull out strings from the resource file. We have

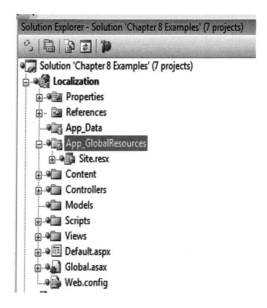

Figure 8.10 Adding an `App_GlobalResource` directory and a default resource file to the project

Listing 8.13   Pulling strings out of the resource file based on the current culture

```
public class HomeController : Controller
{
    public ActionResult Index()
    {
        ViewData["Title"] = GetResource("PageTitle");
        ViewData["Message"] = GetResource("WelcomeMessage");

        return View();
    }

    private string GetResource(string key)
    {
        var httpContext = ControllerContext.HttpContext;
        var culture = Thread.CurrentThread.CurrentUICulture;
        return (string)httpContext.GetGlobalResourceObject("Site", key,
            culture);
    }
}
```

Name	Value
AboutUs	About Us
HomePageLink	Home
PageTitle	Sample ASP.NET MVC Application
WelcomeMessage	Welcome!
*	

Figure 8.11   Our site's resources

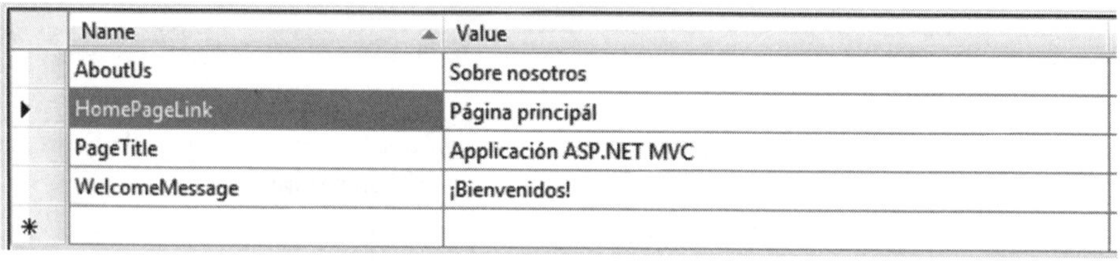

Name	Value
AboutUs	Sobre nosotros
HomePageLink	Página principál
PageTitle	Aplicación ASP.NET MVC
WelcomeMessage	¡Bienvenidos!
*	

Figure 8.12   A localized resource file for Spanish (es-ES)

only defined one, so that is all the users will see. Let's add another. We'll add one for the es-ES culture—Spanish (Spain). To do this, add another resource file in App_Global-Resources, but this time we'll append the culture string to the filename (in this case Site.es-ES.resx). Figure 8.12 shows the contents of this file, and figure 8.13 shows the Solution Explorer view.

We have now added a second resource file that contains the same keys, but the values are localized to the culture in question (in this case Spanish). Let's see what the site looks like in figure 8.14 when we run it.

How did it know which culture we wanted to display? How do Spanish-speaking users see the localized version? In .NET, the current executing thread has a property called

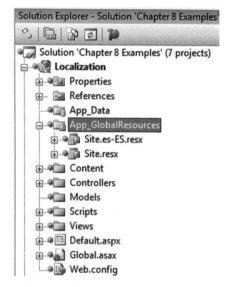

Figure 8.13   Our new resource file is added to the App_GlobalResources folder.

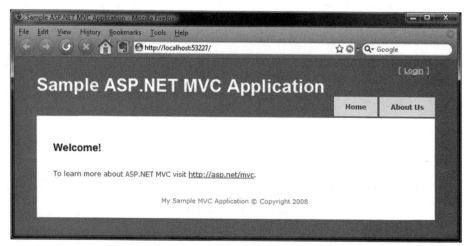

Figure 8.14   Seeing the strings from the resource file live on the site. This browser is Mozilla Firefox with a custom skin.

`CurrentUICulture`. We can set this programmatically, but most web browsers will do the work for us provided we allow them. Here we are using Mozilla Firefox, though all major browsers will allow you to do this. We have gone to Tools > Options > Content (tab) > Languages. Here you can choose your language preference. Figure 8.15 shows that we have added Spanish (es-ES) to the list and moved it to the top. You will also need the `web.config` setting shown in listing 8.14.

Listing 8.14   Enabling autoculture selection from the browser

```
<system.web>
      . . .
      <globalization enableClientBasedCulture="true" uiCulture="auto"
      culture="auto" />
</system.web>
```

After doing this, our browser will submit the culture we prefer to the server. The server reads this and returns the localized resources (if they are available, of course). Figure 8.16 shows that after refreshing the browser, we are greeted with Spanish messages!

The content region of the page has also been localized. To add local resources for a single page, which are accessible on the view, add an `App_LocalResources` folder next to the .aspx files. Figure 8.17 shows this for our *index* view.

It isn't as simple as this. Remember, however, that .aspx views reside in the Views folder because of convention. Due to the highly customizable nature of ASP.NET MVC, there's nothing to stop you from having your views be served from the database, or from another location on disk. This complicates the notion of a "local" resource because "local" is now dynamic!

Luckily Matt Hawley has discovered this (the hard way) and posted his findings on his blog. You can find the post online at http://blog.eworldui.net/post/2008/10/ASP-NET-MVC-Simplified-Localization-via-ViewEngines.aspx. His solution involves deriving

Figure 8.15   Setting our preferred language to Spanish in Firefox

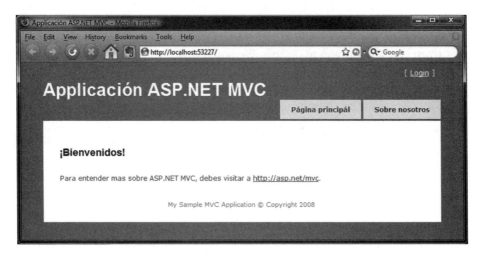

Figure 8.16   Viewing the site with a different preferred language setting in the browser

from the standard `WebFormViewEngine` to create a `LocalizableWebFormViewEngine`. This derived class stores the view path in view data for each view, so when the helper methods invoked from the view require a path, it can be taken directly from `ViewData`. We'll leave the rest of the details to Matt's excellent post.

In these examples, we saw the basic resource API for .NET. In Web Forms, there are additional features in which server controls can declaratively display resources from the current culture. In ASP.NET MVC, none of these exist yet. Fortunately it would be trivial to create additional view helpers to accomplish this.

Localization is an enormous topic, and unfortunately few developers pay attention to it. We have just scratched the surface in this section. If you are building a site that will have users from different countries, be sure to look into localization.

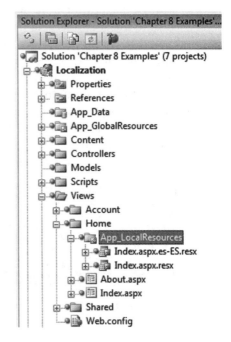

Figure 8.17   Adding local resources for the Index view

8.5   *Implementing ASP.NET site maps*

The last feature we'll visit in this section is the ASP.NET site map. A site map allows you to define the hierarchy of your site in an XML file (called `Web.sitemap`) or another data source of your choosing. On your pages you can include a `SitemapPath` control that displays breadcrumb navigation to the users, allowing them to navigate back to higher level pages.

In ASP.NET MVC, site maps work surprisingly well. You define a sample `Web.sitemap` file, such as that in listing 8.15. This defines the URL hierarchy of the site. You can create a site map file by choosing "Sitemap" on the Add New Item dialog of the project.

Listing 8.15 Defining our site structure in `Web.sitemap`

```
<?xml version="1.0" encoding="utf-8" ?>
<siteMap xmlns="http://schemas.microsoft.com/AspNet/SiteMap-File-1.0" >
    <siteMapNode url="/home" title="Home"  description="">
        <siteMapNode url="/home/index" title="Index"  description="" />
        <siteMapNode url="/home/about" title="About Us"  description="" />
        <siteMapNode url="/home/contact" title="Contact Us"
            description="" />
        <siteMapNode url="/home/legal" title="Legal" >
        <siteMapNode url="/home/legal?section=privacy"
            title="Privacy Policy" />
        <siteMapNode url="/home/legal?section=terms"
            title="Terms &amp; Conditions" />
        </siteMapNode>
    </siteMapNode>
</siteMap>
```

Now that ASP.NET knows about our site structure, we can display the current breadcrumb path to the user, using the standard `SiteMapPath` server control from Web Forms (listing 8.16). Luckily, this control does not require any server-side form tag (nor `ViewState` or post backs). It renders just as you would expect it to. Figure 8.18 shows the result running in the browser.

Listing 8.16 Using the server control to display our current path in the site map

```
<div id="main">
    <asp:SiteMapPath ID="smp" runat="server"  />
    <asp:ContentPlaceHolder ID="MainContent" runat="server" />
</div>
```

We have placed this control in the master page, so every page of our site will get the current site map path displayed at the top, above the content. You can see the result in figure 8.18.

As you can see, our breadcrumb links look good and they help the user navigate back through the higher layers of the site hierarchy. There is only one facet of the site map story that does not work well. Can you guess what it is? That's right: it's those pesky hard-coded URLs! If we change our routing structure, this `SiteMapPath` control will display the wrong links, and our site will be broken. Take care when restructuring URLs in your site.

We can choose to live with this and update it when our routes change (which is actually reasonable, because routes aren't expected to change often), or we can implement

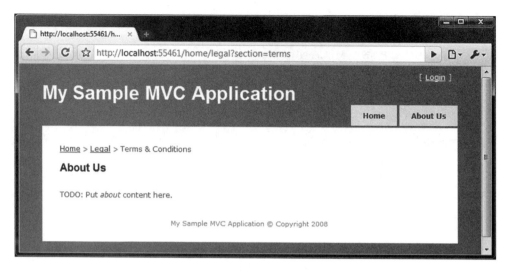

Figure 8.18   Displaying the site map breadcrumbs on the master page

our own custom `SitemapProvider`; one that knows about the controllers, actions, and routes in our web application. This is beyond the scope of this book, but can be left as an exercise you might want to try.

8.6   Summary

As you have seen in this chapter, some features we have used in the past take tweaking to function. Others have limitations or do not work at all. But you can harness the core features of the ASP.NET runtime to your advantage. We hope this chapter has helped you better distinguish between the Web Forms world and the ASP.NET MVC world. Many of the examples in this chapter were purely exploratory, such as the ASP.NET server controls. The section on ASP.NET Caching demonstrated how you can cope with some of the APIs that are not testable out of the box.

We have intentionally skipped over the ASP.NET AJAX feature. Where does AJAX fit into all of this? That happens to be the topic of our next chapter. Read on.

AJAX in ASP.NET MVC

This chapter covers

- Discussing our view on AJAX
- Reviewing difficulties with Web Forms
- Getting to know JavaScript libraries
- Performing simple HTML replacement
- Using JSON and XML responses

AJAX, or *asynchronous JavaScript and XML*, is a term coined by Jesse James Garret describing a clever new technique to make web applications more dynamic. AJAX introduced a new era of web applications. It's a technique that uses the browser's JavaScript capability to send a request to the server asynchronously. This enables applications to become richer and more user-friendly by updating small sections of the page without requiring a brutal full-page refresh. In today's web, the vast majority of major websites have leveraged this technique to their advantage. Users are demanding this type of rich, seamless interaction with websites. You aren't going to let them down, are you?

AJAX is definitely here to stay. With ASP.NET Web Forms, developers have disagreed on how to best apply AJAX to their sites. Many popular code samples and AJAX libraries seemed to fit well for the PHP and Ruby on Rails examples, but they did not translate as well to the ASP.NET platform. This was mainly due to the page-centric request

lifecycle and the lack of control over HTML DOM identifiers. A Web Forms–friendly
framework called ASP.NET AJAX was released by Microsoft in early 2007 to moderate
success. Many developers found it overly complicated and cumbersome. ASP.NET
AJAX and its associated control toolkit depend deeply on the postback behavior of Web
Forms. For ASP.NET MVC applications there are more fitting frameworks available.

In this chapter we'll examine how the AJAX technique is applied to ASP.NET MVC
in a less complicated and more natural way than with Web Forms. You'll see how to
leverage an increasingly popular, lightweight JavaScript library called jQuery. You'll
learn a few types of methods commonly used with AJAX, along with the strengths and
weaknesses of each. Although an introduction to AJAX is provided, you'll be best
served by at least an introductory knowledge of the subject.

9.1   *Diving into AJAX with an example*

An example is the best way to describe how AJAX works. We'll create a simple HTML
page that has a button on it. When the button is clicked, an AJAX request will be sent
to the server. The response will be a simple message, which we'll display to the user.
No browser refresh will occur. Take a look at our HTML page in listing 9.1

> **Listing 9.1   A simple HTML page**

```html
<html>
  <head>
    <title>Ajax Example 1</title>
    <script type="text/javascript" src="ajax-example1.js"></script>
  </head>

  <body>                                                      Issue an Ajax
    <h1>Click the button to see the message...</h1>              request
    <input type="button" value="Whack! " onclick="get_message();" />    ◁

    <div id="result"></div>      ◁⎤ Display
  </body>                          ⎦ result here
<html>
```

This is a basic HTML page with a button on it. When the user clicks the button, the
server should get the message without refreshing the page, and display it to the user.
Listing 9.2 shows the contents of the referenced JavaScript:

> **Listing 9.2   Simple JavaScript file**

```javascript
function get_message()
{                                                 Get XML HTTP
    var xhr = getXmlHttpRequest ();    ◁⎤ Request object

    xhr.open("GET", "get_message.html", true);   ◁── Prepare request

    xhr.onreadystatechange = function() {   ◁── Set up callback function

        if(xhr.readyState != 4) return;   ◁── ReadyState 4 means we're done

        document.getElementById('result').innerHTML = xhr.responseText;   ◁
    };                                              Populate page with result
```

```
    xhr.send(null);    ⟵─ Fire AJAX request
}

function getXmlHttpRequest()
{
    var xhr;                                          ⎤ Check for IE
    if(typeof ActiveXObject != 'undefined'){  ⟵──┘ implementation(s)

        try {
            xhr = new ActiveXObject("Msxml2.XMLHTTP");
        } catch(e) {
            xhr = new ActiveXObject("Microsoft.XMLHTTP");
        }
    } else if(XMLHttpRequest) {                    ⎤ This works for
        xhr = new XMLHttpRequest();        ⟵──┘ other browsers
    } else {
        alert("Sorry, your browser doesn't support Ajax");
    }

    return xhr;
}
```

The resulting page looks like figure 9.1.

If you're thinking that the previous example contains a lot of code for a simple AJAX request, you're not alone. The simple act of creating the XMLHttpRequest object isn't consistent across browsers. We'll see how to clean that up later. First, let's see how this example would be applied in ASP.NET Web Forms.

Figure 9.1 The highlighted text remains, indicating the request was submitted asynchronously. Firebug (shown at the bottom of the browser window) also allows us to inspect AJAX calls for better debugging . Get Firebug at http://getfirebug.com/.

Unobtrusive JavaScript

You might notice throughout this chapter that we prefer unobtrusive JavaScript. This means that the functionality of the page degrades gracefully in the absence of JavaScript. We also adhere to common JavaScript standards, such as `document.getElementById('myDiv')` rather than the nonstandard `document.myDiv` or others.

Have you ever seen code that looks like this?

```
<a href="javascript:window.open('…')">info</a>
```

The `href` attribute is supposed to point to a document, not contain JavaScript code. Other times we see this:

```
<a href="javascript:void(0)" onclick="window.open(…)">info</a>
```

We still have that funky JavaScript string where it doesn't belong, and this time we're using the `onclick` handler of the tag. This is marginally better, but if you followed unobtrusive scripting, you'd end up with something like this:

```
<a href='info.html' class='popup'>info</a>
```

With JavaScript enabled, we can loop over all links with a class of `'popup'` and attach an `onclick` event handler that calls `window.open()` with the link's `href` property. If JavaScript is disabled, the link functions normally, and the user can still see the info. html page. We get the benefit of graceful degradation in the absence of JavaScript and separation of behavior from presentation.

In some cases the examples show what is most easily displayed in book format; in practice, it's worthwhile to follow the unobtrusive JavaScript principles.

For more information on unobtrusive JavaScript, see Jeremy Keith's excellent book *DOM Scripting: Web Design with JavaScript and the Document Object Model*.

9.2   *AJAX with ASP.NET Web Forms*

If we take the example in listings 9.1 and 9.2 and apply it to Web Forms, we may hit some bumps. First is the issue of the actual web request. Earlier we specified the URL to be get_message.html, but in reality this is probably going to be a dynamic page. Let's assume that we used get_message.aspx and the message actually came from a database. ASP.NET pages go through the page lifecycle events and render the template (.ASPX) that we have defined. These templates represent a full HTML document; however, we only wanted to render the message. We could instead utilize a custom `IHttpHandler` to intercept a different file extension and not use the page template. This would look something like listing 9.3.

Listing 9.3   A custom AJAX `HttpHandler`

```
public class AjaxHandler : IHttpHandler
{
    public bool IsReusable
```

```
    {
        get { return true; }
    }

    public void ProcessRequest(HttpContext context)
    {
        if (context.Request.QueryString["operation"] == "get_message")
        {
            context.Response.Write("yuck");
            context.Response.ContentType = "text/plain";
        }

        context.Response.End();
    }
}
```

Quickly we can see that using `Response.Write()` from our code is a cumbersome way to render content for an AJAX request when the logic is nontrivial. As the number and size of the AJAX request/responses increase, `Response.Write()` becomes very difficult to maintain. The *Law of Demeter* violation also increases the difficulty of unit testing this handler class. We'd like to use the templating power of ASPX, without using full HTML documents.

Law of Demeter

The Law of Demeter, or Principle of Least Knowledge, has been heavily discussed since Karl J. Lieberherr presented it to the OOPSLA conference of 1988. The Law of Demeter is as follows:

"For all classes C, and for all methods M attached to C, all objects to which M sends a message must be instances of classes associated with the following classes:

The argument classes of M (including C).

The instance variable classes of C.

(Objects created by M, or by functions or methods which M calls, and objects in global variables are considered as arguments of M.)"

It has been simplified since then and can be summarized by saying "only talk to your immediate friends." A line of `something.something.something()` is the telltale sign of a Law of Demeter violation.

You can read the original OOPSLA88 paper at http://www.ccs.neu.edu/research/demeter/papers/law-of-demeter/oopsla88-law-of-demeter.pdf.

We might come across another bump in the road in the callback function. When the request comes back from the server, we get the element with the ID of `result` and update its contents with the response text. If our target element is a server control—such as a `TextBox`, `Panel`, or `Label`—ASP.NET will generate the ID for us. Thus we are

AJAX return values

The *X* in *AJAX* stands for *XML*, but that doesn't mean we have to return XML for our AJAX calls. There are multiple options for return values. Some are better for over-the-wire performance, some are easy to create on the server-side, and some are easy to consume with JavaScript. You should choose the one that fits your needs best.

Simple return values can be passed, such as in the example in this chapter, or partial HTML snippets can be returned to be added to the DOM. Often you need to work with structured data. XML documents can be returned, and although they are easy to create on the server they are not a common choice due to the additional overhead and complexity of parsing XML in the web browser with JavaScript. Using JSON is a better solution for representing data.

JSON strings are native representations of JavaScript objects. They only need to be passed to the `eval()` method to be evaluated as and returned as usable objects. For more information on the JSON format, see http://json.org.

When you want to take advantage of templates, you can return HTML fragments and update the HTML directly with the result. This option tends to be the simplest, since you do not have to parse any data. This approach can cause issues later on if you refactor your views; you'll have to ensure that every piece of injectable HTML still works with the updated DOM of your new template.

Always choose the most appropriate method of response given your scenario.

forced to generate this ID using some method of `<%= theControl.ClientID %>`, which will give us the correct identifier. This means we either need to pass in the ID to the JavaScript function, or generate the entire function definition inside our ASPX page so that we can execute the snippet in our example.

With ASP.NET MVC we can do better. We have complete control over our HTML, and as such have responsibility for naming our elements in a way that will not collide with other elements on the page. We also have a better method of having templates for our results, so that we may return an HTML fragment for an AJAX call and not rely on `Response.Write()`.

9.3　*AJAX in ASP.NET MVC*

In ASP.NET MVC our AJAX scenario is much cleaner. We have control over the rendered HTML, so we can choose our own element IDs and not rely on ASP.NET server controls to generate them for us. We can also choose to render views that can be plain text, XML, JSON, HTML fragments, or even JavaScript that can be run on the client. Let's take a more complicated scenario and see how it looks in ASP.NET MVC.

Most of the examples in this chapter will utilize an excellent JavaScript library called jQuery. jQuery is becoming increasingly popular for its simplicity and elegant syntax. It has been so popular, in fact, that Microsoft has included jQuery as one of the default JavaScript libraries for ASP.NET MVC projects. The Microsoft AJAX client library that comes with ASP.NET AJAX is also used for a few of the AJAX helpers, most notably `<% Ajax.BeginForm() %>`. We'll see how this functions later in this chapter.

jQuery is a JavaScript library that makes JavaScript development more concise, more consistent across browsers, and more enjoyable. jQuery has a powerful selector system, where you use CSS rules to pinpoint and select elements from the DOM and manipulate them. The entire library is contained in a single minified JavaScript file (jquery.js) and can be placed in the ~/Scripts directory of your MVC project. ASP.NET MVC ships with jQuery, so you can use it right out of the box.

The following sidebar is a quick primer on how to use jQuery. You can use many other excellent JavaScript libraries with the ASP.NET MVC Framework as well. Prototype, script.aculo.us, dojo, mootools, YUI, and so on, all have strengths and weaknesses; jQuery will be included in all MVC projects by default. At the time of writing the current version of jQuery is 1.3.2.

The first example in this chapter used a button click to fire off the request. There were no parameters sent to the server, so the same message would always be returned. This is hardly a useful way to build AJAX applications. A more realistic approach (and one that is quite popular) is to take a form and hook into the onsubmit event. The form values are sent via AJAX instead and the standard form submission is canceled. Jeremy Keith calls this technique Hijax.

9.3.1 *Hijaxing Code Camp Server*

Our first example will cover a small feature in Code Camp Server. We'll implement the Hijax technique. Let's take a look at the user story for this feature:

> *As a potential speaker, I would like to add sessions to the conference (with a name and description) so that the organizer can review them and approve the ones that fit. I would like the interaction to be seamless so that I can add multiple sessions very quickly.*

Figure 9.2 is the form (in Code Camp Server) where you can add sessions to a conference. It consists of two textboxes, a dropdown list, and a submit button. When the form is submitted, a track is created and added to the conference, and the page is rendered again with a styled list of current tracks.

When you submit the form, the session is added, and the user is redirected back to `/session/index` to view the updated table. The HTML behind this form looks like this:

```
<% using(Html.BeginForm("add", "session",
        FormMethod.Post, new{id="new_session"})) { %>
<fieldset>
    <legend>Propose new session</legend>
    <label for="title">Title</label>
    <input type="text" name="title" />

    <label for="description">Description</label>
    <textarea name="description" rows="3" cols="30"></textarea>

    <label for="level">Level</label>
```

```
<select name="level">
    <option selected="selected" value="100">100</option>
    <option value="200">200</option>
    <option value="300">300</option>
    <option value="400">400</option>
</select>

    <input type="submit" value="Add" />
</fieldset>
<% } %>
```

It's important to ensure that your application works without AJAX, because your users might decide to run with JavaScript turned off, or they might be using a mobile

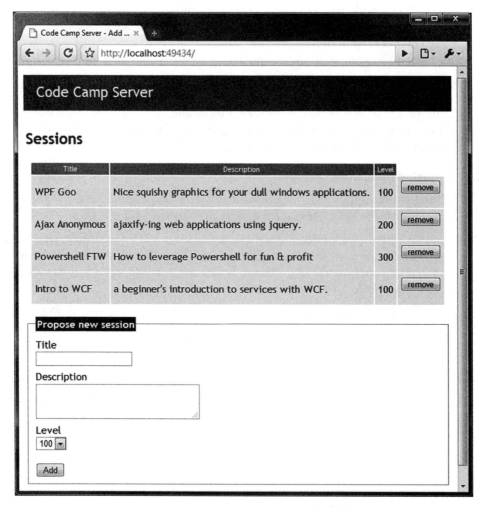

Figure 9.2   These form values are serialized and sent to the server via AJAX. The result is a seamless method of adding sessions without a page refresh. When you disable JavaScript it still works the old way.

A jQuery primer

To use jQuery, you must reference the `jquery.js` JavaScript file in the `<head>` element of your page.

The `$()` function accepts a string and is used to

- Select elements by ID or CSS selector (i.e. `$('#myDiv')` => `<div id="myDiv" />`)
- Select elements within some context (i.e. `$('input:button', someContainer)`)
- Create HTML dynamically (i.e. `$('<span>updating...</span>')`)
- Extend an existing element with jQuery functionality (i.e. `$(textbox)`)
- Execute a function once the entire DOM is ready (i.e. `$(do_stuff)` => executes `do_stuff()`) when the DOM has been loaded (without waiting for images to load).

To have some code executed when the DOM is ready, rather than putting the script at the bottom of the page, you can put it in the `<head>` this way:

- `$(document).ready(function() { /* your code here */ });`

This is the same as

- `$().ready(function() { /* your code here */ });`

It can be shortened even further like so:

- `$(function { /* your code */ });`

There's usually a shorter way of doing *anything* in jQuery. The nice thing about `$(document).ready` is that it will fire as soon as the DOM is loaded, but it doesn't wait for images to finish loading. This results in a faster startup time than with `window.onload`.

The `$.ajax([options])` function can be used to send AJAX requests to the server. `$.get()` and `$.post()` are also useful simplifications of the `$.ajax()` function.

To serialize a form's values into `name1=val&name2=val2` format, use `$(form).serialize()`.

I have just scratched the surface here. For a real introduction to jQuery, visit the jQuery website. I highly recommend the book *jQuery in Action* by Bear Bibeault and Yehuda Katz, also from Manning, for more serious studies.

For more detailed information, see the documentation online at http://docs.jquery.com.

browser without JavaScript support. Our example works, so we can now focus on spot-welding AJAX onto this form without touching the HTML. We can apply a simple jQuery script that will hijack this form post and provide the seamless AJAX experience instead (when the user has enabled JavaScript). This is called *progressive enhancement*.

Let's see how that is implemented. When the user clicks the submit button the browser physically posts to the server. We need to cancel this action so the browser doesn't go anywhere. If we add an `onsubmit` JavaScript handler to the form and call `event.preventDefault()`, we can capture the form post and circumvent the *actual* post operation. We can then gather the form values and submit the form post instead with AJAX. Listing 9.4 shows the setup for the JavaScript.

> **Listing 9.4   The jQuery script that sets up the form hijacking**

```
$(document).ready(function() {
    $("form#new_session").submit(function(event) {
        event.preventDefault();                      Setup form's
        hijack(this, update_sessions, "html");       onsubmit handler
    });
});

function hijack(form, callback, format) {
    $("#indicator").show();
    $.ajax({
        url: form.action,
        type: form.method,
        dataType: format,                            Send form
        data: $(form).serialize(),                   data via AJAX
        completed: $("#indicator").hide(),
        success: callback
    });
}

function update_sessions(result) {                   This is the
    $("#session-list").html(result);                 callback function
    $("#message").hide().html("session added")
        .fadeIn(2000)
        .fadeOut(2000);
}
```

NOTE   *Warning*   Notice in the previous listing that we called `event.prevent-Default()`. This effectively removes the actual form submit behavior. You can also accomplish this by returning `false` from the function. Be careful when using `return false` in your event handlers. If an error occurs before our `return false` statement, it won't be passed down to the caller and the browser will continue with the form post behavior. At the very least, surround this behavior in a `try {} catch {}` block and alert any errors that occur. Detecting and tracking down JavaScript errors after the browser has left the page is difficult and annoying. With jQuery, using `event.preventDefault()` is both easier and safer.

This script can reside in a separate file referenced by the page or in a script tag of the `<head>` element. It's sometimes common to see `<script>` tags in the middle of the `<body>`, but it's good to try to place scripts in the `<head>` to keep things tidy. These scripts are loaded before other DOM content, so if page load times become a problem, consider placing them at the bottom of the page.

Notice how the AJAX call is made. The $.ajax() method accepts a number of options for customizing the call. Isn't this a lot cleaner than our manual approach (figure 9.3)? For more simplified AJAX calls you might opt to use $.post() or $.get(). Read up on the jQuery documentation to see the various options available to you.

Now, the form submits via AJAX when JavaScript is enabled, which is what we were aiming for. Nobody loses functionality in the absence of JavaScript, but rather the experience is enhanced with JavaScript. The best part about this Hijax technique is that it's purely additive; you simply apply the extra JavaScript to an existing functioning form to enhance it with asynchronous behavior.

Figure 9.3   When an AJAX call is initiated Firebug shows it in the Console. You can use this tool to inspect the actual request and response of an AJAX call. Firebug is invaluable when doing AJAX development.

Listing 9.5 shows the SessionController actions in detail. Notice how we are reusing the same actions for both full layout and partial HTML requests. This is implemented as a partial view _list.ascx. This user control is embedded in the full layout, and rendered independently for partial requests.

Listing 9.5   The actions for SessionController

```
public ActionResult Index()
{
```

```
    var sessions = _sessionRepository.FindAll();

    if(Request.IsAjaxRequest())                    Render partial
        return View("_sessionList", sessions);     for AJAX requests

    return View(sessions);
}

[AcceptVerbs(HttpVerbs.Post)]                                        ❶
public ActionResult Add(string title, string description, string level)
{
    var session = new Session
    {
        Id = Guid.NewGuid(),
        Title = title,
        Description = description,
        Level = level
    };

    _sessionRepository.SaveSession(session);

    if(Request.IsAjaxRequest())                    AJAX requests
        return Index();                            need partial view

    return RedirectToAction("index");
}
```

The Index action checks to see whether the request is an AJAX request. If so, it will render the user control that represents the HTML fragment being displayed. If it's a regular request, the full HTML document (with the template) will be rendered.

The Add action is decorated with an AcceptVerbs attribute ❶ to protect it from GET requests. If this is an AJAX request—which is defined by an extra HTTP header in the request—the response needs to be the updated session list HTML. In the standard case without AJAX, the browser should redirect to the Index action.

The AJAX technique that we've applied here is both easy to implement (with the help of jQuery) and easy to understand. This is probably the most common method of applying AJAX. Don't believe me? This is essentially what the beloved UpdatePanel does in ASP.NET AJAX. We hear advertisements for other commercial AJAX components for "no-touch AJAX" or "zero-code AJAX" all the time. This is basically the technique they're using. Your authors firmly believe that "no-code" solutions are great for some scenarios, but they break down and become difficult to work with in more complex situations. It's often better to leverage a simple framework that lets you explicitly control the AJAX integration to give you the flexibility to adapt your application to increasingly complex functionality requirements. Here we've applied a simple script than can be reused on other pages to enhance a page with AJAX.

This example returned a snippet of HTML to the client. Sometimes we don't want HTML as our return value. HTML is the heaviest of the choices because it contains all of the formatting along with the data. Our example returned the entire rendered table. If over-the-wire performance is a concern (for example, if you intend to have users on slow connections or you have a lot of data to transfer) then you might opt for a lighter-weight representation of the data. If updated display information is needed,

JavaScript can dynamically build DOM elements to represent the data. Although more difficult, the flexibility and power exists when necessary.

There are two more common choices in data formats for JavaScript calls: XML and JSON. JSON is much lighter weight than XML. Plaintext is also sometimes useful if you don't need any structure to your data.

9.3.2 AJAX with JSON

Our next example will be a speaker listing. We'll see the names of the speakers in a list. If the user clicks a speaker's name, he will be directed to a speaker detail page. Figure 9.4 illustrates the speaker list. Figure 9.5 shows the speaker details.

Let's provide a richer user experience by applying AJAX to the speaker listing page. We'd like to enhance the speaker listing to show the speaker details next to the name when the user hovers over the name with the mouse.

To accomplish this, we'll leverage JSON as our transfer format. Why JSON? First off, our previous example used HTML, which we can all agree is verbose over the wire. If this is a concern, then we should be transmitting data only, leaving presentation to the client. One choice might be to represent the data using XML. Let's take a look at a sample XML document in listing 9.6:

Listing 9.6   An XML document representing a speaker contains a lot of noise

```
<speaker>
    <id>313bd98d-525c-4566-bfa1-7a4f8b01ef7b</id>
    <firstName>Ben</firstName>
    <lastName>Scheirman</lastName>
    <bio>Ben Scheirman is a Principal Consultant with Sogeti in Houston, TX.</
      bio>
    <picUrl>/content/ben.png</picUrl>
</speaker>
```

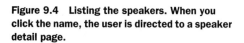

Figure 9.4   Listing the speakers. When you click the name, the user is directed to a speaker detail page.

Figure 9.5   The speaker details are shown on a separate page.

There is a lot of noise text in there (such as all of the closing tags). The same example represented in JSON looks like listing 9.7.

Listing 9.7   A JSON string representing a speaker is much more lightweight

```
({
    "id":"313bd98d-525c-4566-bfa1-7a4f8b01ef7b",
    "firstName":"Ben",
    "lastName":"Scheirman",
    "bio":" Ben Scheirman is a Principal Consultant with Sogeti in Houston,

       TX.",
    "picUrl":"/content/ben.png"
})
```

The JSON format is easy to understand, once you understand the basic rules. At the core, and object is represented as in figure 9.6.

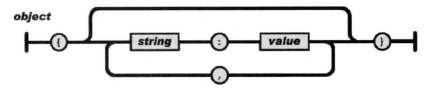

Figure 9.6   The JSON object diagram shows us a simple way of understanding the format. Taken from http://json.org.

Isn't the JSON representation more concise? Sure it might be a tad harder to read, but this is primarily for machines to consume, not humans. JSON documents will require fewer bytes to transmit (21 percent fewer in the earlier example), leading to less strain on the server and faster download times for your users. But this isn't the only reason that JSON is a better choice. JSON *is* JavaScript. Your result can be evaluated and treated as a first-class JavaScript object. (This evaluation is much faster than parsing XML as well.) Take your pick: get a real JavaScript object, or deal with XML parsing and manipulation.

A number of .NET JSON libraries can make your life easier. I've used JSON.NET by NewtonSoft, which is free to use and works well. You can download it at http://www.codeplex.com/json. The ASP.NET MVC Framework also includes a mechanism for serializing objects into JSON, which we'll see in a minute.

Now that we have settled on the JSON format for our AJAX feature, how do we get the controller to render it? Let's see how we can accommodate different view formats in our controllers.

9.3.3   *Adding alternate view formats to the controller*

Currently we have a controller action that finds the speaker from our repository and renders a "detail" view, passing the speaker in as `ViewData`. We want to take advantage of this action, but alter the view that gets rendered. We still want to get a speaker based on the name, but in our AJAX call we'd like the server to return a JSON string instead of an HTML document. Listing 9.8 shows the original controller action.

Listing 9.8 The controller action before any modifications

```
public ActionResult Details(string id)
{
   var speaker = _repository.FindSpeakerByName(id.Humanize());
   return View(speaker);
}
```

The ID passed in is a "URLized" representation of the name. Thus, "Ben Scheirman" becomes "ben-scheirman" in order to have cleaner URLs. This method is not safe for names that are already hyphenated (those would have to be escaped) or contain any other special characters, but for our simple example it works. We perform the reverse operation, called Humanize(), to get the actual name to search for.

NOTE Rather than searching for a single record by name, we could instead have a pseudokey stored in the database for use as a unique, human-readable, URL-friendly identifier. This is sometimes called a *slug*. This would avoid the problem of hyphenated names or names with invalid URL characters. We might also choose to add additional information to the route, such as the primary key. If we employed this technique, our URL would look like /speakers/13/ben-scheirman. The 13 would be a unique identifier, and the remaining segment of the URL would exist simply for the benefit of readability. Refer to chapter 5 for more information on creating custom routes like this.

In our AJAX case, we don't want an entire view to be returned from the action. This would result in a large HTML document being returned in an AJAX call. For an AJAX call, we want to return the JSON data directly. We'll leverage the same technique we did in listing 9.5 and notify the action about the type of request. We can also use this opportunity to allow for multiple formats to be rendered.

The modified controller action shown in listing 9.9 accepts an optional format as an argument. Valid values would be html (the default), partial (for html fragments), xml, and json. Our view can choose to respond to any one or all of those formats.

Listing 9.9 A modified controller action that accepts an optional format

```
public ActionResult Details(string id, string format)
{
   var speaker = _repository.FindSpeakerByName(id.Humanize());

   if(format == "json")
      return Json(speaker);        ❶

   return View(speaker);
}
```

The Json() method ❶ returns a JsonResult from the action and contains the object formatted as JSON.

TIP   You can send anonymous objects to the `Json()` method and have your object serialized to JSON format correctly. This is useful when you want to return JSON data that does not directly map to a class in your project. For example, this is valid:

```
return Json( new { Name="Joe", Occupation="Plumber" } );
```

To test out our different rendering formats, we'll open up the same speaker detail page from before, but this time we'll add ?format=json to the end of the URL as shown in figure 9.7. The MVC Framework will match up querystring and form parameters to action arguments if the names are the same. We could easily add more formats, such as XML. In the event that `format` is omitted (as in our original URL) then this value will be `null`.

Figure 9.7   Seeing our JSON result from the browser

Now that we have our JSON-enabled AJAX action ready for use, let's see how we can modify the speaker listing page to consume this.

9.3.4   *Consuming a JSON action from the view*

The first task is to hook into the *mouseover* and *mouseout* events of each list item. When the user hovers over a list item, as coded in listing 9.10, an AJAX call will be made to get the speaker details (as JSON) and construct a small detail box alongside the link.

Listing 9.10   Hooking up hover behavior on each of the links

```
$(document).ready(function() {
  $("ul.speakers a")
    .mouseover(function() {
```

```
        show_details(this);
    }).mouseout(function() {
        hide_details(this)
    });
});
```

It may not be apparent at first glance, but the $("ul.speakers a") function in listing 9.10 is a CSS selector that returns multiple elements. We attach a handler to each element's mouseover and mouseout events.

Next we have to actually do something when the user hovers over the link. I added a hidden <div> tag to each list item that serves as the container for the speaker's detailed information. The show_details() function, in listing 9.11, should show this box along with an AJAX loading indicator. When the data comes back from the server, we'll build elements to display the information.

Listing 9.11   When the user is hovering over the link

```
function show_details(link)
{
    var box = $(link).next();        ❶

    box.show();                      ❷
    box.html('');

    $('<img/>').attr('src' '/content/load.gif')              ❸
            .attr('alt', 'loading...').appendTo(box);

    var url = link.href
            .replace(/http:\/\/[^\/]+\//, "")               ❹
            .replace(/\?format=html/, "?format=json");

    $.getJSON(url, null, function(data) {
        loadSpeakerDetails(box, data);                      ❺
    });
}
```

This function has a lot going on, so let's break it down for each step. The link itself is passed in to the function, and we know that the "box" (the container where we'll put the user details) is the very next node in the DOM, so we use the jQuery next() function to retrieve it ❶. We then clear its contents and display it ❷. The next line creates an image tag pointing to load.gif and appends it inside the box element ❸. To retrieve the JSON object for the speaker details we have to use the same URL as the link, but we need to replace the format to specify json, so we use a regular expression to do the replacement for us ❹. We issue an AJAX GET request for the URL ❺. The callback for this AJAX operation is the next function, loadSpeakerDetails, as shown in listing 9.12.

Listing 9.12   Creating the HTML to display the speaker details

```
function loadSpeakerDetails(box, speaker)
{
    box.html('');      ⟵─ Clear loading graphic
```

```
$('<img/>')
    .attr("src", speaker.PictureUrl)
    .attr("alt", "pic")
    .attr("style", "float:left;margin:5px")
    .appendTo(box);

$('<span/>')
    .attr("style", "font-size: .8em")
    .html(speaker.Bio).appendTo(box);

$('<br style="clear:both" />').appendTo(box);
}
```

Image to display speaker picture

Span to hold speaker bio

In this function we are simply creating a few HTML elements to display the user details, and we are adding them to the box element. The last thing to do is hide the box, as coded in listing 9.13, when the user leaves the link region.

Listing 9.13   When the user leaves the link

```
function hide_details(link)
{
    $(link).next().hide();
}
```

Using jQuery in these examples has allowed us to be productive and expressive, while not worrying about cross-browser JavaScript quirks and incompatibilities. The resulting code is more durable and more concise. A good JavaScript library such as jQuery is a must in any web developer's tool belt.

All of the pieces are now tied together, and we can see the results of our work. In figure 9.8 you can see AJAX call at the bottom (in the Firebug window), and the page gives us the information we need without any page redirects or refreshes. How refreshing!

Figure 9.8   Our finished AJAX-enabled page

9.3.5   *AJAX helpers*

The ASP.NET MVC Framework ships with a couple of AJAX helpers that you can use to quickly create AJAX behaviors on your site. Just as the HTML helpers are accessed with `<%= Html.HelperName() %>`, the AJAX helpers are accessed via `<%= Ajax.HelperName() %>`. In order to utilize these helpers in your application you must reference Microsoft-Ajax.js and MicrosoftMvcAjax.js, which are included in the project template in the /scripts folder. It's safe to reference these in combination with jQuery.

The first AJAX helper that we'll examine is `Ajax.ActionLink`. This helper provides the ability to invoke an action asynchronously and update an element on the page. The usage is simple:

```
<%= Ajax.ActionLink("Click here", "GetMessage", new AjaxOptions {
    UpdateTargetId = "message_container",
    InsertionMode = InsertionMode.Replace
}) %>
```

This will render a link with displayed text *Click here*. When the user clicks the link the `GetMessage` action will be invoked via AJAX. The response from this action (probably some HTML fragment) will be placed in an element with ID `message_container`. The available parameters you can pass to the `AjaxOptions` class to customize the behavior of the link are listed in table 9.1.

Table 9.1   AJAX options available

HttpMethod	Can be `"GET"` or `"POST"`. The default is `"GET"`.
UpdateTargetId	The element that will receive the content.
InsertionMode	Can be `InsertBefore`, `InsertAfter`, or `Replace`.
OnBegin	JavaScript function to be called before invoking the action.
OnComplete	JavaScript function to be called after the response comes back.
OnFailure	JavaScript function to be called in the event of an error.
OnSuccess	JavaScript function to be called if no errors occur.
Confirm	Confirmation message to provide an OK/Cancel dialog before proceeding.
Url	URL to use if the anchor tag has a different destination than the AJAX request.
LoadingElementId	An element that displays AJAX progress. The element should be marked as `visibility:hidden` initially.

NOTE   *Warning*   It's tempting to put a simple JavaScript expression in the `OnBegin` handler or its counterparts; however, this causes a syntax error in the generated `onclick` handler for the anchor tag. Make sure you simply reference the JavaScript function by name (without parentheses) like this: `OnBegin = "ajaxStart"`

The AJAX link is just one of the helpers that invokes an action asynchronously. It's useful in scenarios where the logic is very simple, such as notifying the server of an action, or retrieving a simple value. For more complicated scenarios, where there is data to be sent to the server, an AJAX form is more appropriate.

The AJAX form is achieved through an AJAX helper called `Ajax.BeginForm`. It behaves similar to the Hijax technique from earlier in this chapter. Usage is similar to the AJAX action link:

```
<% using(Ajax.BeginForm("AddComment", new AjaxOptions{
        HttpMethod = "POST",
        UpdateTargetId = "comments",
        InsertionMode = InsertionMode.InsertAfter})) { %>

    <!-- form elements here -->
<% } %>
```

The same `AjaxOptions` class applies to this helper, and is used in the same way. In this example the form is appending comments to an element on the page.

NOTE   *The using() block?*   The using block might look a bit strange to you. It's purely optional; however, it does give you the benefit of automatically entering your closing form tag through the magic of the `IDisposable` interface. You are free to do it the other way, like this:

```
<% Ajax.BeginForm(); %>
</form>
```

It looks a bit unbalanced. The choice is yours.

The AJAX helpers can quickly give you AJAX behaviors, although they have a couple of drawbacks that are difficult to ignore. First, you can see that even simple examples require many lines of code—code that is mixed in with your HTML markup. For more advanced scenarios you can easily eat up ten lines or more, which detracts from readability. Second, the JavaScript is hidden from you, so you cannot reliably trap errors that occur as a result of your JavaScript handlers. Server errors will be trapped by the `OnError` handler; if your `OnBegin` code throws an error, your AJAX behavior cannot be completed. Because of these deficiencies many will choose to write the JavaScript by hand and get more control over the AJAX interaction. The jQuery samples in this chapter should have given you all you need to create the same effect with pure jQuery. That said, the AJAX helpers allow you to get quick AJAX functionality for minimal effort.

9.4   *Summary*

AJAX is an important technique to use with today's web applications. Using it effectively means that the majority of your users will get a better experience, but it does not prevent users with JavaScript disabled from accessing the site. This is sometimes referred to as progressive enhancement. Unfortunately, with raw JavaScript the technique is cumbersome and error prone. With good libraries such as jQuery, Prototype, script.acul.ous, Mochikit, and others, you can be much more productive.

In this chapter you have learned how to apply AJAX in different ways: using partial HTML replacement and JSON. You have learned how to hijack a form submission and provide a more seamless AJAX experience for those users who support AJAX, while continuing functionality for those who don't. Throughout this chapter you have seen how to apply jQuery, a productive JavaScript library.

Next up, we'll take a look at hosting and deployment options for ASP.NET MVC.

Hosting and deployment 10

This chapter covers

- Understanding server environment requirements
- Revealing hosting options in IIS
- Configuring different environments
- Creating push-button deployments

Running an ASP.NET MVC application in Visual Studio is as easy as hitting F5, but what about deploying the application? In a Windows-hosted environment, web applications are typically deployed to Internet Information Services (IIS). But several different versions of IIS are on the market, each with different configurations and options for hosting an ASP.NET MVC application. With new features like routing, in some versions of IIS hosting presents new challenges that did not exist with Web Forms applications.

Beyond server environment and hosting scenarios, deploying an application presents an entirely different set of challenges. Manual deployments are fraught with problems, as human errors become more prevalent. Automation eliminates these eleventh-hour problems by removing the human factor from deployments. Each deployment environment is slightly different, because connection strings, configuration settings, and server environments can vary. By introducing change management into our automated deployment process, we can ensure we install the correct application with the correct environment settings.

In this chapter the reader will learn options for hosting in the different IIS versions supported today. The reader will learn how to simplify deployment through an xcopy deployment strategy, and automate deployment through build automation tools. With these build automation tools, the reader will see how to take advantage of configuration management to automate configuration changes to the various deployment environments.

10.1 Deployment scenarios

In most scenarios, deploying an ASP.NET MVC application involves deployment to a Windows Server OS environment. Occasionally, it is necessary to deploy to older environments such as Windows Server 2000 or Windows XP, with older versions of IIS. Table 10.1 shows Windows OSs and the version of IIS available.

Windows Operating System	IIS version
Windows 2000	IIS 5.0
Windows XP Professional	IIS 5.1
Windows XP Professional x64 Edition	IIS 6.0
Windows Server 2003	IIS 6.0
Windows Vista	IIS 7.0
Windows Server 2008	IIS 7.0
Windows 7	IIS 7.5
Windows Server 2008 R2	IIS 7.5

Table 10.1 Windows and IIS versions

For all practical purposes, there are only two types of hosting environments we need to worry about:

- IIS 7.0+
- Not IIS 7.0+

Deploying to an IIS 7.0 environment to support the routing features of ASP.NET MVC requires far less configuration than the older versions of IIS. Most of the configuration decisions for IIS 6 and older versions revolve around routing, where your deployment decision could affect how you configure your routes.

Before we look at IIS deployment options, let's look at the hosting requirements for an ASP.NET MVC application. In addition to having IIS installed, the target machine will need to have the following software installed:

- .NET Framework 3.5
- .NET Framework 3.0
- .NET Framework 2.0

The 3.5 version of the .NET Framework includes Service Pack 1 of both .NET Framework 3.0 and 2.0. In addition to the .NET Framework, supporting software such as SQL Server may need to be installed. Note that .NET 3.5 Service Pack 1 is not required, though 3.5 SP1 does include the ASP.NET Routing feature, which both MVC and Web Forms applications can take advantage of.

Later in this chapter, we'll look at how the .NET 3.5 SP1 affects our deployment strategy. But first, we'll see how to deploy to an IIS environment using XCOPY deployment.

10.2 *XCOPY deployment*

Regardless of the version of IIS used, not every file in your solution needs to exist in the final destination on the server. Those familiar with Web Forms deployments know not to deploy code-behind files. The same holds true for MVC deployments. For an MVC-only website, the files needed are

- Global.asax
- Web.config
- Content files (JavaScript, images, static HTML, etc.)
- Views
- Compiled assemblies
- MVC assemblies
- System.Web.Abstractions.dll (not needed with .NET 3.5 SP1)
- System.Web.Mvc.dll
- System.Web.Routing.dll (not needed with .NET 3.5 SP1)

Deployments themselves can be difficult. Add complexities like installers, and deployments can become even more difficult to execute and maintain. Installers usually need a person logged in to the target machine to run them, and automation of installers is possible but still difficult. Log files from a botched installation usually consist of output from the MSI logger, which can be extremely verbose and indecipherable.

For many application deployment scenarios, an installer is unnecessary. Assuming the target machine is already configured correctly, simply copying over files is sufficient to deploy the application. This type of deployment is called *XCOPY deployment*. The term originated from the XCOPY DOS command, which allowed copying of multiple files in one command, along with many other options.

XCOPY deployment can significantly reduce the complexity of a deployment, as no one needs to perform a manual installation on the target server. Although the term *XCOPY* refers to a specific DOS command, it also applies to any technology that copies files.

As mentioned earlier, XCOPY deployments do not have to use a specific technology. Batch files, NAnt scripts, MSBuild scripts and third-party products such as FinalBuilder are all popular choices for creating XCOPY deployments. Particularly appealing are the latter choices, which include features that assist in automated deployments. Later in this chapter, we'll look at taking advantage of NAnt to perform deployment tasks, in

Choosing an installation strategy

Although an XCOPY deployment is the simplest choice, it's not always the right choice. XCOPY deployments are designed to copy files to the destination machine, and nothing more. Some IT environments require a specific deployment technology for a variety of reasons, such as traceability, logging, and reversibility.

XCOPY deployments work well for most web scenarios, but provide no out-of-the-box "uninstall" capabilities. Although other mechanisms exist to roll back an installation, some IT governance teams prefer the reliability of an installer for rolling back changes.

In practice, however, an installer is only as good as the developer who created it. It is still important to have test environments to ensure the installer works before trying it in production.

Modern installer products allow endless customization, such as IIS configuration, SQL configuration, and custom actions. The learning curve for these types of products is not trivial, leaving many teams to assign one member to be the installer. If this person leaves the team for any reason, often both the installer tool and the actions it performs need to be entirely rediscovered and relearned.

addition to copying files. But first, let's look at deploying an ASP.NET MVC application to an IIS 7 environment.

10.3 *Deploying to IIS 7*

Before we look at automating our deployments, we need to configure our server to host an ASP.NET MVC website. An MVC website needs a location on the target machine's hard drive. For this book, the location is unimportant, so we'll choose something simple: C:\websites\MVCSample. Our sample application will have no dependencies on a database, but later we will look at how to incorporate a database into our deployment strategy.

Our controller for this sample application will be simple but incorporate some common routes, as shown in listing 10.1.

Listing 10.1 Our simple controller

```
public class ProductController : Controller
{                                                        Dummy list
    private static readonly Product[] Products =   ◁──┘  of products
        new[]
        {
            new Product {Id = 1, Name = "Basketball",
                Description = "You bounce it."},
            new Product {Id = 2, Name = "Baseball",
                Description = "You throw it."},
            new Product {Id = 3, Name = "Football",
                Description = "You punt it."},
```

```
                    new Product {Id = 4, Name = "Golf ball",
                        Description = "You hook or slice it."}
                };
            public ActionResult List()
            {
                ViewData["Products"] = Products;

                return View();
            }
            public ActionResult Show(int id)
            {
                var product = Products.FirstOrDefault(p => p.Id == id);

                ViewData["Product"] = product;

                return View();
            }
        }
    }
```

Parameterless action

One parameter, from RouteData

Navigating to the List action renders the screen shown in figure 10.1.

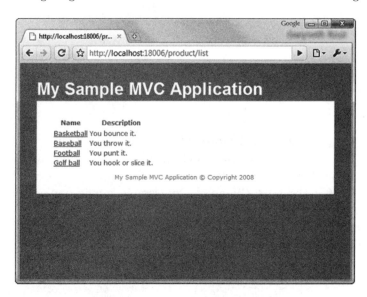

Figure 10.1   Running the MVC application locally allows us to use "pretty" URLs, with no extensions.

To deploy this ASP.NET MVC application to an IIS 7 box, we'll first create a local folder and move all our deployment files over. For this sample application, the folder structure is

- C:\Websites\MVCSample
  - \bin
    - Iis7DeploymentSample.dll (our compiled application assembly)
    - System.Web.Abstractions.dll (only needed when .NET 3.5 SP1 is NOT installed)

- – System.Web.Mvc.dll
- – System.Web.Routing.dll (only needed when .NET 3.5 SP1 is NOT installed)
- – \Content
  - – Site.css
- – \Views
  - – \Product
    - – List.aspx
    - – Show.aspx
  - – \Shared
    - – Error.aspx
    - – Site.master
  - – Web.config
- – Default.aspx
- – Global.asax
- – Web.config

When content is in place, we can configure a new website in the IIS Manager by clicking Add Web Site…, as shown in figure 10.2.

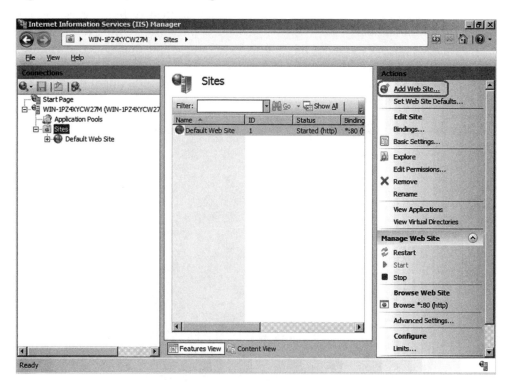

Figure 10.2   Add Web Site in the IIS 7 Manager console

In the Add Web Site dialog that comes up, we'll need to configure the

- Site name
- Application pool
- Physical path
- Binding

For the site name, I chose an arbitrary name that did not exist, "MVCSample." In the application pool dialog, any application pool will suffice as long as it is configured as a .NET 2.0 application pool. In IIS 7/7.5 it is preferred to use *integrated mode*, although with a wildcard mapping, *classic mode* can be made to work as well. ASP.NET MVC is not supported to run on lower versions of ASP.NET. We won't look at application pool strategies, but with IIS 6 onward, IIS supports multiple websites, each with a shared or individual application pool. The physical path will point to our C:\Websites\MVCSample directory. Finally, I chose simply to bind to port 81 for this website. Typically in production scenarios, the host name would be configured. The final configuration values are shown in figure 10.3.

Now that our website is configured and started, we can navigate to our MVC application, as seen in figure 10.4.

Besides extra configuration steps, such as security or binding, we did not have to perform additional steps to get our MVC application running under IIS 7. The new managed architecture of IIS 7 allows us to have simple deployments. Additionally, our URLs look exactly the same as they did when running locally out of Visual Studio, without .aspx or other extensions. IIS 7 supports "pretty" URLs out of the box, with no configuration necessary.

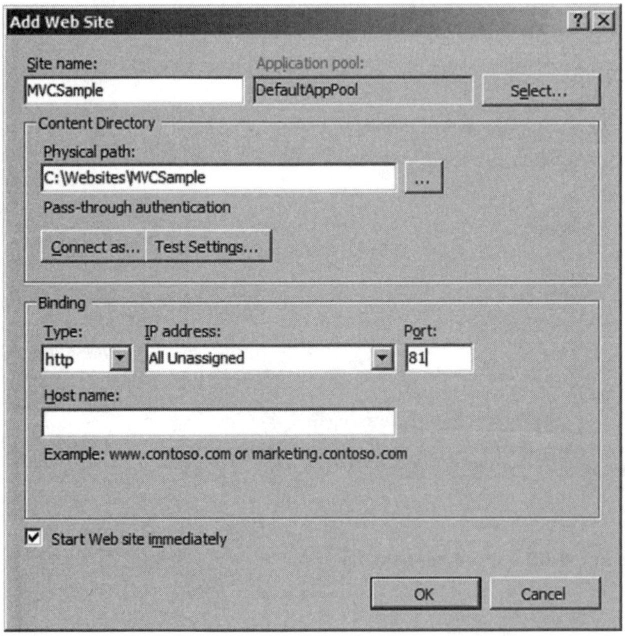

Figure 10.3
Final configuration values for the IIS 7 MVC deployment

**Figure 10.4
MVC application
deployed in IIS 7**

In the next section, we'll examine configuration options available in IIS 6/5, and how we can achieve the same effect of pretty URLs.

10.4 Deploying to IIS 6 and earlier

When we deploy our MVC application to IIS 6 and earlier, we can consider a few options concerning routes. IIS 6 and earlier use ISAPI filters, which map file extension requests to ISAPI handlers. Extensions, such as .aspx and .ascx, map to the ASP.NET ISAPI handler, but extensions in the pretty, extension-less MVC URLs do not. By the time ASP.NET handles the request, IIS has already chosen an ISAPI handler for the request, and the selection may not be ASP.NET. Unfortunately, developing custom ISAPI filters requires C/C++ knowledge. Although some open source projects exist for writing managed ISAPI filters, it is not as easy as creating a custom `IHttpHandler` or `IHttpModule` implementation.

Out of the box, ASP.NET MVC applications will not work in IIS 6. Getting an MVC application to run successfully in an IIS 6 environment requires either changes to our routes or extra configuration steps in IIS. Our four choices for deploying to IIS 6 are

- Configure routes to use the .aspx extension
- Configure routes to use a custom extension (such as .mvc)
- Use a wildcard mapping with selective disabling
- Use URL rewriting

The last choice offers the most flexibility, but does require the use of third-party software. Each option requires more configuration in IIS, which may not be available in your deployment environment. First, let's look at the easiest deployment option and configure our routes to use the .aspx extension.

10.4.1 *Configuring routes to use the .aspx extension*

When we install ASP.NET in IIS, by default the aspnet_isapi.dll ISAPI filter is set up to handle requests to .aspx extensions. By configuring our routes to use the .aspx extension, we'll avoid needing to configure extra mapping settings in IIS for our MVC application. To configure our routes to use the .aspx extension, we need to change the default route configuration to look like listing 10.2.

Listing 10.2 Route configuration with the .aspx extension

```
routes.MapRoute(
    "Default",                                              IIS 7 deployments
    "{controller}.aspx/{action}/{id}",          ◁──┐       don't need extension
    new { controller = "Product", action = "List", id = "" }
);
```

After the `{controller}` element, we insert the .aspx extension into the route configuration. Note that the extension is outside the brackets, and before the first backslash. Deploying the application with the route configuration changes produces the result shown in figure 10.5.

Unfortunately, using this deployment option produces ugly, nonintuitive URLs. Note the URL, http://localhost:81/product.aspx/show/4, now has the extension immediately after the controller name. For those accustomed to extensions at the end of the URL, this URL can be confusing. Although we did not have to perform any additional configuration in IIS, the outcome is an ugly URL. The strategy introduced in chapter 6 for actions serving multiple formats (XML and JSON) becomes more challenging, as IIS may or may not have these extensions routing to ASP.NET. One of the benefits of using MVC over Web Forms is pretty URLs, which have now been lost with this deployment strategy. Our next option is to use a custom extension, which introduces a slight cosmetic change to the resulting URLs.

**Figure 10.5
Using the .aspx
configuration
produces
modified URLs.**

10.4.2 *Configuring routes to use a custom extension*

Instead of mapping our routes to the .aspx extension, a custom extension could reduce the confusion of users accustomed to Web Forms URLs. We'll configure our routes to use the .mvc extension instead of .aspx, as seen in listing 10.3.

Listing 10.3   Route configuration using the custom .mvc extension

```
routes.MapRoute(
    "Default",
    "{controller}.mvc/{action}/{id}",
    new { controller = "Product", action = "List", id = "" }
);
```

This configuration differs from the previous .aspx route configuration in the extension only. When it comes to deploying this route configuration, we need to perform additional steps in IIS. Since IIS is not configured to handle requests from the .mvc extension, we'll need to add a mapping that will enable the ASP.NET ISAPI filter to handle the .mvc extension. To map the new extension, follow these steps, as shown in figures 10.6 and 10.7:

1. Create the website with the default configuration.
2. In the Home Directory tab in the Properties dialog for the website, click Configuration....

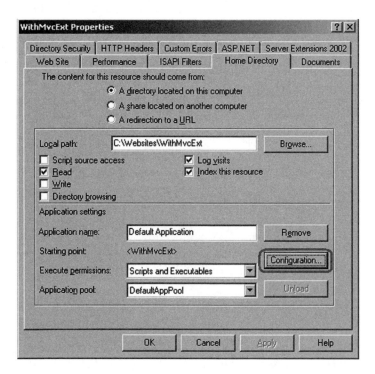

Figure 10.6   Website properties dialog

3 In the Mappings tab in the Application Configuration dialog, click Add....

4 In the Add/Edit Application Extension Mapping dialog:

a Enter the path to aspnet_isapi.dll in the Executable textbox. This is typically at C:\WINDOWS\Microsoft.NET\Framework\v2.0.50727\aspnet_isapi.dll. Use the .NET 2.0 version of the dll.

b Set the Extension value to .mvc. Make sure the extension has the leading dot.

c Select All verbs in the Verbs section. If you know the HTTP verbs you wish to support, provide a comma-separated list of the verbs in the Limit to section.

d Uncheck the Verify that file exists option. The requested URLs will not map to a location on disk, and IIS responds with a 404 if you don't uncheck this value.

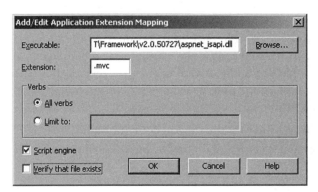

**Figure 10.7
Configuration values
for the new .MVC IIS
extension mapping**

5 Click OK on all of the configuration dialogs.

Now that we have configured IIS to allow ASP.NET to handle requests for the .mvc extension, we can use the MVC application. Our new URL is http://localhost:82/product.mvc/show/4, which is only a slight cosmetic change from the previous option. Although using the .mvc extension might prevent some users from getting confused between Web Forms .aspx URLs and .mvc URLs, these new URLs still go against normal URL conventions. In normal URL conventions, only querystring parameters follow an extension. Instead of using a custom extension, our next option uses a wildcard mapping.

10.4.3 *Using wildcard mapping with selective disabling*

With the next two options, we won't have to perform any special route configuration. In fact, we can deploy the same MVC application to both IIS 7 and IIS 6 and previous versions with the wildcard mapping option. We no longer need an extension in our route configuration, and the URLs used for development will be identical to the URLs used for production on IIS 6.

With wildcard mapping, all requests are routed to a single ISAPI filter. We'll configure the aspnet_isapi.dll filter to be this single filter. To create the wildcard mapping:

1 Create the website with the default configuration.

2 In the Home Directory tab in the Properties dialog for the website, click Configuration....

3 In the Mappings tab in the Application Configuration dialog, click Insert….

4 In the Add/Edit Application Extension Mapping dialog:

  a Enter the path to aspnet_isapi.dll in the Executable textbox. The path is typi-
     cally C:\WINDOWS\Microsoft.NET\Framework\v2.0.50727\aspnet_isapi.dll. Use
     the .NET 2.0 version of the dll.

  b Uncheck the Verify that file exists option and ensure the configuration
     matches that shown in figure 10.8.

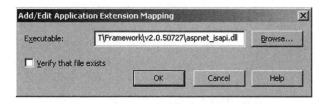

**Figure 10.8 Configuring
wildcard mapping to map
to ASP.NET**

5 Click OK on all configuration dialogs.

After this configuration change, we can navigate to our MVC application, without special extensions. Our URL is now http://localhost:83/product/show/4, matching the
URL that we see in IIS 7 deployments. This wildcard mapping has one unfortunate
side effect: all requests are now handled by ASP.NET, which does not perform as well as
IIS for many file types. For example, static files such as images, CSS, and JavaScript files
now pass through ASP.NET.

  We can configure subdirectories to remove the wildcard mapping. Because all
static content for deployed websites usually exists in subdirectories like *Content*, *Scripts*,
and others, we can perform extra configuration steps to allow IIS to handle these
static files, instead of IIS. Figures 10.9, 10.10, and 10.11 illustrate some of the steps.
For each subdirectory, we'll need to

1 Right-click the subfolder and click Properties in the IIS Management Console.

2 In the Directory tab in the Properties dialog, click the Create button. This will create an application for this folder, and will enable the Configuration… button.

3 In the Directory tab in the Properties dialog, click the Configuration… button.

4 In the Mappings tab of the Application Configuration dialog, click the Remove
   button in the Wildcard application maps section. This will remove the wildcard
   mapping we configured at the root earlier.

5 Click OK to return to the Application Configuration dialog.

6 In the Directory tab in the Application Configuration dialog, click Remove.
   This will remove the Application from the subfolder.

7 Click OK on all configuration dialogs.

When you repeat these steps for each subfolder, you prevent IIS from using the wildcard mapping in these subfolders. Because the only way to enable the Configuration… button is to create an application, we have to temporarily configure the

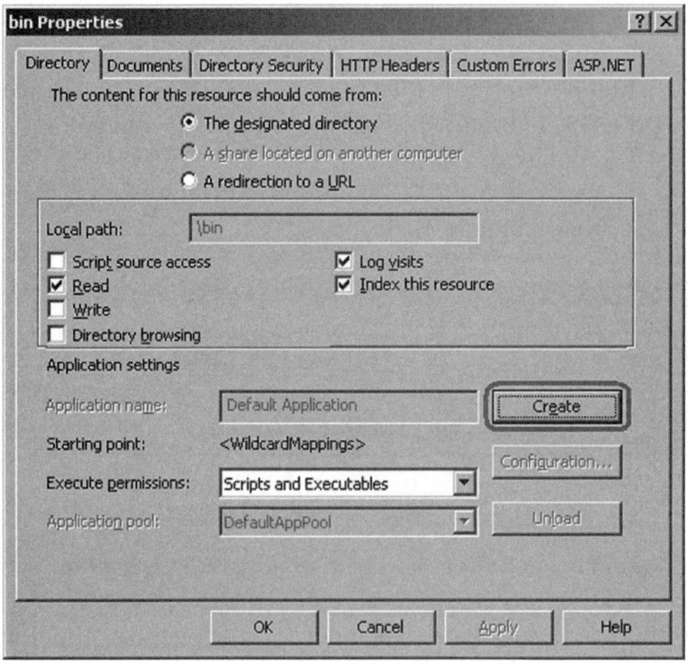

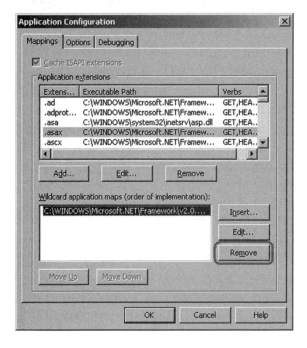

Figure 10.9   Creating an application for a subfolder temporarily

subfolder as an application. Removing the application after configuration does not remove our custom configuration, however. Our changes are safe, although we had to perform extra temporary configuration to get there.

Figure 10.10   Removing the wildcard mapping from a subfolder

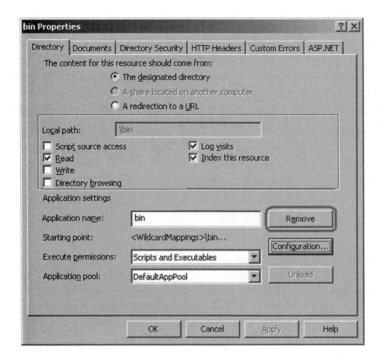

Figure 10.11 Removing the application from the subfolder

Although this option requires a bit of configuration in IIS, it does not require any additional software. Our route mappings do not need to change, and we get to keep our pretty, extension-less URLs. Whenever we add another subfolder, we'll need to repeat the extra configuration steps to ensure ASP.NET does not handle requests it does not need to. Sometimes, we need more control over our URLs than IIS 6 and earlier versions allow right out of the box. In the next section, we'll look at URL rewriting to handle both MVC requests and additional URL rewriting scenarios.

10.4.4 Using URL rewriting

URL rewriting is a sizable topic, which covers resource management support, search engine optimization, and canonicalized URLs. In many other web application servers, URL rewriting is a first-class, built-in feature, or easily configured and customizable add-on. In IIS 6 and earlier, there was no built-in URL rewriting ability. For IIS 7, Microsoft released an `HttpModule` that allowed configuration directly from the IIS Manager. Regardless of the version of IIS used, URL rewriting is a vital function for many websites.

Since URL rewriting is not available for IIS 6 and earlier out of the box, we'll need to use a third-party extension for rewrites. Two popular URL rewrite ISAPI extensions are

- Helicon Tech's ISAPI_Rewrite—http://www.isapirewrite.com/
- Ionic's Isapi Rewrite—http://www.codeplex.com/IIRF/

Helicon Tech has one free and one fully supported edition of its product. The Ionic extension is free and open source, so we'll configure our application using that.

Why should I care about URL rewriting?

URL rewriting is a general term for the ability to intercept URL requests and transform them. For resource management, such as RSS links, URL rewriting can permanently redirect requests to the new RSS URL, while remaining transparent to the subscribers. In many ASP.NET websites, many URLs point to the same page. For example, all of the following URLs resolve to the same page:

- http://codeplex.com
- http://codeplex.com/
- http://codeplex.com/default.aspx
- http://www.codeplex.com
- http://www.codeplex.com/
- http://www.codeplex.com/default.aspx

Yet they all resolve to different URLs, with a couple exceptions. Differing URL resolution has the potential to lower search engine results, as many pages point to the same content. With URL rewriting, all of the example URLs can be redirected to one canonical URL. We can allow extension-less routes in our MVC application, and set ourselves up for further vital URL rewriting scenarios.

First, we'll need to download the latest version of the filter from CodePlex. Once we have the latest binaries, we are ready to configure our MVC application to use the ISAPI Rewrite module. The general idea behind our URL rewriting strategy is to

- Configure ISAPI Rewrite to add an .aspx extension to our URLs.
- IIS will see a request for .aspx, and hand it off to ASP.NET.
- Configure our web application to remove .aspx extensions. For existing Web Forms environments, we'll need to pick a different extension and then configure IIS to handle that extension.

Because our web application removes the .aspx extension before the MVC route handler processes the request, we won't need to change our routing configuration. To configure ISAPI rewrite, we'll need to

1 Modify our web application to remove the .aspx extension at the beginning of the request. We can place the code in listing 10.4 in the Global.asax.cs file.

Listing 10.4   Removing the .aspx extension on each request

```
protected void Application_BeginRequest(Object sender, EventArgs e)
{
    HttpApplication app = sender as HttpApplication;
    if (app != null)
    {
        if (app.Request
            .AppRelativeCurrentExecutionFilePath          Only requests for
            .Contains(".aspx"))                            .aspx resources
```

```
        {
            app.Context.RewritePath(
                app.Request.Url.PathAndQuery.Replace(".aspx", ""));
        }
    }
}
```

2 Create the website with the default configuration, and deploy our application as normal.

3 Create a folder to hold the ISAPI extension. We'll use *C:\inetpub\isapirewrite*.

4 Copy the IsapiRewrite4.dll to the newly created folder.

5 In the newly created folder, create an IsapiRewrite4.ini file and add the contents in listing 10.5. Save this file when you have finished editing it.

Listing 10.5   The URL rewriting rules

```
RewriteRule  ^/(\w+)(?!/Content)(/[A-Za-z0-9_-]+)$      /$1$2.aspx      [I]

RewriteRule  ^/(\w+)(?!/Content)(/[A-Za-z0-9_-]+)(/.*)?$  /$1$2.aspx$3  [I]
```

6 Open the Properties dialog for the website containing the MVC application in IIS Manager.

7 In the ISAPI Filters tab in the Properties dialog, click Add….

8 Enter a name for the Filter name value, and the path to the IsapiRewrite4.dll for the Executable value as shown in figure 10.12.

Figure 10.12   Configuring the ISAPI Rewrite filter

9 Click OK on all of the IIS configuration dialogs.

10 Restart ISS.

We can now navigate to our website with pretty URLs in the form http://localhost:84/ product/show/4. For more detailed configuration options, consult the readme included with the download from CodePlex. The download includes configuration examples, as well as instructions for enabling logging and other advanced features. Although we had to make a small change to our Global.asax.cs file, the routes remained the same, without any extensions. In addition, all URL-generating action helpers still generate pretty URLs, ensuring that no end user ever sees a URL with the .aspx extension. With the URL rewriting extension in place, we can now employ its features to address canonical URLs, forwarding, and other rewriting concerns. The one caveat to keep in mind with this approach is that requests for real Web Forms pages, such as Default.aspx, will no longer be served. If you have chosen this approach, you will likely not be affected by this caveat.

With our application deployed and configured, we'll take a look at automating deployments.

10.5   *Automating deployments*

On launch night, tensions are high as the smallest mistake could bring your website down. To eliminate the human mistakes that inevitably occur, we would like to automate as much as possible. Ideally, we could simply push a button, and our website would be updated in moments. How this happens depends largely on the deployment environment. Regardless of the deployment environment, any good deployment strategy requires the use of continuous integration.

10.5.1   *Employing continuous integration*

Working in an environment without an automated integration process can be hectic, and nerve-racking. Because "it works on *my* machine" does not suffice in a deployment scenario, we need a set of practices to ensure our code always works, and is always ready to deploy. To achieve continuous integration, Martin Fowler laid out a set of practices to adhere to (from http://www.martinfowler.com/articles/continuous-Integration.html):

- Maintain a single source repository (use source control).
- Automate the build.
- Make your build self-testing.
- Make sure everyone commits every day.
- Every commit should build the mainline on an integration machine.
- Keep the build fast.
- Test in a clone of a production environment.
- Make it easy for anyone to get the latest executable.
- Ensure everyone can see what's happening.
- Automate deployment.

We won't cover all of the continuous integration practices in this book, as entire books have been written on this topic. In addition to adhering to these practices, the "check-in dance" ensures that no one inadvertently breaks the build. The check-in dance steps are

1. Run the local build.
2. Announce to the team you are integrating (for large changes).
3. Pull down the latest version of the mainline. Merge any conflicts.
4. Run the local build.
5. If successful, commit the changes, providing a descriptive comment.
6. Wait for the server build to be successful.
7. If the build fails, drop everything and fix it.

Depending on the development environment, there are several continuous integration server tools and technologies to employ. One popular continuous integration stack includes

- Subversion (SVN) for source control
- NAnt for build automation
- NUnit for testing
- CruiseControl.NET for the continuous integration server

Which tool we use does not matter as much as the practices the tools enforce, although we would like our tools to introduce as little friction as possible into the development environment. If we have to wait for a slow or unreliable source control server, our practices are less likely to be followed. Whichever build technology we decide to use, the result of each build should be a single deployment file, checked in to source control at the end of a successful server build. To enable push-button XCOPY deployments, we'll next look at some key NAnt features.

10.5.2 *Enabling push-button XCOPY deployments*

In an intranet environment, XCOPY deployments can be as simple as setting up a network share on the deployed machine. In other situations, the deployment file, whether it is an installer or self-contained .zip file, must be copied over manually or pulled down from source control. Regardless, if the files can be pushed from a network share, or pulled manually on the server, our deployment package will include

- The complete application
- The build tool, if used (NAnt)
- A deployment script
- A batch file to kick the process off

Our automated continuous integration build creates and checks in this deployment package. When we have a deployment package in source control, it enables us to deploy any version of our application as needed. With a tool like CruiseControl.net, it is possible to automate the deployment of the latest version of the application as needed.

NAnt, along with the sister project NAntContrib, provides dozens and dozens of tasks out of the box, which can be compiled together to create a single deployment script. These tasks are

- Source control tasks
- IIS tasks
- File and directory tasks such as creation, deletion, and copying
- Zip tasks
- XML manipulation tasks

With a manual process in place, we can start automating one step at a time with NAnt tasks, until the entire deployment process is automated. Many teams already employ a build process in the form of a Word document or wiki entry, detailing the manual steps.

It is only a matter of finding the corresponding NAnt task for each manual task, and the deployment is automated. If no NAnt task exists for a particular operation, NAnt provides the Exec task, which can execute anything that can execute in the command line. The key NAnt tasks for deployments include

- `unzip`
- `copy`
- `exec`
- `xmlpoke`

We'll need the `unzip` task to unzip the deployment package originally checked in to source control. If this is a manual pull of the deployment package, we can unzip the package manually. The `copy` task is used to copy the complete application to the correct deployed directory, performing an XCOPY deployment in one automated task. The `exec` task is used for a variety of scenarios, such as restarting IIS, stopping and starting services, registering assemblies, and so on. The `xmlpoke` task is used to manage deployment configurations by manipulating key configuration files, such as the Web.config file. In the next section, we'll examine how to manage multiple deployment configurations with NAnt and `xmlpoke`.

10.5.3 *Managing environment configurations*

Development teams often deploy their applications in multiple environments. For any given project, there are at least two environments: production and development. Many teams integrate to one or more test environments before releasing to production. Among these different environments, the deployment must change. Some environments require merely a connection string change, and others require debug flags, configuration values, email addresses, and more. In an automated deployment, the deployment script must take into account the different environment settings. Notably, it must know what environment it is deploying to, and what changes to make to the application to match that environment.

With NAnt, managing all of these environment configurations is straightforward. Deployments are kicked off with a batch file, which merely starts NAnt. The deployment package zip file contains

- Dev.bat
- CommonDeploy.bat
- deployment.build
- NAnt\
- website\
- database\

The NAnt folder contains the entire runtime distribution of NAnt. We include the distribution to avoid an environmental setup step on every server to which we deploy. The website folder contains the complete application that we XCOPY deploy to the correct folder on the server. The deployment.build is the NAnt build script that contains the complete deployment script. The Dev.bat file is a bootstrapper file that calls CommonDeploy.bat. In listing 10.6, the bootstrapper file Dev.bat call overrides the deploy directory and connection string properties by setting environment variables, and then calls the CommonDeploy.bat script.

Listing 10.6   Setting the environment configuration in Dev.bat

```
SET driverClass=NHibernate.Driver.SqlClientDriver
SET connectionString=Data Source=.\sqlexpress;Initial
    Catalog=TODO;uid=sa;pwd=TODO
SET localConnectionString=Data Source=.\sqlexpress;Initial
    Catalog=TODO;uid=sa;pwd=TODO
SET dialect=NHibernate.Dialect.MsSql2005Dialect
SET websiteTargetDir=\\TODO

SET databaseServer=TODO\sqlexpress
SET databaseName=TODO
SET databaseIntegrated=false
SET databaseUsername=sa
SET databasePassword=TODO                        ⊢── SET command
                                                     declares variables
SET shouldReloadDatabase=true      ◁──┘

CommonDeploy.bat
```

In the Dev.bat file, we set up the environment variables for the environment configuration values (some of which still need to be filled in). With one CommonDeploy.bat batch file that runs off environment variables, we can create additional bootstrapper batch files for each target environment. The end of the Dev.bat batch script calls into the CommonDeploy.bat script, which provides a common bootstrapper file on top of NAnt, shown in listing 10.7 below.

Listing 10.7   Bootstrapper CommonDeploy.bat file overriding NAnt properties

```
nant\nant.exe
-buildfile:deployment.build                           ⊢── Use previously set
-D:should.reload.database="%shouldReloadDatabase%"  ◁──┘  environment variables
-D:driver.class="%driverClass%"
-D:connection.string="%connectionString%"
-D:local.connection.string="%localConnectionString%"
-D:dialect="%dialect%"
-D:website.target.dir="%websiteTargetDir%"
-D:database.server="%databaseServer%"
-D:database.name="%databaseName%"
-D:database.integrated="%databaseIntegrated%"
-D:database.username="%databaseUsername%"
-D:database.password="%databasePassword%"
-D:test.database.name="%testDatabaseName%"
-D:excel.server.path="%excelServerPath%"
```

This entire command is in a single CommonDeploy.bat file, calling NAnt, using environment variables set up by a previous environment-specific batch file (Dev.bat in our case). The "-D" command-line switches for NAnt allow us to override properties with the correct deployed values. Because our deployment database will most likely require a different connection string than our local configuration, we need to use NAnt to override this value during deployment. A portion of the deploy.build file is in listing 10.8 below.

Listing 10.8   Deployment.build NAnt script with the deploy target

```
<target name="deploy">                                    Call another target

    <call target="rebuildDatabase" if="${should.reload.database}" />

    <xmlpoke                                      Change the
        file="website/bin/hibernate.cfg.xml"      connection string
        xpath="${connection.string.path}"
        value="${local.connection.string}">
        <namespaces>
            <namespace prefix="hbm"
                uri="urn:nhibernate-configuration-2.2"></namespace>
        </namespaces>
    </xmlpoke>

    <copy todir="${website.target.dir}" overwrite="true"    Copy all
        includeemptydirs="true" >                           website files
        <fileset basedir="website">
            <include name="**" />
        </fileset>
    </copy>

</target>
```

The first items to notice in this NAnt script are the XML attribute values in the format `${some.value.here}`. These are NAnt properties, whose values were defined earlier through our bootstrapper file. When the CommonDeploy.bat file executes, the command-line switches set these property values with the appropriate environmental settings. Finally, the "deploy" target performs the actual deployment. An NAnt target is a named group of tasks, similar to a method in C#.

The actual CodeCampServer NAnt deployment script is considerably larger, but performs these common deployment steps:

1 Applies environmental configuration to various configuration files
2 Rebuilds the local database
3 Populates the local database with test data
4 Removes the existing application
5 Copies files to target location

Each step in the deployment.build script first echoes a message to the console, for informational and debugging purposes. Although CodeCampServer's current build script is large, it was built up over time to support the various configuration and deployment needs. Deployment scripts can be as simple as copy and delete tasks; it depends on each deployment scenario.

10.6 *Summary*

With the new routing abilities of ASP.NET MVC came new deployment challenges. Although IIS 7 supports extensionless, pretty URLs out of the box, earlier versions of IIS do not. However, we have a variety of deployment options with earlier versions of IIS, some of which enable pretty URLs. URL rewriting is the most powerful of these deployment options, as it opens up new scenarios in URL canonicalization and seamless resource management.

When we configure our environment, we must devise a reliable deployment strategy to ensure the right application is deployed with the correct configuration. At the heart of a solid deployment strategy is continuous integration, which includes practices such as automated deployments and self-testing builds. With free, widely used open source tools such as CruiseControl.NET, NAnt, NUnit, and others, we can build an automated build and deployment server. By packaging NAnt, a build script, and a bootstrap batch file, we can harness the flexibility and power of NAnt to deploy and configure our application to multiple environments, up to and including production.

Next, we'll examine existing MVC frameworks, including the .NET based MonoRail and Ruby on Rails, and examine how they compare with the newcomer, ASP.NET MVC.

Exploring MonoRail
and Ruby on Rails

This chapter covers

- Castle MonoRail
- Castle ActiveRecord
- Castle Windsor
- Ruby on Rails
- ActionPack

Model-View-Controller as a pattern emerged about 20 years ago in the Smalltalk community. Since then, numerous representations of the MVC pattern for almost every visual technology and language have developed. Combined with object-oriented programming, the MVC pattern provides a powerful separation of concerns between view technologies and the logic to interpret and react to user input. The MVC pattern is certainly not new, nor is ASP.NET MVC the first MVC framework to exist on the ASP.NET platform.

Many alternative MVC frameworks position themselves as full-stack MVC frameworks, where everything from database to deployment to hosting is included in the framework. Full-stack frameworks can greatly reduce the amount of development time needed to create an application, as all components are designed to work together to create one seamless development experience.

In this chapter, we will examine MVC frameworks built for both .NET and other platforms. We will dive into MonoRail, which is a popular MVC framework built on .NET and is part of the larger Castle Project. Next, we will explore another popular web framework, Ruby on Rails. Ruby on Rails is built on the dynamic language of Ruby, and uses the strong opinions of the framework's developers to guide the end user down well-trodden paths. By the end of this chapter, you will be familiar with two major MVC frameworks used today and their primary features, benefits, and advantages.

11.1 MonoRail

MonoRail is a .NET MVC implementation inspired by the Ruby on Rails ActionPack component. MonoRail is part of a larger open source project, Castle. The Castle Project includes several other enterprise application components, including an IoC container implementation in Windsor/MicroKernel, as well as an Active Record implementation. With the ActiveRecord piece, the Castle Project provides a powerful full-stack web development framework.

As MonoRail has seen more releases and has been under active development for many years, it is natural that MonoRail provides a richer feature set than ASP.NET MVC. But because many components in Castle are not coupled strictly to MonoRail, many features of Castle and even MonoRail can be used in ASP.NET MVC. It is possible to develop a MonoRail and ASP.NET MVC application side by side in one project. But before we examine how to combine Castle features with ASP.NET MVC, let's take a closer look at what MonoRail provides.

11.1.1 Feature overview

Before we look at more advanced features of MonoRail, let's look at a baseline application that incorporates many of the same features as ASP.NET MVC. This example will use quite a few features from MonoRail, which we will cover in detail. First, let's look at a simple controller that displays a list of people in listing 11.1:

Listing 11.1 A simple `PeopleController` using MonoRail

```
[Layout("default")]                                              ❶
public class PeopleController : SmartDispatcherController      ❷
{
    public void List()        ❸
    {
        Person[] people = Person.FindAll();

        PropertyBag["people"] = people;        ❹
    }
}
```

We will skip all the configuration needed for MonoRail, as it is fairly similar to ASP.NET MVC configuration. In listing 11.1, we created the `PeopleController` by declaring a class and inheriting from `SmartDispatcherController` ❷. SmartDispatcherController is similar in functionality to the base `Controller` class in ASP.NET MVC, and holds references to common `HttpContext` runtime components as well as other items needed for the view. Next, we declared a single action, `List` ❸. Any public method becomes an action in a `SmartDispatcherController`, with automatic naming conventions tying URLs to actions. MonoRail also provides support for fine-grained control over the action name relative to the method name. At the top of the class, we tell MonoRail that we're going to use the "default" layout with the `Layout` attribute ❶. There will be a corresponding "Layout" view template in our project.

Inside the action method, we use the `Person` class to query the database to return all people. The `Person` class uses ActiveRecord, another Castle component that we'll cover in the next section. Finally, we add an entry in the `PropertyBag` ❹ with the people array returned from the database. `PropertyBag` is analogous to the `ViewData` property in ASP.NET MVC. When we want to pass data to the view, we use the `PropertyBag`. One important difference between actions in MonoRail and actions in ASP.NET MVC is that the MonoRail actions return void, instead of an `ActionResult` object. In MonoRail all actions alter the state of the controller, and that state is interpreted by the dispatcher after all actions have been executed.

MonoRail, like ASP.NET MVC, supports multiple view engines. For our example, we will use the popular NVelocity view template framework. Listing 11.2 shows our simple table of people:

Listing 11.2   NVelocity template for listing people

```
<h2>People</h2>

#foreach($person in $people)        ❶
#beforeall                          ❷
    <table class="datatable">
        <thead>
            <tr>
                <th>Name</th>
                <th>Email</th>
                <th>Website</th>
                <th>Comments</th>
            </tr>
        </thead>
        <tbody>
#odd        ❸
            <tr style="background-color: #eee">
#even       ❹
            <tr>
#each       ❺
                <td>$person.GetName()</td>
                <td>$person.Contact.Email</td>
                <td><a href="$person.Website">$person.Website</a></td>
                <td>$person.Comment</td>
#after      </tr>
```

```
#afterall
        </tbody>
    </table>
#end
```

In the view template, we provide only the snippet of template code to show the list of people. This template is part of a parent "default" layout, which we specified earlier in our controller with the Layout attribute. In the template, the #foreach section does the work. The #foreach section will loop over all the people in the $people identifier ❶, which looks in the PropertyBag for the actual underlying object. The #beforeall section creates the initial table HTML elements, the header columns, and the start of the table body ❷.

Next, we see two interesting sections: an #odd ❸ and an #even ❹ section. As would be expected, the #odd section is used before each odd-numbered section, and the #even is used before each even section. Next, we supply the individual table cells with data in the #each section ❺. Each table cell uses the $person identifier, defined in the #foreach section. The $person is a Person object, so we can access the properties and methods as if we were working in C#. The result of this template is shown in figure 11.1.

Because of the #odd and #even templates, we were able to apply specific row alternating styles in our table. Unlike other ASP.NET controls, we were able to work efficiently in HTML, putting the <tr> element only in the #odd and #even sections. The Layout attribute allowed us to put our entire common HTML in one template, shown in listing 11.3.

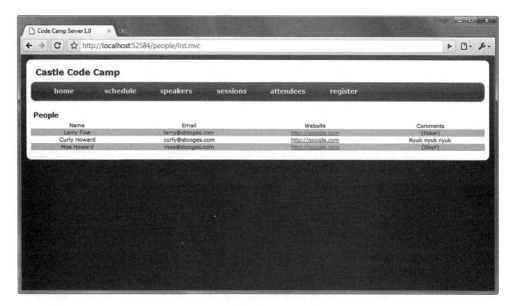

Figure 11.1 Displaying all people with the NVelocity templating engine

Listing 11.3   The common default template

```
<!DOCTYPE html PUBLIC "-//W3C//DTD XHTML 1.1//EN" "http://www.w3.org/TR/
    xhtml11/DTD/xhtml11.dtd">
<html>
<head>
    <meta http-equiv="Content-Type"
        content="text/html; charset=iso-8859-1" />
    <title>Layout</title>
    <link rel="stylesheet" href="$siteRoot/css/stylesheet.css" />
    <link rel="stylesheet" href="$siteRoot/css/themes/green.css" />
</head>
<body>
    <div id="frame">
        <div id="frame-header"></div>
        <div id="content">
            <div id="header">
                <h1>Castle Code Camp</h1>
            </div>
            <div class="cleaner"></div>
            <div id="navigationWrapper">
                <div id="leftNavigationEndCap"></div>
                <ul id="navigationMenu">
                    <li><a href="#">home</a></li>
                    <li><a href="#">schedule</a></li>
                    <li><a href="#">speakers</a></li>
                    <li><a href="#">sessions</a></li>
                    <li><a href="#">attendees</a></li>
                    <li><a href="#">register</a></li>
                </ul>
                <div id="rightNavigationEndCap"></div>
                <div class="cleaner"></div>
                <div id="contentWrapper">
                    $childContent
                </div>
            </div>
        </div>
        <div id="frame-footer"></div>
    </div>
</body>
</html>
```

> **$siteRoot similar to "~" in ASP.NET**

> **$childContent variable is a placeholder**

Our custom content comes from the $childContent placeholder inside the <div>
content element. All views needing to use this common layout will use the Layout
attribute to specify the common default layout. Now that we have our first simple controller, action, and view under our belt, let's explore some of the more interesting features of MonoRail.

FILTERS

In many MVC projects, we tend to see similar code appearing at the beginning or end-
ing of many actions. Whether it's authorization code, session checks, or repository
calls, the code tends to clutter the actual work of the action. When this code is duplicated at the beginning of many actions, we can create a filter to house our code. Filters are special classes we can use to decorate our controller actions to ensure the

filter is executed at a specific time during the request. We can tell MonoRail to execute the filter before, after, or both before and after the action executes.

In our application, we will create a filter that prevents nonadministrators from viewing the List action we created in the last section. First, we need to create a class that implements IFilter. IFilter has only one method, Perform, which returns a Boolean that tells MonoRail whether or not the action should continue executing. In listing 11.4, our filter checks the role and redirects if the user does not belong to the correct role.

Listing 11.4 Authorizing users and performing redirections

```
public class AuthorizationFilter : IFilter
{
    public bool Perform(ExecuteWhen exec, IEngineContext context,
        IController controller, IControllerContext controllerContext)
    {
        if (context.CurrentUser.IsInRole("Administrator"))     ❶
        {
            return true;
        }

        context.Response.Redirect("home", "index");     ❷
        return false;
    }
}
```

MonoRail will pass in any contextual information that the filter might need to perform its work, including when the filter is executing in the ExecuteWhen parameter, execution context information such as the Session, Response, and Request objects in the IEngineContext parameter, the executing IController, and the current IControllerContext. In our example, we check to see if the CurrentUser belongs to the Administrator role ❶. If so, we return true and our action continues executing. If not, we redirect the user to the index action on the home controller ❷, returning false so that the action does not continue to execute.

To use this filter on a controller, you'll need to use MonoRail's FilterAttribute to decorate any controller where we want this filter to execute. You can decorate both actions and controllers with a filter, depending on whether you want the filter to execute for every action in your controller, or only for specific actions. In listing 11.5, we decorate the controller with our filter using the ExecuteEnum.BeforeAction parameter, so that every action on this controller will have the AuthorizationFilter executed before it.

Listing 11.5 Decorating our controller to prevent unauthorized execution

```
[Layout("default")]
[Filter(ExecuteWhen.BeforeAction, typeof(AuthorizationFilter))]     ❶
public class PeopleController : SmartDispatcherController
{
    public void List()
```

```
    {
        Person[] people = Person.FindAll();

        PropertyBag["people"] = people;
    }
}
```

The `Filter` attribute allows us to tell MonoRail which filter to use, as well as when that filter should execute. In listing 11.5, we directed MonoRail to execute the `Authoriza-tionFilter` before each action ❶.

There is still a slight problem with our filter: it gives zero feedback to the end user that anything was wrong! Unauthorized users are silently redirected back to the home page, whether or not intentionally accessing blocked actions. This can be very frustrating for an end user of the application, but easily remedied by use of the `Flash`, as we'll see in the next section.

FLASH

In the last section, we created an `AuthorizationFilter` that ensured that only authorized users were able to access certain controllers and actions. If the user did not belong to a certain role, we redirected them back to the home page. We did not give them any indication of what happened or why, which would lead to their considerable confusion and annoyance. To mitigate the user's potential confusion, we can show them a short message at the top of the screen. In the Web Forms days, we would use `Session` to store these types of values. Because our error message needs to live until the next action is executed, we need to store the error message in a durable container.

`Session` presents a slight problem to developers for messages like these. What about subsequent actions? If our view looks into `Session` for an item, we need to make sure that we clear that value out, so that we don't keep seeing error messages pop up well after they occurred. For messages that need to live only until the next action, we can use MonoRail's `Flash` object. `Flash` is a dictionary-like object, much like `Session`, whose contents are durable only until the next action is executed. `Flash` contents don't last beyond the next action, analogous to `TempData` in ASP.NET MVC. Both `Flash` and `TempData` are implemented using `Session` under the covers.

`Flash` is perfect for error messages, as we only want them displayed on the very next (or current) action executed. For our `AuthorizationFilter`, we want a message displayed after the user gets blocked from an action. In listing 11.6, we add an error message to `Flash`.

> **Listing 11.6   Adding an error message to `Flash`**

```
public class AuthorizationFilter : IFilter
{
    public bool Perform(ExecuteWhen exec, IEngineContext context,
        IController controller, IControllerContext controllerContext)
    {
        if (context.CurrentUser.IsInRole("Administrator"))
        {
            return true;
        }
```

```
        context.Flash["error"] =                              | Put message
            "You are not authorized to view this page.";      | in Flash
        context.Response.Redirect("home", "index");
        return false;                                    ◁──┐ Cancel current
    }                                                        | request
}
```

After our message is in `Flash`, we check for that item in our templates. The ideal place for messages like these would be our default layout, as all other views use the default layout at this time. In listing 11.7, we modify our default layout to show the `Flash` error if it exists.

Listing 11.7 Displaying the `Flash` error message

```
<div id="contentWrapper">
                                            | Display error
#if ($Flash.error)                     ◁──┘ message from Flash
        <div class="flash error">
            $Flash.error
        </div>
#end

  $childContent

</div>
```

Because we want the error message to display only when it actually exists, we wrap the entire `Flash` output in a `#if` statement. Now that we have a meaningful error message when the user attempts to navigate to an unauthorized action, our page will display useful information, as shown in figure 11.2.

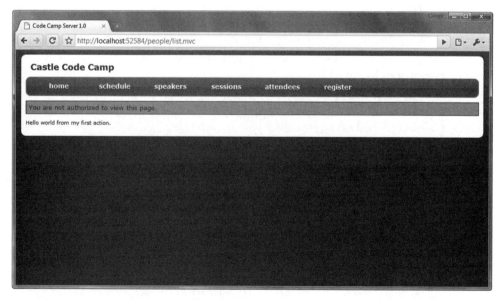

Figure 11.2   Error message displayed after an attempt to access an unauthorized action

After we refresh this page, the error message goes away. The contents of Flash live only until the next action is executed, and are purged after the action executes. In MonoRail, we have granular control over the Flash lifetime, so Flash messages can live on or get purged earlier if needed. But for simple items like error messages, the default Flash behavior provides nice behavior that Session will not.

Up to this point, our application has behaved quite nicely. But exceptions are a fact of life in .NET, and production-ready applications need to handle exceptions gracefully. By default, an ugly yellow error page shows in the event of an unhandled exception in ASP.NET. Although Web Forms allows for custom error pages to be defined in Web.Config, there isn't much built-in control for more complex behavior. In the next section, we'll look at unhandled exceptions and rescues.

RESCUES

Exceptions and errors are realities in application development, but they don't have to create an overtly negative user experience. Out of the box, Web Forms does not provide much to prevent a negative experience for unhandled exceptions. Even the greenest of ASP.NET developers becomes familiar with the "yellow screen of death," the ugly default error page that ASP.NET displays in the event of an unhandled exception. Configuration allows us to create a custom error page, but any additional configuration is severely limited. ASP.NET allows custom error pages per HTTP status code, but this is not nearly enough to provide custom error pages, as all exceptions generate a 500 Internal Server Error status code. The custom error page is global to the site, and cannot be easily configured per request.

Because MonoRail is in complete control of the entire request, as well as executing the controller actions, MonoRail is in a much better position to provide finer grained control over exception pages. This control comes in the form of *rescues*. A rescue is simply an attribute applied to either the controller or action level, with the name of the view that should be displayed in the event of an exception. MonoRail also allows exception-specific rescues, where different exceptions route to different rescue views, as shown in listing 11.8.

Listing 11.8   Rescues defined per exception and action

```
[Layout("default")]                                            Rescue for all
[Rescue("generalerror")]                              ◁        exceptions
[Rescue("specificerror", typeof(ApplicationException))]   ◁┐   Rescue
public class ErrorController : SmartDispatcherController       for specific
{                                                              exception type
    public void Error1()
    {
        throw new Exception("Something wicked this way comes.");
    }

    public void Error2()
    {
        throw new ApplicationException(
            "Something specifically wicked this way comes.");
    }                                                       Rescue declared
                                                      ◁┐    for specific action
    [Rescue("actionerror")]
    public void Error3()
```

```
    {
        throw new SystemException("System error.");
    }
}
```

Not only do we define type-specific rescues on the controller, we can effectively override the default rescue by providing rescues at the action level. After we have the rescues defined in our code, we need to create the views for each corresponding rescue. These rescue views reside in a special Rescues folder in the Views folder. Our simple rescue view for the `generalerror` rescue is shown in listing 11.9.

Listing 11.9 Our default rescue view

```
<h2>Unexpected error happened</h2>

<p>
Please review the details below.  If this error
continues, please contact your adminstrator.
</p>

<pre>
#set($exc = $context.LastException)         ❶
<strong>$exc.GetType().Name</strong>

Message:
$exc.Message
</pre>
```

The `LastException` property from the `$context` object contains the `Exception` object originally thrown in the action ❶. We only show the exception type name, but all information on the `Exception` object is available to us, including stack trace and other custom data. Because our rescue view still uses the default layout defined at the controller level, we get stylized error pages, as shown in figure 11.3.

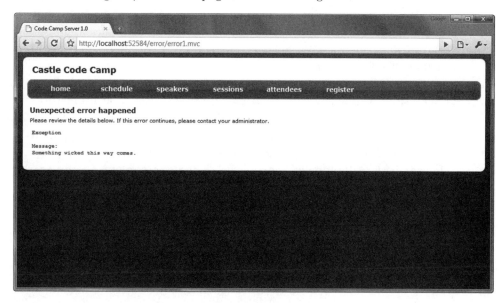

Figure 11.3 General error rescue matching site design

Even with rescues, an end user might see the "yellow screen of death." Rescues do not preclude developers from creating a custom ASP.NET error page for their websites. The probability for this page being shown is much lower, as most exceptions originate from actions.

Showing only static pages is not an interesting application. Data access and separation of concerns are necessary in any medium-to-large application. In the next section, we'll tour some of the additional components of the Castle framework to see how Castle tackles these two areas.

11.1.2 *ActiveRecord and Windsor*

Besides MonoRail, the other two major components of the Castle framework are ActiveRecord and Windsor. As Castle aims to be a full-stack web framework, it supplies two other pieces to the web application puzzle besides the MVC component. Active-Record fills in the puzzle pieces for data access, by providing a full-featured Active Record pattern implementation. For managing dependencies and component lifetime, Castle supplies the Windsor container.

ACTIVERECORD

Databases and data access are nearly ubiquitous in web applications. But how should we expose the database to our web application? The .NET Framework exposed `Data-Sets` from the first release as a means of moving data to and from the database. Unfortunately, `DataSets` are quite clunky, as their structure mirrors the physical structure of the database. Moreover, individual components were not easily disconnected from their source.

Because .NET is a fully object-oriented platform, many developers took the route of creating classes to represent their models in the application, while providing mapping layers to map data in and out of these custom classes. As anyone who has written mapping layers can attest, the task of creating a robust mapping layer is quite daunting. Most development frameworks mitigate the object-relational mapping (ORM) problem through open source libraries. .NET is no different in that regard, as several mature ORM frameworks are available today.

With the power of these ORM frameworks comes more responsibility on the developer's side to understand how to configure and use these frameworks. For many classes of applications with a simple model, it is not necessary to completely separate the object model from the database mapping. The Active Record pattern is used in those applications to provide one-to-one mapping structures from the object model to the database. Additionally, the objects themselves contain all the mapping logic needed to both hydrate and persist.

In the Castle framework, an Active Record implementation, known as ActiveRecord, is available to developers. ActiveRecord is built on top of a proven ORM framework, NHibernate. Instead of configuration files, you decorate your ActiveRecord classes with attributes to describe the mapping. Typically, ActiveRecord is used in greenfield development, where the database does not yet exist.

We still have to provide XML configuration for ActiveRecord, but this is only for configuration items such as the SQL dialect (NHibernate supports multiple databases, including Oracle and SQL Server) and connection string. After these configuration values are defined, we can start creating our ActiveRecord classes. Active Record pattern implementations are usually simplified by inheriting from a base class. In Active-Record's case, the base class is `ActiveRecordBase`. This base class provides the Active Record functionality, such as persistence, searching, deletion, and retrieval; `Active-RecordMediator` is a preferred method over `ActiveRecordBase` in many cases. Our first ActiveRecord class will be the `Person` object, used for both `Speakers` and `Attendees` in the Code Camp Server application. First, we need to create the `Person` class, as shown in listing 11.10.

Listing 11.10 Empty `Person` class tied to ActiveRecord

```
[ActiveRecord]
public class Person : ActiveRecordBase<Person>
{
}
```

For most configurations, that's all need to describe the table mapping for an entity. By default, ActiveRecord will assume the same table name as the class name. This can be overridden by setting properties on the `ActiveRecord` attribute. In addition to the `ActiveRecord` attribute, the `Person` class inherits from the `ActiveRecordBase<T>` class, which provides strongly typed functions such as `Create`, `Delete`, `Save`, `Find`, and `Update`. But to use an ActiveRecord class, we'll first need to define the primary key of the entity. This is as simple as creating a property and decorating the property with the `PrimaryKeyAttribute`, as shown in listing 11.11.

Listing 11.11 Adding a primary key to our ActiveRecord `Person` class

```
[ActiveRecord]
public class Person : ActiveRecordBase<Person>
{
    [PrimaryKey(PrimaryKeyType.GuidComb)]        ❶
    public virtual Guid Id { get; set; }
```

By applying the `PrimaryKeyAttribute`, we are directing `ActiveRecord` to use the `Id` property as the identity of this entity, for both persistence and determining transience. If a `Person` is created, but not yet saved, it is in a transient state and its `Id` will be the default value. We also supply an additional configuration setting, to use a special `Guid` generation algorithm optimized for database persistence in a clustered index ❶. No additional configuration files or modeling diagrams need to be changed. The entire configuration for our database persistence for the `Person` class is made up of these attributes. But a `Person` with only an `Id` is not interesting; let's fill out some of the other `Person` attributes. In listing 11.12, we add the rest of our `Person` attributes, excluding the `Contact`:

Listing 11.12   Filling out the other `Person` attributes

```
[ActiveRecord]
public class Person : ActiveRecordBase<Person>
{
    [PrimaryKey(PrimaryKeyType.GuidComb)]
    public virtual Guid Id { get; set; }

    [Property]                                    ❶
    public virtual string Website { get; set; }

    [Property]
    public virtual string Password { get; set; }

    [Property]
    public virtual string PasswordSalt { get; set; }

    [Property]
    public virtual bool IsAdministrator { get; set; }

    [Property]
    public virtual string Comment { get; set; }
```

Each new property we add to the ActiveRecord class is decorated with the `Property-Attribute` ❶. The `PropertyAttribute`, among other things, contains mapping options for cases where the property name does not match the database column name. For the most part, ActiveRecord attributes directly expose the underlying NHibernate configuration options, which are quite extensive. But for most scenarios, especially in new application development, there is little need to provide additional configuration.

We have one final piece of the puzzle for our `Person` entity: the `Contact` object. The `Contact` object does not have an identity of its own. The `Contact` at its heart is a group of related properties from the `Person` object. It is an example of a domain-driven design *value object*, as covered in chapter 2. When using ORMs like NHibernate and ActiveRecord, it is common to group a set of related properties into a mapping called a component, which can then have its own behavior. With ActiveRecord, these components are configured through the `NestedAttribute`, as seen in listing 11.13.

Listing 11.13   The nested `Contact` component configured on the `Person` class

```
[ActiveRecord]
public class Person : ActiveRecordBase<Person>
{
    private Contact _contact = new Contact();

    [Nested]                          ⟵┐ Group columns
    public virtual Contact Contact      │ into a single type
    {
        get { return _contact; }
        set { _contact = value; }
    }
}
```

The `NestedAttribute` tells ActiveRecord that this property is not defined by a single database column, but is instead composed of many database columns. With this in mind, the `Contact` class does not need as many attributes as the `Person` class, nor does it need to inherit from `ActiveRecordBase`, as seen in listing 11.14.

Listing 11.14 The configured `Contact` component

```
public class Contact : IEquatable<Contact>
{
    private string _firstName = string.Empty;
    private string _lastName = string.Empty;
    private string _email = string.Empty;

    [Property]
    public virtual string FirstName
    {
        get { return _firstName; }
        set { _firstName = value; }
    }

    [Property]
    public virtual string LastName
    {
        get { return _lastName; }
        set { _lastName = value; }
    }

    [Property]
    public virtual string Email
    {
        get { return _email; }
        set { _email = value; }
    }
}
```

The `Contact` class merely needs to configure its individual properties. The `IEquatable` implementation is functionality for other domain behavior, and is not needed by components.

We have looked at the basics of defining our ActiveRecord implementations, but should the querying and saving reside directly in our controller actions? Ideally, we would like to create individual service and repository classes that can house all these concerns. In the next section, we will take a closer look at Castle Windsor, which allows us to take advantage of SoC, the dependency inversion principle, but keep the burden of locating and building objects off calling code.

CASTLE WINDSOR

In our controller actions, we are primarily concerned with handling input, handing off to services to process the request, and finally choosing a view for display based on the results of that operation. Although ActiveRecord provides true rapid application development, we do not always want to see queries, saving, and other logic directly inside our controller actions. If we do not take care to break out concerns into distinct classes, our controller actions will quickly resemble the `SaveButton_Click` or `Page_Load` events we have seen from Web Forms.

Instead, we can break out these concerns into individual classes. For example, instead of calling directly into our ActiveRecord class to retrieve all `Person` objects, we can create a simple abstraction on top of this concept in the form of an IPerson-Repository, as shown in listing 11.15.

Listing 11.15 The `IPersonRepository` interface

```
public interface IPersonRepository
{
    Person[] FindAll();
}
```

The implementation of IPersonRepository is quite simple. It uses the ActiveRecord FindAll method to return all Person objects in the database, as shown in listing 11.16. There is a good argument for also using ActiveRecordMediator in the repository if you prefer that your entities not be bound to ActiveRecord.

Listing 11.16 The `PersonRepository` implementation using ActiveRecord

```
public class PersonRepository : IPersonRepository
{
    public Person[] FindAll()
    {
        return Person.FindAll();          FindAll comes from
    }                                     ActiveRecordBase
}
```

This implementation is not that interesting until we consider the impact on our People-Controller, which needs to use the PersonRepository to find the list of people. But how should the PeopleController get its instance of IPersonRepository? Should it instantiate it itself, or use a Factory or Builder pattern? What happens if the implementation of IPersonRepository has dependencies of its own? All of these decisions are too much for the PeopleController to manage. Instead, we will assume that "something" gives the IPersonRepository implementation to our PeopleController. To make it clear that PeopleController depends on IPersonRepository, we will make this dependency required by the constructor, as shown in listing 11.17.

Listing 11.17 The `PeopleController` using the `IPersonRepository`

```
public class PeopleController : SmartDispatcherController
{
    private readonly IPersonRepository _personRepository;

    public PeopleController(IPersonRepository personRepository)
    {
        _personRepository = personRepository;          IPersonRepository
    }                                                   is required

    public void List()
    {
        Person[] people = _personRepository.FindAll();

        PropertyBag ["people"] = people;
    }
```

The interesting aspect of this implementation is that the `PeopleController` is no longer directly coupled to how the `Person` array is found. We could have used ADO.NET, LINQ to SQL, or NHibernate. By separating the database concern from `People-Controller`, we have allowed each class to grow independently. As long the `IPerson-Repository` contract is fulfilled, the `PeopleController` will function properly. But how did the `IPersonRepository` get there? Something had to know to create the correct implementation at runtime and wire the `PeopleController` up properly. That "something" is Windsor, Castle's IoC container.

Castle Windsor provides the wiring up of dependencies, as well as strong support for lifetime management and runtime configuration of components. But before we can take advantage of Windsor, we need to tell Windsor about the components in our application. We have several options for providing this configuration, including programmatically, XML configuration files, or even a Boo domain-specific language (DSL). For compile-time safety, we will go with the programmatic option. Our first step is to create a `WindsorContainer`, which will house all our component registration code, as shown in listing 11.18.

Listing 11.18 Our `WebContainer` with component registration

```
public class WebContainer : WindsorContainer
{
    public WebContainer()
    {
        RegisterFacilities();
        RegisterComponents();
    }

    private void RegisterComponents()
    {
        AddComponent("home.controller", typeof(HomeController));      ⟵ Add named
        AddComponent("people.controller", typeof(PeopleController));     components
        AddComponent("error.controller", typeof(ErrorController));
        AddComponent("person.repository", typeof(IPersonRepository),
            typeof(PersonRepository));
    }

    protected void RegisterFacilities()
    {
        AddFacility("monorail", new MonoRailFacility());
    }
}
```

In the `RegisterFacilities` method, we register the `MonoRailFacility`, a Windsor facility designed especially for MonoRail integration. This facility ensures that controller lifetime is correct, and registers other components needed for managing controller dependencies. We place all of our component registration code in the `RegisterComponents` method. To register each component, we use the `AddComponent` method. We register each controller, as well as the `IPersonRepository` interface and implementation.

At runtime, Windsor examines PeopleController and notes that it requires an IPersonRepository implementation. Because we also registered the IPersonRepository interface and PersonRepository implementation, Windsor knows to wire up the PersonRepository implementation to the PeopleController. Note that we never specified that PeopleController should get a PersonRepository in our component registration. Component registration is separate from dependency specification. It is up to each component to expose its required dependencies, which is simply through a constructor. In this fashion, the wiring up of dependencies is completely separate from the use of the dependency, as we saw in our PeopleController.

Finally, we need to reference Castle.MonoRail.WindsorIntegration.dll. Then create the container and instruct MonoRail to use Windsor to resolve controller instances. The most straightforward manner to do this is to modify our Global.asax implementation, as shown in listing 11.19.

Listing 11.19   Providing the WindsorContainer to MonoRail through Global.asax

```
public class Global : System.Web.HttpApplication, IContainerAccessor    ❶
{
    private static IWindsorContainer _container;

    protected void Application_Start(object sender, EventArgs e)
    {
        _container = new WebContainer();
    }

    protected void Application_End(object sender, EventArgs e)
    {
        _container.Dispose();
    }

    public IWindsorContainer Container    ❷
    {
        get { return _container; }
    }
}
```

To expose our WebContainer implementation to MonoRail, we need to implement the IContainerAccessor interface ❶. This interface has one member, the Container property ❷. This Container property returns the private WebContainer instance, which is created and disposed of at the Start and End application events. The final piece to configure is in the Web.config file, to tell MonoRail to use Windsor integration, as shown in listing 11.20.

Listing 11.20   Configuring MonoRail to use Windsor integration

```
<monorail useWindsorIntegration="true">    ❶
<controllers>
<assembly>MonoRailExample</assembly>
</controllers>
<viewEngines viewPathRoot="Views">
<add type="Castle.MonoRail.Framework.Views.NVelocity.NVelocityViewEngine,
```

```
➡    Castle.MonoRail.Framework.Views.NVelocity"/>
    </viewEngines>
    </monorail>
```

With the `useWindsorIntegration` attribute value configured ❶, MonoRail will now use the `IContainerAccessor` to access the `IWindsorContainer`. All controller instantiation will go through our `WebContainer`.

Many of these MonoRail and Castle components and features can be taken advantage of directly inside ASP.NET MVC. In the next section, we will examine some of the key features of Castle and MonoRail that can enhance an ASP.NET MVC application.

11.1.3 *MonoRail and Castle features available in ASP.NET MVC*

During the first few preview releases of ASP.NET MVC, many components of MonoRail did not have had an equivalent counterpart in ASP.NET MVC. ASP.NET MVC has caught up in many areas, but some components are still missing. Because of the modular nature of ASP.NET MVC, however, quite a few features of MonoRail and Castle can be used directly in an ASP.NET MVC application.

In chapter 6, we learned how to integrate Castle Windsor as a `ControllerFactory`. All of the power of Windsor is available by supplying the Windsor `ControllerFactory` implementation to ASP.NET MVC.

Additionally, all of the power of Castle ActiveRecord is available for use in ASP.NET MVC. Because no Castle component (Windsor, MonoRail, or ActiveRecord) has a dependency on another, using ActiveRecord or Windsor in an ASP.NET MVC application will not force any dependency on MonoRail.

Besides the major Castle components, many of the components of MonoRail are available in ASP.NET MVC. These include the view engines, NVelocity and Brail. Originally part of MonoRail, both of these view engines have been adapted to execute against ASP.NET MVC, and are part of the open source MVCContrib project. Eventually, many other features of MonoRail will show up in ASP.NET MVC. For the missing features, it would be easier to look toward MonoRail for inspiration, rather than trying to adapt MonoRail components to run directly inside ASP.NET MVC. Often when we want to use existing features of MonoRail in an ASP.NET MVC application, it is easier to use MonoRail instead.

For inspiration, MonoRail relied heavily on another MVC framework, Ruby on Rails. In the next section, we'll examine the core philosophy behind Rails and how this philosophy shaped the design of Rails.

11.2 *Ruby on Rails*

Ruby on Rails is perhaps the most popular MVC framework used today. Shortly after the 2004 release of the framework, the Rails community exploded to include numerous community websites, dozens of books, and many conferences held worldwide. Unlike many other MVC frameworks, Ruby on Rails is a harvested framework, one that was extracted from a real-world application: 37signals' application Basecamp. Because Ruby on Rails is a harvested framework, all its features have been used in a production environment and all are needed. Any feature that goes well outside the existing design is probably not needed at all.

Ruby on Rails incorporates two central design philosophies, *convention over configuration* and the *DRY* (don't repeat yourself) principle. Ruby on Rails is built to directly support agile development and at its core is the Agile Manifesto. Unlike rapid application development (RAD) frameworks like Web Forms or VB6, Rails supports testability and SoC directly out of the box. Its design attempts to minimize duplication as much as possible, so that the common scenarios require as little code as necessary to function properly.

In this section, we will take a short tour through the major components and design philosophies of Ruby on Rails. Although this section is not meant to be an introduction to the Ruby language, you will recognize its constructs because you're already familiar with the object-oriented paradigm.

11.2.1 Convention over configuration and "the Rails way"

The easiest way to explain the convention-over-configuration philosophy and the DRY principle is to see a simple example in action. First, we will start with defining the model. In our Code Camp domain, we have `Person`, `Conference`, `Session`, `TimeSlot` and `Track` entities. Of these, `Person` and `Conference` are the core pieces of our model. Without these, none of the other entities can exist. In an ASP.NET MVC application, creating these initial models can be quite a daunting task. We need to create the controller, the model class, a view, and some sort of mapping layer code. With NHibernate, this might mean the repository and a mapping file. In Rails, creating a model is accomplished through a generator.

But before we even think about our model, we need a Rails site to work against. After installing Ruby and Rails, we can create a Rails development site from the command line, as shown in listing 11.21.

Listing 11.21   Creating our Rails application from the command line

```
D:\Dev>rails codecampserver_onrails
      create
      create    app/controllers
      create    app/helpers
      create    app/models
      create    app/views/layouts
      create    config/environments
      create    config/initializers
      create    db
      create    doc
      create    lib
      create    lib/tasks
      create    log
      create    public/images
      create    public/javascripts
      create    public/stylesheets
      create    script/performance
... more output
```

We removed the bulk of the output for brevity, but we can see that one command from the command line creates the entire skeleton for our new application. The rails command is far more powerful than the Visual Studio `Add New Project` command—it creates the full-stack environment for our new application:

- A home for our application in the "app" folder
- Environment configuration
- A home for the content of our application (JavaScript, images, CSS)
- A bevy of helpful Ruby scripts used throughout development
- Build scripts
- Migration scripts
- Tests

The initial starting point for a Rails application is light-years ahead of anything Visual Studio can give you to start with. Now that we have our Rails application created, it is time to generate our first model. In Visual Studio, we would normally accomplish this through the File > New dialog, and create a single class. In some cases, a wizard might pop up to give us more options. In Rails, we can use the scripts created for us in the previous step to generate exactly what we need. In listing 11.22, we use the resource generator to create a starting point for our `Person` model.

Listing 11.22   Using a generator to create the `Person` model

```
D:\Dev\codecampserver_onrails>ruby script\generate resource person
      exists  app/models/
      exists  app/controllers/
      exists  app/helpers/
      create  app/views/people
      exists  test/functional/
      exists  test/unit/
  dependency  model
      exists     app/models/
      exists     test/unit/
      exists     test/fixtures/
      create     app/models/person.rb
      create     test/unit/person_test.rb
      create     test/fixtures/people.yml
      create     db/migrate
      create     db/migrate/20081103024758_create_people.rb
      create  app/controllers/people_controller.rb
      create  test/functional/people_controller_test.rb
      create  app/helpers/people_helper.rb
       route  map.resources :people
```

The generator caused interesting things to happen. We can see that a person.rb file was created in the app\models folder, as well as a test file for that model. The generator also created a people folder in the views folder, correctly figuring out the plural for person. A controller/test pair, a helper, and a migration script were also generated. That is quite a few files for one command! The concepts of DRY and convention over configuration are strong influencers for this design, as the same files are almost always needed each time we create a new model. We are never forced to use these generators, but life can be much easier if we follow the conventions laid out.

One of the files created is the migrations file. In Rails, every database change is managed through a migration script. This migration script is not a SQL script, but rather an internal domain-specific language (DSL). That is, our migration script is written in Ruby. By using Ruby instead of SQL, we are able to shield ourselves from the different SQL dialects of the various SQL products supported by Ruby. In each migration script, we create both up and down scripts, so that our changes can be rolled back at any time. Rails manages the migrations through the clever use of timestamps and record keeping. Since the file was created with a timestamp, Rails can keep track of which scripts should be executed on any developer or production environment.

First, we will fill in the columns we need for our Person class, which included name attributes, password attributes, and other information. In listing 11.23, we see our basic Person table through the migration DSL.

Listing 11.23   The `CreatePeople` migration script

```
class CreatePeople < ActiveRecord::Migration
  def self.up
    create_table :people do |t|
      t.string :first_name
      t.string :last_name
      t.string :email
      t.string :website
      t.string :password
      t.string :password_salt
      t.boolean :is_administrator
      t.timestamps
    end
  end
  def self.down
    drop_table :people
  end
end
```

Annotations:
- Inherit from ActiveRecord::Migration
- Used to upgrade a database
- Create people table
- Used to downgrade a database

We will not go too deeply into the Ruby language, but we can see in our example that we defined two class methods, up and down. In the up method, we call the create_table method to create a People table, with the initial columns. The Active-Record::Migration class contains many methods to manipulate the database, such as creating and dropping tables and columns. To run our migrations, we simply run the migration script through, as shown in listing 11.24.

Listing 11.24   Running the migration script

```
D:\Dev\codecampserver_onrails>rake db:migrate
(in D:/Dev/codecampserver_onrails)
== 20081103024758 CreatePeople: migrating
   =====================================
-- create_table(:people)
   -> 0.2100s
== 20081103024758 CreatePeople: migrated (0.2100s)
   ===========================
```

The `rake db:migrate` command executes the migration script to apply any new database changes to our local database. When we run this script again, no migration scripts execute because our database is up to date. In a team environment, we run the migration script on a regular basis on each of our development machines when we want to update our local database with the newest changes.

Now that we have created a table, we can play around with our model in the Ruby console. The Ruby console is a sandbox that lets us run Ruby code directly against our model. We can create a new `Person` in our application, as shown in listing 11.25.

Listing 11.25 Using the Ruby console to create a new `Person`

```
D:\Dev\codecampserver_onrails>ruby script\console
Loading development environment (Rails 2.1.2)
>> Person.create(:first_name => 'Larry', :last_name => 'Fine', :email =>
    'larry@stooges.com')
=> #<Person id: 1, first_name: "Larry", last_name: "Fine", email:
    "larry@stooges.com", website: nil, password: nil, password_salt: nil,
    is_administrator: nil, created_at: "2008-11-06 01:42:34", updated_at:
    "2008-11-06 01:42:34">
>>
```

The `Person` model class created by the generator earlier has quite a few helpful methods, similar to MonoRail's `ActiveRecordBase` class. In listing 11.25, we call a class method to create a person, with the specified attributes for first name, last name, and email. We did not have to create a new `Person` object, and instead we passed a `Hash` of name-value pairs for the `Person` attributes and values. The `create` method creates a new `Person` and immediately saves it back to the database. If we want a transient `Person`, we can use the initializer instead, as shown in listing 11.26.

Listing 11.26 Using the initializer and the `save` method to create a new `Person`

```
>> curly = Person.new(:first_name => 'Curly', :last_name => 'Howard', :email
    => 'curly@stooges.com')
=> #<Person id: nil, first_name: "Curly", last_name: "Howard", email:
    "curly@stooges.com", website: nil, password: nil, password_salt: nil,
    is_administrator: nil, created_at: nil, updated_at: nil>
>> curly.save
=> true
>>
```

So far, nothing is much different than what we saw in the previous section on Mono-Rail. Rails provides a better total package, such as a build script, but these are items we can fairly easily put on top of our application. Where Rails truly shines is its embrace of the dynamic nature of Ruby combined with the mantras of convention over configuration and the DRY principle. We can see these two ideas in action if we open up our `Person` model, created earlier by the generator. Listing 11.27 shows the entire `Person` implementation.

Listing 11.27 The entire, fully functional `Person` implementation

```
class Person < ActiveRecord::Base    ◁—  Inherit from ActiveRecord::Base
end
```

That's it! Rails defines the `Person` class and inherits it from the `ActiveRecord::Base` type, in just two lines. But in our previous examples, we saw a `Person` object with all sorts of attributes, such as `first_name`, `is_adminstrator`, and others. Where did these extra attributes come from? Since Ruby is a dynamic language, Rails adds these attributes to our class dynamically. Conventions cover the details, leaving much less code for us to write. In our MonoRail example, the `Person` class required dozens of lines of code, none of them interesting.

The base ActiveRecord type, `ActiveRecord::Base`, defines many helpful methods for searching, lifetime management, and everything else we would expect from a fully featured Active Record pattern implementation. But because Ruby is a dynamic language, the Rails developers took advantage of its nature to create powerful conventions to reduce the amount of code needed to get an application up and running. In the next section, we will go deeper into Active Record with a more complex model and more interesting querying scenarios.

11.2.2 *Active Record*

In the last section, we saw the power of convention over configuration and the DRY principle applied to the dynamic nature of Ruby. In this section, we will see how these two ideals shape Rails to support scenarios that, while difficult in a static language, are easy and intuitive in Ruby. Up to this point our model consists of exactly one class, `Person`. If we go back to our original CodeCampServer model, the relationships can get fairly complex, as shown in figure 11.4.

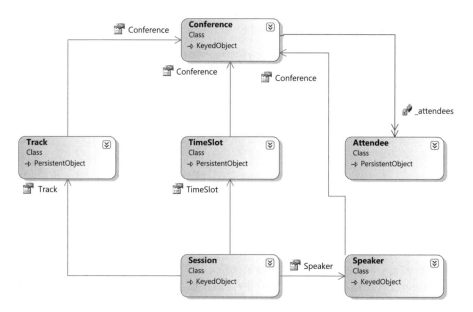

Figure 11.4 The CodeCampServer entities with relationships shown

It is not entirely clear from figure 11.4, which only shows explicit associations through properties and fields, but there are more relationships defined than are programmed for. For example, the `Track` entity has a `Conference`, but does a `Conference` not have many `Tracks`? That relationship must be traversed through a repository or through direct querying. The same problem can be seen with both `Session` and `TimeSlot`; we cannot navigate the web of relationships.

First, we will focus on the relationship between `Conference` and `TimeSlot`. A `Conference` has many `TimeSlots`, and each `TimeSlot` belongs to a `Conference`. When we create the table for `TimeSlot` in our migration script, we must include this relationship in the definition. Our `Conference` schema definition will be fairly straightforward, as shown in listing 11.28.

Listing 11.28 The `Conference` schema migration script

```
class CreateConferences < ActiveRecord::Migration
  def self.up
    create_table :conferences do |t|
      t.string :key
      t.string :name
      t.date    :start_date
      t.date    :end_date

      t.timestamps
    end
  end

  def self.down
    drop_table :conferences
  end
end
```

We added the name, key, and start and end dates for our `Conference` model. For our `TimeSlot` schema definition, we will need to add the foreign key for `Conference` because a `TimeSlot` belongs to a `Conference`. Listing 11.29 shows the `TimeSlot` definition, with the foreign key back to `Conference`.

Listing 11.29 `TimeSlot` schema migration script with foreign key for `Conference`

```
class CreateTimeSlots < ActiveRecord::Migration
  def self.up
    create_table :time_slots do |t|
      t.string   :purpose
      t.datetime :start_time
      t.datetime :end_time
      t.integer  :conference_id

      t.timestamps
    end
  end

  def self.down
    drop_table :time_slots
  end
end
```

To wire up the relationships between the two entities, adding this column will not be enough. Instead, we will need to add information to each model, describing the relationship for each endpoint. Looking back at our relationship diagram, we see that a `Conference` has many `TimeSlots`, and a `TimeSlot` belongs to a `Conference`. To add this relationship to our model, we need to change the `Conference` and `TimeSlot`, as shown in listing 11.30.

Listing 11.30 The `Conference` and `TimeSlot` models include the relationship.

```
class Conference < ActiveRecord::Base          "one" side of
  has_many :time_slots                    ←┘   one-to-many

end

class TimeSlot < ActiveRecord::Base            "many" side of
  belongs_to :conference                  ←┘   one-to-many

end
```

Notice how easy it is to read the models and interpret the relationship between the two. A `Conference` has many `TimeSlots`, and this is represented by the has_many association in our model. On the other side of the relationship, a `TimeSlot` belongs to a `Conference`, so we see the belongs_to association to `Conference`. Because of the Rails convention, Rails knows to look for a column called conference_id on the `TimeSlot` table. We are not forced to use these conventions, and we can override the defaults as needed. In most cases, it is simpler to accept the conventions and move on to building the application.

Now, it would not be a Rails feature if it did not incorporate the dynamic nature of Ruby to provide rich support for this association. We merely described the relationship, but how do we develop against these new relationships? First, we need to create a new `Conference` and `TimeSlot`, as shown in listing 11.31.

Listing 11.31 Creating a `Conference` and `TimeSlot`

```
>> Conference.create(:key => "UCON", :name => "UberCon", :start_date =>
     Date.new(2007, 10, 1), :end_date => Date.new(2007, 10, 3))
=> #<Conference id: 1, key: "UCON", name: "UberCon", start_date: "2007-10-
     01", end_date: "2007-10-03", created_at: "2008-11-09 23:09:22",
     updated_at: "2008-11-09 23:09:22">
>> TimeSlot.create(:purpose => "Morning", :start_time => DateTime.new(y=2007,
     m=10, d=2, h=9, min=0, s=0), :end_time => DatcTime.new(y=2007, m=10,
     d=2, h=10, min=0, s=0))
=> #<TimeSlot id: 1, purpose: "Morning", start_time: "2007-10-02 09:00:00",
     end_time: "2007-10-02 10:00:00", conference_id: nil, created_at: "2008-
     11-09 23:29:14", updated_at: "2008-11-09 23:29:14">
```

In listing 11.31, we created a `Conference` and `TimeSlot`, but did not associate the two. To do so, we can grab the `TimeSlot` we just created and append it to the `Conference`'s `TimeSlots`, as shown in listing 11.32.

Listing 11.32 Appending the "Morning" TimeSlot to the UberCon Conference

```
>> @morning = TimeSlot.find(1)
=> #<TimeSlot id: 1, purpose: "Morning", start_time: "2007-10-02 09:00:00",
    end_time: "2007-10-02 10:00:00", conference_id: nil, created_at: "2008-
    11-09 23:29:14", updated_at: "2008-11-09 23:29:14">
>> Conference.find(1).time_slots << @morning
=> [#<TimeSlot id: 1, purpose: "Morning", start_time: "2007-10-02 09:00:00",
    end_time: "2007-10-02 10:00:00", conference_id: 1, created_at: "2008-11-
    09 23:29:14", updated_at: "2008-11-09 23:31:16">]
```

The append operator (<<) lets us append the TimeSlot we created onto the Conference. The bidirectional association is maintained for us as well. We can inspect the "Morning" TimeSlot and see that the Conference was associated at that end of the relationship as well, as shown in listing 11.33.

Listing 11.33 Maintaining both ends of the relationship

```
>> @morning.conference
=> #<Conference id: 1, key: "UCON", name: "UberCon", start_date: "2007-10-
    01", end_date: "2007-10-03", created_at: "2008-11-09 23:09:22",
    updated_at: "2008-11-09 23:09:22">
```

ActiveRecord and Rails start to show their power in the ability to create smart, scoped searches. We might not know the specific TimeSlot ID for the "Early Morning" TimeSlot, but we can easily do a find for it, as shown in listing 11.34.

Listing 11.34 A scoped search for a specific TimeSlot

```
>> Conference.find(1).time_slots.find_by_purpose("Early Morning")
=> #<TimeSlot id: 3, purpose: "Early Morning", start_time: "2007-10-02
    08:00:00", end_time: "2007-10-02 09:00:00", conference_id: 1,
    created_at: "2008-11-10 00:58:18", updated_at: "2008-11-10 00:58:30">
```

Instead of searching for all TimeSlots with a purpose of "Early Morning", only the TimeSlots of the Conference with ID of 1 are returned. Listing 11.34 also showcases the dynamic nature of Ruby, as the find_by_purpose method did not exist on our original model. It was generated dynamically, and convention pointed to search by the purpose attribute. Convention combined with the dynamic nature of Ruby results in a powerful mechanism derived from succinct code. We merely set up the table schemas and described the relationship, and Rails and ActiveRecord did the rest. We only showcased one type of relationship, the "has_many", but several other types of relationships are supported, each with its own features added strictly to support scenarios for those types of relationships.

We set up a preliminary model for our CodeCampServer, but we have yet to display any HTML. In the next section, we will take a closer look at the Rails view/controller component, ActionPack.

11.2.3 *ActionPack*

In the previous section, we looked at the ActiveRecord component of Rails, and discovered how to create rich models with little code. These models are not very useful if no end user can interact with them. With Rails, this interaction is coordinated through ActionPack, which manages the request cycle and routing. A user types a URL or clicks a link to generate a request to Rails. Through routing configuration, Action-Pack will direct the request to the correct action on the correct controller. After the action executes on the controller, the view generates the HTML that eventually travels back down to the client. In addition to the routing component, ActionPack includes a controller and view component, aptly named `ActionController` and `ActionView`.

Part of our resource generator in the previous section generated entries in the routing configuration and created a blank controller and view. This initial routing configuration, which we will not need to change, is shown in listing 11.35.

Listing 11.35   Routing configuration

```
ActionController::Routing::Routes.draw do |map|
  map.resources :time_slots

  map.resources :conferences

  map.resources :people                    Default route similar
                                           to ASP.NET MVC
  map.connect ':controller/:action/:id'
  map.connect ':controller/:action/:id.:format'
end
```

Because many requests will follow the same format, the first `map.resources` calls set up resource mappings for several default actions, such as `new`, `create`, `show`, and others. Like ASP.NET MVC, routes are defined in order of precedence, so the less specific rules are defined last. In our Rails CodeCampServer, we want to show a single `Conference`, and a table with all of its `TimeSlots`. We could additionally provide links for `Sessions` and `Attendees`, as well as actions for registering. In our simplified application, we will just look at the `Conference` and `TimeSlot` relationship.

For our simple `Conference` page, we first need to handle the request for a single `Conference` in an action on our `ConferenceController`. We need to grab the ID passed into the URL, and use ActiveRecord to find that `Conference`, as shown in listing 11.36.

Listing 11.36   Defining the show action to find a single Conference

```
class ConferencesController < ApplicationController          Inherit from
  def show                                     An action    ApplicationController
    @conference = Conference.find(params[:id]) method
  end
end
```

The result of the find is put into a variable, which will be available for the view to use. For our view, which will look similar to the Web Forms views in ASP.NET MVC, we will use embedded Ruby in HTML to create our final HTML delivered to the client. The view, whose name and location match the action name and controller name, is shown in listing 11.37.

Listing 11.37   The full `Show Conference` view

```
<!DOCTYPE html PUBLIC "-//W3C//DTD XHTML 1.1//EN" "http://www.w3.org/TR/
    xhtml11/DTD/xhtml11.dtd">
<html>
<head>
    <meta http-equiv="Content-Type"
        content="text/html; charset=iso-8859-1" />
    <title>Layout</title>
    <%= stylesheet_link_tag 'style-2column' %>
    <%= stylesheet_link_tag 'master' %>
</head>
<body>
    <div id="header">
        <div id="logo">
            <h1>Rails Code Camp</h1>
            <p>Powered by
                <a href="http://codecampserver.org">Code Camp Server</a>
            </p>
        </div>
        <div id="menu">
            <ul>
                <li>Home</li>
                <li>Schedule</li>
                <li>Speakers</li>
                <li>Attendees</li>
                <li>Sponsors</li>
            </ul>
        </div>
    </div>
    <div id="page">
    <div id="content">
        <h1><%= @conference.name %></h1>
        <h2>aka <%= @conference.key %></h2>
        <p>
            kicks off at <%= @conference.start_date %>
            <br />
            shuts it down at <%= @conference.end_date %>
        </p>
        <h3>Time Slots</h3>
        <table>
            <thead>
                <tr>
                    <th>Purpose</th>
                    <th>Start Time</th>
                    <th>End Time</th>
                </tr>
            </thead>
        <tbody>
        <% for time_slot in @conference.time_slots %>
            <tr>
```

```
                        <td><%= time_slot.purpose %></td>
                        <td><%= time_slot.start_time %></td>
                        <td><%= time_slot.end_time %></td>
                    </tr>
                <% end %>
                </tbody>
            </table>

        </div>

        <div id="sidebar">
        </div>
        </div>
        <div id="footer">
            <!-- Footer -->
        </div>
    </body>
</html>
```

Embedded Ruby looks nearly identical to Web Forms, with the exception that we are using Ruby instead of C#. We use output embedding tags (<%= %>) to directly output strings, for the Conference name, key, and dates. Without the equals, the tags become evaluation embedding tags, where we can put any Ruby code. In this case, we used evaluation embedding to create a for loop to loop over the Conference's TimeSlots. The final rendering of this page is modified in listings 11.38 and 11.39 and can be seen by navigating to http://localhost:3000/conferences/show/1 and in figure 11.5.

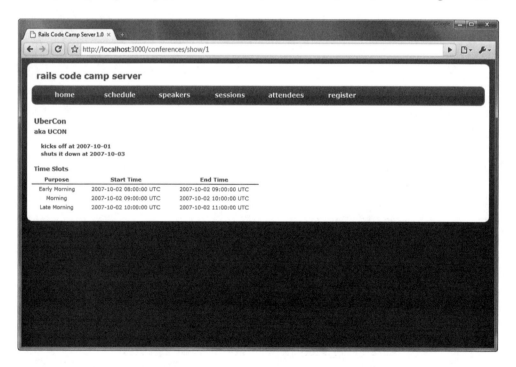

Figure 11.5   Our view conference page

The rendering in figure 11.5 shows the time slots in the correct sort order. We did not sort them directly in the view, because `TimeSlot` order is a fundamental aspect of the relationship between a `Conference` and its `TimeSlots`. ActiveRecord lets us manipulate this ordering aspect, as shown in listing 11.38.

Listing 11.38   The new `Conference` to `TimeSlot` relationship incorporating order

```
class Conference < ActiveRecord::Base                    Include sort order
  has_many :time_slots, :order => "start_time ASC"    ◁─┘ in association

end
```

We supply a small SQL fragment describing the correct order of `TimeSlots` belonging to a `Conference`, which now corrects the order of `TimeSlots` we see in the `Show Conference` view. Much like ASP.NET MVC and MonoRail, ActionView allows us to combine common views into layouts. Because all pages show the same layout, we will create a view with a convention-based name, called `application.html.erb`. We could create controller-specific layouts as needed, but for our purposes, a site-wide layout is more than sufficient. Our application layout is shown in listing 11.39, which looks very similar to the master page in our ASP.NET MVC application. The main difference is the use of the Ruby `yield` keyword to denote child content.

Listing 11.39   The application layout

```
<!DOCTYPE html PUBLIC "-//W3C//DTD XHTML 1.1//EN" "http://www.w3.org/TR/
    xhtml11/DTD/xhtml11.dtd">
<html>
<head>
    <meta http-equiv="Content-Type"
        content="text/html; charset=iso-8859-1" />
    <title>Rails Code Camp Server 1.0</title>
    <%= stylesheet_link_tag 'themes/green' %>
    <%= stylesheet_link_tag 'stylesheet' %>
</head>
<body>
    <div id="frame">
        <div id="frame-header"></div>
        <div id="content">
            <div id="header">
                <h1>rails code camp server</h1>
            </div>
            <div class="cleaner"></div>
            <div id="navigationWrapper">
                <div id="leftNavigationEndCap"></div>
                <ul id="navigationMenu">
                    <li><a href="#">home</a></li>
                    <li><a href="#">schedule</a></li>
                    <li><a href="#">speakers</a></li>
                    <li><a href="#">sessions</a></li>
                    <li><a href="#">attendees</a></li>
                    <li><a href="#">register</a></li>
                </ul>
```

```
                    <div id="rightNavigationEndCap"></div>
                    <div class="cleaner"></div>
                    <div id="contentWrapper">
                        <%= yield %>
                    </div>
                </div>
            </div>
            <div id="frame-footer"></div>
        </div>
    </body>
</html>
```

With the child content removed, our Show Conference view becomes small, and rather easy to understand without the entire page layout HTML getting in the way. The final Show Conference view is shown in listing 11.40.

Listing 11.40   The condensed Show Conference view

```
<div class="dataDoubleWideContainer mt10">
    <h2><%= @conference.name %></h2>
    <h3>aka <%= @conference.key %></h3>
    <p>
        kicks off at <%= @conference.start_date %>
        <br />
        shuts it down at <%= @conference.end_date %>
    </p>
    <h4>Time Slots</h4>
    <table class="display">
        <thead>
            <tr>
                <th>Purpose</th>
                <th>Start Time</th>
                <th>End Time</th>
            </tr>
        </thead>
        <tbody>
        <% for time_slot in @conference.time_slots %>
            <tr>
                <td><%= time_slot.purpose %></td>
                <td><%= time_slot.start_time %></td>
                <td><%= time_slot.end_time %></td>
            </tr>
        <% end %>
        </tbody>
    </table>
</div>
<div class="cleaner"></div>
```

In this section of Ruby on Rails, we barely scratched the surface of capabilities in each of the major areas of Rails. Because MonoRail was inspired by Rails, many of the features in MonoRail have their own counterpart in Rails, such as validation, partials, flash, filters, as well as other features not found in MonoRail. The combination of Ruby, convention over configuration, and the DRY principle form a powerful full-stack framework.

Choosing an MVC framework

A quick, but rather useless recommendation is "it depends." Each framework has its strengths and weaknesses, and often the platform decision is out of your hands. Additionally, you will have to consider other aspects such as deployment, support, your current team's skills, and so on. If you are already on a team developing with ASP.NET, it will be a nontrivial undertaking to switch to Ruby on Rails.

MonoRail, with its integration with Windsor and ActiveRecord, provides a more complete solution than ASP.NET MVC. Because ASP.NET MVC is a Microsoft product, you will have access to a much wider community, even if MonoRail is more mature by many years. Some companies, for whatever reason, tend to discourage open source tooling, even when there is commercial support available for MonoRail.

The Ruby on Rails question will be more difficult. Rails is a complete ecosystem, and one that currently does not run on .NET. If you choose Rails, you will be switching programming languages, IDEs, hosting environments, and so on. The Rails community is huge, with bookstores dedicating large sections to books on the subject. If your IT shop is 100 percent Microsoft, the decision has already been made for you. Even in those situations, we encourage you to try out Rails on personal or pet projects, as Rails is built to get you up and going quickly.

11.3 Summary

MVC as a pattern extends back several decades, and has existed in the web space since nearly the beginning of the web. Since ASP.NET MVC leaned heavily on existing MVC frameworks, including MonoRail and Ruby on Rails, an examination of these frameworks is helpful for new ASP.NET MVC developers to understand the mistakes, challenges, and problems solved by preexisting communities and frameworks. These existing frameworks will continue to serve as bellwethers in MVC framework design, and many features will cross-pollinate among the different frameworks. For many features not yet incorporated into ASP.NET MVC, application developers can look to existing frameworks for clues on how to solve problems that most likely arose years before in other communities.

In some cases, another framework might be a better fit for a given situation. Because each MVC framework has different advantages and disadvantages, only through understanding which options are available can we make an informed decision on which framework to use. In this chapter, we reviewed two of the more widely used MVC frameworks, and gained a deeper understanding of the motivation behind each framework as well as their influence on ASP.NET MVC design.

In the next chapter, we will examine a collection of best practices harvested from CodeCampServer and other ASP.NET MVC applications in production today.

Best practices

12

This chapter covers

- Designing maintainable controllers, filters, and actions
- Building maintainable views with minimum duplication
- Designing and testing routes
- Testing MVC components

Although the ASP.NET MVC Framework is young in the .NET space, the MVC pattern applied to web applications is not. We have presented thus far techniques already used in many other MVC Frameworks, but some areas in the ASP.NET MVC Framework require extra attention. The ASP.NET MVC Framework is open-ended and extensible for customization, but not all usage and customization is appropriate. Not every approach to solving a problem will lead to elegant, maintainable results. Many of the examples on the web work well for simple problems, but break down quickly in a large production application or slightly complex small applications. In this chapter, we examine the major feature areas and extension points of ASP.NET MVC to discover what parts to use, what parts to avoid, and how to get the most out of our design by following best practices.

12.1 Controllers

As the entry point for the main control of a request, controllers that lack careful design can quickly resemble their predecessors (the old `Page_Load` event) in complexity and opacity. Duplication shows up early in an application with even the slightest complexity, and the best approach is to remove different kinds of duplication. Multiple copy-and-paste commands add up and obscure the true intent of an action method. Using the wrong technique to remove duplication can wind up hiding the mechanism of a request and leading to difficulty in maintenance and troubleshooting.

The designers of ASP.NET MVC studied many mature MVC frameworks to determine the best method of providing extension points and removing duplication. When a request comes in from the outside world, we might have a group of actions we want to restrict to certain roles. Or entire areas of our application might require an authenticated user. Patterns, extensions, and techniques can help a great deal in such situations. In this section, we look at ways to make our controllers easier to develop and maintain. The first of these patterns is the Layer Supertype, applied to controllers.

12.1.1 Layer Supertype

As an application grows, patterns emerge in your controllers—a filter applied to a common group of controllers, or a set of views that need the same data. Because a controller is just a class, nothing technically stops us from using additional supertypes between our concrete controller and the `Controller` type. In these cases, we can employ the Layer Supertype pattern. As the name suggests, a Layer Supertype is a supertype (base class) for all types in that layer. This supertype contains all the common behavior that applies across an entire layer.

In CodeCampServer, the Layer Supertype is the `SmartController` type, shown in figure 12.1.

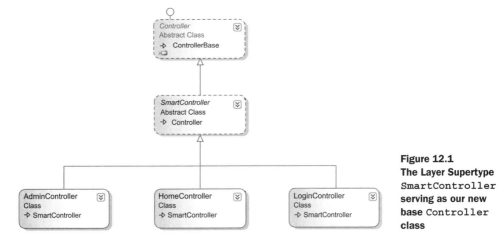

**Figure 12.1
The Layer Supertype**
`SmartController`
**serving as our new
base** `Controller`
class

One popular use for a Layer Supertype in an MVC application is to gather common filters in one location. Because filters applied to a base type at the class level also apply to derived types, a Layer Supertype is a great choice to use as a common filter. The SmartController uses several filters:

- Authentication filter
- Url referrer filter
- Assembly version filter
- User group filter

To display the view, the authentication filter adds the current user in session to View-Data. Athough we want this common behavior across many actions and views, it would be painful to put this filter on every controller. We would likely forget some controllers. In addition, maintenance of a filter declared on a large group of controllers is duplication that should be avoided. The other filters perform similar operations, and they place relevant information into ViewData so that the views can use the information.

A Layer Supertype is trivial to create: you declare a new controller, mark it as abstract, and place it between the concrete controller type and the MVC base Controller type. Any new controller you create can then inherit directly from our Layer Supertype, as shown in listing 12.1.

> **Listing 12.1   CodeCampServer Layer Supertype and a derived controller**

```
public class ScheduleController : SmartController

[AuthenticationFilter]
public abstract class SmartController : Controller
```

Instead of always beginning an application using the Layer Supertype pattern, keep in mind that it is most appropriate for larger applications or complex layers within an application. Trivial applications often do not need this pattern, but CodeCampServer is an example of an application that benefits from it. Every concrete controller has the SmartController in its inheritance chain. In addition to common filters, Layer Supertypes also hold common helper methods or properties.

12.1.2 *Filters*

As described in chapter 3, filters allow us to implement common behavior among many actions or controllers. Not all common behavior belongs in a filter. Filters are only one way of eliminating duplication in ASP.NET MVC. Filters are best at eliminating duplication in action methods and ensuring common behavior is executed among common controllers and actions.

In many web applications, access to certain areas is restricted to authenticated users. If anonymous users attempt to access these areas, they are redirected from these secured resources. To create this authentication, we need two items. First we need an IAuthorizationFilter implementation to perform the filter behavior. Second, we need an implementation of the AuthorizeAttribute to trigger our custom behavior. The custom filter is shown in listing 12.2.

Listing 12.2   Our custom authorization filter implementation

```
public class EnforceAuthenticationFilter : IAuthorizationFilter
{
    private readonly IUserSession _userSession;      ❶

    public EnforceAuthenticationFilter(IUserSession userSession)
    {
        _userSession = userSession;
    }

    public void OnAuthorization(AuthorizationContext filterContext)
    {
        if (_userSession.GetCurrentUser() == null)
        {
            filterContext.Result = new RedirectResult ("/");     ❷
        }
    }
}
```

Our authentication filter depends on an `IUserSession` ❶, whose implementation is merely a wrapper around `Session`. We need to implement one `IAuthorizationFilter` method—`OnAuthorization`. In this method, the `AuthorizationContext` gives us access to contextual data about the request and inherits from `ControllerContext`. The `AuthorizationContext` also gives us a `Result` property that allows us to provide an optional `ActionResult` to execute. In the previous example, we redirect the user to the home page by setting the `Result` property to a new `RedirectResult` ❷. This happens only when we don't have a current user. Otherwise, the filter does nothing, and the request proceeds as normal.

To apply this filter to our controllers and actions, we need an `AuthorizeAttribute` implementation, shown in listing 12.3.

Listing 12.3   Custom authorization filter delegating to the filter implementation

```
public class EnforceAuthenticationAttribute : AuthorizeAttribute
{
    public override void OnAuthorization(
        AuthorizationContext filterContext)
    {
        var authFilter = IoC.Resolve<EnforceAuthenticationFilter>();

        authFilter.OnAuthorization(filterContext);
    }
}
```

The `EnforceAuthenticationAttribute` inherits from `AuthorizeAttribute`, overriding the `OnAuthorization` behavior to instantiate and call into our `EnforceAuthenticationFilter` for the actual behavior we want. The final step is to apply our new attribute to the controllers we want to enforce authentication on, as shown in listing 12.4.

Listing 12.4   Decorating our controller with the custom authorization attribute

```
[EnforceAuthentication]
public class SecuredController : Controller
{
```

With this filter applied, we prevent anonymous users from taking any action on our `SecuredController`, as well as any derived controllers. How do we know when it's necessary to create a filter? Common, orthogonal behavior fits best into action filters. In listing 12.3, authorization happens for a wide variety of controllers and actions, but this behavior often does not relate to the other behavior in an action. This orthogonal behavior is best abstracted through a filter. In other cases, copying and pasting the same code between actions is another sign that a filter might be appropriate.

Filters can be overused and misapplied, especially as their behavior is not as explicit as code inside an action method. But applied correctly, filters are a great way to add site-wide behavior with little code and little impact on your controllers.

Why separate filters from attributes?

Many examples show the work of the filter being done directly inside of the filter attribute. The custom filter attribute class is the only piece required to implement a custom filter, but we often create a separate filter from the attribute because of the nature and limitations of attributes. If you choose to use a container or factory to locate dependencies, you will not have control over the instantiation of your attribute class. One common workaround is to define two constructors, one that takes the filter's dependencies, and one that calls into the container or factory to supply implementations at runtime. This leads to nontrivial bugs, as your attribute's constructor can be called at nonobvious times, such as in reflection scenarios used by unit testing frameworks.

If your filter does not use dependencies, having two separate classes is overkill. But as soon as you start including dependencies in your filter, take the extra step of separating the attribute from the filter.

12.1.3 *Smart binders*

The model binders in ASP.NET MVC are useful out of the box. They do a great job of taking request and form input and hydrating fairly complex models from them. But a custom binder can also remove another common form of duplication—loading an object from the database based on an action parameter. Most of the time, this action parameter is the primary key of the object or another unique identifier. Instead of putting this repeated data access code in all of our actions, we can use a custom model binder that can load the persisted object before the action is executed. Our action can then take the persisted object type as a parameter instead of the unique identifier.

One problem with the MVC model binder implementation is that we can match our custom model binder for a single type. In an application with dozens of entities, it is easy to forget to register the custom model binder for every type. For example, CodeCampServer uses a common base type (PersistentObject) for all entities in the system. Ideally, we could register the custom model binder just once, or just leave it up to each custom binder to decide whether or not it should bind.

To accomplish this, we need to replace the default model binder with our own implementation. Additionally, we can define an interface, IFilteredModelBinder, for our new binders, as shown in listing 12.5.

Listing 12.5   The IFilteredModelBinder interface

```
public interface IFilteredModelBinder : IModelBinder
{
    bool IsMatch(Type modelType);
}
```

The IFilteredModelBinder inherits from the MVC IModelBinder interface, and adds a method through which implementations can perform custom matching logic. In our case, we can look at the base type of the model type passed in to determine if it is a PersistentObject type. To use custom filtered model binders, we need to create a DefaultModelBinder implementation, as shown in listing 12.6.

Listing 12.6   A smarter model binder

```
public class SmartBinder : DefaultModelBinder
{
    private readonly IFilteredModelBinder [] _filteredModelBinders;

    public SmartBinder (
        params IFilteredModelBinder [] filteredModelBinders)        ❶
    {
        _filteredModelBinders = filteredModelBinders;
    }

    public override object BindModel (                             ❷
        ControllerContext controllerContext,
        ModelBindingContext bindingContext)
    {
        foreach (var modelBinder in _filteredModelBinders)         ❸
        {
            if (modelBinder.IsMatch(bindingContext.ModelType))
            {
                return modelBinder.BindModel (controllerContext,
                    bindingContext);                               ❹
            }
        }
        return base.BindModel (controllerContext, bindingContext);
    }
}
```

Our new SmartBinder class takes an array of IFilteredModelBinders ❶, which we'll fill in soon. Next, it overrides the BindModel method ❷. BindModel loops through all of the supplied IFilteredModelBinders, and checks to see if any match the ModelType from the `ModelBindingContext` ❸. If it is a match, we execute and return the result from `BindModel` for that `IFilteredModelBinder` ❹. The complete class diagram is shown in figure 12.2.

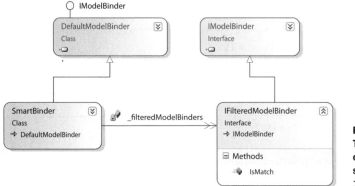

**Figure 12.2
The class diagram
of our `SmartBinder`
showing the relationship to
`IFilteredModelBinder`**

Now that we have a new binder that can match on more than one type, we can turn our attention to our new model binder for loading persistent objects. This new model binder will be an implementation of the `IFilteredModelBinder` interface. It will need to do a number of things in order to return the correct entity from our persistence layer:

1 Retrieve the request value from the binding context
2 Deal with missing request values
3 Create the correct repository
4 Use the repository to load the entity, and return it

We won't cover the third item in much depth, as this example assumes that an IoC container is in place. The entire model binder needs to implement our `IFiltered-ModelBinder`, and is shown in listing 12.7.

Listing 12.7   The `EntityModelBinder`

```
public class EntityModelBinder : IFilteredModelBinder
{
    public bool IsMatch(Type modelType)         ❶
    {
        return typeof(PersistentObject).IsAssignableFrom(modelType);
    }

    public object BindModel (
        ControllerContext controllerContext,
        ModelBindingContext bindingContext)
    {
        ValueProviderResult value =
            bindingContext.ValueProvider [bindingContext.ModelName];   ❷

        if (value == null)        ❸
            return null;
```

```
        if (string.IsNullOrEmpty(value.AttemptedValue))
            return null;

        var entityId = new Guid(value.AttemptedValue);

        Type repositoryType = typeof(IRepository<>)
            .MakeGenericType(bindingContext.ModelType);
        var repository = (IRepository)IoC.Resolve(repositoryType);
        PersistentObject entity = repository.GetById(entityId);

        return entity;
    }
}
```

In listing 12.7 we implement our newly created interface, IFilteredModelBinder. The additional method, IsMatch ❶, returns true when the model type being bound by ASP.NET MVC is a PersistentObject, our base type for all model objects persisted in a database. Next, we have to implement the BindModel method by following the steps laid out just before listing 12.7. First, we retrieve the request value from the ModelBindingContext ❷ passed in to the BindModel method. The ModelBindingContext contains a dictionary of strings to ValueProviderResults in the ValueProvider property. If the ValueProviderResult does not exist, or the attempted value does not exist, we won't try to retrieve the entity from the repository ❸. Although the entity's identifier is a Guid, the attempted value is a string, so we construct a new Guid from the attempted value on the ValueProviderResult ❹.

Now that we have the parsed Guid from the request, we can create the appropriate repository from our IoC container ❺. But because we have specific repositories for each kind of entity, we don't know the specific repository type at compile time. However, all of our repositories implement a common interface, as shown in listing 12.8.

Listing 12.8 The common repository interface

```
public interface IRepository<TEntity>
    where TEntity : PersistentObject
{
    TEntity GetById(Guid id);
}
```

We want the IoC container to create the correct repository given the type of entity we are attempting to bind. This means we need to figure out and construct the correct Type object for the IRepository we create. We do this by using the Type.MakeGenericType method to create a closed generic type from the open generic type IRepository<>.

Open and closed generic types

An open generic type is simply a generic type that has no type parameters supplied. IList<> and IDictionary<,> are both open generic types. To create instances of a type, we must create a closed generic type from the open generic type. A closed generic type is a generic type with type parameters supplied, such as IList<int> and IDictionary<string, User>.

When we have the closed generic type for IRepository using the ModelBinding-Context.ModelType property, we can use our IoC container to create an instance of the repository to call and use. Finally, we call the repository's GetById method and return the retrieved entity from BindModel. Because we cannot call a generic method at runtime without using reflection, we use another nongeneric IRepository interface that returns only objects as PersistentObject, as shown in listing 12.9.

Listing 12.9   The nongeneric repository interface

```
public interface IRepository
{
    PersistentObject GetById(Guid id);
}
```

All repositories in our system inherit from a common repository base class, which implements both the generic and nongeneric implementations of IRepository. Because some places cannot hold references to the generic interface (as we encountered with model binding) the additional nongeneric IRepository interface supports these scenarios.

We have our SmartBinder and EntityModelBinder, which bind to entities from request values, but we still need to configure ASP.NET MVC to use these binders instead of the default model binder. To do this, we set the ModelBinders.Binders.Default-Binder property in our application startup code, as shown in listing 12.10.

Listing 12.10   Replacing the default model binder

```
protected void Application_Start()
{
    ModelBinders.Binders.DefaultBinder =
        new SmartBinder (new EntityModelBinder ());
```

At this point, we have only a single filtered model binder. In practice, we might have specialized model binders for certain entities, classes of objects (such as enumeration classes), and so on. By creating a model binder for entities, we can create controller actions that take entities as parameters, as opposed to just a Guid, as shown in listing 12.11.

Listing 12.11   Controller action with an entity as a parameter

```
public class ConferenceController : Controller
{
    public ViewResult Show(Conference c)
    {
        return View(c);
    }
}
```

With the EntityModelBinder in place, we avoid repeating code in our controller actions. This repetition would obscure the intent of the controller action with data access code that is not relevant to what the controller action is trying to accomplish.

12.1.4 *Hardcoded strings*

ASP.NET MVC often uses dictionaries to pass information and data among different layers. With all these dictionaries floating around, the possibility for hardcoded, duplicated strings increases. Dictionaries are useful when we cannot specify an exact contract for the data to pass between two objects. For example, the controller uses `ViewData` to pass information to the view. But `ViewData` at its heart is nothing more than an enhanced dictionary. If we hardcode our strings in the controller, such as in the listing 12.12 example, we run the risk of brittle and unmaintainable code.

Listing 12.12 Hardcoded string in a controller

```
public ActionResult Register()
{
    ViewData ["PasswordLength"] = MembershipService.MinPasswordLength;

    return View();
}
```

In this case, the `ViewData` key, `"PasswordLength"`, is used no less than six times in the entire sample ASP.NET MVC project! If we ever decided to change this key to something else, we could attempt a global find and replace, but we still run the risk of changing the wrong keys. Repeating this key could cause problems for future maintainers, who might not understand where the key is used. So you wind up with a key value that is never changed, for fear of breaking the application.

Instead, with some static fields and a little organization, we can make sure that this key appears once as a string in our application, as shown in listing 12.13.

Listing 12.13 Organized view data keys

```
public static class Keys
{
    public static class ViewData
    {
        public static readonly string PasswordLength = "PasswordLength";
    }
}
```

When we want to use a certain dictionary key, we go to the one place in our application where these keys are defined. The changed controller action is shown in listing 12.14.

Listing 12.14 Using a single location for a dictionary key

```
public ActionResult Register_after()
{
    ViewData[Keys.ViewData.PasswordLength] =
        MembershipService.MinPasswordLength;

    return View();
}
```

In our view, we'll use the same reference to ensure that we have the key value only once in our application. If we decide to rename the value of this key, or its reference, we won't break any existing controllers, views, or tests. Hardcoded strings work well, until the values are repeated. Some developers go as far as changing their IDE font color settings for strings to be bright and recognizable, as a visual cue to the developer indicating use of hardcoded strings.

12.1.5 *Separated view models*

In many applications, the model we pass to the view is our domain model. A screen to show conference information might need only a single `Conference` object to display what it needs. In other cases, we might need more information than what is available on our domain model. A search results screen might need paging information, the number of results returned, and perhaps a list of matched terms. On an edit screen, we may want to include validation on our objects. If users can enter quantities in their shopping carts, how can we ensure they entered valid numbers?

Let's take a simple example: when editing a conference, we are required to enter the maximum number of attendees. This would be represented on our domain model as shown in listing 12.15.

Listing 12.15   Conference model

```
public class Conference : PersistentObject
{
    public int MaxAttendees { get; set; }
}
```

When it comes to binding this to our edit view, we'll have a slight problem. If we make our `Conference` the same model as the one our edit view uses, what happens if a user enters an invalid numerical value, or nothing at all? Model binding either won't work, or will only bind the default to our `MaxAttendees` property. In order to properly handle all use cases, our `MaxAttendees` property can only be a string. This is a case of the view's concerns leaking into our domain model, a situation to be avoided if all possible.

The other option is to create a separate view model type for our views from the domain model. We'll create a specialized class, just for that one view. We can shape that type however we like, and allow the view to shape our view model however we want. The advantage of a separated view model is that our views won't influence the domain model in any way. For less complex applications, this separation is not necessary and overcomplicates the design. As complexity of the views increases, the design of the views has more and more impact on our domain model, unless the view model and domain model are separated.

But the information from our domain still needs to get to the views, and to do this, we can simply transform our domain model into the view model, as shown in listing 12.16.

Listing 12.16   Transforming the domain model to view model

```
public ActionResult Edit(Conference conference)
{
    var editModel = new EditConference
```

```
    {
        Id = conference.Id,
        MaxAttendees = conference.MaxAttendees.ToString()
    };
    return View(editModel);
}
```

Our `Edit` action, which is used to edit a `Conference`, takes a `Conference` domain object as a parameter (using the model binding techniques of the last section). Next, we create an `EditConference` view model object from our `Conference`. In our `Edit-Conference` type, `MaxAttendees` is a string, so we can properly handle malformed input. Finally, we return a `ViewResult` with the `EditConference` object as our model for that view. To handle the final form post for editing, our `Edit` POST action now takes the `EditConference` as a parameter, as shown in listing 12.17.

> **Listing 12.17 The edit action for posting conference updates**

```
[AcceptVerbs(HttpVerbs.Post)]
public ActionResult Edit(EditConference conference)
{
```

One interesting side effect of crafting custom view models is that our views and controllers start to become much more strongly typed. Instead of receiving a bag of form variables, we have a single object to deal with. Instead of myriad dictionary key-value pairs, we have properties on a real type. We do have to write code to process the `Edit-Conference` object and map it to our `Conference` object, but this is something we would need to do in any case. Using an OOM (object-object mapper) such as AutoMapper can save you from writing the lion's share of mapping code. By separating our `EditConference` type from the `Conference` type, we allow each to grow independently, with the only coupling between the two being our mapping code. The view can shape the `EditConference` model, and our domain can shape the `Conference` model. In practice, we found that our domain model and view models start with a similar shape, but start to diverge as our views became more and more complex. As we introduced master pages, partials, AJAX, caching, and so on, a separated view model allowed us to contain the complexity of our views, without affecting the design of our domain model.

12.1.6 *Validation*

Because validation can take so many forms, it's a tricky subject. For a single screen for adding a conference, you might have to enforce several rules:

- Maximum attendees must be a number.
- Maximum attendees is required.
- Maximum attendees cannot exceed what the building's fire code allows.
- A large conference cannot be cancelled without approval of a majority of the organizers.

As we can see, there is no black-and-white distinction among different rules. We must enforce the rule that the "maximum attendees" value entered by the user is a number, but what about it being a required field? That starts to bleed into business rules validation. Validation and business rules include a wide spectrum, from invariants such as type checking and required fields, all the way to complex workflow logic. Validation frameworks work well with the UI end of the spectrum, where we are validating user input for further business rule checking. This distinction is not altogether concrete, especially when we want to tie business rule violations to specific user interface elements.

But validation frameworks help to consolidate and standardize user input validation, providing a common interface for executing and reporting validation errors. There are many validation frameworks in .NET, from the Validation Application Block from the Microsoft Patterns and Practices group, to Data Annotations, originating from ASP.NET Dynamic Data, to open source offerings such as Castle Validators. Each is configured through attributes.

We can use the Castle Validators for data type and required field validation, as shown in listing 12.18.

Listing 12.18 Our `EditConference` model with validation attributes applied

```
public class EditConference
{
    public Guid Id { get; set; }

    [ValidateNonEmpty]
    [ValidateInteger]
    public string MaxAttendees { get; set; }
```

Castle Validators won't execute automatically as part of an ASP.NET MVC request, unless we specifically code them to do so. But we don't want to have to code this validation for every controller action that needs validation. Instead, we can modify our custom model binder to do the validation. When our controller action processes the bound model, it can examine `ModelState` to determine if any validation errors occurred, and take appropriate action. To add our Castle Validator logic to model binding, we'll need to override the `OnModelUpdated` method, as shown in listing 12.19.

Listing 12.19 The modified default model binder with Castle Validator

```
protected override void OnModelUpdated (
    ControllerContext controllerContext,
    ModelBindingContext bindingContext)
{
    var runner = new ValidatorRunner (new CachedValidationRegistry());    ❶
    if (!runner.IsValid(bindingContext.Model))                             ❷
    {
        var summary = runner.GetErrorSummary(bindingContext.Model);        ❸

        foreach (var invalidProperty in summary.InvalidProperties)
        {
```

```
        foreach (var error in summary
            .GetErrorsForProperty(invalidProperty))
        {
            bindingContext.ModelState
                .AddModelError(invalidProperty, error);     ❹
        }
    }
  }
}
```

To run validation against our model, we'll first need to create the `ValidatorRunner` ❶, the class responsible for executing the validation logic. The `IsValid` method ❷ takes our model, and returns a boolean indicating whether or not validation was successful. If not, we call the `GetErrorSummary` method ❸, looping through the invalid properties and errors for each property, adding the individual error message to the `ModelState` errors collection ❹. Castle Validators have their own structure for representing validation errors, which we have to translate into ASP.NET MVC's mechanism for representing model errors. In our `Edit` action that accepts the form post, we need only to inspect the `ModelState` for any errors, and show the original edit view if validation failed, as shown in listing 12.20.

Listing 12.20   Handling validation errors in our controller action
---

```
[AcceptVerbs(HttpVerbs.Post)]
public ActionResult Edit(EditConference conference)
{
    if (!ModelState.IsValid)
        return View(conference);
```

In our view, we can use the normal `HtmlHelper` methods to display any validation errors or summaries, as we are using the built-in `ModelState` for Castle Validator validation messages. With our custom model binder, we were able to provide seamless integration between a third-party validation framework and ASP.NET MVC. Our views have no knowledge of any validation framework underneath, allowing us to mix and match validation frameworks to our needs. In the next section, we'll examine ways to ensure our views are easy to deal with in complex and long-term maintenance scenarios.

12.2   Views

It is easy to underestimate the effort needed to create and maintain the HTML markup and code in an MVC application. Although the view is responsible *only* for creating and displaying HTML, duplication exists just as much in views as it would in other layers in our application. We'll look at techniques for reducing duplication as well as using lambda expressions and strongly typed views to eliminate magic strings.

12.2.1   Strongly typed views

Here is one view, one model. When a view accepts only one model type, it allows us to make optimizations along that vector, such as the generic `HtmlHelper` and expression-based HTML generation. Strongly typed views are straightforward to use: when we use the View method in an action method, we pass in the model object. On the view side, we can inherit from the generic System.Web.Mvc.ViewPage<TModel base type. Moving away from the dictionary-based view model to a strongly typed model with real properties eliminates many of the pesky runtime errors that crop up due to relying on a weak contract of dictionary keys, which are not compile-safe. With dictionary keys, we have to rely on the strength (and correctness) of our controller unit tests to ensure our views don't break. Strongly typed views also bring another developer convenience: IntelliSense. When we access the Model property in a view, IntelliSense can pick up all members from the underlying model type.

Strongly typed views don't force us away from the dictionary-based ViewData. Both can exist in a single view, though these occurrences should be the exception, not the rule. We'll have to handle some scenarios slightly differently, such as filters used for populating ViewData. With a strongly typed view, we want to limit the filters being used in this manner. Instead, we can use the RenderAction method inside of a view to grab common information that is not already in the existing view model. It may seem strange to call another action inside of a view, but this provides a way for the template of a page to organize other information that may need to appear on many pages. When we use filters for populating ViewData, we are introducing a strong, but not obvious, coupling from the view to the controller. When we look in a view and see access to ViewData through a key-value pair, it is difficult to trace back and understand where this value came from, and why. With strongly typed views and RenderAction, we can enforce strongly typed views throughout our application, regardless of how we organize our views into partials.

Current ASP.NET MVC demos and examples rely heavily on dictionaries to pass data around. Overreliance on these mechanisms can lead to a brittle application, and just the introduction of compile-time safety in strongly typed views is a welcome safety net for reducing bugs.

12.2.2 *Fighting duplication*

When using Web Forms, we had many different avenues for reducing duplication and providing common visual components. Many of these same avenues exist for MVC; some are new, and some are deprecated. There are at least four ways to consolidate HTML in ASP.NET MVC:

1 Master pages
2 Partials
3 RenderAction
4 Extending HtmlHelper

In addition to these four, there are more exotic ways to render HTML in a view, such as subcontrollers and partial requests. The most common mechanisms are the four listed, and each has its sweet spot.

For site-wide layout, master pages are the ideal choice. Using content placeholders, we can create a common layout for our site, and individual pages can insert content for each placeholder. Master pages can be nested, allowing us to construct general layouts, as well as layouts for sections of a website. The administrative section might have the same header and footer, but a different toolbar and main section layout, whereas the rest of the site might have a preference-generated toolbar, with a sidebar for bookmarks. With master pages, interaction with `ViewData` should be kept to a minimum, as interactions would create a coupling from controller design to view design. Master page design should not affect controller/action design.

Every time you start to copy and paste HTML, stop yourself. This could be an opportunity to refactor that common markup into a partial. Partials, which can themselves be strongly typed, are perfect for small, repeated bits of markup used in more than one view. Partials have their own `ViewData`, which must be supplied by a parent view, and therefore the calling action. If this information is already available in the single view model given to the view through `ViewData`, partials are an appropriate mechanism for consolidating HTML. If you must resort to filters to supply a partial's `ViewData`, your controllers will start to become more and more intimate with the design of your view.

`RenderAction` is an excellent alternative to using the combination of a filter and a partial, because it effectively displays markup and data that is completely orthogonal to your main controller action. A logon widget displayed on every page needs login information. But if your main controller action is displaying a list of products, it muddies the concern of our controller to include the name of the current user. We can put the name of the current user in `ViewData` through a filter, but our view is no longer completely strongly typed. On the view side, we'll see a call to `RenderPartial` and passing in the user's name. Using this method, you will likely not be able to understand from where the information is coming. If you have to search for usages of a dictionary key value, that is likely an indication of too much indirection. With `RenderAction`, the view creates a minipipeline, calling an action with all of the action's filters executed. The choice of locating data for the subview is relegated to the other controller.

We have the choice of extending `HtmlHelper`. The choice between using a partial and extending `HtmlHelper` is fairly clear. If the piece of HTML is only one or two elements, the `HtmlHelper` is an ideal choice. A common scenario for input elements is to include a label alongside the form element. This repetitive HTML gets tedious to write over and over. We can encapsulate this into a single `HtmlHelper` extension, as shown in listing 12.21.

Listing 12.21 Extending `HtmlHelper` to include labels

```
public static string TextBoxWithLabelFor<TModel, TProperty>(
    this HtmlHelper<TModel> htmlHelper,
    Expression<Func<TModel, TProperty>> expression,
    string label)
    where TModel : class
{
    string labelHtml =
```

```
        string.Format("<label for=\"{0}\">{1}:</label>",     ❶
            ExpressionHelper.GetInputName(expression),     ❷
            label);
    string textboxHtml = htmlHelper.TextBoxFor(expression);

    return labelHtml + " " + textboxHtml;
}
```

In our extension, we craft custom HTML for the label ❶, but lean on helpers from
the MVC Futures assembly to assist in creating both the textbox and the value of the
label's `for` attribute ❷. The markup then becomes much easier to read, as shown in
listing 12.22.

Listing 12.22   Using the `HtmlHelper` extension in a view

```
<% using (Html.BeginForm()) { %>
    <div>
        <%= Html.TextBoxWithLabelFor (c => c.MaxAttendees, "Max Attendees")
        %>
        <%= Html.ValidationMessageFor(c => c.MaxAttendees) %>
        <p>
            <input type="submit" value="Submit" />
        </p>
    </div>
<% } %>
```

The MVC Futures assembly contains quite a few extensions that are useful with
strongly typed views. We can combine and extend the provided extensions in new and
interesting ways. We could add support for validation error messages, asterisks for
required fields, or custom HTML for certain kinds of output. We could create extensions for dates to include a calendar picker, or autocomplete functionality for user
pickers. Code looks bad in markup, and markup is hard to distinguish in code. If you
find yourself piecing together lots of HTML in an `HtmlHelper` extension, you may want
to look at partials. If your partial is small, or contains logic, an `HtmlHelper` can provide
a cleaner mechanism for the containing view.

   To fully take advantage of views in ASP.NET MVC, it helps to understand the different ways we can refactor, extend, and improve how we craft HTML. Not all mechanisms are appropriate in every scenario, and often, the choice between options is not
always clear. Views should never get so complicated that it is difficult to move from a
partial to an `HtmlHelper` extension or a `RenderAction` call to a filter and a partial. In
the next section, we'll examine ways to reduce the number of magic strings present in
our application through use of expressions.

12.2.3 *Embracing expressions*

Magic strings permeate the ASP.NET MVC Framework. They are magic because they
represent a property or a well-known attribute, but there is no connection to the original information. When using magic strings, you are prone to the following types of
errors: misspelling, refactoring, and renaming bugs. Even the default template
included in ASP.NET MVC is riddled with magic strings. Because C# is a statically typed

language, we can leverage the type and symbol checking if we use symbols instead of strings to make relationships among code. As an exercise, let's examine one view in the sample, the LogOn.aspx page, in listing 12.23.

Listing 12.23 Magic strings in a view

```
<h2>Log On</h2>
<p>
    Please enter your username and password.
    <%= Html.ActionLink ("Register", "Register") %>    ❶
    if you don't have an account.
</p>
<%= Html.ValidationSummary("Login was unsuccessful. Please correct the errors
    and try again.") %>
<% using (Html.BeginForm()) { %>
    <div>
        <fieldset>
            <legend>Account Information</legend>
            <p>
                <label for="username">Username:</label>    ❷
                <%= Html.TextBox("username") %>    ❸
                <%= Html.ValidationMessage("username") %>    ❹
            </p>
            <p>
                <label for="password">Password:</label>
                <%= Html.Password("password") %>
                <%= Html.ValidationMessage("password") %>
            </p>
            <p>
                <%= Html.CheckBox("rememberMe") %>
                <label class="inline" for="rememberMe">Remember me?</label>
            </p>
            <p>
                <input type="submit" value="Log On" />
            </p>
        </fieldset>
    </div>
<% } %>
```

We can see several examples of magic strings:

- The `ActionLink` call refers to a method on a controller ❶, and will break if the method name changes.
- All labels refer to a parameter name on a method ❷, which will break if the name changes.
- All input elements refer to a parameter name on a method ❸.
- All validation messages refer to a parameter name on a method ❹.
- Labels, input elements and validation messages must line up, or the page will break.

Fighting these magic string errors is easy–don't use them! Instead, we can use expression-based methods and strongly typed views. Consider the action method that would accept a form post from the page using the view in listing 12.23. One approach is for the action method to accept each form field as an individual parameter. Another approach would be to create a single view model type to represent the entire form, as shown in listing 12.24.

Listing 12.24   Our new view model form type

```
public class LogOnForm
{
    public string Username { get; set; }
    public string Password { get; set; }
    public bool RememberMe { get; set; }
    public string ReturnUrl { get; set; }
}
```

Our view can then be changed to a strongly typed view for our `LogOnForm`. All HTML generation can now use expressions pointing to a property instead of magic strings, as shown in listing 12.25.

Listing 12.25   Using expressions in our view

```
<h2>Log On</h2>
<p>
    Please enter your username and password.
    <%= Html.ActionLink<AccountController>(c => c.LogOn_after(null),
        "Register") %>                                                    ❶
    if you don't have an account.
</p>
<%= Html.ValidationSummary("Login was unsuccessful. Please correct the errors
    and try again.") %>

<% using (Html.BeginForm()) { %>
    <div>
        <fieldset>
            <legend>Account Information</legend>
            <p>
                <%= Html.TextBoxWithLabelFor(
                    form => form.Username, "Username") %>        ❷
            </p>
            <p>
                <%= Html.PasswordWithLabelFor(
                    form => form.Password, "Password") %>        ❸
            </p>
            <p>
                <%= Html.CheckBoxWithLabelFor(
                    form => form.RememberMe, "Remember me") %>       ❹
            </p>
            <p>
                <input type="submit" value="Log On" />
            </p>
        </fieldset>
    </div>
<% } %>
```

We have introduced many changes in this view:

- The ActionLink call now refers to a method on a controller ❶.
- The username input element is generated from an expression ❷.
- The password input element is generated from an expression ❸.
- The "remember me" input element is generated from an expression ❹.

Despite all these changes, our final HTML has not changed. However, our view is now much less susceptible to subtle bugs, which can only be caught at runtime. With strongly typed views and expression-based HTML generation methods, we can feel comfortable that refactoring will work properly and view compilation will fail if we rename or remove a controller action or view model property. Not all instances of magic string usage are eliminated in the MVC Futures assembly. Additional extensions are easily added as necessary if they don't already exist in the MvcContrib project. For instance the MvcContrib.FluentHtml assembly can assist with HTML generation.

Magic strings are insidious sources of runtime bugs, and should be eliminated wherever you find them. Common usages of magic strings come in the form of representing method, property, or parameter names as strings in your application. These should be red flags for developers, and replaced with compile-safe, IntelliSense, and refactoring-friendly expressions. In the next section, we'll examine more usages of expressions for dealing with routes.

12.3 Routes

Routing is perhaps the biggest innovation of the ASP.NET MVC project—so big, in fact, it was included in the .NET Framework 3.5 SP1 release, well ahead of the ASP.NET MVC release. Like any new tool, routing is easy to abuse. Unless routes are tested thoroughly, changes to routes can break existing URLs. When URLs become public, changing them can break links, bookmarks, lower search rankings, and anger end users. Designing of custom routes and URL patterns should come from actual business requirements. In this section, we'll examine some common sense practices for routes, as well as some practices to ensure we don't break our application in the process.

12.3.1 Testing routes

When we do need custom routes, we need to ensure both that the routes we are creating are correct, and any existing routes are not modified. We can start off with the built-in routes, and lock those down with tests. The default route is shown in listing 12.26.

Listing 12.26 Default route in a new application

```
routes.IgnoreRoute("{resource}.axd/{*pathInfo}");

routes.MapRoute(
    "Default",
    "{controller}/{action}/{id}",
    new { controller = "Home", action = "Index", id = "" }
);
```

For many applications, this route is sufficient and does not necessarily need to be tested on its own. If we added additional routing behavior, we would want to ensure that existing routes that follow this format are not broken. Before we start writing tests, we need to think of a few scenarios. The following URLs should work in the default sample application:

- /—maps to `HomeController.Index()`
- /home—maps to `HomeController.Index()`
- /home/about—maps to `HomeController.About()`

To make things more interesting, we'll add a simple `ProductController` to list, view, and search products, as shown in listing 12.27.

Listing 12.27   Simplified product controller

```
public class ProductController : Controller
{
    public ViewResult Index()
    {
        var products = new[]
        {
            new Product {Name = "DVD Player"},
            new Product {Name = "VCR"},
            new Product {Name = "Laserdisc Player"}
        };
        return View(products);
    }

    public ViewResult Show(int id)
    {
        return View(new Product {Name = "Hand towels"});
    }

    public ViewResult Search(string name)
    {
        return View("Show", new Product {Name = name});
    }
}
```

With our new controller, we want to support more interesting URL scenarios:

- /product/show/5—maps to `ProductController.Show`
- /product/SomeProductName—maps to `ProductController.Search(Some-ProductName)`

Out of the box, the built-in routes support the first scenario, but not the second. Before we start messing around with our routes, we need to add tests to our existing scenarios. Testing routes is possible, but much easier with the testing extensions of the open source project, MvcContrib. We'll test the first scenario, as shown in listing 12.28.

Listing 12.28   Testing a blank URL

```
[Test]
public void Should_map_blank_url_to_home()
```

```
{
    "~/".Route().ShouldMapTo<HomeController>(c => c.Index());
}
```

Using extension methods, first transforms a string into a `Route` object with the `Route` extension method. Next, we use the `ShouldMapTo` extension method to assert that a route maps to the `Index` method on `HomeController`. `ShouldMapTo` is a generic method, taking an expression. It is similar to other expression-based methods such as `Html.ActionLink`. The expression is used to perform strongly typed reflection, as opposed to doing something like passing the controller and action name in as strings, which will fail under refactoring scenarios. Unfortunately, this test does not pass yet, as we have not called anything to set up our routes. We'll accomplish this in a test setup method to be executed before every test, as shown in listing 12.29.

Listing 12.29　Registering the routes in a setup method

```
[TestFixtureSetUp]
public void Setup()
{
    MvcApplication.RegisterRoutes(RouteTable.Routes);
}
```

With our setup in place, our test now passes. The next scenarios we want to test are the other built-in scenarios, as shown in listing 12.30.

Listing 12.30　Testing the built-in routing scenarios

```
[Test]
public void Should_map_home_url_to_home_with_default_action()
{
    "~/home".Route().ShouldMapTo<HomeController>(c => c.Index());
}

[Test]
public void Should_map_home_about_url_to_home_matching_method_name()
{
    "~/home/about".Route().ShouldMapTo<HomeController>(c => c.About());
}

[Test]
public void
    Should_map_product_show_with_id_to_product_controller_with_parameter()
{
    "~/product/show/5".Route().ShouldMapTo<ProductController>(
        c => c.Show(5));
}
```

With default scenarios added, we can now proceed with modifying our route to support the special case of a search term directly in the URL. Before we get there, let's make sure our routes don't already support this scenario by adding a test to verify the functionality. After all, if this test passes, our work is done! The new test is shown in listing 12.31.

Listing 12.31   New scenario routing product search terms

```
[Test]
public void Should_map_product_search_to_product_controller_with_parameter()
{
    "~/product/SomeProductName"
        .Route()
        .ShouldMapTo<ProductController>(c => c.Search("SomeProductName"));
}
```

Alas, our test fails, and our work is not yet done. The test fails with the message "Mvc-Contrib.TestHelper.AssertionException : Expected Search but was SomeProduct-Name." To make our test pass, we need to add the appropriate changes to the routes, as shown in listing 12.32.

Listing 12.32   Additional route for searching products

```
routes.MapRoute(
    "SearchProduct",
    "product/{name}",
    new { controller = "Product", action = "Search" }
);
```

With this addition to our routes, our new test passes, along with all the other tests. We were able to add a new route to our routing configuration with the assurance that we would not break the other URLs. Since URLs are now generated through routes in an MVC application, testing our routes becomes of utmost importance. The test helpers in MvcContrib wrapped all the ugliness that usually comes along with testing routes. In the next section, we'll examine action names and custom routes.

12.3.2 *Action naming*

Although the default routes in an MVC application match a URL to a method name on a controller, the defaults can be changed. As shown in section 12.3.1, we can map the second URL segment to a parameter on a specific action. When using the MVC extension points of the `ActionNameSelectorAttribute` and `ActionMethodSelectorAttribute`, the name of an action method on a controller does not exactly match the method name. The two concepts of *action name* and *action method* name are completely separate, and can be configured independently. We can configure an action method as shown in listing 12.33 to modify the action name.

Listing 12.33   Modifying the action name for an action method

```
public class ChangedActionNameController : Controller
{
    [ActionName("Foo")]
    public ActionResult Index()
    {
        return View();
    }
}
```

In the controller shown in listing 12.33, we specified that the action method should be different from the action name. The action name, (originally the action method name, "Index"), is now "Foo". Navigating to /changedactionnname /changedactionname/index now results in a 404 Not Found error. The action name is now "Foo", and we can only access this action through /changedactoinname/foo. As view names correspond to action names, not action method names, our view is named "Foo.aspx".

But in most applications, we are better served adhering to the convention that action names match action method names. If method names differ from action names, we can no longer use expression-based URL generators. Our URL generation is now susceptible to subtle refactoring and renaming errors. This can be alleviated by introducing global constants for action names, but it still creates a string-based system, with another level of indirection between action methods and action names, that is not needed in many cases.

Consistency in action naming can reduce the complexity in your system. If your system is generally resource-based; that is, controllers are designed around individual entities (a `ProductController` and a `UserController`), RESTful-style action names introduce both discoverability on the client side, and predictable design on the developer side. Given a controller designed for products, the user interactions we might want to support include

- Listing products
- Showing one product
- Creating a new product
- Editing an existing product
- Deleting a product

Translated into controller actions, these would map to

- Index
- Show
- New
- Edit
- Delete

Because MVC action methods can be configured to accept only certain HTTP verbs, such as POST, we can design our controller with a set of overloaded action methods, one for viewing a form and one for receiving the posted form. If we had some sort of `Widget` resource in our system, our `WidgetsController` would look similar to listing 12.34.

Listing 12.34   A RESTful-style controller for managing `Widget` resources

```
public class WidgetsController : Controller
{
    public ActionResult Index()
    {
```

```
˥n View();


        ɔnResult Show(int id)


            .ɘw();


    ᴜic ActionResult New()        ❶
    {
        return View();
    }

    [AcceptVerbs(HttpVerbs.Post)]                    ❷
    public ActionResult New(WidgetForm widget)
    {
        return RedirectToAction("Index");
    }

    public ActionResult Edit(int id)
    {
        return View();
    }

    [AcceptVerbs(HttpVerbs.Post)]
    public ActionResult Edit(WidgetForm widget)
    {
        return RedirectToAction("Index");
    }
}
```

Actions that support GET and POST verbs, the New and Edit actions, can be overloaded so that one method responds to GET requests ❶ and the other responds to POST requests ❷. To be clear, these actions don't match the definition of REST. However, the design would be simpler if all of the controllers dealing with a resource looked the same. If we went to a real RESTful architecture, using MvcContrib's SimplyRestfulRouteHandler, we could support all of the standard REST actions and corresponding HTTP verbs. Regardless of whether we want to adopt REST, having every action that shows a single entity or resource called Show makes new features easier to learn and makes the application easier to maintain.

12.4 *Testing*

The separation of concerns that the MVC pattern provides significantly increases testability for .NET web applications. Because controllers are normal classes, and actions are merely methods, we can load and execute actions and then examine the results. Even though testing controllers is simple, we must consider an important caveat. When we test a controller action, we are only able to write assertions for the behavior we can observe. The true test of a working application is running it in a browser, and there are significant differences between viewing a page in a browser and asserting results in a controller action test. We can assert that the correct view is chosen, but we cannot assert that the correct view is shown at runtime. We can assert that we put correct information into ViewData, but we cannot ensure that the view uses all of the information we give it. We also cannot assert that all possible controller code paths place the necessary objects into `ViewData`. With action filters, it is quite possible that a view will need data that is not present. Controller action tests don't run the entire MVC engine, so things like ActionFilters are not executed. Although action unit tests add value, they don't replace end-to-end application-level testing. Before we examine the last mile of testing in UI tests, let's see how we can lock down the behavior in the rest of our MVC application through unit testing.

12.4.1 *Controller unit tests*

For controllers to be maintainable, they should be as light and skinny as possible, delegating all real domain work to other services. Our controller tests will reflect this choice, as assertions will be small and target only the following:

- What `ActionResult` was chosen
- What information was passed to the view, in `ViewData` or `TempData`

All other web-related information, whether it is security, cookies, or session variables, should be encapsulated in a domain-specific and domain-relevant interface. Although it eases testing, encapsulation and separation of concerns are the most significant reasons to leave these other `HttpContext`-related items out of controllers. The simplest example of a controller action is one that simply passes data into a view, as shown in listing 12.35.

Listing 12.35 A simple action

```
public ViewResult Index()
{
    var products = _productRepository.FindAll();

    return View(products);
}
```

In this example, `productRepository` is a private field of type `IProductRepository`, as shown in listing 12.36.

Listing 12.36 The controller with its dependency

```
public class ProductsController : Controller
{
    private readonly IProductRepository _productRepository;

    public ProductsController(IProductRepository productRepository)
    {
        _productRepository = productRepository;
    }
```

When we test the `ProductsController`, we don't need to supply the actual implementation of the `IProductRepository` interface. For the purposes of a unit test, we are testing only the `ProductsController` and no external dependency used. To maximize the localization of defects, our unit tests should test only a single class. We don't want a controller unit test to fail because we have a problem with our local database. In a unit test, we'll have to pass a test double into the `ProductsController` repository. A test double is a stand-in for an actual implementation, but one that we can manipulate to force our class under test to execute specific code paths. Our controller unit test will need to set up the stubbed `IProductRepository` with dummy data, and then assert that the right action result is used, the right view is chosen, and the right data is passed to the view, as shown in listing 12.37.

Listing 12.37   Testing our `Index` action

```
[Test]
public void Index_should_use_default_view_and_repository_data()
{
    var products = new[]                                    ❶
    {
        new Product {Name = "Keyboard"},
        new Product {Name = "Mouse"}
    };

    var repository = Stub<IProductRepository>();            ❷
    repository.Stub(rep => rep.FindAll()).Return(products); ❸

    var productsController = new ProductsController(repository); ❹

    ViewResult result = productsController.Index();         ❺

    result.ViewName.ShouldEqual(string.Empty);             ❻
    result.ViewData.Model.ShouldEqual(products);           ❼
}
```

We set up product data for our test ❶. The values inside don't matter for the purposes of our unit test, but aid in debugging if our test fails for an unknown reason. We create a stub of our `IProductRepository` by calling a method on our base test class ❷. This method is a wrapper around Rhino Mocks, a popular test double creation and configuration framework. After we create a test double of our `IProductRepository`, we stub out the call to `FindAll` to return our array of `Products` we created earlier ❸. With the stubbed `IProductRepository`, we create a `ProductsController` ❹.

With all of the classes and test doubles set up for our unit test, we can execute our controller action and capture the resulting `ViewResult` object ❺. We assert that the `ViewName` should be an empty string ❻ (signifying we use the Index view), and that the model passed to the view is our original array of products ❼. Our test passes with the implementation of our action shown in listing 12.35.

A two-line action method is tested easily, but is not very interesting. In a more interesting scenario, we edit a model, then post it to a form. We expect several things to happen:

- Check the model state for errors
- If errors exist, show the original view
- If not, save the model and redirect back to the index

Let's start with the error path, where a user entered incorrect information. We'll assume that model state errors are populated through other means as a result of validation, perhaps through a model binder or action filter. For the purposes of our test, shown in listing 12.38, the means of validation is not important, but rather, how the controller behaves under this condition.

Listing 12.38 Testing the edit action when errors are present

```
[Test]
public void Edit_should_redirect_back_when_model_errors_present()
{
    var badProduct = new Product { Name = "Bad value" };

    var repository = Stub<IProductRepository>();

    var productsController = new ProductsController(repository);
    productsController                                                    ❶
        .ModelState.AddModelError("Name", "Name already exists");

    var result = productsController.Edit(badProduct);                     ❷

    result.AssertViewRendered().ViewName.ShouldEqual(string.Empty);       ❸
    repository.AssertWasNotCalled(rep => rep.Save(badProduct));           ❹
}
```

To force our controller into an invalid model state, we need to add a model error to `ModelState` with the `AddModelError` method ❶. After setting up our controller, we invoke the `Edit` action ❷, and examine the result returned. We assert that a view is rendered with the `AssertViewRendered` method ❸, which returns a `ViewResult` object. The `ViewName` on the `ViewResult` should be an empty string, signifying the `Edit` view is rerendered. Finally, we assert that the `Save` method on our repository was not called ❹. This negative assertion ensures we don't try to save our `Product` if it has validation problems. Normally, we would create a separate presentation model specifically for the form, but in this example, we use our domain model directly. We tested the error condition, and now we need to test our controller in the positive condition that our model didn't have any validation problems, as shown in listing 12.39.

Listing 12.39 Testing our controller action when no errors are present

```
[Test]
public void Edit_should_save_and_redirect_when_no_model_errors_present()
{
    var goodProduct = new Product { Name = "Good value" };

    var repository = Stub<IProductRepository>();

    var productsController = new ProductsController(repository);

    var result = productsController.Edit(goodProduct);           ❶

    result
        .AssertActionRedirect()                                  ❷
        .ToAction<ProductsController>(c => c.Index());           ❸

    repository.AssertWasCalled(rep => rep.Save(goodProduct));
}
```

In this test, we set up our dummy product and controller in a manner similar to the last test, except this time we don't add any model errors to our `ModelState`. We invoke the `Edit` action with the product we created ❶, and then verify values on the result. We use the MvcContrib project's `AssertActionRedirect` ❷ to assert that the result of our action redirects to another action, specifically to the `Index` action. The `ToAction` method allows us to assert that we redirect to a specific action using a strongly typed expression ❸. Because we use expressions here, our test won't break if we rename the `Index` action method name. To make both of these tests pass, our action looks like listing 12.40.

Listing 12.40   Implementation of the `Edit` action

```
[AcceptPost]
public ActionResult Edit(Product product)
{
    if (!ModelState.IsValid)          ❶
    {
        return View(product);         ❷
    }
    _productRepository.Save(product);

    return this.RedirectToAction(c => c.Index());        ❸
}
```

In our `Edit` action, we check for any `ModelState` errors with the `IsValid` property ❶, and return a `ViewResult` with our original `Product` ❷. Our `Edit` view likely will use styling to highlight individual model errors and display a validation error summary. If there are no validation errors, we save the `Product` and redirect back to the `Index` action ❸. With our controller's behavior locked down sufficiently, we can feel confident we can modify our `Edit` action in the future and know if our change breaks existing functionality. In the next section, we'll examine strategies for testing custom model binders.

12.4.2   *Model binder unit tests*

Custom model binders eliminate much of the boring plumbing that often clutters action methods with code not pertinent to the true purpose of the action method. But with this powerful tool comes the need for thorough testing. Our infrastructure needs to be rock solid, as it can execute on a large majority of requests. Testing model binders is not as straightforward as testing action methods, but it is possible. The amount of testing needed varies depending on what you are doing with your custom model binder. Simply implementing the `IModelBinder` interface likely means you'll only need to worry about one single `BindModel` method and only a `ModelBindingContext` during testing. Inheriting from `DefaultModelBinder` is a bit more challenging, as any code we add will execute alongside other code that we don't own. We must ensure that any behavior we add works correctly in the context of the other responsibilities of the base `DefaultModelBinder` class. The `DefaultModelBinder` class design has extensibility in mind, and key extension points are available through specific method overrides, but we still need to test these methods in the context of an entire binding operation (such as a single BindModel call).

In section 12.1.3, we examined creating a custom model that bound entities from a repository, as shown in listing 12.41.

Listing 12.41   Entity model binder implementation

```
public object BindModel (
    ControllerContext controllerContext,
    ModelBindingContext bindingContext)
{
    ValueProviderResult value =
        bindingContext.ValueProvider [bindingContext.ModelName];

    if (value == null)
        return null;

    if (string.IsNullOrEmpty(value.AttemptedValue))
        return null;

    var entityId = new Guid(value.AttemptedValue);

    Type repositoryType = typeof(IRepository<>)
        .MakeGenericType(bindingContext.ModelType);
    var repository = (IRepository)IoC.Resolve(repositoryType);

    PersistentObject entity = repository.GetById(entityId);

    return entity;
}
```

We didn't add any tests in our original example, so let's add some now. We have several guard clauses protecting against bad input. However, we didn't include the check for a user or part of our application puting an invalid GUID into the querystring (or form variable). Rather than allow an exception to be thrown during binding, we would like to handle this by returning null, as shown in the test in listing 12.42.

Listing 12.42   Test for bad GUID values

```
[Test]
public void Should_resolve_bind_to_null_when_guid_not_in_correct_format()
{
    var valueProviderDictionary = new ValueProviderDictionary(null)
    {
        {
            "ProductId",
            new ValueProviderResult ("NotAGuid", "NotAGuid", null)      ❶
        }
    };

    var bindingContext = new ModelBindingContext      ❷
    {
        ModelName = "ProductId",
        ValueProvider = valueProviderDictionary
```

```
    };

    var binder = new EntityModelBinder ();
    object model = binder.BindModel (null, bindingContext);

    model.ShouldBeNull();
}
```

Our model binder uses only a `ModelBindingContext`, not the `ControllerContext`. We need only focus on creating a `ModelBindingContext` representative of an invalid GUID value. First, we create a `ValueProviderDictionary`, with a single entry for a `ProductId` parameter ❶. For the raw and attempted values in the `ValueProviderResult`, we'll substitute bad GUID values, to force our model binder to throw an exception. With our `ValueProviderDictionary` assembled, we can create our `ModelBindingContext` ❷, using the same `ModelName` as was used in our `ValueProviderDictionary`. Because we use the `ModelName` directly to look up `ValueProviderResults` in our model binder, any mismatch will cause our custom model binder to not execute the code we are interested in. When we execute this unit test, it fails with a `System.FormatException`, because our model binder is not yet able to handle invalid GUIDs. To make our test pass, we can either parse the input string using regular expressions, or use a `try...catch` block. For simplicity, we'll use the exception handling method, with the additions shown in listing 12.43.

Listing 12.43   Modifying the GUID parsing code to handle invalid values

```
Guid entityId;

try
{
    entityId = new Guid(value.AttemptedValue);
}
catch (FormatException)          ❶
{
    return null;
}
```

With these changes, our test now passes. We surrounded our original GUID constructor with a `try..catch` block for the specific `FormatException` type thrown when the parsed value is not of the right format ❶. There are other interesting scenarios we could add tests for, but all of them employ the same technique of creating a `Model-BindingContext` representative of a certain model-binding scenario. Unit tests for model binders go quite a long way to proving the design of a model binder, but still don't guarantee a working application.

Model binders are one cog in a larger machine, and only through testing that larger part can we have complete confidence in our model binders. It can often take quite a bit of trial and error to get the model binder to function correctly. When it is working correctly, we need only to construct the context objects used by our model binder in our unit test to recreate those scenarios. Unfortunately, merely looking at a model binder may not show you how to construct the context objects it uses. A common test failure is a `NullReferenceException`, where a call to an MVC framework method requires other supporting objects in place. The easiest way to determine what pieces your model binder needs in place is to simply write a test and see if it passes. If it does not pass because of an exception, keep fixing the exceptions, often by supplying test doubles, until your test passes or fails due to an assertion failure. In the next section, we'll examine testing action filters.

12.4.3 *Action filter unit tests*

The story for testing action filters is very similar to that for testing model binders. Unit testing is possible, and its difficulty is directly proportional to how much the filter relies on the context objects. Generally, the deeper the filter digs in to the context object, the more we'll need to be set up or mocked in a unit test. Table 12.1 illustrates the types of filters and the context objects used for each.

Table 12.1 Filters and their supporting context objects

Filter type	Method	Context object
IActionFilter	OnActionExecuted	ActionExecutedContext
	OnActionExecuting	ActionExecutingContext
IAuthorizationFilter	OnAuthorization	AuthorizationContext
IExceptionFilter	OnException	ExceptionContext
IResultFilter	OnResultExecuted	ResultExecutedContext
	OnResultExecuting	ResultExecutingContext

Each context object has its own difficulties for testing, as each has its own dependencies for usage. All context objects have a no-argument constructor, and a unit test may be able to use the context object as is without needing to supply it with additional objects. Although your filter may use only one piece of the context object, you may find yourself needing to supply mock instances of more pieces, as many of the base context object constructors have null argument checking. You may find yourself far down a long path that leads to supplying the correct dependencies for a context object, and these dependencies may be several levels deep. Let's add tests to the filter shown in listing 12.44.

Listing 12.44 Simple action filter

```
public class CurrentUserFilter : IActionFilter
{
    private readonly IUserSession _session;

    public CurrentUserFilter (IUserSession session)
    {
        _session = session;
    }
```

```
    public void OnActionExecuting(ActionExecutingContext filterContext)
    {
        ControllerBase controller = filterContext.Controller;
        User user = _session.GetCurrentUser();
        if (user != null)
        {
            controller.ViewData.Add(user);
        }
    }

    public void OnActionExecuted(ActionExecutedContext filterContext)
    {
    }
}
```

In this filter, we have the requirement that a User object is needed for a component in the view, likely for displaying the current user in a widget. Our CurrentUserFilter depends on an IUserSession, whose implementation contains the logic for storing and retrieving the current logged in user from the session. Our filter retrieves the current user and places it into the controller's ViewData. The controller is supplied through the ActionExecutingContext object. If possible, during unit testing, we prefer to use the no-argument constructor and supply any additional pieces by merely setting the properties on the context object. The ActionExecutingContext type has setters for the Controller property, so we'll be able to use the no-argument constructor and not worry about the larger, parameter-full constructor. Our complete unit test, shown in listing 12.45, is able to create a stub implementation for only the parts used in our filter.

Listing 12.45 Action filter unit test

```
[TestFixture]
public class CurrentUserFilterTester : TestClassBase
{
    [Test]
    public void Should_pass_current_user_when_user_is_logged_in ()
    {
        var loggedInUser = new User();

        var userSession = Stub<IUserSession>();                          ❶
        userSession.Stub(session => session.GetCurrentUser())            ❷
            .Return(loggedInUser);

        var filterContext = new ActionExecutingContext        ❸
        {
            Controller = Stub<ControllerBase>()       ❹
        };

        var currentUserFilter = new CurrentUserFilter (userSession);     ❺
        currentUserFilter.OnActionExecuting(filterContext);

        filterContext.Controller.ViewData                    ❻
            .Get<User>().ShouldEqual(loggedInUser);
    }
}
```

Our `CurrentUserFilter` depends on an implementation of an `IUserSession` interface ❶, which we supply using the `Stub` method. The `Stub` method comes from the `TestClassBase` class, and is a wrapper around Rhino Mocks' `CreateStub` method. Next, we stub the `GetCurrentUser` method on our stub `IUserSession` to return the `User` object created earlier ❷. Because the actual implementation of `IUserSession` requires the full `HttpContext` to be up and running, by supplying a fake implementation, we get much finer control over the inputs to our filter object.

Next, we create our `ActionExecutingContext` ❸, but call only the no-argument constructor. The controller can be any controller instance, and we again use Rhino Mocks to create a stub implementation of `ControllerBase` ❹. Rhino Mocks creates a subclass of `ControllerBase` at runtime, which saves us from using an existing or dummy controller class. In any case, the `ControllerBase` provides `ViewData`, so we don't need to provide any stub implementation for that property. With our assembled `ActionExecutingContext` and stubbed implementation of `IUserSession`, we can create and exercise our `CurrentUserFilter` ❺. The `OnExecutingMethod` does not return a value, so we need to examine only the `ActionExecutingContext` passed in. We assert that the controller's `ViewData` contains the same logged-in user created earlier ❻, and our test passes!

Getting to this point required trial and error to understand what the context object requires for execution. Because filters are integrated and specific to the MVC framework, it can be fruitless to try to write filters test-first, as only the fact that the complete website is up and running proves the filter is working properly. We supplied dummy implementations of the context objects, but constructed them in a way that the MVC framework will likely not use. In the next section, we'll examine how to automate tests with the entire website up and running through automated UI tests.

12.4.4 Testing the last mile with UI tests

In this chapter thus far, we examined testing individual components of ASP.NET MVC, including routes, controllers, filters, and model binders. Although unit testing each component in isolation is important, the final test of a working application is interaction with a browser against a live instance. With all of the components that make up a single request, whose interaction and dependencies can become complex, it is only through browser testing that we can ensure our application works as desired from end to end. While developing an application, we often launch a browser to manually check that our changes are correct and produce the intended behavior.

In many organizations, manual testing is formalized into a regression testing script to be executed by development or QA personnel before a launch. Manual testing is slow and quite limited, as it can take minutes to execute a single test. In a large application, regression testing is minimal at best and woefully inadequate in most situations. Fortunately, many free automated UI testing tools exist. Some of the more popular tools are listed here:

- WatiN (http://watin.sourceforge.net/)
- Watir (http://wtr.rubyforge.org/)
- Selenium (http://seleniumhq.org/)
- QUnit (http://docs.jquery.com/QUnit)—for testing JavaScript

In addition to these open source projects, many commercial products on the market provide additional functionality or integration with bug reporting systems or work item tracking systems, such as Microsoft's Team Foundation Server. However, the tools are not tied to any testing framework, so integration with an existing project is rather trivial.

In this section, we'll examine UI testing with WatiN, which provides easy integration with unit testing frameworks. WatiN, an acronym of *web application testing in .NET*, is a .NET library that provides an interactive browser API to both interact with the browser, by clicking links and buttons for example, as well as find elements in the DOM.

Testing with WatiN usually involves interacting with the application to submit a form, then checking the results in a view screen. Because WatiN is not tied to any specific unit testing framework, we can use any unit testing framework we like. The testing automation platform Gallio (http://www.gallio.org/) provides important additions that make automating UI tests easier:

- Test steps for logging individual interactions in a single test
- Running tests in parallel
- Ability to embed screenshots in the test report (for failures)

To get started, we need to download and install Gallio. Gallio includes an external test runner (Icarus), as well as integration with many unit testing runners, including Test-Driven.NET, ReSharper, and others. Also included in Gallio is MbUnit, a unit testing framework which we'll use to author our tests. With Gallio downloaded and installed, we need to create a Class Library project and add references to both Gallio.dll and MbUnit.dll. Next, we need to download WatiN and add a reference in our test project to the WatiN.Core.dll assembly. With our project references done, we are ready to create a simple test. One of the most basic, but useful scenarios in our application is to test to see if we can log in to our application. Testing manually, this would mean

1 Navigating to the login URL
2 Entering username and password
3 Clicking the Log in button
4 Checking that the login widget at the top of the screen has the correct name

Because we'll want common functionality and configuration in all of our test classes that use WatiN, we'll create a base test class, as shown in listing 12.46.

Listing 12.46 Web test base class

```
[TestFixture]
[ApartmentState (ApartmentState.STA)]
```

```
public class WebTestBase
{
}
```

The first attribute on our `WebTestBase` class should be familiar; it is the MbUnit attribute for tagging a class as a `TestFixture`. The next attribute is not as well known. Because WatiN uses COM to communicate with Internet Explorer (IE), and the COM IE wrapper is not thread-safe, we must configure our unit test runner to use a single-threaded apartment (STA). Each unit test runner is configured differently and in MbUnit's case, we use the `ApartmentStateAttribute` with and `ApartmentState` value of `ApartmentState.STA`. With this attribute applied to our `WebTestBase` class, we need to configure this setting only once in our test project, as long as all of our tests use `WebTestBase` as a base class.

Next, we can create a new test that performs the steps listed earlier in this section, as shown in listing 12.47.

Listing 12.47   Testing the login screen

```
public class LoginScreen : WebTestBase
{
    [Test]
    public void Can_log_in_successfully()
    {
        using (var ie = new IE ("http://localhost:8082/Login"))      ❶
        {
            ie.TextField (Find.ByName ("Username")).TypeText("admin");       ❷
            ie.TextField (Find.ByName ("Password")).TypeText("password");

            ie.Button(Find.ByName ("login")).Click();

            Assert.IsTrue(ie.ContainsText ("Joe User"));
        }
    }
}
```

Our `LoginScreen` class inherits from the `WebTestBase` class created earlier. In the `LoginScreen` test class, we define one test, "Can_log_in_successfully." Inside this test, we first create a new instance of the WatiN `IE` object ❶. The `IE` class has a constructor that takes a URL as a parameter, which causes the IE browser to immediately launch at the specified URL. We hardcoded the correct starting URL so that the IE browser immediately navigates to the login screen. If the starting URL needs to be configured, we could pull this information from a configuration file. The lifetime of the `IE` object is wrapped in a using statement block, to ensure that our COM resources are disposed of properly.

The `IE` object is our primary source of interaction with the browser. It includes a variety of methods to locate elements in the DOM, as well as methods to interact with the browser's periphery, such as cookies, dialog boxes, and so on. Our interaction will deal mainly with locating and manipulating DOM elements, but other browser interaction is available if needed. Back in our test, the next two lines use the `TextField` method ❷ to locate the HTML INPUT elements of type TEXT. The `TextField` method takes a variety of arguments, each enabling a different way to search for elements. With ASP.NET MVC, we can use the `Constraint` overload, and use the `Find` static class to build a `Constraint` object to match the element we need. Other options include a string for an element ID, a regular expression, or a custom callback function. For our purposes, we'll stick mainly with the `Find.ByName` constraint. With ASP.NET Web Forms, it was more common to use regular expressions, as element ID and names were not entirely deterministic. The MVC framework gives us complete control over element IDs and names.

The `TextField` method returns a single `TextField` object. We use the `TypeText` method to fill in text into both the username and password fields. In this test, we didn't set up any login information beforehand, and we know that this login information will work for a clean build of CodeCampServer. Typically, we'll set up all entities needed for a test in a setup method. After filling in the username and password, we use the `Button` method in combination with the `Find.ByName` constraint to locate the login button and click it with the `Click` method. If our login is correct, we'll be redirected in the browser to the home page, and our user's name will appear at the top. To verify this, we use the `ContainsText` with our user's name and assert that our user's name is found.

With our basic test in place, we can execute this test in the Gallio Icarus test runner, shown in figure 12.3.

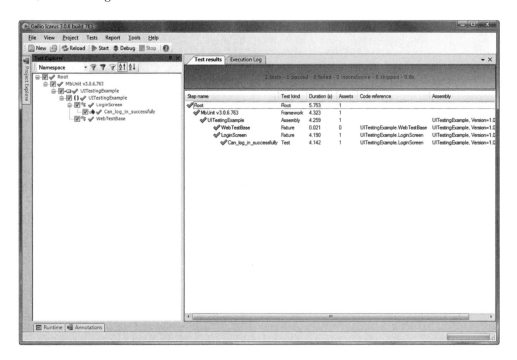

Figure 12.3   Simple passing login screen test

In our test, we referenced all of the input elements by name, but how did we know what name to look for? In older browsers, this meant viewing the HTML source. In modern browsers, including IE8 and Chrome, a built-in HTML inspector picks HTML elements by clicking them to bring the specific HTML element into a readable interface. Google's Chrome HTML inspector, shown in figure 12.4, allows us to click an element on the browser to determine relevant information, such as element names.

Figure 12.4   Google Chrome HTML inspector with our login button highlighted

Other browsers have extensions for this purpose, including Firebug (http://getfirebug.com/) for Firefox, and the IE Web Developer Toolbar (http://www.microsoft.com/downloads/details.aspx?familyid=E59C3964-672D-4511-BB3E-2D5E1DB91038) for versions previous to IE8. With these tools, we need only to click elements on a live browser and inspect their element names or IDs for our UI tests. In figure 12.4, we have the login button from our login screen selected, leaving guesswork or hunting through our project behind.

But what if our test fails? One of the features of MbUnit is the ability to embed images into test reports, and one of the features of WatiN is to capture images. First, we'll create a failing test in as shown in listing 12.48.

Listing 12.48   Intentional test failure

```
[Test]
public void Intentional_failure()
```

```
{
    using (var ie = new IE ("http://localhost:8082/Login"))
    {
        ie.TextField (Find.ByName ("Username")).TypeText("admin");
        ie.TextField (Find.ByName ("Password")).TypeText("password");

        ie.Button(Find.ByName ("login")).Click();

        Assert.IsTrue(ie.ContainsText ("Joe Schmoe"));
    }
}
```

For this intentionally failing test, we change the text of the name asserted to an incorrect name, "Joe Schmoe." Running this test proves our failure, but we would like to capture the screenshot as part of the failure. Because we created the `WebTestBase` class earlier, we can centralize all failure behavior in one place. We can create a teardown method, run after every test, and check to see if there were any failures in our test. If so, we take a screenshot using WatiN and embed the image into Gallio's test results. To accomplish all of this, we'll need to make more modifications to our `WebTestBase` class, as taking a screenshot requires the original instance of the `IE` object. Because our original test had the `IE` object in a `using` block, it won't be available to our teardown method without modifications to our test. Instead of instantiating our IE object in each test, we'll do so in our `WebTestBase` in a `SetUp` method, as shown in listing 12.49.

Listing 12.49   Modified `WebTestBase` setting up the `IE` object

```
protected IE Browser { get; private set; }

[SetUp]
public void SetUp()
{
    Browser = new IE ("http://localhost:8082/Login");
}
```

Before each test executes, we create an `IE` instance and assign it to our protected `Browser` property. Our original failing test now needs to use the `Browser` property instead of creating the `IE` object itself, as shown in listing 12.50.

Listing 12.50   Modifying the failing test to use the `Browser` property

```
[Test]
public void Intentional_failure()
{
    Browser.TextField (Find.ByName ("Username")).TypeText("admin");
    Browser.TextField (Find.ByName ("Password")).TypeText("password");

    Browser.Button(Find.ByName ("login")).Click();

    Assert.IsTrue(Browser.ContainsText ("Joe Schmoe"));
}
```

With our `IE` object now managed by our base test class, we can introduce a `TearDown` method to check for test failures and capture screenshots. Even if we didn't include the screenshot concept, we still need to add code in a teardown method to dispose of our IE instance properly. Our `TearDown` method is shown in listing 12.51.

Listing 12.51 `Teardown` **method with image capturing and logging**

```
[TearDown]
public void TearDown()
{
    try
    {
        if (TestContext.CurrentContext
                .Outcome.Status == TestStatus.Failed)          ❶
        {
            var writer = TestLog.Writer.Default;               ❷
            using (writer.BeginSection("Test failed on this page"))  ❸
            {
                writer.Write("Url: ");
                using (writer.BeginMarker(Marker.Link(Browser.Url)))  ❹
                {
                    writer.WriteLine(Browser.Url);
                }
                var imageCapturer = new CaptureWebPage (Browser);  ❺
                var image = imageCapturer
                    .CaptureWebPageImage(false, false, 100);       ❻
                writer.EmbedImage("Failure.png", image);
            }
        }
    }
    finally
    {
        Browser.Close();          ❼
        Browser = null;
    }
}
```

In a `try-finally` block, we separate the image capturing and logging from managing the IE instance. The IE browser should always be discarded at teardown, regardless of whether an exception happens during image capturing ❼. The `try-finally` block ensures our IE instance is disposed of properly. Inside the `try` block, we first check Gallio's test status in the `TestContext` object ❶. We only want to capture screenshots in the event of a failing test. Next, we create a reference to the default log writer for Gallio ❷. Gallio supports multiple nested log streams for complex test reports, but in our case, the default will suffice.

To create sections in our log output, we use the `BeginSection` method ❸. We might have more sections logged detailing the steps executed in our test, so a separate section for the error helps distinguish it in the final report. We also write the original URL of the screen with the error for informational purposes. Using the `Marker.Link` method ❹ generates a clickable link in the final report, helpful to quickly traverse to the failing screen. We are ready to capture the image.

We create a `CaptureWebPage` object ❺, passing in the IE instance stored in our test class. Next, we create an `Image` object and capture a screenshot using the

`CaptureWebPageImage` method. We use the `EmbedImage` method ❻ on our log writer object, providing the image object and a file name. Running this test in our Icarus test runner gives us a nice screenshot of our failure, as shown in figure 12.5.

Gallio is a powerful tool for creating UI tests when combined with WatiN. We can create a wrapper over the WatiN browser calls, which can be difficult to read, as well as more fluent calls that take advantage of strongly typed views, expressions, and Gallio's test steps. With test steps and a simple wrapper, we can log all interaction with IE as a sort of test script, so that we can easily read exactly what our test performed, and exactly where it failed in the context of a user's actions, instead of a stack trace. We might rather know that a test failed when the user clicked Submit Order, rather than receive a line number in a file. With Gallio and WatiN, this is possible. Tests that might take weeks to execute manually can finish in an hour.

UI tests are much, much slower than unit and integration tests, but they are vital in ensuring our application works end to end. Because of the speed of these tests, their use should be reserved for scenario-based tests, happy-path or black-box testing, and regression tests. Unless care is taken to ensure strongly typed tests and to avoid the magic strings we examined earlier, UI tests become quite brittle. It's worth noting that most applications are not easily testable without modifications. Just as we have to design our code for testability, we need to design our UI for testability. This might include putting IDs or special class names around certain data-driven elements, or sharing the view types with our UI tests to ensure that the exact same HTML element names are used for both HTML generation and UI testing. These changes don't affect

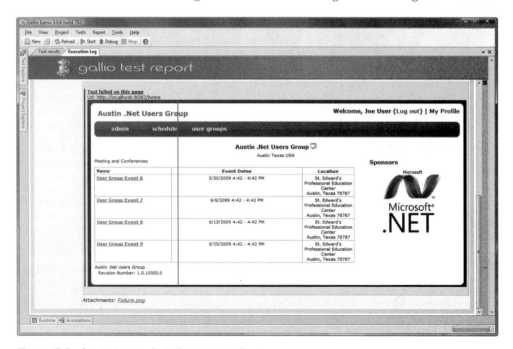

Figure 12.5   Our test report including a screenshot

the end-user experience, and allow us as developers to focus on adding value, rather than fixing brittle tests.

12.5 Summary

In this chapter, we explored many of the extension points and major feature areas of ASP.NET MVC and discovered how best to take advantage of these areas in a maintainable manner. Although not every practice applies in every context, it is important to consider all the options available, and the benefits and tradeoffs of each before proceeding with a design. If you go down a path with filters and magic strings in View-Data, you might not like the end result. Instead, we can consider the long-term viability of each option and choose the most appropriate path for each situation. Some practices are strongly recommended for a maintainable and easily testable codebase, such as strongly typed views. Others, such as convention-based, REST-style action names are appropriate only in resource-centric applications.

Duplication is one of the biggest causes of development attrition, whether using ASP.NET MVC or another framework. The techniques used to remove duplication have changed from classic Web Forms, from custom model binders, to action filters and partials in our views. Although each of these extension points is powerful, none is appropriate in every context. We examined many of the options for eliminating duplication in our controllers and views, as well as elaborating on the right contexts for each of these options.

We focused on testing these extension points. Because these extension points can be executed on every request, it is vital to ensure that these extension points behave as desired. However, the true test of a working MVC application is using it in a browser. We finished our testing discussion by examining UI testing with WatiN and Gallio, taking advantage of features in both products to capture screenshots from failures and logging meaningful test messages. In the next chapter, we'll examine a variety of real-world scenarios in the form of in-depth recipes.

Recipes
13

By now you have seen all of the components of the ASP.NET MVC Framework. Surely you have asked yourself, *How do I do ____ in ASP.NET MVC?* Certainly with a new paradigm it's natural to feel a bit lost when trying to implement functionality in your first application. This chapter is geared toward giving you concrete examples, or recipes, for achieving common functions such as automatic validation or data access. Take these examples verbatim and use them in your applications, or simply learn from them and apply the techniques in your own way. We start with client-side functionality, move through extending validation, and through a comprehensive data access recipe. We finish by replacing the built-in view engine that comes with ASP.NET MVC, and try out the Spark view engine.

13.1 jQuery autocomplete text box

It's not uncommon for text boxes to automatically suggest items based on what we type. The results are further filtered as we type to give us the option to select an

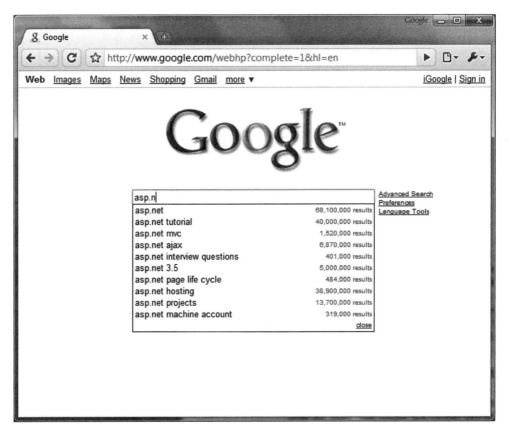

Figure 13.1 Google Suggest filters options as you type.

available item with the mouse or keyboard. One of the first examples of this in the wild was Google Suggest as shown in figure 13.1.

A rudimentary implementation of this automatic suggestion feature would be to monitor key presses and fire off AJAX requests for each one. Of course this means that a fast typist would trigger many requests, most of which would be immediately discarded for the next request coming in 5 milliseconds. An effective implementation will take into account a typing delay and also provide keyboard/mouse support for selecting the items.

Luckily jQuery has an extensive list of plugins available. One such plugin is Dylan Verheul's autocomplete.

NOTE *Dylan Verheul's autocomplete* You can download the autocomplete plugin at http://www.dyve.net/jquery/ with a few others, including googlemaps and listify.

The basic idea is that you have a simple text box on your page. The jQuery plugin adds the behavior necessary to handle key press events and fire the appropriate AJAX requests to a URL that will handle the request. The URL points to a controller action, and by convention the response is formatted so that the plugin could handle the response.

Assume for our purposes that we want to filter U.S. cities in the text box. The first step is to add a controller, action, and view for displaying the UI for this example. Ensure that jQuery (in this case jquery-1.2.6.js) and jquery.autocomplete.js are referenced at the top of the view (or master page).

```
<script type="text/javascript" src="../../scripts/jquery-1.2.6.js"></script>
<script type="text/javascript" src="../../scripts/jquery.autocomplete.js">
    </script>
```

Next, add the text box. In this example we'll call it `city`.

```
<%= Html.TextBox("city") %>
```

Package this up with a simple controller (listing 13.1), and the result will be similar to that show in figure 13.2.

Listing 13.1   Controller and action for displaying our test page

```
public class HomeController : Controller
{
    public ActionResult Index()
    {
        return View();
    }
}
```

Now we add a little JavaScript to add the autocomplete behavior.

```
<script type="text/javascript">
    $(document).ready(function() {
        $("input#city").autocomplete('<%= Url.Action("Find", "City") %>');
    });
</script>
```

Place the script in the <head> of the page. You can see that the URL for the autocomplete behavior is specified as `Url.Action("Find", "City")`. This will point to a `Find()` action on the `CityController`. We'll need to write this controller and action, as shown in listing 13.2.

Figure 13.2   Our simple view with a text box

NOTE   *Local Data Mode*   The autocomplete plugin can also filter local data structures. This is useful when you have a limited set of data, and you want to minimize requests sent to the server. The autocomplete plugin in local mode is also much faster, because there is no AJAX request being made behind the scenes. The only downside is that you must render the entire array onto the view.

Listing 13.2 Action to find cities from an autocomplete AJAX request

```
public class CityController : Controller
{
    private readonly ICityRepository _repository;

    public CityController()
    {
        string csvPath =
            System.Web.HttpContext.Current          Load CSV file
            .Server.MapPath("~/App_Data/cities.csv");  containing citites

        _repository = new CityRepository(csvPath);   Load CSV into
    }                                                 repository

    public CityController(ICityRepository repository)  Testable
    {                                                  constructor
        _repository = repository;
    }                                    Autocomplete sends
                                         parameter 'q'
    public ActionResult Find(string q)
    {                                              Return
        string[] cities = _repository.FindCities(q);  raw text
        return Content(string.Join("\n", cities));
    }
}
```

The details of the CityRepository can be found in the code samples provided with the book. For now, we'll focus on the new Find(string q) action. Because this is a standard action, you can navigate to it in your browser and test it out. Figure 13.3 shows a quick test.

Now that we are sure that the action is returning the correct results, we can test the text box. The JavaScript we added earlier hooks up to the key press events on the text box and should issue queries to the server. Figure 13.4 shows this in action.

The drop-down selections are unformatted by default, which makes them a little ugly. CSS magic will make it look nicer. Listing 13.3 shows sample CSS for this transformation.

**Figure 13.3
A simple HTTP GET for the action with a filter of "hou" yields the expected results.**

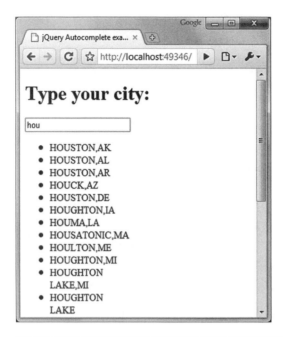

Figure 13.4   The results are displayed in a \<ul\> tag. We can apply CSS to make it look nicer.

Listing 13.3   CSS used to style the autocomplete results

```
<style type="text/css">
    div.ac_results ul
    {
        margin:0;
        padding:0;
        list-style-type:none;
        border: solid 1px #ccc;
    }

    div.ac_results ul li
    {
        font-family: Arial, Verdana, Sans-Serif;
        font-size: 12px;
        margin: 1px;
        padding: 3px;
        cursor: pointer;
    }

    div.ac_results ul li.ac_over
    {
        background-color: #acf;
    }
</style>
```

The options of the autocomplete plugin enable you to configure it to your needs. For the case that we've shown here, it's as simple as this:

```
$(your_textbox).autocomplete('your/url/here');
```

Figure 13.5 shows the autocomplete in action, and table 13.1 shows the various options for the plugin.

Figure 13.5 The styled drop-down results look much nicer. The selected item is highlighted and can be chosen with the keyboard or mouse.

Table 13.1 Common options for the plugin

`inputClass`	This class will be added to the input box.
`resultsClass`	The class to apply to the results' container. Default value is "ac_results".
`loadingClass`	The class to apply to the input box while results are being fetched from the server. Default is "ac_loading."
`lineSeparator`	The character used to separate the results. The default is \n.
`minChars`	The minimum number of characters before sending a request to the server. Default is 1.
`delay`	The delay after typing when the request will be sent. Default is 400 ms.

To set these options, include them in a dictionary as the second argument to the autocomplete method like this:

```
$("input#city").autocomplete('<%= Url.Action("Find", "City") %>', {
    minChars : 3,
    delay : 300
});
```

This type of functionality is immensely useful for selecting from large lists. It keeps your initial page size down by not loading all of these items at once and is user-friendly.

13.2 *Automatic client-side validation*

The ASP.NET MVC Framework includes support for model validation; however the support doesn't include client-side validation. The `ModelBinders` that you learned about in chapter 3 can be combined with validation attributes, such as those provided in the `System.ComponentModel.DataAnnotations` namespace. The Castle Project also has a good set of validation attributes that you can use on your classes. These provide simple ways of declaring properties as required, or requiring certain input.

We'd like to extend this to automatically render the appropriate JavaScript validation so that you can define your rules once, and have them used in client-side and server-side model validation.

Our preference is to use the Castle Validation attributes. These can be downloaded at http://castleproject.org. The attributes are easy to use. You simply add the appropriate attribute to the property that needs the rule, as shown here:

```
public class Person
{
    [ValidateNonEmpty]
    public string Name {get;set;}
}
```

To validate the instance of the class, you run it through the `ValidationRunner` class. All of these classes come from the `Castle.Components.Validator` namespace.

Do I place these attributes on my domain model?

Ask two developers this question and you'll probably get two different answers. There are good arguments from both sides. From one perspective, declarative validation is elegant, requires little code, and works well for simple, data-oriented models. The other perspective sees value in not allowing domain entities to enter an invalid state. The perspective favors methods that convey behaviors for state changes rather than properties with getters and setters.

The decision of whether or not to add validation attributes to your domain model is contextual. If you're using a view model—that is, specific classes dedicated for representing the data displayed or entered on your UI—they're great.

View model objects are inherently data oriented, and they provide a realistic representation of the data gathered from the UI. Because you always validate user input before letting it creep into your system, this is a perfect place for declarative validation attributes.

If you're using your domain entities on your view directly, then you might favor the validation attributes within your domain model. If complexity requires you to create view models to interact with the UI and map to your domain entities, then you'll probably want to avoid placing these attributes in your domain model and rely instead on validating the view models.

Let's use an example from Code Camp Server. When users register for a conference, they need to fill in their name and contact information. These values will eventually map to domain entities, but initially they are populated in a view model object called NewAttendeeForm. This class contains all of the properties that are needed to gather user input from the view.

```
public class NewAttendeeForm
{
    public string FirstName { get; set; }
    public string LastName { get; set; }
    public string Email { get; set; }
    public string Url { get; set; }
    public string Notes { get; set; }
}
```

After adding the validation attributes, our class now looks like this:

```
public class NewAttendeeForm
{
    [ValidateNonEmpty]
    public string FirstName { get; set; }

    [ValidateNonEmpty]
    public string LastName { get; set; }

    [ValidateNonEmpty, ValidateEmail]
    public string Email { get; set; }

    [ValidateRegExp("http://(\w+?\.)+\w{3}")]
    public string Url { get; set; }

    public string Notes { get; set; }
}
```

The properties FirstName, LastName, and Email are all required. There is a built-in validator for email address validation for our Email property. We want to verify that the Url property is correctly formatted. Please excuse the naïve regular expression for the URL. The proper URL regular expression is enormous and not necessary for this example. Now that we have the validation attributes specified, we can implement instance validation inside of a custom model binder. Listing 13.4 shows a custom model binder for constructing and validating a class decorated with Castle Validators.

Listing 13.4 Custom Castle Validation ModelBinder

```
public class CastleValidationBinder : DefaultModelBinder
{
    public override object BindModel(ControllerContext controllerContext,
        ModelBindingContext bindingContext)
    {
        object model =                                              Copy values
            base.BindModel(controllerContext, bindingContext);      onto object

        if (model == null) return model;

        var validator =                                             ❶
            new ValidatorRunner(new CachedValidationRegistry());
```

```
        if (!validator.IsValid(model))        ❷
        {
            var summary = validator.GetErrorSummary(model);
            foreach (string invalidProperty in
            summary.InvalidProperties)                    ❸
            {
                foreach (string error in
                summary.GetErrorsForProperty(invalidProperty))

                {
                    var modelState = bindingContext.ModelState;
                    modelState
                        .AddModelError(invalidProperty, error);    ❹
                }
            }
        }

        return model;
    }
}
```

You can see from listing 13.4 that a ValidationRunner class is created ❶, which then inspects the model ❷. If the model object is found to be invalid, it loops over the properties found to be in error ❸. Each property might have more than one broken rule (such as our Email property), so we need to loop over these. After we have a specific error and property name, we add it to ModelState so that the view can take advantage of it ❹.

We can enable this model binder for our view model by adding the following line to Application_Start in Global.asax.cs:

```
ModelBinders.Binders.Add(typeof(NewAttendeeForm),
    new CastleValidationBinder());
```

We might instead choose to make this the new default model binder, using

```
ModelBinders.Binders.DefaultBinder = new CastleValidationBinder();
```

At this point we have a complete functioning model binder that will validate the model as it's created. Now consider the following action:

```
[AcceptVerbs(HttpVerbs.Post)]
public ActionResult Index(NewAttendeeForm newAttendeeForm)
{
    if(!ModelState.IsValid)
    {
        return View();
    }

    TempData["message"] = "You were successfully registered";
    return RedirectToAction("index");
}
```

The newAttendeeForm will be created (and validated) with our custom model binder. If errors are found, they will be present in ModelState. This completes the server-side validation; however we still need to add client-side validation to avoid having to POST to the server just to get simple validation errors.

In the view, we'll need a simple helper that will output the appropriate JavaScript to automatically validate the form fields. The rules will come from the same attributes we defined earlier. We'll leverage a jQuery plugin called jQuery.validation.js. You can get this file from http://bassistance.de/jquery-plugins/jquery-plugin-validation/.

Using jquery.validation

The jQuery Validation plugin requires jQuery 1.2.6 or greater. This plugin validates a form as simple as

```
$("#myForm").validate();
```

The rules for the form can be passed in as arguments to the validate method like this:

```
$("#myForm").validate({
    rules:{
        username:{
            required:true,
            minlength:3
        }
    }
});
```

Some rules can be applied directly to a form element, like this:

```
<input type="text" id="username" class="required" minlength="3" />
```

Custom rules can also be added. We'll see an example of this later on.

The submit button of the form will now trigger client-side validation for the form. If any fields are found to be invalid, the form POST will be cancelled, and the user will have an opportunity to correct the error.

Now that we know the basics of the validation plugin, we can write a helper class to automatically output the required JavaScript based on the validation attributes we placed on our model.

The basic idea is that we'll pass in the model into a helper method. The helper will look for the attributes decorated on the class and return any JavaScript needed to validate each one.

We'll start by writing a function to get the validation attributes from a property:

```
private static AbstractValidationAttribute[] GetValidationAttributesFor(
    PropertyInfo property)
{
    return (AbstractValidationAttribute[])property.GetCustomAttributes(
        typeof(AbstractValidationAttribute), true);
}
```

Next, we'll write a function that will take the attribute and property and return the JavaScript required to validate it.

```
private static string GetAttributeValidation(PropertyInfo property,
    AbstractValidationAttribute attrib)
```

```
{
    if (attrib is ValidateNonEmptyAttribute)
        return AddCssClass(property.Name, "required");

    if (attrib is ValidateEmailAttribute)
        return AddCssClass(property.Name, "email");

    if (attrib is ValidateRegExpAttribute)
    {
        var validator = (RegularExpressionValidator) attrib.Build();
        return string.Format(
            "$('#{0}').rules('add', {{regex:'{1}'}});",
            property.Name, validator.Expression);
    }

    return string.Empty;
}
```

Here we're handling three of the validation attributes (the ones that are easy to handle in JavaScript). Creating the first two (ValidateNonEmptyAttribute and Validate-EmailAttribute) is as simple as adding a CSS class. The regular expression validation is not built in, so we have to add a custom function for this. The custom validation script is defined like this:

```
$.validator.addMethod(              | Validator
'regex',                          ⟵──┘ name
function(value, element, regexp) {    ⟵─ Validation function
        var check = false;
        var re = new RegExp(regexp);
        return this.optional(element) || re.test(value);
    },
'Please check your input.');    ⟵─ Error message
```

We'll have to add this function along with our other validation script. The AddCss-Class() method we saw earlier simply uses jQuery to add a CSS class to the specified element:

```
private static string AddCssClass(string name, string className)
{
    return string.Format("$('#{0}').addClass('{1}');",
name,
className);
}
```

Armed with these pieces of code, we can finally write our helper. The entire helper is shown in listing 13.5.

Listing 13.5   Helper for the client-side validation for Castle `Validation` attributes

```
public static class ValidationHelpers
{
    public static string ClientValidationFor<T>(this HtmlHelper<T> html,
        T model) where T : class
    {
        var js = new StringBuilder();
```

```
            js.AppendLine("<script type='text/javascript'>");
            js.AppendLine(CustomRegexRule);
            js.AppendLine("$(function() {");
            js.AppendFormat("$('form').validate();");

            var properties = typeof (T).GetProperties();

            foreach(var property in properties)
                foreach(var attrib in GetValidationAttributesFor(property))
                    js.AppendLine(GetAttributeValidation(property, attrib));

            js.AppendLine("});");
            js.AppendLine("</script>");
            return js.ToString();
        }

        private const string CustomRegexRule =
            @"$.validator.addMethod('regex', function(value, element, regexp) {
                    var check = false;
                    var re = new RegExp(regexp);
                    return this.optional(element) || re.test(value);
                }, 'Please check your input.');";

        private static AbstractValidationAttribute[]
            GetValidationAttributesFor(PropertyInfo property)
        {
            return (AbstractValidationAttribute[])property.GetCustomAttributes(
                typeof(AbstractValidationAttribute), true);
        }

        private static string GetAttributeValidation(PropertyInfo property,
            AbstractValidationAttribute attrib)
        {
            if (attrib is ValidateNonEmptyAttribute)
                return AddCssClass(property.Name, "required");

            if (attrib is ValidateEmailAttribute)
                return AddCssClass(property.Name, "email");

            if (attrib is ValidateRegExpAttribute)
            {
                var validator = (RegularExpressionValidator) attrib.Build();
                return string.Format("$('#{0}').rules('add',
                    {{regex:'{1}'}});", property.Name, validator.Expression);
            }

            return string.Empty;
        }

        private static string AddCssClass(string name, string className)
        {
            return string.Format("$('#{0}').addClass('{1}');",
                name, className);
        }
    }
```

Usage of our helper is incredibly simple. On the view in question, we'll simply add

```
<%= Html.ClientValidationFor(Model) %>
```

We pass in the `Model` property, which means our view is defined as `ViewPage<New-AttendeeForm>`.

Of course we'll also have to add the `<%@ Import Namespace="..." %>` to the top of the view for our helper to be recognized. Listing 13.6 shows our sample view.

Listing 13.6   Using automatic client-side validation helper in the view

```
<%@ Page Title="" Language="C#" MasterPageFile="~/Views/Shared/Site.Master"
    Inherits="System.Web.Mvc.ViewPage<NewAttendeeForm>" %>
<%@ Import Namespace="AutomaticValidation.Models"%>
<%@ Import Namespace="AutomaticValidation.Helpers"%>

<asp:Content ID="Content1" ContentPlaceHolderID="MainContent" runat="server">

    <h2>Register for the conference!</h2>              Add validation
                                                       scripts
    <%= Html.ClientValidationFor(Model) %>     ←──┘

    <%= Html.ValidationSummary("Registration was unsuccessful. Please correct
    the errors and try again.") %>                     ←──┐ Display ModelState
    <% using (Html.BeginForm()) {%>                         errors
        <fieldset>
            <label for="FirstName">FirstName:</label>
            <%= Html.TextBox("FirstName") %>
            <%= Html.ValidationMessage("FirstName", "*") %>

            <label for="LastName">LastName:</label>
            <%= Html.TextBox("LastName") %>
            <%= Html.ValidationMessage("LastName", "*") %>

            <label for="Email">Email:</label>
            <%= Html.TextBox("Email") %>
            <%= Html.ValidationMessage("Email", "*") %>

            <label for="Blog">Blog:</label>
            <%= Html.TextBox("Blog") %>
            <%= Html.ValidationMessage("Blog", "*") %>

            <label for="Comments">Comments:</label>
            <%= Html.TextBox("Comments") %>
            <%= Html.ValidationMessage("Comments", "*") %>

            <input type="submit" value="Register" />
        </fieldset>
    <% } %>
</asp:Content>
```

The client-side validation script will now be rendered with the view. We still need to retain the server-side validation summary, in case the user doesn't have JavaScript enabled. Never rely on client-side validation. It's a friendly addition to forms; however it's no replacement for solid validation on the server.

If we run our view and start to enter invalid data, we'll see it right away. Figure 13.6 shows it running.

The validation helper that we created demonstrates a fairly easy way of getting JavaScript validation free. This allows us to define the rules in one place (the attributes) and use them both in server-side and client-side validation. The implementation that

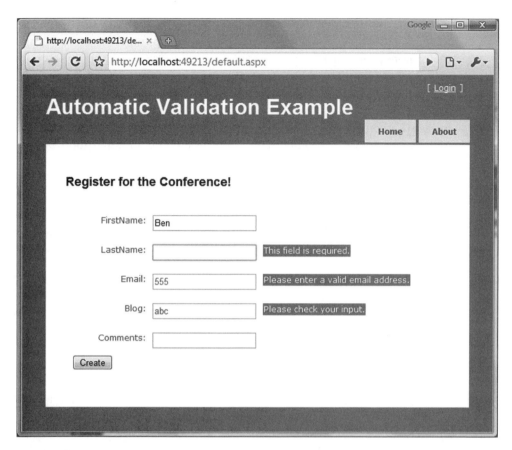

Figure 13.6   Seeing our client-side validation in action, we notice that the error messages automatically show up without a trip to the server.

we created still has room for improvement. For example, custom error messages are not yet implemented. In addition, we handle only three of the dozens of validation attributes that are present in the Castle validation library.

NOTE   *xVal Validation Framework*   Steve Sanderson (http://blog.codeville.net) started a project to fill this need. It's called the xVal Validation Framework. This project allows you to define your rules in a variety of ways (Castle validators, DataAnnotations attributes, custom). It also allows you to utilize one of a few client-side validation libraries, such as jQuery Validation and LiveValidation. The xVal Framework is much richer in functionality. Consider using it in your projects for more flexibility. Download it at http://xval.codeplex.com.

13.3   *Data access with NHibernate*

Even though the ASP.NET MVC Framework is focused on the presentation layer, many developers work on small applications that do not need several layers of business logic and separation between the presentation layer and the data store. For these small applications, simpler separation patterns may be appropriate; however, many small applications grow much larger than originally anticipated. When this happens, SoC is critical to the long-term maintainability of the software. NHibernate is a popular object-relational mapper. It makes data access with relational databases trivial. As with anything new, there is a learning curve associated with understanding the method of configuring the mapping between objects and tables. This recipe demonstrates how to configure and leverage NHibernate when developing an application whose UI takes advantage of the ASP.NET MVC Framework.

13.3.1 *Functional overview of reference implementation*

Our reference implementation is on top of the default project template. The functionality that is added is the capability to track visits to the site. Each page tracks visitors. The site tracks the following pieces of data:

- URL
- Login name
- Browser
- Date and time
- IP address

We see in figure 13.7 that by running the application the most recent visits are displayed at the bottom of the page. Each page displays the recent visits.

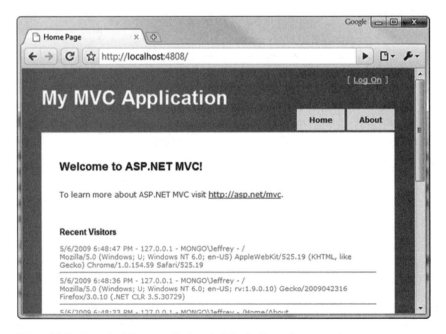

Figure 13.7   Recent visitors are displayed at the bottom of every page.

We have intentionally kept the scope of this recipe small so we can focus on the usage of NHibernate as the data access library that allows us to persist and retrieve `Visitor` objects. Before we go into each layer of the application, let's review the architecture of this application at a high level.

13.3.2 *Application architecture overview*

At a broad level, this application uses DDD inside an Onion Architecture. At a high level, the application is composed of a domain model at its core. Figure 13.8 shows a reference layout of Onion Architecture.

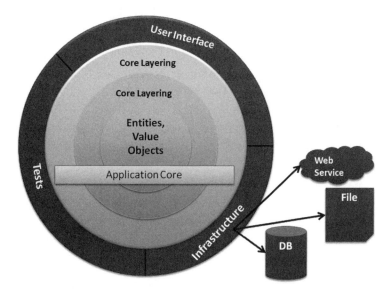

Figure 13.8 The Onion Architecture uses the concept of an application core that doesn't depend on external libraries, such as NHibernate.

The solution structure implements the decoupling strategy that Onion Architecture requires. In figure 13.9, you can see the solution structure with the Core project's references expanded. This application has a simple core, and the libraries referenced to implement the core are straightforward. Notice that there is no reference to NHibernate.dll from the Core project. It's important that the Core remain portable and not coupled to external libraries that will change over time. As with everything in software, this is a trade-off. You may feel comfortable coupling to some libraries, but evaluate the consequences carefully.

Figure 13.9 The Core project has minimal references and no external dependencies.

If we expand more of the projects, we see that no project references the Infrastructure project except for IntegrationTests, which is not deployed to production anyway. Figure 13.10 shows the solution fully expanded. Only the Infrastructure project references NHibernate.dll; no project references Infrastructure. When we examine the UI project, we'll see how the application is organized at runtime to function properly. Note that this recipe is not focused on automated testing, so many of the necessary automated tests are omitted for the sake of brevity.

Now that we understand how the application is structured at a high level, we'll explore each layer bit by bit. We'll begin with the domain model.

13.3.3 *Domain model—the application core*

The domain model is the most important part of the application. Without the domain model, all of the pertinent concepts would be represented only in the UI. Our particular domain model contains a single aggregate made up of a single entity, the `Visitor`. The code for the `Visitor` class is shown in listing 13.7.

Figure 13.10   No project references Infrastructure. This arrangement is important for decoupling.

Listing 13.7 `Visitor` class is domain model for this recipe.

```
using System;

namespace Core
{
    public class Visitor
    {
        public virtual Guid Id { get; set; }
        public virtual string PathAndQuerystring { get; set; }
        public virtual string LoginName { get; set; }
        public virtual string Browser { get; set; }
        public virtual DateTime VisitDate { get; set; }
        public virtual string IpAddress { get; set; }
    }
}
```

We have no business logic here, and at first glance it looks just like a data structure. All other concerns have been left out in an effort to include only abstractions and logic that are necessary for leveraging NHibernate in a loosely coupled way.

The `Visitor` class contains properties for all of the pieces of information that we want to record. The `Id` property exists as an identifier for the particular visit. We could certainly use `Int32` as the ID, but in a data persistence environment, that forces a dependency on the data store for the generation of a unique `Int32` value. Sometimes this is appropriate, but in DDD, the developer errs on the side of giving responsibility to the domain model, not the data store. In line with that, the `Id` is a `Guid`, and the application will generate a `Guid` before attempting to save to the database.

The mechanism for persisting or retrieving a `Visitor` is called a *repository*. The repository will save our entity as well as retrieve it. It can also represent filtering operations. In our domain model, we have an `IVisitorRepository`. This interface is seen in listing 13.8.

Listing 13.8 The repository defines the persistence operations.

```
namespace Core
{
    public interface IVisitorRepository
    {
        void Save(Visitor visitor);
        Visitor[] GetRecentVisitors(int numberOfVisitors);
    }
}
```

With our repository, we are able to save a visitor as well as get the most recent visitors. We can ask for a specific number of recent visitors. In figure 13.10, you see that the Core project doesn't contain any class that implements `IVisitorRepository`. This is important because the class that actually does the work represented by the interface will be responsible for the persistence, which is not a domain model concern. Persistence is infrastructure. I could imagine that this functionality would work equally well if I persisted the data to a file instead of the database. The mechanism of persistence is not a concern for the domain model; therefore, the class responsible for it is not in the Core project.

The concern that is in the Core project, however, is a factory that is capable of locating or creating an instance of `IVisitorRepository`. The `VisitorRepository-Factory` is responsible for returning an instance of our repository. Listing 13.9 shows that the knowledge of how to create the factory doesn't reside with this class. This factory class merely represents the capability to return the class.

Listing 13.9 Factory offers capability to get repository.

```
using System;

namespace Core
{
    public class VisitorRepositoryFactory
    {
        public static Func<IVisitorRepository> RepositoryBuilder =        // Initialize at application startup
            CreateDefaultRepositoryBuilder;

        private static IVisitorRepository CreateDefaultRepositoryBuilder()
        {
            throw new Exception("No repository builder specified.");      // Throw if factory not initialized
        }
        public IVisitorRepository BuildRepository()
        {
            IVisitorRepository repository = RepositoryBuilder();          // Use delegate to build repository
            return repository;
        }
    }
}
```

To even the inexperienced eye, this class doesn't seem useful alone. When `BuildFactory()` is called, an exception will be thrown. Out of the box, the domain model doesn't know the implementation of `IVisitorRepository` that will be used, so there is no way to embed this knowledge into compiled code. The `public static RepositoryBuilder` property will have to be set to something useful before the factory will work properly. We'll see how this is accomplished after all the pieces have been introduced.

This explicit factory is not necessary if you're using an IoC container that has been left out for the sake of simplicity. This domain model is simple. This is all there is. The next step is to understand how we configure NHibernate to automatically persist our entity to the database.

13.3.4 *NHibernate configuration—infrastructure of the application*

There is little code to write in order to leverage NHibernate for seamless persistence. NHibernate is a library, not a framework; the difference is important. Frameworks provide templates of code in which you then fill in the gaps to create something useful. Libraries are usable without providing templates. NHibernate doesn't require your entities to derive from a specific base class or the implementation of a specific interface. NHibernate can persist any type of object as long as the configuration is correct.

This section will walk through the configuration of NHibernate so that we can save and retrieve the `Visitor` object.

Before we dive into the configuration, let's example the implementation of the `IVisitorRepository` interface specified in the domain model. The purpose for starting with this class is to demonstrate how little code is actually written when calling NHibernate to perform a persistence operation. Listing 13.10 shows the `Visitor-Repository` class located in the Infrastructure project.

Listing 13.10   Repository implementation coupled to NHibernate APIs

```
using System.Collections.Generic;
using System.Linq;
using Core;
using NHibernate;

namespace Infrastructure
{
    public class VisitorRepository : IVisitorRepository
    {
        public void Save(Visitor visitor)
        {
            ISession session = GetSession();
            session.SaveOrUpdate(visitor);
        }

        public Visitor[] GetRecentVisitors(int numberOfVisitors)
        {
            IList<Visitor> visitors = GetSession()          Use HQL
                .CreateQuery(                               to select
                    "select v from Visitor v order by v.VisitDate desc"   Visitors
                    ).SetMaxResults(numberOfVisitors)
                .List<Visitor>();

            return visitors.ToArray();              Return array
        }                                           of Visitors

        private ISession GetSession()
        {
            var cache = new SessionCache();         Retrieve session
            ISession session = cache.GetSession();  from cache
            return session;
        }
    }
}
```

This class is a total of 34 lines long, and many lines are largely whitespace. The code that leverages the NHibernate APIs is limited. Now that we see what it looks like to call NHibernate, we'll walk through the configuration process of NHibernate and explore each step. We'll start with the main configuration.

LIKE ANY .NET APPLICATION, NHIBERNATE NEEDS CONFIGURATION

The beginning of the configuration process is the hibernate.cfg.xml file. This file is the same name as that used by the Hibernate library in Java. Because NHibernate started as a port from Hibernate, this is just one of the many similarities. Knowledge of one largely translates directly to the other.

The contents of the hibernate.cfg.xml file can also be put into the web.config file or app.config file. For simple applications, embedding this information into the .NET configuration file may be adequate; we should emphasize that this example stresses separation so that when applied to a medium-sized application, the code and configuration don't run together. We have seen web.config files grow large, and it's trivial to store the NHibernate configuration in a dedicated file. Listing 13.11 shows the contents of the hibernate.cfg.xml file.

Listing 13.11   Hibernate.cfg.xml file contains database connection information.

```
<hibernate-configuration xmlns="urn:nhibernate-configuration-2.2">
  <session-factory>
    <property name="connection.driver_class">
         NHibernate.Driver.SqlClientDriver
    </property>
    <property name="connection.connection_string">
         server=.\SQLExpress;database=NHibernateSample;
         Integrated Security=true;
    </property>
    <property name="show_sql">false</property>
    <property name="dialect">
         NHibernate.Dialect.MsSql2005Dialect
    </property>
    <property name="adonet.batch_size">100</property>
    <mapping assembly="Infrastructure" />
  </session-factory>
</hibernate-configuration>
```

This is a simple configuration, and there are many other options offered with the NHibernate documentation (http://nhforge.org/doc/nh/en/index.html). The most obvious piece of information is the connection string. Also, the driver class and dialect specify the details of the database engine used. This sample uses SQL Server 2005, but these values would change if you wanted to use any version of Oracle, SQLite, or the many other database engines supported out of the box.

The show_sql property will output each SQL query to the Console as the statement is being sent to the database. This is useful for debugging. The adonet.batch_size controls how many updates, deletes, or inserts will be sent to the database in a single batch. It's more efficient to send multiple statements in a single network call than to make a separate network call for each statement. NHibernate will do this automatically. The last, but most important configuration item is the assembly where NHibernate can find the mapping files. We are telling NHibernate to look in the Infrastructure project to find the mappings.

THE NHIBERNATE MAPPING FILES—SIMPLE BUT POWERFUL

NHibernate requires at least one mapping file. You can put the mappings for many entities in a single mapping file, but it's a better practice to segment out each "class" node. The class node represents an entity. Figure 13.11 shows the Infrastructure project.

We are about to explore the Visitor.hbm.xml file, which contains the mapping information for the Visitor class. First, notice the four files that are linked into the project:

- Hibernate.cfg.xml
- Log4Net.config
- Nhibernate-configuration.xsd
- Nhibernate-mapping.xsd

These files do not belong to the project directly; they are linked from elsewhere. We do this because multiple projects need the same copy of these files. The first example that needs linked files is the IntegrationTests. It will contain tests for all data access. To test the data access, the tests need to leverage the same configuration as the application.

We have already covered the hibernate.cfg.xml file. The Log4Net.config file contains Log4Net configuration information that is broadly applicable to any type of application. If you're not familiar with Log4Net, you can find more information at http://logging. apache.org/log4net/index.html. The two files provide the schema for the NHibernate configuration and the NHibernate mapping files. When added to the project, they enable Visual Studio to provide XML IntelliSense when you are editing these files. It makes the editing process smooth. We edit mapping files most heavily. Without this XML IntelliSense, it would be cumbersome to maintain these XML files.

Let's now turn to the mapping file for the `Visitor` class. We'll open the Visitor.hbm.xml file and examine its structure, as shown in listing 13.12.

Figure 13.11   The Infrastructure project contains the Visitor.hbm.xml mapping file.

Listing 13.12   Visitor.hbm.xml file contains mapping for the `Visitor` class.

```xml
<?xml version="1.0" encoding="utf-8" ?>
<hibernate-mapping xmlns="urn:nhibernate-mapping-2.2"
          namespace="Core" assembly="Core">

    <class name="Visitor" table="Visitors" dynamic-update="true">
        <id name="Id" column="Id" type="Guid">
            <generator class="guid.comb"/>
        </id>
        <property name="PathAndQuerystring" length="4000" not-null="true"/>
        <property name="LoginName" length="255" not-null="true"/>
        <property name="Browser" length="4000" not-null="true"/>
        <property name="VisitDate" not-null="true"/>
        <property name="IpAddress" not-null="true"/>
    </class>
</hibernate-mapping>
```

The first node is pretty standard and declares the NHibernate XML namespace. Then, the default namespace and assembly are declared. Without these, the class name would have to be fully qualified, and when mapping files get more complex than this, you want to avoid having to fully qualify type names.

The class node contains the information about how to persist the `Visitor` class. We want the table name to be different from the class name, so we declare it. If we did not declare the table name, NHibernate would use the class name.

The id node is special, and it has to be the first property mapped on an entity. This will become the primary key on the table, and there are many ways to handle it. The generator node has many options, including SQL Server "identity" and Oracle "sequence" functionality. We want the object to have a value in the Id property before being persisted, so we are configuring NHibernate to generate a Guid for us before issuing the INSERT statement to the database. The guid.comb generator is special, and it generates GUIDs in sequential order so that the clustered index on the primary key column has little to do when absorbing a new record inserted into the table. This sequencing sacrifices a bit of uniqueness in the GUID algorithm, but in this context, the only thing that is important is that the GUID be unique for this particular table. You can read more about the COMB GUID from the inventor, Jimmy Nilsson: http://www.informit.com/articles/article.aspx?p=25862.

The rest of the properties are largely self-explanatory. They have names, constraints, and the strings can have a length specified. If you're all right with the column name being the same as the property name on the class, then a column attribute is unnecessary. When you have all the properties mapped, you're ready to move on. If you have a more complex class structure, you will want to review all your mapping options in the documentation at http://nhforge.org/doc/nh/en/index.html.

INITIALIZING THE CONFIGURATION

There are two main abstractions in NHibernate: ISessionFactory and ISession. A session factory creates a session. A session is meant to be used for a single transaction. You should use and then quickly dispose of NHibernate sessions. The session factory is intended to be kept for the life of the application so that it can be used to create all sessions. The interface is the abstraction, but the implementation provided by NHibernate requires some understanding. The code in listing 13.13 shows how to create the session factory that will be used for the life of the application.

Listing 13.13 A Configuration object creates a session factory.

```
var configuration = new Configuration();              Configure NHibernate
configuration = configuration.Configure();            using XML configuration
SessionFactory = configuration.BuildSessionFactory();
                                                      Build and cache
                                                      session factory
```

The session factory is expensive to create. By expensive, we mean that it accesses the file system and parses XML from embedded resources inside DLLs. The configuration object is going to read the hibernate.cfg.xml file (out-of-process call), and then it will build the session factory using this configuration. When building the session factory, it will retrieve all the mapping files from within the DLL files (out-of-process call). Each mapping file will be parsed using the XML DOM, and then it uses reflection on all the types to ensure that every property declared in the mapping files actually exists on the types referenced. If lazy loading is enabled (the default), it will also check that all public properties and methods are marked virtual. If you prefer not to mark them virtual, disable lazy loading. With most applications, it takes several seconds to create the session factory; this operation is not something you want to do often. If you create the session factory for every web request, your web application will slow down dramatically. We push the session factory instance in a static variable so we can hold on to it for the life of the application.

The NHibernate session, on the other hand, is cheap. We'll create and destroy many of these objects. In a stateful application, we'll use a session for a single transaction or user operation. For a web application, we'll use one session per web request. We'll cover the web application usage is just a bit. The code for the creation of a session is shown in listing 13.14.

Listing 13.14   The session is inexpensive to create.

```
ISession session = SessionFactory.OpenSession();       ◁──┐ Session factory
                                                          provides the session
```

Before we can move on to the code that uses all this, we have to have a database. We have declared our connection string, and with the mapping, NHibernate knows the table structure. We can proceed to create our database schema manually, or we can get NHibernate to help us out. After creating an empty database named "NHibernate-Sample" inside SQL Server Express, as declared by the connection string, we can execute the code shown in listing 13.15 to have NHibernate create our schema.

Listing 13.15   NHibernate generates database from mappings.

```
using NHibernate.Cfg;
using NHibernate.Tool.hbm2ddl;
using NUnit.Framework;

namespace IntegrationTests
{
    [TestFixture]
    public class DatabaseTester
    {
        [Test, Explicit]
        public void CreateDatabaseSchmea()
        {
            var export = new SchemaExport(new Configuration().Configure());
            export.Execute(true, true, false, true);
        }
    }
}
```

We are using an NUnit test fixture as an easy launching point for this code. It makes it trivial to run the code snippet. After running this test, we'll see the output in the output windows similar to listing 13.16.

Listing 13.16   Output from schema export shows table DDL

```
------ Test started: Assembly: IntegrationTests.dll ------

if exists (select * from dbo.sysobjects where id = object_id(N'Visitors') and
    OBJECTPROPERTY(id, N'IsUserTable') = 1) drop table Visitors
create table Visitors (
```

```
 Id UNIQUEIDENTIFIER not null,
  PathAndQuerystring NVARCHAR(4000) not null,
  LoginName NVARCHAR(255) not null,
  Browser NVARCHAR(4000) not null,
  VisitDate DATETIME not null,
  IpAddress NVARCHAR(255) not null,
  primary key (Id)
)
```

```
1 passed, 0 failed, 0 skipped, took 6.86 seconds.
```

The NUnit test lives in the IntegrationTests project. This project also links in the hibernate.cfg.xml file to leverage the same configuration. Figure 13.12 shows the IntegrationTests project structure. We have kept it minimal for the sake of simplicity.

Notice the `VisitorRepositoryTester` class. You can probably guess what this class does. That's right! It contains the automated testing necessary to ensure that the repository implementation functions as expected. We can't write unit tests for data access. Data

Figure 13.12   The IntegrationTests project contains tests for all the mappings and repositories.

access, by its very nature, is an integration test concern. Not only are we integrating a third-party library, NHibernate, but we are also expecting another process to be running on our network, server, or workstation. SQL Server must be up and running. It also must contain the correct schema. If anything is wrong along the way, the tests will fail. Because of this arrangement, these integration tests are larger than we would expect for simple unit tests. Even so, keep them as small as possible, and only test the data access. Listing 13.17 shows the code for the `VisitorRepositoryTester`.

Listing 13.17   Integration test verifies mappings and database are correct

```
using System;
using Core;
using Infrastructure;
using NHibernate;
using NHibernate.Cfg;
using NUnit.Framework;
using NUnit.Framework.SyntaxHelpers;

namespace IntegrationTests
{
    [TestFixture]
    public class VisitorRepositoryTester
    {
        [Test]
        public void When_saving_should_write_to_database()
        {
            var config = new DataConfig();      <──── Configure NHibernate
```

```
        config.PerformStartup();
        config.StartSession();

        var visitor = new Visitor      ◁── Create new Visitor
        {
            Browser = "1",
            IpAddress = "2",
            LoginName = "3",
            PathAndQuerystring = "4",
            VisitDate = new DateTime(2000, 1, 1)
        };

        var repository = new VisitorRepository();
        repository.Save(visitor);                    ◁── Save Visitor

        config.EndSession();         │ Create new
        config.StartSession();       │ session                    │ Reload
                                                                   │ Visitor
        ISession session = new SessionCache().GetSession();   ◁──
        var loadedVisitor = session.Load<Visitor>(visitor.Id);

        Assert.That(loadedVisitor, Is.Not.Null);
        Assert.That(loadedVisitor.Browser, Is.EqualTo("1"));
        Assert.That(loadedVisitor.IpAddress, Is.EqualTo("2"));   │ Assert
        Assert.That(loadedVisitor.LoginName, Is.EqualTo("3"));   │ correct
        Assert.That(loadedVisitor.PathAndQuerystring,            │ data
            Is.EqualTo("4"));
        Assert.That(loadedVisitor.VisitDate,
            Is.EqualTo(new DateTime(2000, 1, 1)));
    }

    public void SetUpNewSession()
    {
        new DatabaseTester().CreateDatabaseSchmea();
        var configuration = new Configuration();
        configuration = configuration.Configure();
        ISessionFactory factory = configuration.BuildSessionFactory();
        new SessionCache().CacheSession(factory.OpenSession());
    }
  }
}
```

These tests are essential to ensuring that every query generated by NHibernate is tested and retested with every build. Because configuration changes will change the queries that are generated, tests are important for the stability of the application. When we run this test, we see that it passes, as shown in figure 13.13.

You now know the basics of persisting with NHibernate. All NHibernate coupling should remain in the Infrastructure project. Remember that none of the other projects have a reference to Infrastructure, so the rest of the code is not coupled to this particular data access library. This decoupling is important because data access methods change very frequently. You do not want to couple your application to infrastructural concerns when they are likely to change frequently.

Now that we have covered both the Core and Infrastructure, we'll see how this ties together in the UI.

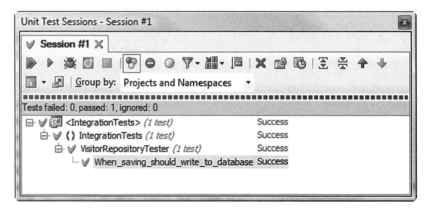

Figure 13.13   When the repository test passes, we know the mapping is correct.

13.3.5   *UI leverages domain model*

Now that the domain model and the NHibernate infrastructure are set up and functioning, we can turn our attention once again to the ASP.NET MVC project. We have left the project close to the default template in an effort to keep it simple as well as call out the additions necessary to enable the saving of every visitor to the site. Figure 13.14 shows the structure of the UI project.

From figure 13.7 you can recall that each page on the site shows the most recent visitors to the site at the bottom. To share this view on each page, we have wired up a partial view to the master page, Site.Master. We have covered this capability in previous chapters, so we won't cover it in depth here.

At the highest level, we have added an action filter attribute to each controller. If the site contains many controllers, we would consider introducing a Layer Supertype for all controllers and applying the filter to just that controller. In this example, the project contains only the HomeController and Account-Controller. The HomeController is shown in listing 13.18. Notice the action filters applied at the class level.

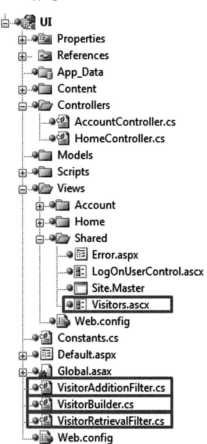

Figure 13.14   The additions to the project are boxed. We have added several files to support the capture and display of visitors.

Listing 13.18 Action filters applied to controller to keep concerns separated

```
using System.Web.Mvc;

namespace UI.Controllers
{
    [HandleError]
    [VisitorAdditionFilter(Order = 0)]       ❶
    [VisitorRetrievalFilter(Order = 1)]      ❷
    public class HomeController : Controller
    {
        public ActionResult Index()
        {
            ViewData["Message"] = "Welcome to ASP.NET MVC!";

            return View();
        }

        public ActionResult About()
        {
            return View();
        }
    }
}
```

We have introduced two filters, the VisitorAdditionFilter ❶, and the Visitor-RetrievalFilter ❷. We have applied the Order optional parameter to ensure that they are executed in the intended order. It may be confusing, but the order the attributes are applied to the class is not the execution order. We want to persist a new visitor before we get the list of recent visitors and pass the objects to a view. Listing 13.19 shows both of the action filters.

Listing 13.19 Action filters interact with domain model.

```
using System.Web.Mvc;
using Core;

namespace UI
{
    public class VisitorAdditionFilter : ActionFilterAttribute
    {
        private readonly IVisitorRepository _repository;

        public VisitorAdditionFilter(IVisitorRepository repository)
        {
            _repository = repository;
        }

        public VisitorAdditionFilter() :
            this(new VisitorRepositoryFactory().BuildRepository())   ❶
        {
        }

        public override void OnResultExecuting(           ❷
            ResultExecutingContext filterContext)
        {
            var builder = new VisitorBuilder();
```

```
                    Visitor visitor = builder.BuildVisitor();     ❸
                    _repository.Save(visitor);
                }
            }
        }

        using System.Web.Mvc;
        using Core;

        namespace UI
        {
            public class VisitorRetrievalFilter : ActionFilterAttribute
            {
                private readonly IVisitorRepository _repository;

                public VisitorRetrievalFilter(IVisitorRepository repository)
                {
                    _repository = repository;
                }

                public VisitorRetrievalFilter() : this(
                    new VisitorRepositoryFactory().BuildRepository())    ❶
                {
                }

                public override void OnResultExecuting(     ❷
                    ResultExecutingContext filterContext)
                {
                    Visitor[] visitors = _repository.GetRecentVisitors(10);
                    filterContext.Controller                            ❹
                      .ViewData[Constants.ViewData.VISITORS] = visitors;
                }
            }
        }
```

Each of the filters is simple. Most of the code is just for managing the dependency of the IVisitorRepository and building the repository from the factory ❶. The three lines of work that are interesting are in the OnResultExecuting method ❷. We build the visitor and save it ❸. Then we get the recent visitors and push them into view data ❹. The VisitorBuilder class is not shown, but it's a simple one that constructs a Visitor and populates it with information from the HttpRequest. The next interesting file is the Visitors.ascx partial view located in /Views/Shared/Visitors.ascx. Listing 13.20 shows this partial view.

Listing 13.20 Partial view is strongly typed and displays recent visitors.

```
<%@ Control Language="C#"
    Inherits="System.Web.Mvc.ViewUserControl<Visitor[]>" %>
<%@ Import Namespace="Core"%>
<div style="text-align:left">
<h3>Recent Visitors</h3>
    <%foreach (var visitor in ViewData.Model){%>
        <%=visitor.VisitDate%> -
        <%=visitor.IpAddress%> -
        <%=visitor.LoginName%> -
```

```
        <%=visitor.PathAndQuerystring%><br />
        <%=visitor.Browser%><hr />
    <%}%>
</div>
```

This partial is added to the page via the master page. The array of visitors is expected to be in `ViewData.Model` so that the array can be rendered the default way. At the bottom of the master page, the following code passes just the visitor array to the partial: `<%Html.RenderPartial(Constants.Partials.VISITORS, ViewData[Constants.ViewData.VISITORS]); %>`.

We use the constants so that the views do not contain duplicate string literals. Since logging and displaying visitor information are cross-cutting concerns for the application, we have taken steps to keep the logic factored out so that it can be shared across all controllers in the application. Let's review what we have done:

- Kept the persistence logic behind an interface that doesn't belong to the UI project
- Leveraged action filters so that no single controller is responsible for knowing how to interact with `IVisitorRepository`
- Created a partial view to own the layout of the recent visitors
- Delegated to the partial view from the master page so that individual views don't have to care about it

All the pieces are now in place to be pulled together.

13.3.6 *Pulling it together*

If you have been keeping a close eye on the code up to this point, you have noticed that we do not have a default way to create the NHibernate repository instance of `IVisitorRepository` that lives in the Infrastructure project. Our UI project doesn't reference the Infrastructure project at all. This section walks through the process of wiring up these decoupled pieces.

The first piece is in the web.config file. Inside the httpModules node, we have registered an extra module:

```
<add name="StartupModule" type="Infrastructure.NHibernateModule, Infrastructure,
➥    Version=1.0.0.0, Culture=neutral"/>
```

This module kicks off the process of creating the session factory. It also hooks the `BeginRequest` and `EndRequest` events and creates and destroys NHibernate sessions for each web request. Listing 13.21 shows the code for NHibernateModule.cs, which lives in the Infrastructure project.

Listing 13.21 `NHibernateModule` **kick-starts NHibernate.**

```
using System;
using System.Web;

namespace Infrastructure
{
```

```
public class NHibernateModule : IHttpModule
{
    private static bool _startupComplete = false;
    private static readonly object _locker = new object();

    public void Init(HttpApplication context)
    {
        context.BeginRequest += context_BeginRequest;
        context.EndRequest += context_EndRequest;
    }

    private void context_BeginRequest(object sender, EventArgs e)
    {
        EnsureStartup();
        new DataConfig().StartSession();
    }

    private void context_EndRequest(object sender, EventArgs e)
    {
        new DataConfig().EndSession();
    }

    private void EnsureStartup()
    {
        if (!_startupComplete)
        {
            lock (_locker)
            {
                if (!_startupComplete)
                {
                    new DataConfig().PerformStartup();
                    _startupComplete = true;
                }
            }
        }
    }

    public void Dispose()
    {
    }
}
```

Annotations: **Open session when request starts** (pointing to `new DataConfig().StartSession();`), **End session when request ends** (pointing to `new DataConfig().EndSession();`).

The DataConfig class (not shown) will create a session and store it in the cache. Listing 13.22 shows the SessionCache.cs file as well as an important method from DataConfig.cs.

Listing 13.22 Session cache keeps session in HttpContext items.

```
using System.Collections;
using System.Web;
using NHibernate;

namespace Infrastructure
{
    public class SessionCache
    {
        private const string SESSION_KEY = "NHIBERNATE_SESSION";
```

```
        private static readonly IDictionary _cacheStore = new Hashtable();

        public ISession GetSession()
        {
            var session = (ISession) GetCacheStore()[SESSION_KEY];
            return session;
        }

        public void CacheSession(ISession session)
        {
            GetCacheStore()[SESSION_KEY] = session;
        }

        private static IDictionary GetCacheStore()
        {
            if (HttpContext.Current != null)
                return HttpContext.Current.Items;

            return _cacheStore;
        }
    }
}
                                                        Part of
private void InitializeRepositories()  ⟵――  DataConfig.cs
{
    Func<IVisitorRepository> builder =
        () => new VisitorRepository();
    VisitorRepositoryFactory.RepositoryBuilder = builder;
}
```

Now that we have a session factory, and we have a session, our application can call NHibernate and communicate with the database. Aside from the NHibernate initialization, we have the initialization of the VisitorRepositoryFactory. In CodeCampServer, we use StructureMap as our IoC container. IoC tools provide these factories automatically, but because this sample doesn't leverage the IoC container, we had to provide this startup logic explicitly. There are several ways to do that. Another popular way is to declare an interface for the factory and keep an implementation around. Use your judgment when choosing a technique. The important thing is that no project should reference the Infrastructure project. We have kept NHibernate completely off to the side so that the rest of the application doesn't care how the data access is happening.

There is one final missing piece required before we can run this application from Visual Studio using CTRL + F5. The web.config file refers to a class in the Infrastructure project, but because there is no reference, the Infrastructure assembly will not be in the bin folder of the website. We could copy it explicitly every time we compile, but that will get tiresome. The solution is to have Visual Studio copy it every time it's compiled by adding the following lines to the Infrastructure.csproj file as a post-build event such as the command in listing 13.23.

Listing 13.23 Post-build event copies assemblies and config files.

```
xcopy /y  ".\*.dll" "..\..\..\UI\bin\"
xcopy /y  ".\log4net.config" "..\..\..\UI\"
xcopy /y  ".\hibernate.cfg.xml" "..\..\..\UI\bin\"
```

By setting up the three commands shown in listing 13.23, we have configured the Infrastructure project to copy two important configuration files as well as the necessary binaries to the UI project's `bin` folder. Not only will the Infrastructure assembly be copied, the NHibernate assemblies will be copied as well. This ensures that when the UI project is run from Visual Studio, you will be greeted with a running application that is saving and showing visitors as in figure 13.15.

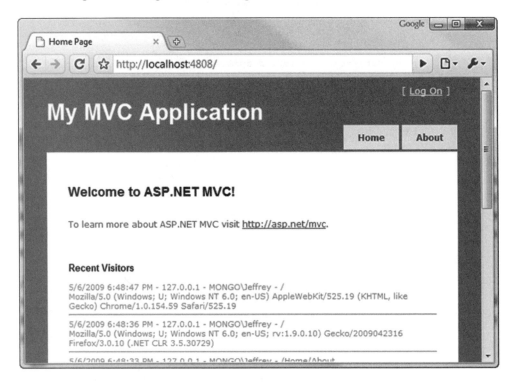

Figure 13.15   The application works as expected after being wired together.

Because of this post-build step, the application has all the required assemblies and configuration files. This reduces the pain of copying these files manually every time they change. This is just one type of automation required when you truly commit to decoupling your applications.

13.3.7   *Wrapping up data access with NHibernate*

In this recipe, you have seen how to structure your solution, configure NHibernate, use the repository pattern from ASP.NET MVC, and wire up loosely coupled code at runtime. This recipe presents a vastly simplified example, but the patterns contained within are appropriate in medium-to-large applications as well.

Configuring and using NHibernate is easy. It's also easy to couple to it and get in trouble. Whether it's NHibernate or any other data access library, do not couple your application to it. Keep your core clean and your UI separated. All data access should be behind interfaces and tested separately. For more advanced usages of NHibernate with ASP.NET MVC, you can open the CodeCampServer solution, which is included with this book's code download at www.manning.com/ASP.NETMVCinAction.

13.4 Designing views with the Spark view engine

By default, an ASP.NET MVC application uses the `WebFormViewEngine` to locate and render views. But we are not forced to use Web Forms to design and render our views. One of the extension points of ASP.NET MVC is the ability to swap out the default `IViewEngine` for a different implementation. With a different view engine, we get a different experience in defining and developing views. Popular alternative view engines supported in ASP.NET MVC through various open source efforts include

- Brail
- NHaml
- NVelocity
- Spark

But why would we want to investigate other view engines? One issue with the `WebForm-ViewEngine` is that you do not have many options for server-side coding except with complex languages such as C# and VB.NET. Although these languages are quite powerful, seeing code interspersed with markup is ugly. Creating a simple loop of HTML requires a `foreach` loop and curly braces mixed with our HTML tags. For more complex view logic, it becomes nearly impossible to understand what is going on. The `WebFormViewEngine` suffices in many situations, but it's obvious that it was not built with MVC-style applications in mind, where we are almost guaranteed to need code in our views. Although this code is strictly view-centric, it's still unavoidable.

These alternative view engines are designed to be view engines, rather than holdovers from the Web Forms days. Each is optimized for designing an MVC view, and many are ported versions of other, established view engines for other, established MVC frameworks. For example, NHaml is a port of the popular (and extremely terse) Haml view engine. Another view engine, designed for both ASP.NET MVC and MonoRail, is Spark (http://sparkviewengine.com/). Spark provides a unique blend of C# code in line with HTML, disguised as XML elements and attributes. There are disadvantages to some view engines, such as the lack of IntelliSense and a slightly less integrated feel in Visual Studio. Spark provides integration with Visual Studio, including IntelliSense and a view compiler. The view compiler ensures that at least we do not have to wait for runtime exceptions to expose typos and bugs in our views. In this section, we examine the major features of Spark to see the advantages it has over the default view engine. But first, we'll walk through the installation and configuration process.

13.4.1 Installing and configuring Spark

The latest release can be found at Spark's CodePlex site, at http://sparkviewengine. codeplex.com/. The release includes the following:

- The Spark assemblies we need in our MVC project
- Documentation
- Samples
- Installer for Visual Studio IntelliSense

To get Spark running in our MVC project, we need only the binaries. However, the IntelliSense is quite helpful, so we'll run the installer before launching Visual Studio. Next, we add references to both the `Spark` and `Spark.Web.Mvc` assemblies, shown in figure 13.16.

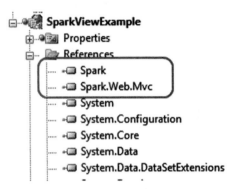

With our Spark assembly references added to our project, we can configure ASP. NET MVC to use Spark as our view engine. Spark has additional configuration, which we can either place in our Web.config file or in code. For this example, we'll configure Spark in code, but the Spark documentation has full examples of both options. Our Spark configuration is shown in listing 13.24.

Figure 13.16   Adding the Spark assembly references to our project

---

Listing 13.24   Spark configuration code

```
var settings = new SparkSettings()
    .SetDebug(true)
    .AddAssembly("SparkViewExample")
    .AddNamespace("System")
    .AddNamespace("System.Collections.Generic")
    .AddNamespace("System.Linq")
    .AddNamespace("System.Web.Mvc")
    .AddNamespace("System.Web.Mvc.Html");

ViewEngines.Engines.Add(new SparkViewFactory(settings));
```

We place the code into the `Application_Start` method in our Global.asax.cs file, as the Spark configuration and MVC view engine configuration only need to happen once per application domain. In the first section, we create a `SparkSettings` object, configuring the compilation mode, and adding our project assembly and various assemblies for compilation. This section should look similar to configuring the `WebFormViewEngine` in our Web.config file. Next, we add a new `SparkViewFactory` instance to the `System.Web.Mvc.ViewEngines.Engines` collection. The `ViewEngines` class allows additional view engines to be configured for our application. To the `SparkViewFactory` instance we pass our `SparkSettings` object created earlier. That is all it takes to configure Spark! Now that Spark is configured, we can move on to creating views for our example.

13.4.2 *Simple Spark view example*

On the controller and model pieces of our MVC application, we won't see any changes with our new view engine. We want to show a list of `Product` model objects, shown in listing 13.25.

Listing 13.25   Simple `Product` model

```
public class Product
{
    public string Name { get; set; }
    public string Description { get; set; }
    public decimal Price { get; set; }
}
```

Again, the Spark view engine places no specific constraints on our model, nor our controller action, shown in listing 13.26.

Listing 13.26   A `ProductController` for displaying `Product` objects

```
public class ProductController : Controller
{
    public ViewResult Index()
    {                                       ┐ Create dummy
        var products = new[]          ◁────┘ products
        {
            new Product {
                Name = "Toothbrush",
                Description = "Cleans your teeth",
                Price = 2.49m
            },
            new Product {
                Name = "Hairbrush",
                Description = "Styles your hair",
                Price = 10.29m
            },
            new Product {
                Name = "Shoes",
                Description = "Protects your feet",
                Price = 55.99m
            },
        };                                  ┐ Send products
        return View(products);        ◁────┘ to the view
    }
}
```

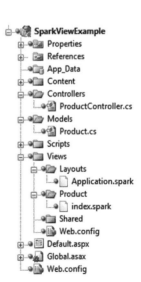

Figure 13.17   Complete folder structure for our Spark views

We show only a dummy list of products for our Spark views to display. To create our Spark views, the folder structure is similar to our structure for other view engines. In the root Views folder, we create a Product folder to correspond to our `ProductController`. Additionally, we create Layouts and Shared folders, as shown in figure 13.17.

In Spark, view files use the.spark file extension. This is mainly so that the file extension doesn't conflict with other view engines in the IDE or at runtime.

Spark supports the concept of layouts, which are similar in nature to the Web Forms master pages. By convention, the default layout name is Application.spark, found in either the Layouts or Shared folder. To start, we'll create just a text file in Visual Studio named Application.spark (instead of a Web Form or other template). This is shown in figure 13.18.

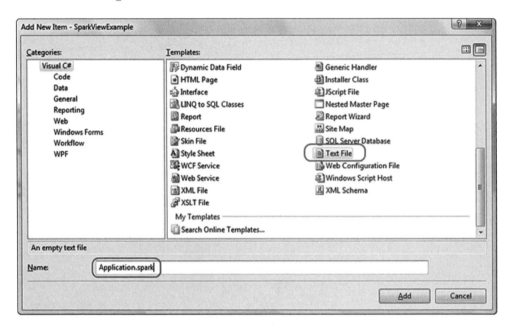

Figure 13.18   Adding an Application.spark layout for our views

We choose the Text File template as we don't want any of the built-in functionality with something like a Web Forms template; we need only a blank file. Inside our base layout, we need to place a couple of links as well as provide a placeholder for the actual child content. Our entire layout is shown in listing 13.27.

Listing 13.27   Entire Application.spark layout template

```
<!DOCTYPE html PUBLIC "-//W3C//DTD XHTML 1.0 Strict//EN" "http://www.w3.org/
    TR/xhtml1/DTD/xhtml1-strict.dtd">
<html xmlns="http://www.w3.org/1999/xhtml">
<head>
    <title>Spark View Example</title>
    <link href="~/Content/Site.css" rel="stylesheet" type="text/css" />
</head>
<body>
    <div class="page">
        <div id="header">
```

```
                <div id="title">
                    <h1>My MVC Application</h1>
                </div>
                <div id="logindisplay">
Welcome!
                </div>
                <div id="menucontainer">
                    <ul id="menu">
                        <li>${Html.ActionLink("Home", "Index", "Home")}</li>
                        <li>${Html.ActionLink("About", "About", "Home")}</li>
                    </ul>
                </div>
            </div>
            <div id="main">

                <use content="view"/>

                <div id="footer">
                </div>
            </div>
        </div>
</body>
</html>
```

The first interesting item is the `"link"` element linking to our CSS file. It uses the familiar tilde (`"~"`) notation to note the base directory of our website, instead of relative path notation (`"../../"`). We can rebase our website and redefine what the tilde means in our Spark configuration if need be. This method is helpful in web farm or content-delivery network (CDN) scenarios. The next interesting item is our familiar `Html.ActionLink` calls, but this time, we enclose the code in the `${}` syntax. This syntax is synonymous with the `<%= %>` syntax of Web Forms. However, if we place an exclamation point after the dollar sign, using `$!{}` instead, any `NullReferenceExceptions` will have empty content, instead of an error screen. This is one advantage of Spark over Web Forms, where a null results in an error for the end user, even though missing values are normal. The last interesting piece of our layout is the `<use content="view"/>` element. The named content section, "view," defaults to the view name from our action. In our example, this would be an Index.spark file in a Product folder. We can create other named content sections, for a header, footer, sidebar, and anything else we might need in our base layout. Like master pages, we can nest our layouts as much as our application demands.

With the layout in place, we can create our action-specific view, shown in listing 13.28.

Listing 13.28 Spark view for the `Index` action

```
<viewdata model="SparkViewExample.Models.Product[]" />
<var styles="new [] {'even', 'odd'}" isCurrent="false" />
<h2>Products</h2>
<table>
    <tr>
        <th>Name</th>
        <th>Price</th>
```

```
        <th>Description</th>
    </tr>
    <var i="0">
    <tr each="var product in ViewData.Model" class="${styles[i%2]}">
        <td>${product.Name}</td>
        <td>${product.Price}</td>
        <td>${product.Description}</td>
        <set i="i+1" />
    </tr>
    </var>
</table>
```

In the Index view, we want to loop through all of the Products in the model, display-ing a row for each Product. With Web Forms, we would need to put in `<% %>` code blocks for our for loop. With Spark, we have cleaner options. First, we use the `<view-data />` element to tell Spark that we are using a strongly typed view, and our model type is an array of Products. Spark also supports the key-based ViewData dictionary. Next, we create local styles and isCurrent variables with the `<var />` element. Each attribute name becomes a new local variable, and the attribute value is the value assigned. These two variables will help us create alternating row styles.

Next, we put normal HTML in our view, including a header, table, and header row. With Spark, special Spark XML elements are interspersed with HTML elements, mak-ing our view look cleaner without C#'s distracting angle brackets. After the header row, we create a counter variable to help in the alternating row styles. We need to iter-ate through all the Products in our model, creating a row for each item. In Web Forms, this is accomplished through a foreach loop. In Spark, we need only to add an each attribute to the HTML element we want to repeat, giving the snippet of C# code to iterate in each attribute's value. The class element in our row element is set to an alternating style, using a counter to switch between odd and even styles.

Inside our row, we use the ${} syntax to display each individual product. Because we installed the Spark Visual Studio integration, we get IntelliSense in our views, as demonstrated in figure 13.19.

To complete the alternating row styles, we increment the count using the `<set />` element. This element lets us assign values to variables we created earlier in our view. In addition to the each attribute and `<set />` element, Spark provides complex

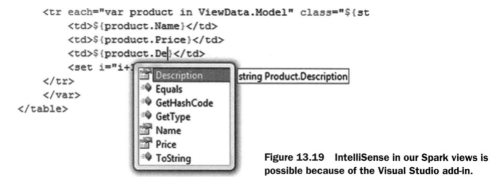

Figure 13.19 IntelliSense in our Spark views is possible because of the Visual Studio add-in.

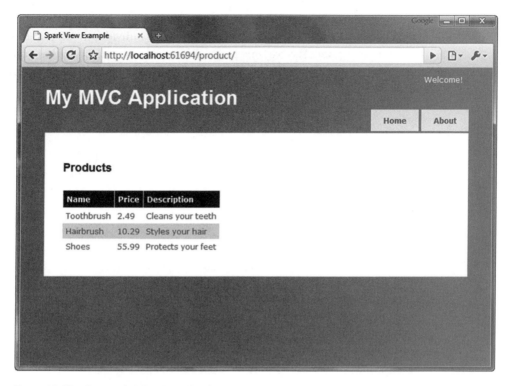

Figure 13.20 Our running Spark application

expressions for conditional operators (if...else), macros, and more. With our Spark view complete, our view renders as expected in the browser, as shown in figure 13.20.

Because of the ASP.NET MVC architecture, we can swap out view engines without needing to change our controllers or actions. As we saw in this section with the Spark view engine, many view engines provide a cleaner way to create views in our MVC application. The Spark view engine gives us a terser, more readable markup, blending code and HTML seamlessly. Because Spark supports compiling views and IntelliSense, we do not need to give up all the nice integration that Web Forms offers. The decision to choose a different view engine is still quite important, as it has long-term technical and non-technical ramifications. Alternative view engines should be another option to investigate for MVC applications, as they offer compelling alternatives to the default WebFormViewEngine.

13.5 *Summary*

In this chapter, you have seen how the ASP.NET MVC Framework can dovetail with other libraries and tools. Because this framework is based on interfaces and abstractions, it's simple to mesh other libraries and techniques in your web applications.

Here, we have reviewed client-side extension techniques with jQuery, one way to perform client-side validation, a method to leverage NHibernate with an ASP.NET

MVC application, and an alternate view engine that integrates with the framework as well as Visual Studio. These recipes can be applied individually or together. They have several moving parts, so we encourage you to explore the code that comes with this book. Feel free to use and extend the code as you apply it to your own ASP.NET MVC applications.

index

MORE TITLES FROM MANNING

The Art of Unit Testing
with Examples in .NET
by Roy Osherove

ISBN: 1-933988-27-4
320 pages
$39.99
May 2009

Building Domain Specific Languages
in BOO
by Ayende Rahien

ISBN: 1-933988-60-6
400 pages
$49.99
September 2009

For ordering information go to www.manning.com